The Ultimate WHM Guide

By Travis Newton

The Ultimate WHM Guide

First published: June 2024

Edition: First

Revision: 1.2

ISBN: 9798326391582

To provide feedback on this book, please visit

https://www.nodespacebooks.com/whm

Dedicated to my Wife, who has graciously put up with the chore of being my editor. And to my kids, who have enjoyed being Junior Editors helping edit Daddy's books. *Stay curious.*

About the Author

Travis Newton is a seasoned professional in the web hosting industry, having been an active user of cPanel and WHM since 2006. His journey began when he launched his first web hosting company, driven by a passion for technology and a commitment to providing exceptional service. Over the years, Travis has amassed extensive experience in managing and optimizing web hosting environments, making him a respected expert in the field.

In addition to his technical expertise, Travis is the founder and owner of NodeSpace Hosting, a company that prides itself on delivering high-quality hosting solutions tailored to the needs of small businesses. Under his leadership, NodeSpace Hosting has become synonymous with reliability, innovation, and superior customer support.

Travis's deep understanding of cPanel's intricacies and his practical experience managing a successful hosting service provide him with unique insights that he shares in this book. His goal is to help others master cPanel and WHM to enhance their web hosting experiences and achieve their business objectives.

Through this book, Travis offers readers the benefit of his years of experience. Whether you are beginning with a simple reseller account or a seasoned administrator with a dedicated server, Travis's guidance will prove invaluable.

You can connect with Travis on social media:

@travis@nodespace.social

@travisatnodespace

@travisatnodespace

Table of Contents

Quick Index

Since this book is more of a reference manual rather than one to be read from cover-to-cover, you can use this section to help you find common tasks.

I want to…	Section Number
Update the system	24.12
Recompile Apache	24.14
Install/remove PHP version	24.14.1.3
Install/remove PHP module	24.14.1.4
Everything email	25
Manage backend processes ("task manager")	26.1
Show disk usage	26.3
Manage AutoSSL (Let's Encrypt SSL certificates)	28.3

1 Introduction to WHM

Welcome to *The Ultimate WHM Guide*! This book compliments my other book, *The Ultimate cPanel Guide*. If you're reading this book, it probably means you've decided to look into reseller hosting or get a VPS/dedicated server and install cPanel/WHM on it either to start a web hosting business, provide hosting services for clients, or just to host multiple websites.

1.1 Who This Book is For

This book is for people who have some technical knowledge. While I do my best to keep things simple, there is some expectations that you would know more than the average user that *The Ultimate cPanel Guide* aims towards. At the very least you should know:

- What a domain name is.
- What DNS records are.
- Basic Linux commands (if you use a VPS or dedicated server)
- Basic usage of cPanel.

If you don't have a basic understanding of these topics, you may find it hard to follow. However, if you are serious about this venture, we all had to start somewhere!

If you don't feel that you're willing to take on some or most of the tasks in this book, I strongly urge you to return this book (I won't be offended) and purchase a fully managed hosting solution.

WHM, which stands for Web Host Manager, is the companion software to cPanel. cPanel is a control panel software that web hosting companies will install on a server to allow people to manage their websites. It's the business side of things. If you're reading this book, it probably means that you are already familiar with cPanel and you're running your own web hosting venture or you are a web developer, marketing agency, or in a position where you are managing multiple cPanel hosting accounts.

1.2 A Word of Caution About Technical Books

I feel like it needs to be said, cPanel is software. This is a book. Whether you're reading this book in dead tree (paper) or electronic format, it's still a book. Software changes at the speed of light while books are kind of time capsules – recording things as they are now. While books can certainly be updated, they won't be updated as fast as cPanel changes. This book was written in **May 2024** and is current and accurate as of then. If something doesn't line up or match exactly, it could be for a few reasons:

1. The feature was deprecated and removed.
2. cPanel replaced the feature with something else.
3. cPanel added new features and shuffled things around.
4. Your web hosting provider disabled it.

Just keep all these points in mind as you move forward. I've written this book to hopefully stand up to most major changes.

1.3 What You Need to Get Started

- **Internet Access:** This may seem obvious, but since cPanel/WHM is web-based software that lives at your hosting provider, you need Internet access. If you don't have Internet access at home, you can generally access the Internet at school, work, coffee shops, airports, and other public places. Just word of warning though: always make sure you're using encryption in public places (e.g. HTTPS).
- **A Modern Web Browser:** While cPanel/WHM should theoretically work with any browser, your best bet is a modern version of Mozilla Firefox, Apple Safari, Google Chrome, Microsoft Edge, or any of the variants of browsers built from those browsers.
- **A Web Hosting Provider with cPanel/WHM:** This one should be obvious. It is hard to use cPanel without cPanel. If you don't have a provider, don't worry. I'll cover how to find a host in the next few pages.
- **Domain & Website:** While picking a domain name and creating a website are not topics for this book, you should have a domain name to get your hosting

account setup. The website, you can either already have or you can build it on your new hosting account. How you build it is up to you.

- **FTP Client:** While not required, it's generally helpful to have a FTP client. I like to use Filezilla as it's free and available for Linux, Mac, and Windows – all systems I use.
- **A Text/Code Editor:** Another optional, but very useful thing to have is a text or code editor like Visual Studio Code, Notepad++, Notepad, or Text Edit.

1.4 Finding cPanel/WHM Web Hosting

If you don't already have any cPanel web hosting, you're going to need it! There are hundreds of thousands of web hosting providers out there. How do you find one?

First, I own a hosting provider – NodeSpace Hosting (`https://www.nodespace.com`). So naturally, I am going to tell you that our cPanel hosting is the best and you should get your hosting through us.

- We offer a 45-day money back guarantee if we're not the right host for you.
- We have up-front and transparent pricing. We don't try to hide what your renewal fee is.
- We don't have "introductory pricing" that we bait you with. We're a web hosting provider, not your cable company and we all know how much people dislike their cable company!
- We don't try to upsell you to the next plan.
- We offer free migrations from (almost) anywhere* – another cPanel host, a provider that doesn't use cPanel, a VPS or dedicated server.
- I have plenty of other reasons, but I don't want to just talk about NodeSpace!

*There are just some websites we cannot transfer. For example, websites that are built on most drag-n-drop website builders are generally proprietary and we cannot transfer. But everything else is generally transferable.

1.4.1 Finding cPanel/WHM Hosting

When you look for web hosting that is going to give you access to WHM, you're going to be looking for a special kind of hosting. Let's explore the different types of hosting options you have.

1.4.1.1 Reseller Hosting

If you're familiar with cPanel shared hosting, then reseller hosting is shared hosting except you're buying your hosting resources in bulk – disk space, bandwidth, and cPanel accounts. Reseller accounts vary in price, but you can expect to pay anywhere from $10 to $100 per month, depending on the package details. You can carve up your allotted resources into packages that you can sell and provide to your own customers at your own price.

Reseller hosting doesn't require you to be a system administrator as your hosting provider will take care of the server hardware. Additionally, you'll be sharing the server with other clients.

If you're looking to keep your hosting company in the shadows as best as possible, you will want to make sure the hosting provider you choose offers **private label** or **white label** reseller hosting. This means that the server hostname is generic and not linked back to the company. For example, if your server hostname was `reseller-lnr.nodespace.com` then your clients would figure out that you were hosting with NodeSpace. Instead, you want a hosting provider that uses server hostnames like `server1.penguinserver.com` as that domain would not be traced back to your hosting provider. Reseller accounts also allow you to brand your own DNS nameservers so you can use your own domain instead of the host's.

Something to note is that a few years ago, cPanel changed the way they licensed cPanel to web hosts. Previously, web hosts were allowed to have as many accounts on their servers as they wanted. Then, cPanel started licensing per user. Likewise, this caused reseller hosting to change. Now reseller accounts typically come with a certain number of cPanel accounts. Once you hit that limit, you have to upgrade your account to the next plan – or ask your host if they can sell you additional cPanel accounts.

When it comes to technical support, having a reseller account means that you're going to have to provide technical support to your own clients. Most hosting providers will not support your customers and require your customers to obtain technical support through you. But don't worry, if you find a situation where you can't fix the problem (such as your client needing a PHP module installed, for example), your hosting provider will be able to help you.

NodeSpace Hosting – Reseller Accounts
Over at NodeSpace, our reseller accounts are provisioned with a certain number of accounts. However rather than forcing you to upgrade to a higher-priced plan with more accounts, we will bill you for any additional accounts beyond what is included with your plan. For example, if your reseller plan includes 5 cPanel accounts, but you end up using 7 cPanel accounts, you will be billed for those 2 additional accounts. If you delete two accounts, we'll remove those two accounts from your next invoice.

Reseller Hosting Takeaways

- Reseller hosting is still shared hosting, just with bulk resources.
- You will probably be limited in the number of cPanel accounts you may create.
- You might have to do some more technical support work than you would on standard shared hosting.
- Just like in shared hosting, your host is responsible for managing and maintaining the server.

1.4.1.2 Virtual Private Server (VPS) Hosting

A virtual private server (commonly called a VPS or even a virtual cloud server) is a virtual machine that the host provisions on to one of their servers. Any number of configurations are available, and the best part is, you get to choose what you want – how many CPUs, how much RAM, how much disk space, and even the operating system. VPS pricing can range from $4 to around $100 per month.

Keep in mind typically when you buy a VPS, you need to know some server administration skills. If Linux isn't your thing, you can buy what is called a Managed VPS. This is where the hosting company will perform administrative tasks for you – but a managed VPS will cost a little more than a regular VPS you manage. You might also find that your host won't include a cPanel license in the cost of your VPS. You'll either have to buy this license from your host or directly from cPanel.

cPanel License – Solo

If you're planning on running only one user account on your VPS, cPanel offers a special license called cPanel Solo. This license will only allow one user to be added to the server (but you can run as many websites from that single account as you would like). This might be a good option if your website has outgrown shared hosting but wouldn't be appropriate for reseller hosting or a dedicated server.

As I previously mentioned, a benefit to a VPS is that you will have all the assigned resources to yourself. Additionally, you get full administrative access to the server. That means you can configure your server how you like it instead of how your host likes it.

VPS hosting is also like a special kind of shared hosting. While your server is yours, you will be sharing the physical hardware with other servers. However, most virtual servers offer some benefits that shared, and reseller hosting don't – if your host needs to perform maintenance, they can typically move your virtual server to different hardware without any downtime. In most cases, you won't even notice!

VPS hosting is also great for larger resellers and web agencies as it provides some independence from the hosting provider.

When it comes to configuring cPanel and WHM, the added benefit is that you will have full control of the server. Your server can use your own domain name for the hostname instead of a generic domain.

VPS Hosting Takeaways

- VPS hosting is an affordable way to get dedicated resources.
- cPanel licensing is typically an extra cost.
- You might need to manage your own server, hire someone to do it, or buy managed VPS services from your hosting provider.
- It's great for sites that have outgrown shared hosting, but aren't big enough to move to a dedicated server and reseller hosting doesn't fit the bill.

1.4.1.3 Dedicated Server Hosting

Dedicated server hosting is very similar to virtual private servers except for one major difference. Unlike with a VPS, dedicated servers you are the only person on the physical hardware that your hosting company provides. Pricing for dedicated servers varies greatly based on several factors but one of the major factors is hardware. You can find dedicated servers generally anywhere from $25 to thousands of dollars per month. The only limit is your budget.

When you shop for a dedicated server, you can build a custom server, picking everything from the CPU, type and amount of RAM, to even how much storage you want – from gigabytes to hundreds of terabytes! Most commonly, you will be able to pick a pre-configured server

Similarly to VPS hosting, dedicated servers come in two flavors: managed by you and managed by your host. A dedicated server you manage yourself will always be a little cheaper than a server managed by your host but when your host manages your server, you don't need to be a system administrator or hire one.

Also like a VPS, cPanel licensing is typically not included. It's important to note the cPanel licensing structure changes a lot for physical hardware. Since you can run a lot of websites on physical hardware, cPanel charges accordingly. The base license you can get, either from your host or directly from cPanel, will allow for up to 100 accounts. Once you pass 100 accounts, you pass into what cPanel calls "bulk accounts" and your host may sell you additional account packs.

If you choose to purchase your license directly from cPanel, then your licensing numbers will be reported automatically monthly. If you go above 100 accounts, you'll be billed the bulk rate for each additional account automatically.

If you're planning on running a very busy website or lots of sites, a dedicated server might be worth the extra cost. Since you are the only one assigned to the hardware, your websites can use the full power of the server. No one else can use it. It's all yours.

When it comes to configuring cPanel and WHM, the added benefit is that you will have full control of the server. Your server can use your own domain name for the hostname instead of a generic domain.

Dedicated Server Takeaways

- Much more expensive option.
- You're the only one using the hardware so you get the full performance.
- cPanel licensing is typically an extra cost.
- You might need to manage your own server, hire someone to do it, or buy managed dedicated services from your hosting provider.
- Perfect for very large sites or if you're planning on hosting a large number of websites.

2 Getting Started With WHM

At this point, you should already have a reseller account, a VPS, or a dedicated server with cPanel/WHM installed. This book won't go into installing cPanel and WHM because logging in is a very simple process and the cPanel documentation covers it very well.

2.1 Logging into WHM

Whether you have signed up for a shared reseller hosting account or you are using a VPS or dedicated server, this process is pretty similar.

If you are using a reseller account, your web hosting provider will have assigned you a username and password. This username and password will also match a cPanel account. When you get both a cPanel account and WHM account, most people will use the cPanel account to host their website and, optionally, billing software. If you are using a VPS or dedicated server, instead of getting a cPanel account, you will get a root user account which is the main user account for the server.

Protect the root user account!

The root user account is a special account. It is the main administrator account to the system. Anyone with this account can take over the server. It is important that the root account is protected and has a secure password.

In order to login to WHM, you can use any of the following methods:

- Using the server's IP address: `https://100.60.100.100:2087/`[1]
- Using the server's hostname: `https://server.example.com:2087/`[2]
- Adding /whm to the end of either the server's IP address or hostname or to your own domain name.

---

[1] I will be using 100.64.100.100 as a placeholder IP for your server. You should of course replace this with the IP address given to you by your hosting provider.

[2] I use the domain "example.com" as a placeholder for primary domains. You'll also see me switch this out for example.net and example.org for secondary domains.

It is important to remember, that WHM's port number is 2087 and cPanel's port number is 2083.

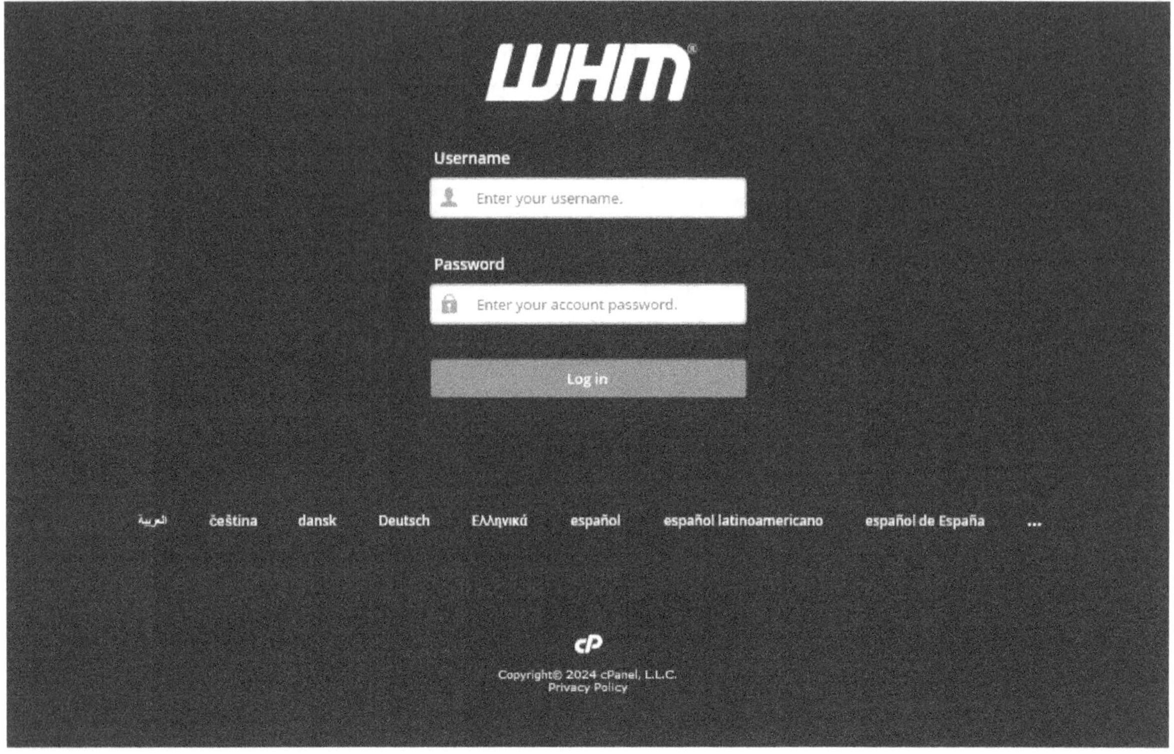

The WHM login page looks like the cPanel login page with a few major differences. The login screen, besides having the WHM logo, is a deep blue color.

Going forward, I am going to be using the root user to access WHM, so the features you see in screenshots will depict permissions available to root. If you're missing a feature or an option, it may be restricted by your hosting provider, or your reseller account doesn't have permissions to use the feature.

2.2 WHM Dashboard

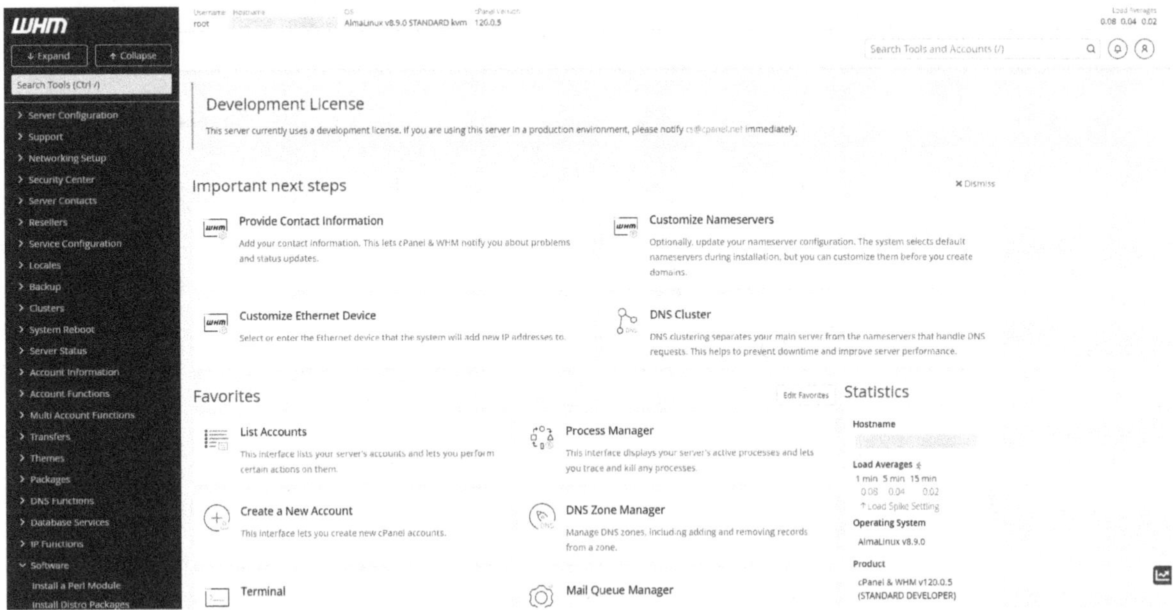

Since the dashboard and tools section is very large, I'll be breaking these up so you're able to clearly see them.

The **Important next steps** section can be dismissed but it contains important steps that you should perform to setup your account.

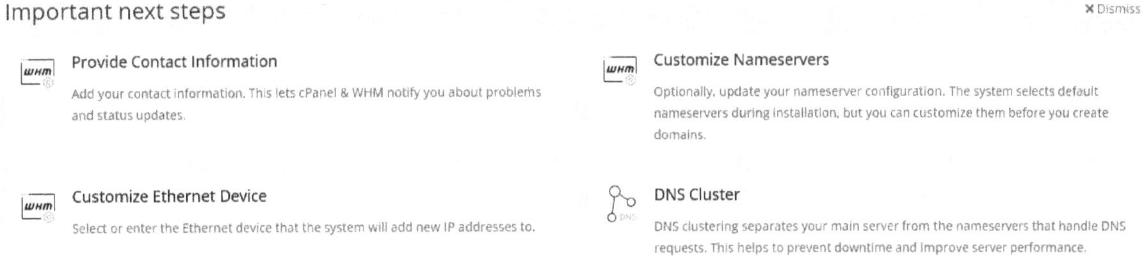

The **Favorites** section can be changed around, but the defaults are shown. On the right, you'll see the **Statistics** section. This will show the server's hostname, load averages, the operating system the server is running, the product version (license type), and your user analytics ID.

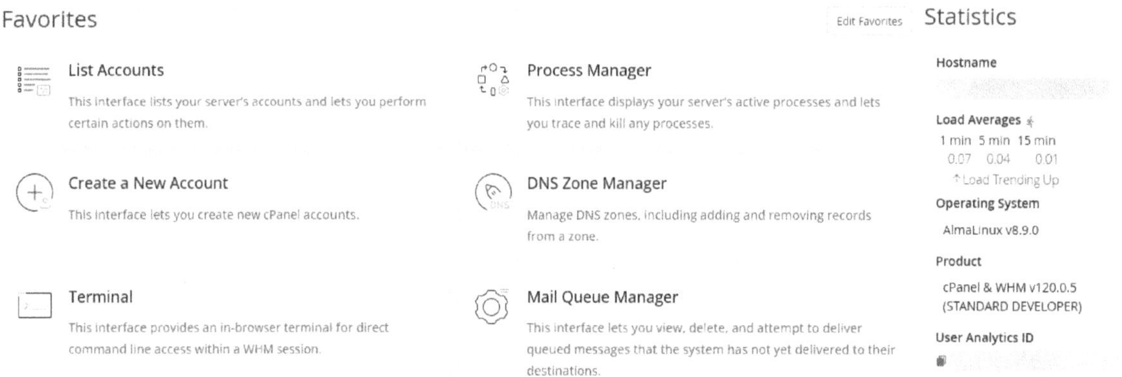

You might notice a lot of these tools are like what you might have seen in cPanel. Just remember that this is the administrative side of things. Also you may not see all of these options if you have a reseller account as your hosting provider may not have the options available to you. But when you are logged in with a root user (such as on a VPS and dedicated server), you will see all these options.

You may also have other options that are not here. This is probably because they are third-party tools. This book will not cover any third-party tools.

Tools

Server Configuration

Basic WebHost Manager® Setup
Change Root Password
Configure cPanel Analytics
Configure cPanel Cron Jobs
Initial Quota Setup
Link Server Nodes
Server Profile
Server Time
Statistics Software Configuration
Terminal
Tweak Settings
Update Preferences
WHM Marketplace

Support

Create Support Ticket
Grant cPanel Support Access
Support Center

Networking Setup

Change Hostname
Resolver Configuration

Security Center

Apache mod_userdir Tweak
SMTP Restrictions
Compiler Access
Configure Security Policies
cPHulk Brute Force Protection
Host Access Control
Manage External Authentications
Manage root's SSH Keys
Manage Wheel Group Users
ModSecurity™ Configuration
ModSecurity™ Tools
ModSecurity™ Vendors
Password Strength Configuration
Security Advisor
Security Questions
Shell Fork Bomb Protection
SSH Password Authorization Tweak
Traceroute Enable/Disable
Two-Factor Authentication

Server Contacts

Contact Manager
Edit System Mail Preferences

Resellers

- Change Ownership of an Account
- Change Ownership of Multiple Accounts
- Edit Reseller Nameservers and Privileges
- Email All Resellers
- Manage Reseller's IP Delegation
- Manage Reseller's Shared IP
- Reseller Center
- Reset Resellers
- Show Reseller Accounts
- View Reseller Usage and Manage Account Status

Service Configuration

- Apache Configuration
- cPanel Log Rotation Configuration
- cPanel Web Disk Configuration
- cPanel Web Services Configuration
- EXIM Exim Configuration Manager
- FTP FTP Server Selection
- Mailserver Configuration
- Manage Service SSL Certificates
- NS1 Nameserver Selection
- Service Manager

Locales

- Configure Application Locales
- Copy a Locale
- Delete a Locale
- Edit a Locale
- XML Locale XML Download
- XML Locale XML Upload
- View Available Locales

Backup

- Backup Configuration
- Backup Restoration
- Backup User Selection
- File and Directory Restoration

Clusters

- Configuration Cluster
- DNS Cluster

System Reboot

Forceful Server Reboot
Graceful Server Reboot

Server Status

Apache Status
Daily Process Log
Server Information
Service Status
Task Queue Monitor

Account Information

List Accounts
List Parked Domains
List Subdomains
List Suspended Accounts
Show Accounts Over Quota
View Bandwidth Usage

Account Functions

Change Site's IP Address
Create a New Account
Email All Users
Force Password Change
Limit Bandwidth Usage
Manage Account Suspension
Manage Demo Mode
Manage Shell Access
Modify an Account
Password Modification
Quota Modification
Raw Apache Log Download
Raw NGINX® Log Download
Rearrange an Account
Reset Account Bandwidth Limit
Terminate Accounts
Unsuspend Bandwidth Exceeders
Upgrade/Downgrade an Account
Web Template Editor

Multi Account Functions

Change Multiple Sites' IP Addresses
Modify/Upgrade Multiple Accounts

Transfers

Convert Addon Domain to Account
Review Transfers and Restores
Transfer or Restore a cPanel Account
Transfer Tool

Themes

Theme Manager

Packages

Add a Package
Delete a Package
Edit a Package
Feature Manager

DNS Functions

Add a DNS Zone
Add an A Entry for Your Hostname
Delete a DNS Zone
DNS Zone Manager
Edit Zone Templates
Email Routing Configuration
DKIM SPF
Enable DKIM/SPF Globally
Nameserver Record Report
Park a Domain
Perform a DNS Cleanup
Set Zone TTL
Setup/Edit Domain Forwarding
Synchronize DNS Records

Database Services

Change Database Root Password
Change Database User Password
Database Map Tool
Edit Database Configuration
Manage Database Access Hosts
Manage Database Profiles
Manage Database Users
Manage Databases
phpMyAdmin
Repair Databases
Show Database Processes
Upgrade Database Version

IP Functions

IPv6 Ranges
Add a New IP Address
Assign IPv6 Address
Configure Remote Service IPs
IP Migration Wizard
Rebuild the IP Address Pool
Show IP Address Usage
Show or Delete Current IP Addresses
Show/Edit Reserved IPs

Software

Install a Perl Module
Install Distro Packages
Module Installers
MultiPHP INI Editor
MultiPHP Manager
NGINX® Manager
Rebuild RPM Database
System Update
Update Server Software
EasyApache 4

Email

Email Deliverability
Filter Incoming Emails by Country
Filter Incoming Emails by Domain
Greylisting
Mail Delivery Reports
Mail Queue Manager
Mail Troubleshooter
Mailbox Conversion
Repair Mailbox Permissions
Spamd Startup Configuration
View Mail Statistics Summary
View Relayers
View Sent Summary

System Health

Background Process Killer
Process Manager
Show Current Disk Usage
Show Current Running Processes

cPanel

Change Log
Customization
Install cPAddons Site Software
Manage cPAddons Site Software
Manage Plugins
Modify cPanel & WHM News
Reset a Mailman Password
Upgrade to Latest Version

SSL/TLS

Generate an SSL Certificate and Signing Request
Install an SSL Certificate on a Domain
Manage AutoSSL
Manage SSL Hosts
Purchase and Install an SSL Certificate
SSL Storage Manager
SSL/TLS Configuration

Market

Market Provider Manager

Restart Services

Database Server
DNS Server
HTTP Server (Apache)
IMAP Server
Mail Server (Exim)
Mailing List Manager (Mailman)
PHP-FPM service for Apache
SSH Server (OpenSSH)

Development

Apps Managed by AppConfig
cPanel Development Forum
cPanel Plugin File Generator
Developer Documentation
Manage API Tokens
Manage Hooks

Plugins

ImunifyAV
WP Toolkit

3 Server Configuration

For VPS/Dedicated Servers

The information in this section applies to VPS and dedicated servers.

The Server Configuration section you will probably fequent, especially if you have a new VPS or dedicated server and need to get the settings just right.

In this chapter, we will review the tools available to help you configure your server.

3.1 Basic WebHost Manager Setup

This section contains basic settings for cPanel and WHM. It will show you all the settings by default, but you'll find settings for contact information, some basic configuration settings for cPanel, and default nameserver setup.

3.1.1.1 Contact Information

Contact Information

Enter one or more email addresses to contact in case a problem arises with this server.

Examples: john@doe.com, john.q.public@anonymous.com, user@host.com

Enter the sender's name you would like to appear on the notification email's "From:" line. This value defaults to *"cPanel on"*, followed by your server's hostname.

Example: DO NOT REPLY - cPanel Notification on DarkOrb Hosting

Enter an email address that accepts replies to notification emails. This setting ensures that customers' responses to do-not-reply emails will not be lost.

Examples: support@example.host, do-not-reply@example.com

Enter one or more cellular phone or pager email addresses to message via email in case a problem arises with this server.

Examples: john@cellphone.com, 8005551212@provider.com, user@host.com

An API Token for the Pushbullet API

The ICQ ID that this server should use for login to ICQ when sending alerts. To disable or fine-tune ICQ notifications, go to Contact Manager. You can register for a new ICQ number here.

The ICQ ID password for sending alerts.

Enter one or more ICQ user identification numbers (comma delimited) you can be reached at in case a problem arises with this server.

Examples: 1234567, 11223344, 1020304

A comma-separated list of http:// or https:// URLs of a system to which you want to send POST notifications as form data with the keys "hostname", "subject", and "body". Query strings will be converted and sent as POST data. For example https://www.cpanel.net/events.cgi?apikey=XXXXX will send apikey via POST. Note that all keys and values must be in URLencoded format. Also, if you use the https://user:password@domain.tld/ format to authenticate to the destination system, you must also URLencode the "user" and "password" keys and values.

Slack WebHook URL. Multiple hooks can be specified by separating with a comma(,). To obtain your own Slack WebHook, please follow the guide at https://api.slack.com/messaging/webhooks

The first box is for supplying one or more email addresses that should be notified in the event of an issue with the server. Multiple email addresses can be entered separated by a comma. For example: `johndoe@example.com, janedoe@example.com, serverteam@example.com`.

The second box is for defining a sender's name for the email, for example, cPanel Server Notification.

The third box will allow you to define an email address that accepts replies to notifications. Generally, a support email address or an information address. A mailbox that will be checked if someone replies to a notification.

The next box is where you can define a Pushbullet API token. Pushbullet is a third-party notification service that is integrated into cPanel and can alert you or your team to problems.

The next three fields are some legacy fields that are really showing the age of cPanel software. They are for configuring ICQ messages. The ICQ service shut down on June 26, 2024, and therefore, these fields are non-operational and will be removed in a future version of cPanel.

The next field is for a "poor man's push notification" service. This relies on some custom code that you would need to write and is out of the scope of this book.

Finally, there is space for a Slack WebHook URL. Slack is a popular messaging platform with companies. Other messaging services also use Slack-compatible webhooks like Mattermost. If you setup a webhook in Slack or Mattermost, you can add that here and the cPanel server will send notifications there.

3.1.1.2 Basic Config

Basic Config

The IPv4 address (only one address) to use to set up shared IPv4 virtual hosts. **We strongly recommend that you only specify an IPv4 address that you have associated with this server.** *Example: 10.11.133.14*	192.198.80.110 *Required*
The IPv6 address (only one address) to use to set up shared IPv6 virtual hosts. **You must enter a valid IPv6 address that you have bound to this server.** *Examples: 2001:db8::10fe:5000 or 2001:db8::*	
The ethernet device onto which new IP addresses are added. Devices detected with at least one IP are listed in the drop-down, or you may specify another device. *Examples: eth0:3, eth1, eth2, venet0:0 (virtuozzo servers)*	(•) ens18 ( ) Other: ens18 *Required*
Enter the location where you wish for new users' home directories to be created. By default all directories matching the "Home Directory Prefix" are checked for available disk space and the directory with the most free space will be used. *Example: /home*	(•) /home *default* ( ) /home
Additional home directories matching the following value will also be used for new home directory creations. (Leaving this value blank disables the feature.) Only mount points are considered. **This option only takes one value.** *Examples: "home" matches /home, /home2, /newhome, /usr/home, /anythingwith/homeinit*	(•) home *default* ( ) home
Automatically create a cgi-bin script alias. This setting can be individually overridden during account creation.	(•) Yes *default* ( ) No
This value defines the caching time for host name lookups for domains hosted on this server. When a caching nameserver queries the authoritative nameserver for a resource record, this value defines the number of seconds before the record will expire. Shorter TTL values can cause heavier loads on the nameserver, but can be useful for zones that contain frequently changing records. The range of values in seconds as defined by RFC 2181 is 0 to 2147483647.	(•) 14400 *default* ( ) 14400 *Required*
This value is similar to the previous setting, but is specifically the value used for newly created zone file's authoritative nameserver entries.	(•) 86400 *default* ( ) 86400 *Required*
Enter the style in which you wish to receive your Apache logs. • **combined** - All information including referers, user agents, and requested files are logged. • **common** - Only information about requested files are logged.	(•) combined *default* ( ) common

The Basic Config section contains settings that could make your server inaccessible or prevent it from working properly. Only adjust these settings if you know what you are doing or if you have been advised to by your server provider.

If you have multiple IP addresses, you can specify a particular IP address that you want cPanel to use. For example, if you are assigned the block `100.60.100.24/29` but you want to use `100.60.100.30` as your primary IP address, you can enter it in this field.

If your server has been assigned an IPv6 block, you can enter a single address into the following field. Keep in mind that this needs to be a single address. While your server might be assigned a /64 or larger, you must enter only a single IPv6 address in this field for cPanel to use.

The next field is for the ethernet adapter to use for additional IP addresses. Commonly, this will just be your server's primary ethernet port, but your hosting provider will tell you for sure.

The next field is for where you want users' home directories to be created. By default, this is `/home`.

If you expand your server, you may want to place additional home directories in another location. If you have a secondary disk, for example, you might mount it as `/home2`. The next field is where you can place that directory and cPanel will place additional home directories in that filesystem.

If you want cPanel to automatically create a cgi-bin script alias, you can set this option to on (default) or off.

The next setting is about DNS caching times for hostname lookups performed by this server. The default is 14400 seconds, but you can change this value if you would like.

The next option is about the TTL value for newly created zone files' Authoritative Nameserver caching. The default value is 86400 seconds.

Finally, the last option is the style in which you want to receive Apache log files. The combined option is default, and it will log additional information about requests. If you're more privacy-oriented, you may decide to change this to common and only information about the requested files are logged. Keep in mind that this may make troubleshooting issues more difficult.

3.1.1.3 Nameservers

Nameservers

The root account's default nameservers used when root creates an account.

Nameserver 1: ns1. .cprap Configure Address Records

Nameserver 2: ns2. .cprap Configure Address Records

Nameserver 3: Configure Address Records

Nameserver 4: Configure Address Records

⚠ Default nameservers of the type `.cprapid.com` are not compatible with `.com` domain registrations. Learn More

This section is for setting the server's default nameservers. By default, cPanel will configure the nameservers to be ns1.server.example.com and ns2.server.example.com. You should change these to the appropriate values for your domain. Don't forget to register your nameservers!

Note

If you're using the temporary domain that cPanel provides for servers when cPanel is freshly installed called cprapid.com, you will probably run into issues. You should switch your server's hostname over to a domain name that you have full control over and make the nameservers match accordingly. For example, if my server was `cpanel1.nodespacehosting.com`, I would make my name servers `ns1.nodespacehosting.com` and `ns2.nodespacehosting.com`.

3.1.2 Registering Nameservers

To use your own private name servers, you will need to register them. These are called Glue Records. To register nameservers, you will need to create these records where you registered your domain. How you do this will vary by domain registrar, but you will need to look for options such as "Register Nameserver", "Custom Nameservers", "Private Nameservers", etc.

If you cannot find the option, consult where you registered your domain for assistance.

3.2 Change Root Password

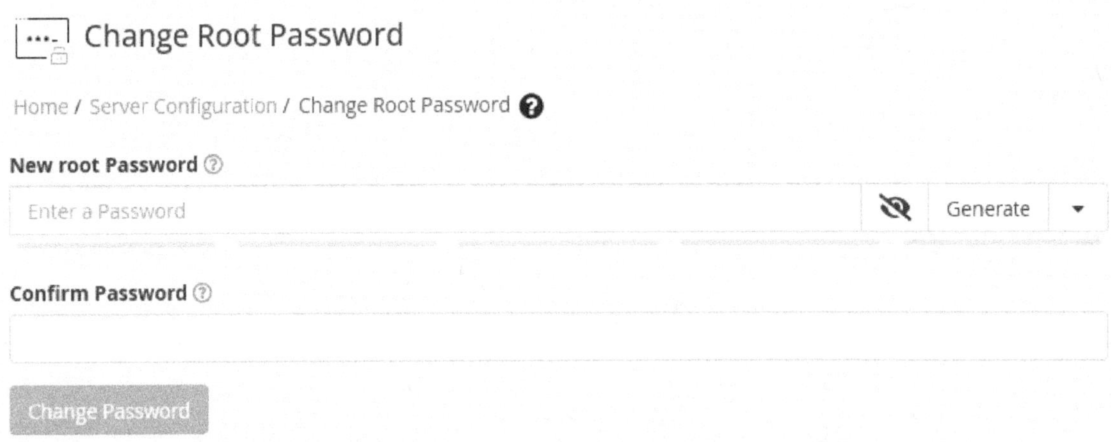

It should be obvious as to what this tool does. It will change your server's root user password to the password that you specify. While you can also change the root password through Linux's `passwd` command, due to the nature of cPanel, it's is best to change the password through the WHM web interface so that it is updated in all cPanel's configurations.

Protect your root password!

Always make sure you choose a very strong root password! Do not use dictionary words, previously used passwords, or insecure passwords! Hackers routinely try to break into servers using root accounts and a weak root password will lead to server compromise. You should use a password that is at least 15 characters and randomly generated. Store this password in a password manager and do not share it with anyone!

3.3 Configure cPanel Analytics

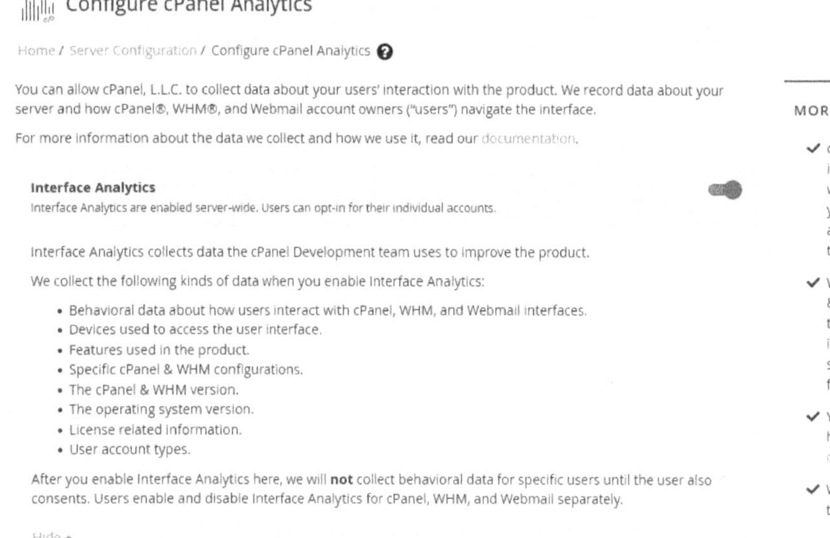

This is a telemetry feature added into cPanel fairly recently. If you recall, I mentioned that on the dashboard for WHM, there was a User Analytics ID. This is what that ID is referring to. Such telemetry sent to cPanel, linked with the User Analytics ID, which is unique per cPanel user, includes:

- How you interact with the web interface.
- Types of devices used to access the web interface (iPhone, laptop, desktop, tablet, etc.)
- The features you use and access.
- Specific configurations.
- Versions of cPanel and the operating system.
- License information.
- User account types.

If you disable analytics here, it will be disabled on all user accounts. Keep in mind that users can enable and disable this telemetry for cPanel, WHM, and Webmail separately.

3.4 Configure cPanel Cron Jobs

cPanel is Linux software and it has tasks that it needs to run on a schedule such as system backups and other various maintenance tasks. This option allows you to customize the timing of the upcp script and backup.

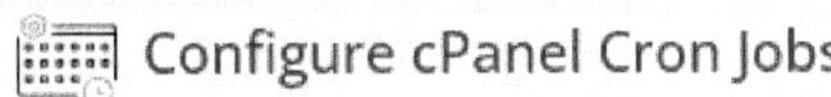

Home / Server Configuration / Configure cPanel Cron Jobs

Cron jobs are scheduled tasks that take place at predefined times or intervals on the server. Set the following variables to configure the cPanel & WHM Cron Jobs below:

Minute: The number of minutes between each execution of the cron job, or the minute of each hour on which you wish to run the cron job. For example, 15 to run the cron job every 15 minutes.
Hour: The number of hours between each execution of the cron job, or the hour each day (in military format) at which you wish to run the cron job. For example, 2100 to run the cron job at 9:00pm.
Day: The number of days between each execution of the cron job, or the day of the month on which you wish to run the cron job. For example, 15 to run the cron job on the 15th of the month.
Month: The number of months between each execution of the cron job, or the month of the year in which you wish to run the cron job. For example, 7 to run the cron job in July.
Weekday: The day(s) of the week on which you wish to run the cron job.

Enter * to indicate that the cron job should run at each interval. For example, a value of 0 indicates Sunday, or a value of 6 indicates Saturday. For example, a process set to run every day at 21:15 (or 9:15pm in 12-hour format) would be set to Minute = 15, Hour = 21, Day = *, Month = *, Weekday = *.

Command: upcp

upcp updates cPanel & WHM. We recommend that you run this script once per day. The script, by default, is set to run at a random time between 9pm and 6am local time. You may set this script to run at any time you wish. We recommend that you set it to run during off-peak hours.

Minute	Hour	Day	Month	Weekday
30	21	*	*	*

Save

Command: backup

backup runs backups on your server. By default, this script runs at 2:00 AM where the server is located, because this is an off-peak time for most servers. We recommend that you set it to run during off-peak hours, early enough to allow your server to finish backups before peak traffic resumes. If you have backups disabled, the script will immediately exit after it runs.

Minute	Hour	Day	Month	Weekday
0	2	*	*	*

Save

cPanel recommends that the `upcp` script run once per day and it is initially randomly set (when cPanel is installed) between 9pm and 6am, server time. If you find that this script is interfering with your server, you can change the time to non-peak times.

The same goes for the backup script. By default, backups, if configured, will run starting at 2am, server's time. If you need to change this to a different time of day, you can make that change here.

3.5 Initial Quota Setup

Home / Server Configuration / Initial Quota Setup

Warning: On servers that use the XFS® filesystem, you **must** reboot the server after you enable quotas.

Warning: enabling quotas on a machine that does not have kernel support for quotas may result in an unbootable system. This should only happen if you have compiled a custom kernel on your machine WITHOUT quota support. Proceed at your own risk.

Proceed >>

If you want to enable disk quotas, you will need to use this tool to enable them. If you don't enable quotas, while your packages can still have quotas, the server will not be able to enforce them.

3.6 Link Server Nodes

Link Server Nodes

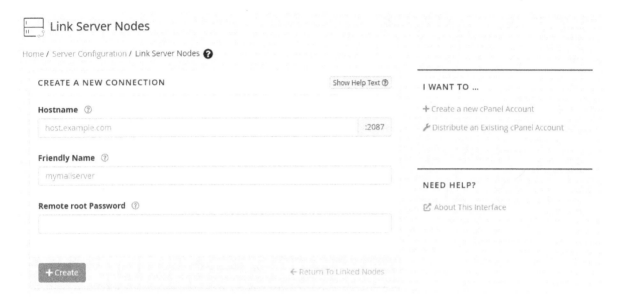

Home / Server Configuration / Link Server Nodes

CREATE A NEW CONNECTION

Show Help Text

Hostname

host.example.com :2087

Friendly Name

mymailserver

Remote root Password

+ Create

← Return To Linked Nodes

I WANT TO ...

+ Create a new cPanel Account

Distribute an Existing cPanel Account

NEED HELP?

About This Interface

The Link Server Nodes feature allows you to create connections from Server A to Server B to manage the functions of Server B through Server A. For example, in a large cPanel environment, you may have 3 servers that run Mail, Databases, and DNS. You can create links to these 3 cPanel servers with those roles in order to allow Server A to manage the features on those servers. For example, if you have a separate mail server, you would need to create a link so that if a user was to create an email account, cPanel would create the account on the cPanel email server.

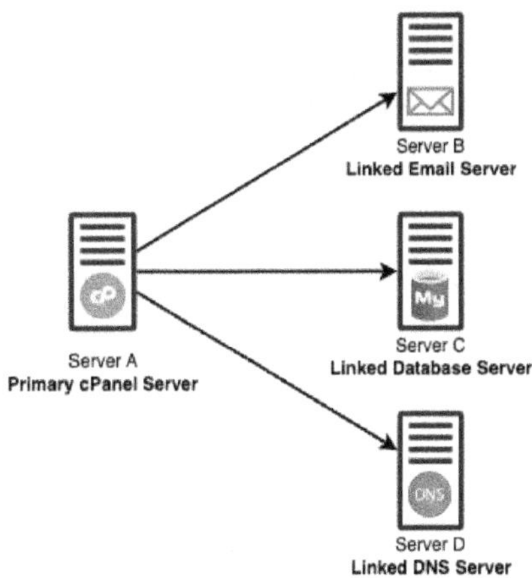

Keep in mind, this feature is still in active development. cPanel only really supports DNS and Mail profiles as of this writing. There are also some "gotchas" where you may not want to use this feature.[3]

3.7 Server Profile

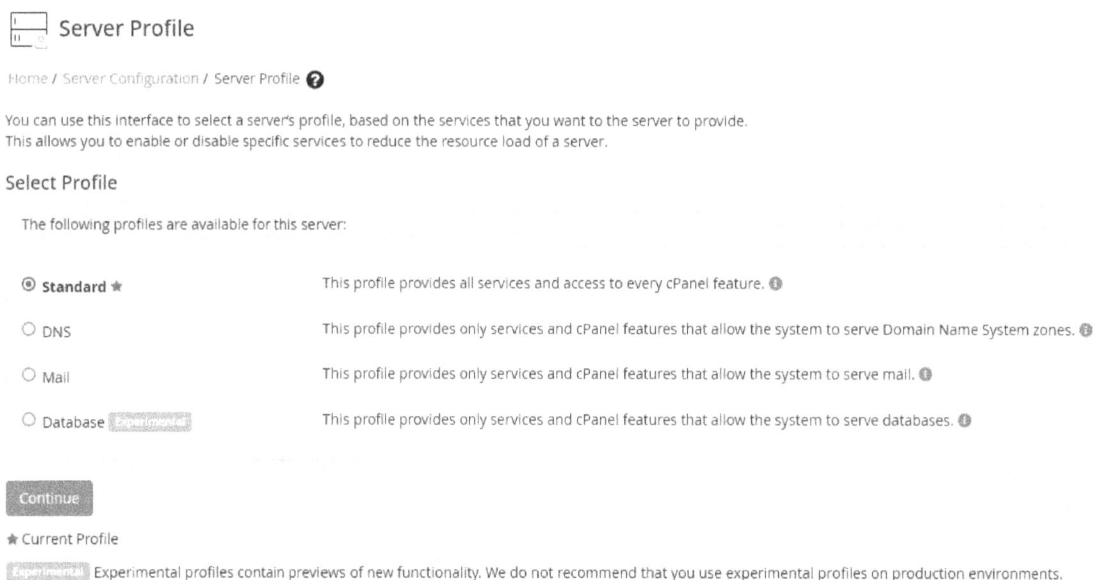

This screen will let you select what server profile you want to use. The default is Standard and it will allow for a full cPanel system – web hosting, email, DNS, and databases all on the same server. Enabling one of the other profiles will turn that server into a specific role for cPanel and then you can link the servers together. This has some benefits, like reducing the load of a single server, but there are some drawbacks as well. These drawbacks and disadvantages are highlighted in the cPanel documentation about the feature (as referenced in Footnote 3).

[3] cPanel lists these limitations in the Mail profile section at https://docs.cpanel.net/whm/server-configuration/server-profile/

3.8 Server Time

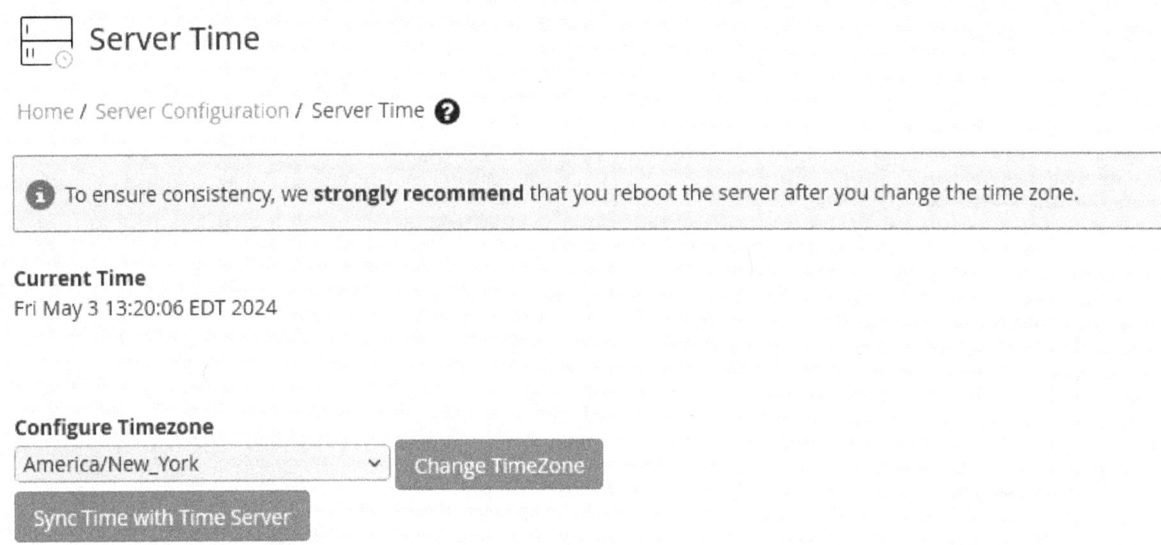

This allows you to set your server to a particular time zone if you notice that the time zone was set incorrectly, or you need to change it. You can also use the button on this page to force your server to sync with cPanel's time server.

3.9 Statistics Software Configuration

cPanel users have website statistics software made available to them. In this tool, you can choose to enable, make available, disable, and manually run tasks to process statistics for users manually.

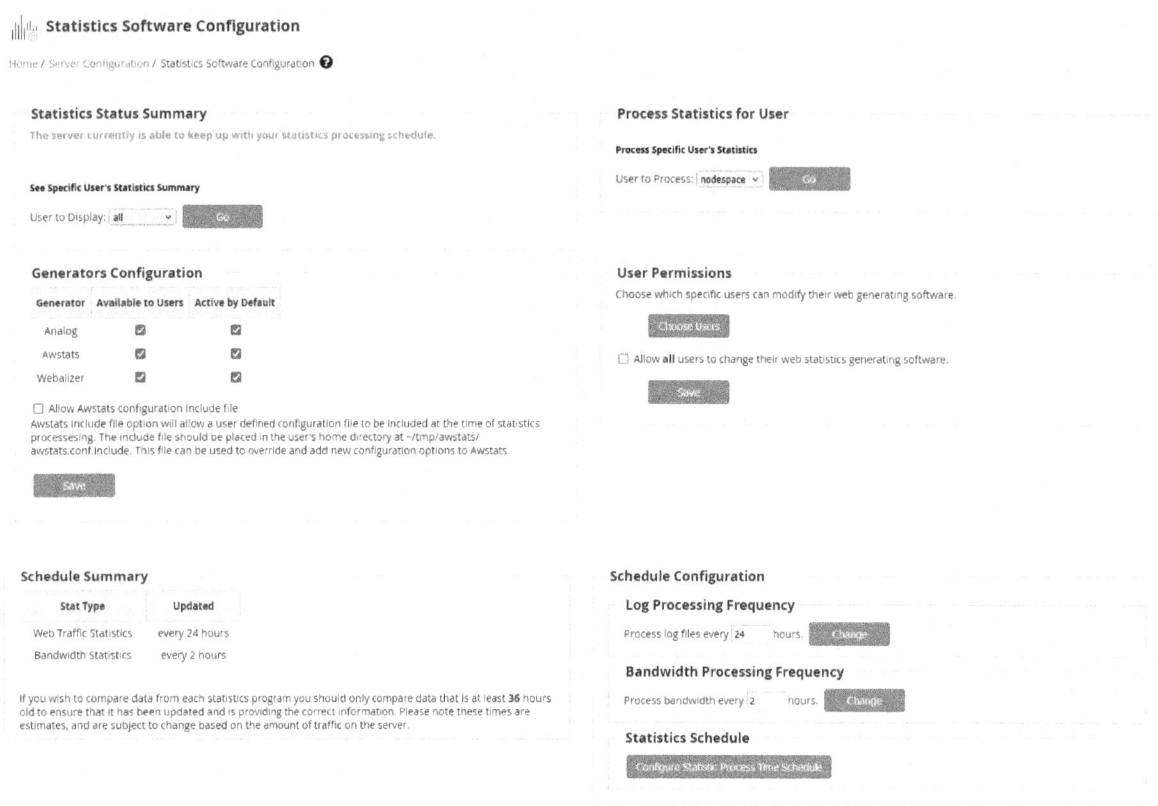

3.9.1 Statistics Status Summary

This tool will show you the status of statistics processing on user accounts, websites, and subdomains.

Legend:

✔: Stats Enabled : Disk Quota Exceeded ✖: Stats Disabled

nodespace	Stats Last Processed at: Fri May 3 08:16:17 2024	Bandwidth Last Processed at: Fri May 3 13:08:28 2024	Stats Processing is keeping up
	analog	awstats	webalizer
	✔ Details	✔ Details	✔ Details
	✔ Details	✔ Details	✔ Details
	✔ Details	✔ Details	✔ Details
	✔ Details	✔ Details	✔ Details
	✔ Details	✔ Details	✔ Details
	✔ Details	✔ Details	✔ Details
	✔ Details	✔ Details	✔ Details
	✔ Details	✔ Details	✔ Details
	✔ Details	✔ Details	✔ Details
	✔ Details	✔ Details	✔ Details

You can also drill down to specific statistics software details and see the processing that has occurred. If there is an error, this section will also outline what the error is. If a customer is saying there is something wrong with their website statistics, you can check here.

3.9.2 Process Statistics for User

This function lets you select a specific user. The process runs in the background while you can continue to do other work in WHM. When the process finishes, you'll be able to view the statistics in the user's cPanel interface. This feature is useful if a customer is having issues with statistics, and you want to manually process the statistics after fixing an issue.

3.9.3 Generators Configuration

This section allows you to enable or disable as well as make active the different statistics generators. cPanel includes three: Analog, Awstats, and Webalizer. By default, all three are available and active. For example, if you only wanted to make Awstats available, you would need to uncheck all the boxes other than Awstats. Then in the cPanel interface, users would only see Awstats. If you wanted to make Awstats the default but not enable Analog or Webalizer, you can uncheck the boxes for these two programs in the "Active by Default" column. This would allow your users to enable these stats programs if they wanted.

Enabling the option "Allow Awstats configuration Include file" will allow your users to configure Awstats via a special configuration file in their home directory. This is an advanced feature that is not enabled by default.

3.9.4 User Permissions

This feature allows you to place some control into your users' hands regarding the statistics software. You can either select specific users or allow all users on the system to be able to modify the statistics software.

When this feature is enabled, users will have a "Metrics Editor" option available in cPanel and from this page, they can choose to have Analog, Awstats, aand Webalizer enabled for any of the websites or subdomains in their account.

Metrics Editor

This interface allows you to choose which stats programs you will use when viewing site statistics.

Domain	☑ Analog	☑ Awstats	☑ Webalizer
	☑	☑	☑
	☑	☑	☑
	☑	☑	☑
	☑	☑	☑
	☑	☑	☑
	☑	☑	☑
	☑	☑	☑
	☑	☑	☑
	☑	☑	☑
	☑	☑	☑

Unchecking an option makes that option not available for viewing statistics for that website or subdomain.

3.9.5 Schedule Summary

This will show you how often the system will update which type of statistic – the two being web traffic and bandwidth. The default timing option is every 24 hours.

3.9.6 Schedule Configuration

If you want to change the frequency or the time that the system processes web traffic statistics and bandwidth statistics, that can be done from this section. It is strongly recommended to leave the default options.

3.10 Terminal

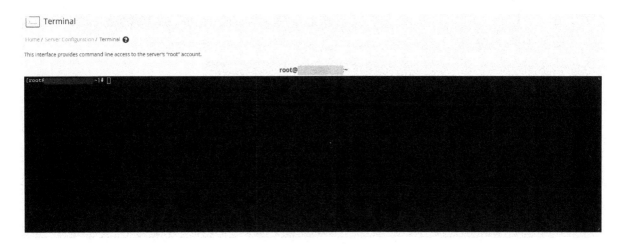

The terminal tool provides a command line interface to the server. This acts just like if you were using SSH, only the tool is able to be accessed from the WHM interface. This allows you to run commands just like you would if you were SSH'd into your server. You can use `vi` or `nano` to edit files, you can run commands, etc.

3.11 Tweak Settings

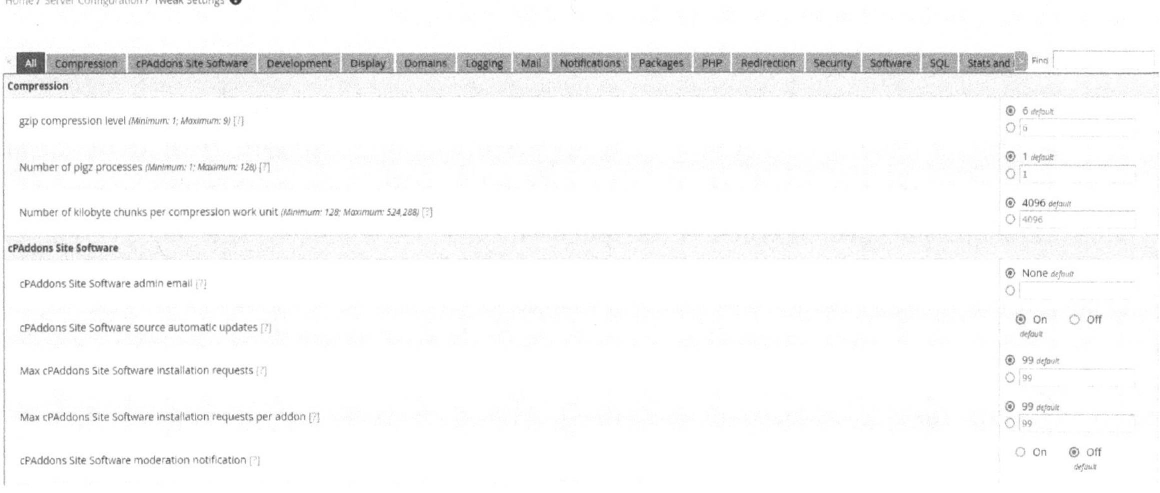

If there is one tool that you will frequently use as a cPanel server administrator, this is it. Tweak Settings is a tool that allows you to quickly provide "tweaks" to various settings. It's very comprehensive and it allows you to make fast changes without delving deeper into the system.

3.11.1Compression

By default, Apache will serve up web pages in a compressed format called gzip. This section let's you make some changes to the compression.

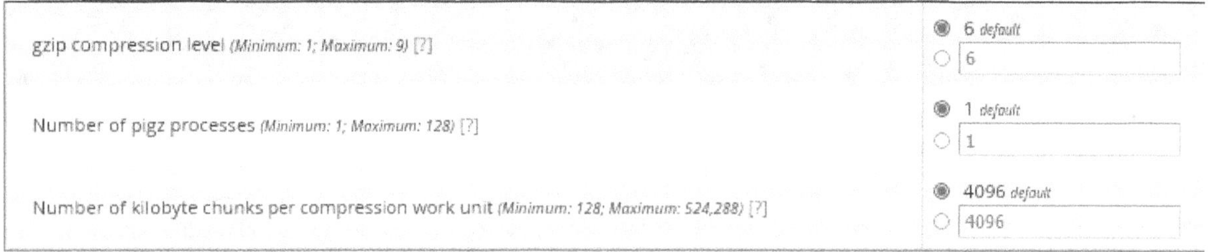

- gzip compression level – the default is 6. Minimum is 1 (virtually no compression), maximum is 9 (higher compression, but will use more of the server's CPU).
- Number of pigz processes – these are the processes that will do the compressing of the HTML. Default is 1 but you should set this to the same number of cores your server has. For example, if your server has 20 cores, you should have 20 pigz processes.
- Number of kilobyte chunks per compression work unit – This is the size (in 1024 byte chunks) of compression work units to be distributed to each pigz process. The default is 4096 which means 4096KB of data will be distributed to each pigz process at a time. If your system has a higher L2/L3 cache, you can adjust this accordingly for better performance.

3.11.2cPAddon Site Software

These settings are related to cPAddon Site Software. cPAddon Site Software is an old "one click installer" that cPanel used to have several software items in back in the day. Over the years, cPanel has basically removed most of the software. While cPanel has yet to officially deprecate this feature, I personally do consider it deprecated and it should be avoided.

cPAddons Site Software admin email [?]	◉ None *default* ○
cPAddons Site Software source automatic updates [?]	◉ On *default* ○ Off
Max cPAddons Site Software installation requests [?]	◉ 99 *default* ○ 99
Max cPAddons Site Software installation requests per addon [?]	◉ 99 *default* ○ 99
cPAddons Site Software moderation notification [?]	○ On ◉ Off *default*
Allow cPAddons Site Software installations from non-cPanel sources [?]	◉ On *default* ○ Off
Allow cPAddons Site Software installations from modified sources [?]	○ On ◉ Off *default*
Notify reseller of cPAddons Site Software installations [?]	◉ On *default* ○ Off
Notify root of cPAddons Site Software installations [?]	◉ On *default* ○ Off
Notify cPanel users when they need to update their cPAddons Site Software installations [?]	◉ Allow users to choose *default* ○ always ○ never

3.11.3 Development

These settings are related to development mode. They should not be enabled on a production system.

Standardized Hooks - Debug Mode [?]	◉ Debug mode is off. *default* ○ Debug mode is on. The system displays information about a hook while it executes, but does not log debug data to the error log. ○ Debug mode is on. The system displays information about a hook while it executes and logs debug data to the error log. ○ Debug mode is on. The system displays information about every stage for every hookable event, even if no hooks exist for that stage.
User Interface - Debug Mode [?]	◉ Debug mode is off. *default* ○ Debug mode is on.

3.11.4 Display

These settings control some of the display features of cPanel. If you have another login theme, you can set that here to be the default. Not every hosting provider creates their own theme. cPanel also ships a "cpanel-legacy" theme, but this should not be enabled. Anything legacy is at risk of removal by cPanel at any time.

The option to Display File Usage Information in the cPanel stats bar is how you can show users their inode count. Keep in mind that cPanel doesn't have any built-in inode restrictions. These items are controlled through addon software like CloudLinux.

The Number of Accounts Per Page takes affect on the List Accounts page. These are the number of accounts you would like to see per page. If you set this value too low, you will have a larger number of pages to flip through if you have a large number of accounts. Set this value too high and you could slow down your browser. 30 is the default. All is fine on small servers.

Display announcement banner allows cPanel to display announcements to users when they login. Typically, these announcements are new features that are released when cPanel updates. The default is On, but you can disable that feature here.

The last option is Display Upgrade Opportunities column in "List Accounts". This feature allows you to provide upselling opportunities to your clients – it'll note which clients are running low on disk space, etc. cPanel does not display this to your clients. The default is Off as this can clutter up the List Accounts page.

3.11.5 Domains

This section has a lot of options regarding how domains are handled on your system. There are a lot of options here, and for most of them the defaults are fine.

Allow users to park subdomains of the server's hostname.

Default: Off. For example, if the server's hostname is "server.example.com", then this option enabled would allow an account to park a domain such as "mywebsite.server.example.com". This is a security risk as it could allow impersonation of your hosting company.

Allow cPanel users to create subdomains across accounts

Default: Off. If this is enabled, it would allow AccountA to create a subdomain of a domain name that AccountB owns. So for example if AccountB owned "example.com", AccountA could create "forums.example.com" even though example.com is not owned by their account. This is a security risk to enable on shared servers.

Allow WHM users to create subdomains across accounts

Default: Off. This is just like the last option except it filters to users who have access to WHM. It is a security risk to enable this feature on shared servers.

Allow Remote Domains

Default: Off. This will allow cPanel to add domains to accounts either as parked or addon domains even if their name servers point elsewhere. This is to "prove" that the user adding the domains owns them or has some control over them (e.g. to prevent spoofing of domains they don't own). However, if a customer is using an external DNS service, such as Cloudflare, with this option enabled, they will not be able to add the domain themselves without first changing the nameservers. However, WHM users can add the domain for the user.

Allow resellers to create accounts with subdomains of the server's hostname.

Default: Off. Just like the first option, this will prevent reseller users from creating accounts with subdomains using the server's hostname. It is recommended to keep this off.

Allow unregistered domains

Default: Off. This option will prevent the system from adding domains that aren't registered. While it's not a security risk, it can be a minor risk to have this enabled. If this setting is disabled, the system will not check if a domain is registered or not.

Automatically add A entries for registered nameservers when creating a new zone

Default: On. This setting will automatically add A records for registered nameservers when a new domain is added to the system. It's recommended to keep this on.

Replace service SSL certificates that do not match the local hostname

Default: On. This option will enable the system to replace service SSL certificates that don't match the hostname. For example, mail.example.com, ftp.example.com. It's recommended to leave this on.

Prevent cPanel users from creating specific domains

Default: On. This setting will cause cPanel to check a list of common domains. If the domain is on that list, it will not add it to the system. It is strongly recommended to keep this option on to prevent spoofing.

Check zone syntax

Default: On. This makes sure that zone files are formatted properly.

Check zone owner

Default: On. This makes sure that zone files are owned by the right account.

Enable DKIM on domains for newly created accounts

Default: On. DKIM is important to helping emails get delivered. cPanel can generate the required DNS records automatically.

Enable SPF on domains for newly created accounts

Default: On. SPF is important to helping emails get delivered. cPanel can generate the required DNS records automatically.

DNS request management application

Default: dnsadmin, auto-detect SSL. Not recommended to change.

Service subdomains

Default: On. This option will generate service subdomains, for example: mail.example.com, ftp.example.com, etc.

Thunderbird and Outlook autodiscover and autoconfig support (enables service subdomain and SRV record creation)

Default: Off. This option might be worth turning on as it will enable email clients to self-discover email settings for email accounts.

Preferred mail service to configure to use for Thunderbird and Outlook autodiscover and autoconfig support

Default: imap.

Host to publish in the SRV records for Outlook autodiscover support.

Default: cpanelemaildiscovery.cpanel.net.

Overwrite custom A records used for service subdomains

Default: Off. If this is enabled, then custom A records that match service subdomains weill be removed when you add or remove a subdomain. Recommended to leave this off.

Overwrite custom SRV records used by Outlook AutoDiscover support

Default: Off. Same as above.

Service subdomain override

Default: On. Allows customers to create cpanel, webmail, webdisk, etc. service subdomains. Recommended to leave this on.

Restrict document roots to public_html

Default: On, Recommended: Off. This setting will restrict all document roots, including subdomains, to use public_html. I recommend turning this off because I like my subdomain document roots to be located just outside public_html. Remember, anything inside public_html can be browsed through the main website domain. This can also affect MultiPHP settings as well.

Share the document root by default when creating a domain

Default: On. This setting controls the check box "Share document root" by default on the "Create a New Domain" page in cPanel.

Always use authoritative (registered) nameservers when creating a new DNS zone.

Default: Off. This will tell cPanel to ignore the configured nameservers for a domain and to use the authoritative ones. It's recommended to keep this off.

3.11.6 Logging

dnsadmin logging level *(Minimum: 0; Maximum: 9)* [?]	◉ 0 *default* ○ 0
Enable verbose logging of DNS zone syncing [?]	○ On ◉ Off *default*
Log successful logins [?]	○ On ◉ Off *default*
Enable cPanel API Log [?]	○ On ◉ Off *default*

The logging settings are related to cPanel's application logs. The defaults are off, but you may want to enable these logs and increase logging verbosity if you suspect you are having problems. On busy servers, this will generate large log files. Keep these off unless you suspect a problem.

3.11.7 Mail

These settings are related to email on the server. Some of these settings should be changed.

Max hourly emails per domain

Default: Unlimited. It is strongly recommended to change this setting for spam prevention. 500 is a safe number, it can be increased to 1000 if needed depending on your client needs.

Number of emails a domain may send per day before the system sends a notification.

Default: Unlimited. It's recommended to change this value based on the previous value.

The mailbox storage format for new accounts

Default: maildir. This is the best option.

Initial default/catch-all forwarder destination

Default: System account. By default, cPanel will use the system account email (the cPanel username) as a catchall account. A lot of customers don't check this account causing it to fill up with spam. If you want to disable this behavior, the best option is Blackhole.

Mail authentication via domain owner password

Default: Off. This setting is a special setting. It allows the cPanel account user who created an email account to login to that account with the cPanel account's password if this option is enabled. Even with this option off, a cPanel account owner can still access email accounts, but will only be able to do so from within the cPanel interface. It's recommended to keep this setting Off.

Include mailman in disk usage calculations

Default: On. This is recommended.

Email delivery retry time

Default: 15 minutes. This is the amount of time the system will wait before retrying email delivery if it fails.

Track email origin via X-Source email headers

Default: On. This will add headers to emails to track the user that sends emails. It's recommended keeping this on for spam prevention, especially on shared servers.

The percentage of email messages (above the account's hourly maximum) to queue and retry for delivery. (Minimum: 100; Maximum: 10,000)

Default: 125%. It's not recommended to change this setting.

Monitor the number of unique recipients per hour to detect potential spammers.

Default: On. You should definitely keep this on, especially on a shared server.

Select the action for the system to take on an email account when it detects a potential spammer.

Default: Take no action. Recommended: Hold outgoing mail. If a potential spammer is detected, this is the action that the system will take.

Number of unique recipients per hour to trigger potential spammer notification.

Default: 500.

Count mailman deliveries towards a domain's Max hourly emails.

Default: No. It's recommended to leave this as default as any users who are using the Mailman software will encounter potential issues.

Maximum percentage of failed or deferred messages a domain may send per hour

Default: Unlimited. Recommended: 100%. This setting is the maximum percentage of a domain's outgoing mail that can consist of failed or deferred messages. Once this setting is reached, the system will temporarily block email.

Number of failed or deferred messages a domain may send before protections can be triggered

Default: 5.

Restrict outgoing SMTP to root, exim, and mailman (FKA SMTP Tweak)

Default: On. This setting restricts outgoing SMTP to special system users. You may find that if you have users that need to connect to an external mail server, this setting needs to be changed to Off.

Prevent "nobody" from sending mail

Default: On. You should definitely leave this on for spam prevention.

Allow users to relay mail if they use an IP address through which someone has validated an IMAP or POP3 login within the last hour (Pop-before-SMTP)

Default: Off. You should leave this off for spam prevention.

Add X-PopBeforeSMTP header for mail sent via POP-before-SMTP

Default: Off. You should only enable this for troubleshooting. Otherwise it is not required to be on.

Enable BoxTrapper spam trap

Default: On. While this feature is not widely used, you can disable it if you would like but you may find a user that does actually use it.

Enable Email Archiving support

Default: Off. If you want to enable Email Archiving support, you can enable this but it's safe to keep it off.

Enable Mailman mailing lists

Default: On. Mailman mailing lists are like discussion forums. Surprisingly, you'll find a few users still using it so you might want to leave this on.

Enable Roundcube webmail

Default: On. You should leave this on as cPanel does not have any other webmail software available. Otherwise, users will have to connect a mail client in order to check email.

Enable Apache SpamAssassin™ spam filter

Default: On. You should only disable this unless you have an external mail filter. In most cases you won't so you should leave this on.

Enable Apache SpamAssassin™ Spam Box delivery for messages marked as spam (user configurable)

Default: On. This will enable a "spam" box in each mailbox. You should leave this on.

Prefix "mail." onto Mailman URLs

Default: Off. If enabled, this will prefix "mail" to any URL that has Mailman configured on it. For example, if you use "lists.example.com", and this is enabled, the Mailman URL will be "mail.lists.example.com".

Default user-defined quota value for new email accounts (Maximum: 4,294,967,296)

Default: 32768 MB. There's no reason to change this unless you feel compelled to.

Default quota option for new email accounts

Default: User-defined. This will change the default quota to the amount specified above.

3.11.8 Notifications

These settings are for system notifications that the system will send to users.

System disk space usage warnings

Default: On.

Account system disk usage "warn" percentage

Default: 82.55%

Account system disk usage "critical" percentage

Default: 92.55%

Disk quota usage warnings

Default: On.

Out of memory warnings

Default: On.

Account disk quota "warn" percentage

Default: 80%

Notify admin or reseller when disk quota reaches "warn" state

Default: Off.

Account disk quota "critical" percentage

Default: 90%

Notify admin or reseller when disk quota reaches "critical" state

Default: On.

Account disk quota "full" percentage

Default: 98%. This is the percentage of quota in which it's reported to the user as completely full. It's best to leave this below 100% to allow for extra space.

Notify admin or reseller when disk quota reaches "full" state

Default: On.

Enable mailbox usage warnings

Default: Off.

Mailbox disk quota "warn" percentage

Default: 80%

Mailbox disk quota "critical" percentage

Default: 90%

Mailbox disk quota "full" percentage

Default: 98%.

Bandwidth limit check

Default: On.

Send notifications when certificates approach expiry.

Default: On. This will send account owners notifications that their SSL certificates are reaching expiration. It can be annoying for some users, but they can turn this off at the account level.

Send bandwidth limit notification emails

Default: On.

Bandwidth usage warning: 70%

Default: Off.

Bandwidth usage warning: 75%

Default: Off.

Bandwidth usage warning: 80%

Default: On.

Bandwidth usage warning: 85%

Default: Off.

Bandwidth usage warning: 90%

Default: Off.

Bandwidth usage warning: 95%

Default: Off.

Bandwidth usage warning: 97%

Default: Off.

Bandwidth usage warning: 98%

Default: Off.

Bandwidth usage warning: 99%

Default: Off.

3.11.9 Packages

These are settings for new package defaults.

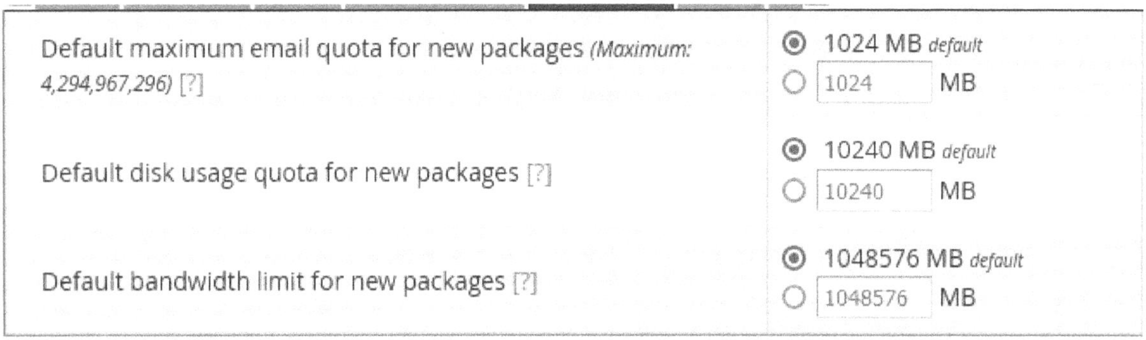

Default maximum email quota for new packages *(Maximum: 4,294,967,296)* [?]	◉ 1024 MB *default* ○ 1024 MB
Default disk usage quota for new packages [?]	◉ 10240 MB *default* ○ 10240 MB
Default bandwidth limit for new packages [?]	◉ 1048576 MB *default* ○ 1048576 MB

3.11.10 PHP

These settings are related to cPanel's built in PHP. Any settings here will not affect websites. This is strictly for the PHP version that runs the cPanel web interface. A common item you may need to enable here is the ioncube PHP loader. For example, Softaculous is a plugin that requires ioncube to be enabled.

cPanel PHP max execution time *(Minimum: 90; Maximum: 500)* [?]	◉ 90 s *default* ○ 90 s
cPanel PHP memory limit *(Minimum: 128; Maximum: 16,384)*	◉ 128 MB *default* ○ 128 MB
cPanel PHP max POST size *(Minimum: 55; Maximum: 2,047)*	◉ 55 MB *default* ○ 55 MB
cPanel PHP max upload size *(Minimum: 50; Maximum: 2,047)*	◉ 50 MB *default* ○ 50 MB
cPanel PHP loader	☐ ioncube ☐ sourceguardian

3.11.11 Redirection

These settings are for redirection when it comes to cPanel and WHM interfaces. For example, you can force a particular hostname or domain name. When a user logs out, you can redirect them to a specific page.

Choose the closest matched domain for which that the system has a valid certificate when redirecting from non-SSL to SSL URLs. Formerly known as "Always redirect to SSL/TLS" [?]	◉ On *default* ○ Off
Non-SSL redirect destination [?]	○ *Hostname* ◉ *Origin Domain Name default*
SSL redirect destination [?]	◉ *SSL Certificate Name default* ○ *Hostname* ○ *Origin Domain Name*
Logout redirection URL [?]	◉ No redirection *default* ○

3.11.12 Security

These settings allow you to tweak the security of your server. Some of these settings may affect quality of life for your users so adjust these carefully, especially after you have already brought users onto the system.

Allow autocomplete for login screens.

Default: On. If you change this setting to "Off" then it will disable the ability for browsers to save details in the Username field on login screens.

Hide login password from cgi scripts

Default: Off. This setting will prevent CGI scripts from within cPanel from obtaining the login password.

Cookie IP validation

Default: strict. Changing this setting will change the way that cPanel and WHM will validate sessions and cookies. Strict validation requires the current IP address and cookie IP address to exactly match. Loose validation only requires that they are in the same /24 network.

Generate core dumps

Default: Off. This setting should remain off unless cPanel support says they need a core dump. Core dumps can contain sensitive information and should not be enabled unless absolutely necessary.

Send passwords when creating a new account

Default: Off. When this option is enabled, cPanel will send account passwords in plaintext over email. Enabling this option is a security risk.

Enable File Protect

Default: On. This will enable the EasyApache FileProtect module which helps improve the security of each user's public_html directory. You should leave this on.

Blank referrer safety check

Default: Off. This will only permit cpanel/whm/webmail to execute functions when the browser provides a referrer. This will probably break integration with SSO systems and billing software. Cookies are required when this option is enabled. If you're using automation software, you should leave this off.

Referrer safety check

Default: Off. This will only permit cpanel/whm/webmail to execute fuctions when the browser provided referrer exactly matches the destination URL. This will probably break integration with SSO systems and billing software. Cookies are required when this option is enabled. If you're using automation software, you should leave this off.

Require SSL for cPanel Services

Default: On. This option will force the server to redirect unencrypted cPanel, Webmail, WHM, and DAV requests to secure ports. You should leave this option "On".

Allow PHP to be run when logged in as a reseller to WHM

Default: Off. This option should be left off as if it is enabled, PHP will run under root. Running things as root, especially PHP, that does not need to be ran as root can be a security risk for a system.

Allow apps that have not registered with AppConfig to be run when logged in as a reseller to WHM.

Default: Off. This option will require an installed app or addon to register with AppConfig before WHM will execute them when logged in as root or a reseller user. It's generally safe to leave this off, but it should be enabled unless you're using an app or addon that hasn't been updated to use this functionality yet.

Allow apps that have not registered with AppConfig to be run when logged in as root or a reseller with the "all" ACL in WHM.

Default: Off. This option will require an installed app or addon to register with AppConfig before WHM will execute them when logged in as root or a reseller user. It's generally safe to leave this off, but it should be enabled unless you're using an app or addon that hasn't been updated to use this functionality yet. Similar to the above function, but applies to ACLs defined with the "all" permission.

This setting allows WHM applications and addons to execute even if an ACL list has not been defined.

Default: Off. This setting will allow apps and addons to run without an ACL list defined in their AppConfig file. Generally safe to leave this off, but you should enable it unless you are using an app or addon that hasn't been updated yet.

This setting allows cPanel and Webmail applications and addons to execute even if a feature list has not been defined.

Default: Off. This setting will permit cPanel and Webmail apps and addons to run without a feature list item defined. Generally safe to leave this off, but should be turned on for increased security unless you run into issues with any apps or addons that haven't been updated yet.

Use MD5 passwords with Apache

Default: On. While it may be tempting to turn this "off" as MD5 passwords aren't considered generally secure anymore, if you turn this off however, you will be limited to crypt-encoded passwords which have a maximum length of 8 characters. MD5 passwords can be any length.

EXPERIMENTAL: Jail Apache Virtual Hosts using mod_ruid2 and cPanel® jailshell.

Default: Off. Jail is a way to better segment the system. By default, Apache will run as the same user for all user accounts. Enabling this feature will cause Apache to run in a chroot jail and it will segment the Apache vhosts from each other. Keep in mind that this is experimental and it may not work as expected in all cases.

Signature validation on assets downloaded from cPanel & WHM mirrors.

Default: Release Keyring Only. This is the option that cPanel will use to validate packages that are downloaded from the repository. Since this is probably a production server, you should use the Release Keyring Only. The Development keyring should only be enabled on development servers.

Default SSL/TLS Key Type

Default: RSA, 2,048-bit. This is the option for the type of certificates that the server will use to generate or request SSL/TLS certificates. RSA 2,048-bit and RSA 4,096-bit are the recommended values. RSA 2,048-bit is the preferred key type to use in most cases.

Generate a self signed SSL certificate if a CA signed certificate is not available when setting up new domains.

Default: On. This setting will make sure that new domains have some type of SSL certificate when they're created, in this case a self-signed SSL. The self-signed certificate will be replaced when the AutoSSL job runs. You should leave this on.

Verify signatures of 3rdparty cPaddons.

Default: Off. This option will validate the GPG signatures of 3rd party addons. Enabling this option will require that all 3rd party addons be signed. If they are not signed or have an invalid signature, they will not install.

Allow deprecated WHM accesshash authentication

Default: Off. This option should only be enabled if you are using older billing software that has not been updated to use cPanel's new API token. Accesshash should be disabled if possible.

Use X-Frame-Options and X-Content-Type-Options headers with cpsrvd

Default: On. This option helps ensure that your cPanel interface cannot be rendered in a <frame>, <iframe>, or <object> tag. This helps prevent clickjacking and this should be kept on.

Enable strict SSH host key checking

Default: Disabled. This option will help prevent man-in-the-middle attacks by validating that every remote system connecting has a valid key in /etc/ssh/ssh_known_hosts file. By using DNS, the system will check if the remote system has SSHFP records in a DNSSEC-signed zone.

Display a message to reboot the server after essential software updates.

Default: On. This will display a message to the root user after the server has installed some software that requires the server to be rebooted for the updates to take effect. For example, Kernel updates.

Enable Content-Security-Policy on some interfaces

Default: Off. Enabling this option will enable the Content-Security-Policy header on some WHM interfaces. This option can help prevent cross-site scripting (XSS) attacks. JavaScript loaded from external sites will be blocked when visiting a CSP-enabled interface. It's recommended to turn this on unless you are finding issues

3.11.13 Software

These are settings that are related to the cPanel daemons and services. In most cases, you won't need to adjust these settings.

Dormant services [?]	☑ cpdavd ☑ cphulkd ☑ cpsrvd ☑ dnsadmin ☑ spamd
Maintenance cPanel RPM Check [?]	◉ On *default* ○ Off
Maintenance cPanel RPM Digest Check [?]	◉ On *default* ○ Off
Enable phpMyAdmin information schema searches [?]	◉ On *default* ○ Off

3.11.14 SQL

The SQL settings are how cPanel interacts with MySQL and MariaDB.

Include databases in disk usage calculations	(●) On *default*	( ) Off
Use INFORMATION_SCHEMA to acquire database disk usage [?]	(●) On *default*	( ) Off
Allow cPanel & WHM to determine the best value for your database service's open_files_limit configuration? [?]	(●) On *default*	( ) Off
Allow cPanel & WHM to determine the best value for your database service's max_allowed_packet configuration? [?]	(●) On *default*	( ) Off
Allow cPanel & WHM to determine the best value for your database service's innodb_buffer_pool_size configuration? [?]	( ) On	(●) Off *default*
Require a username prefix on names of new databases and database users [?]	(●) On *default*	( ) Off
Force short prefix for MySQL and MariaDB databases [?]	( ) On	(●) Off *default*

3.11.15 Stats and Logs

This section contains some configuration items for the statistics and analytics software within cPanel.

Allow users to update Awstats from cPanel	On / Off (default)
Delete each domain's access logs after statistics are gathered [?]	On (default) / Off
Archive logs in the user's home directory at the end of each stats run unless configured by the user. [?]	On (default) / Off
Remove the previous month's archived logs from the user's home directory at the end of each month unless configured by the user. [?]	On (default) / Off
Extra CPUs for server load [?]	0 default / 0
Keep master FTP log file [?]	On / Off (default)
Keep log files at the end of the month [?]	On / Off (default)
Keep stats logs [?]	On / Off (default)
Apache log file chmod value [?]	0640 default / 0640
Show bandwidth usage in megabytes by default in WHM	On / Off (default)
Stats log level *(Minimum: 1; Maximum: 10)* [?]	1 default / 1
Log rotation size threshold *(Minimum: 10)* [?]	300 MB default / 300 MB
The interval, in days, to retain Exim stats in the database *(Minimum: 1; Maximum: 365,000)*	10 default / 10
The number of days to keep records of ModSecurity™ rule hits. (Use zero to keep forever).	7 default / 7
Number of days to retain upcp logs before purging them *(Minimum: 3; Maximum: 999)* [?]	45 default / 45

3.11.16 Stats Programs

This is where you can enable or disable stats programs as well as enable Awstats Reverse DNS resolution if you would like to have DNS names in Awstats.

Awstats reverse DNS resolution	○ On	◉ Off *default*
Enable Analog stats	◉ On *default*	○ Off
Enable Awstats stats	◉ On *default*	○ Off
Enable Webalizer stats	◉ On *default*	○ Off

3.11.17 Status

This section is one of the smallest. The only option is to change the critical load threshold.

Critical load threshold [?]	◉ # of CPUs (autodetect) *default* ○

3.11.18 Support

This section contains configuration items related to support links and sending logs to cPanel.

Display documentation links in cPanel interface	○ On	◉ Off *default*
Send error reports to cPanel for analysis [?]	○ On	◉ Off *default*
Update analysis retention interval *(Minimum: 0)* [?]	○ Disable message retention ◉ 90 days *default* ○ Save indefinitely ○ 90 days	

3.11.19 System

The final section contains a lot of options about different items on the system, mostly cPanel daemons, and other various system-core related settings.

Accounts that can access a cPanel user account: [?]	◉ Root, Account-Owner, and cPanel User *default* ○ Account-Owner and cPanel User Only ○ cPanel User Only
Allow server-info and server-status [?]	
Allow cPanel users to install SSL Hosts.	◉ On *default* ○ Off
Apache non-SSL IP/port [?]	◉ 0.0.0.0:80 *default* ○ 0.0.0.0:80
Apache SSL port [?]	◉ 0.0.0.0:443 *default* ○ 0.0.0.0:443
cPanel & WHM API shell (for developers) [?]	○ On ◉ Off *default*
DNS server reload deferral time *(Maximum: 300)* [?]	◉ 2 s *default* ○ 2 s
HTTPD deferred reload time [?]	◉ 0 s *default* ○ 0 s
The number of seconds between ChkServd service checks. *(Minimum: 60; Maximum: 7,200)* [?]	◉ 300 *default* ○ 300
The number of times ChkServd allows a previous check to complete before termination. *(Minimum: 1; Maximum: 20)* [?]	◉ 2 *default* ○ 2
The option to enable or disable ChkServd HTML notifications. [?]	◉ On *default* ○ Off
The option to enable or disable ChkServd recovery notifications. [?]	◉ On *default* ○ Off
Conserve memory [?]	○ On ◉ Off *default*
Max upload size for CalDAV/CardDAV server *(Minimum: 1)* [?]	◉ 10 MB *default* ○ 10 MB

cpsrvd username domain lookup [?]	○ On ◉ Off *default*
Prevent cpsrvd from serving standard HTTP ports [?]	○ On ◉ Off *default*
Cache disk quota information [?]	◉ On *default* ○ Off
Recursive DNS query pool size [?]	○ Unrestricted ◉ 10 *default* ○ 10
Reverse DNS lookup upon connect [?]	○ On ◉ Off *default*
Maximum age, in days, of content to keep when automatically emptying the users' File Manager Trash [?]	◉ Disabled *default* ○ disabled
Enable optimizations for the C compiler [?]	○ On ◉ Off *default*
Max HTTP submission size *(Minimum: 1; Maximum: 10,240)* [?]	◉ Unlimited *default* ○ MB
File upload required free space [?]	◉ 5 MB *default* ○ 5 MB
Interval, in days, between rebuilds of the FTP quota and disk usage data (applies to Pure-FTPd only) *(Minimum: 1; Maximum: 365,000)* [?]	◉ 30 *default* ○ 30
Depth to recurse for .htaccess checks *(Minimum: 0)* [?]	◉ 2 *default* ○ 2
Account Invites for Subaccounts [?]	◉ On *default* ○ Off
Listen on IPv6 Addresses [?]	○ On ◉ Off *default*

I/O priority level at which bandwidth usage is processed *(Minimum: 0; Maximum: 7)* [?]	◉ 6 *default* ○ 6
I/O priority level at which stats logs are processed *(Minimum: 0; Maximum: 7)* [?]	◉ 7 *default* ○ 7
I/O priority level at which nightly backups are run *(Minimum: 0; Maximum: 7)* [?]	◉ 6 *default* ○ 6
I/O priority level at which cPanel-generated backups are run *(Minimum: 0; Maximum: 7)* [?]	◉ 7 *default* ○ 7
I/O priority level for user-initiated processes *(Minimum: 0; Maximum: 7)* [?]	◉ 6 *default* ○ 6
I/O priority level at which quota checks are run *(Minimum: 0; Maximum: 7)* [?]	◉ 6 *default* ○ 6
I/O priority level at which FTP quota checks are run (when Pure-FTPd is enabled) *(Minimum: 0; Maximum: 7)* [?]	◉ 6 *default* ○ 6
I/O priority level at which email_archive_maintenance is run *(Minimum: 0; Maximum: 7)* [?]	◉ 7 *default* ○ 7
I/O priority level at which dovecot_maintenance is run *(Minimum: 0; Maximum: 7)* [?]	◉ 7 *default* ○ 7
Use cPanel® jailshell by default [?]	○ On ◉ Off *default*
Jailed /proc mount method *(* Choosing this option will create a limited /proc mount for legacy operating systems.)* [?]	○ Always mount a full /proc ◉ * Full /proc for supported operating systems and xenpv *default* ○ * No /proc for supported operating systems and xenpv
Jailed /bin mounted suid [?]	○ On ◉ Off *default*
Jailed /usr/bin mounted suid [?]	○ On ◉ Off *default*
Max cPanel process memory *(Minimum: 4,096)* [?]	○ Unlimited ◉ 4096 MB *default* ○ 4096 MB

Minimum time between Apache graceful restarts. *(Minimum: 10; Maximum: 600)* [?]	(●) 10 *default* ( ) 10
Send language file changes to cPanel	(●) On *default* ( ) Off
Remote WHM timeout *(Minimum: 35)* [?]	(●) 35 s *default* ( ) 35 s
Disk usage/quota bailout time [?]	(●) 60 s *default* ( ) 60 s
Reset Password for cPanel accounts [?]	(●) On *default* ( ) Off
Reset Password for Subaccounts [?]	(●) On *default* ( ) Off
Enable Linux kernel update during nightly maintenance. [?]	( ) On (●) Off *default*
Server Locale [?]	English System Default: English
Send a notification when a user's backup has errors	(●) On *default* ( ) Off
Allow other applications to run the cPanel and admin binaries [?]	( ) On (●) Off *default*
ChkServd TCP check failure threshold [?]	( ) Disable notifications and restarts from TCP checks (●) 3 *default* ( ) 3
Number of seconds an SSH connection related to an account transfer may be inactive before timing out *(Minimum: 1,800; Maximum: 172,800)*	(●) 1800 seconds *default* ( ) 1800 seconds
Do not make changes to the firewall during account modification. [?]	( ) On (●) Off *default*
Do not make changes to the firewall via scripts/configure_firewall_for_cpanel. [?]	( ) On (●) Off *default*
Enforce user account limits for resellers with the "Account Modification" ACL. [?]	( ) On (●) Off *default*
Copy default error documents to docroot for new accounts, addon domains, and subdomains [?]	( ) On (●) Off *default*

3.12 Update Preferences

cPanel is software that updates frequently. As such, cPanel offers different release tiers that you can put your server on in order to control how often you receive updates as well as how long the version is supported.

3.12.1 Current Version

This section will show you the current version of cPanel you have installed as well as details like where your updates come from and the release tier you are on.

Home / Server Configuration / Update Preferences 

You can use this interface to choose when and how the system updates your server. For more information, read our documentation about release tiers and updates.

cPanel & WHM Version

Installed Version:
120.0.8

Hide Additional Details ^

Update From:
httpupdate.cpanel.net
Current Tier:
CURRENT

3.12.2 Release Tier

cPanel offers 5 different release tiers: LTS (Long Term Servicing), STABLE, RELEASE, CURRENT, and EDGE. At first glance, some of these sound very similar, but there are a few differences. You can also use this tool to downgrade cPanel, but keep in mind that you can't downgrade past a certain point. For example, at the time of this writing, the current LTS version is 118.0.11 but the server is running 120.0.8. this means that the server cannot downgrade to 118, but it can "downgrade" to 120.0.5 on the RELEASE channel because 120.0.8 and 120.0.5 are "compatible" with each other. If you cannot change to a particular channel, it means the version you have installed is too new.

You may also notice that most of the time, the channels will align and you'll find they all have either the same version number or STABLE and RELEASE are the same and CURRENT and EDGE are the same. This is just an alignment of the versions from the cPanel developers, and it is a great time to pick a release tier if you want to change.

Tier	Description
LTS	This is an older, stable version of cPanel that is supported for 1 full year. You can expect your server to update this version of cPanel only once per year (exception are major security issues). If you're looking for the most stable over features, then this is the tier. Keep in mind you may not be able to switch to this tier unless your server is running a version that cPanel has designated as the LTS. At which point you'll have a small window of opportunity to switch over.
STABLE	This is a feature-complete, well-tested, and stable version of cPanel. Generally, it is the previous RELEASE tier version. It updates frequently, but not as frequently as RELEASE.
RELEASE	This is the recommended channel to use. You'll receive new features as they are developed and determined to be stable. It's well-tested and in use by the majority of cPanel servers.
CURRENT	This channel is considered "release candidate" meaning it's a test version and it can contain some features and bugs. Generally, it's pretty stable, but it can still receive some bugs and it may have features that don't make it to release.
EDGE	This can be considered a development beta channel and should not be used for production. Things may break and there will definitely be bugs.

Release Tier

Select the release tier to use for updating cPanel & WHM. You **can't** downgrade or select tiers that are older than the currently-installed version.

	Tier	Currently		Description
○	LTS	118.0.11	⚠	A well-tested and proven version that cPanel, L.L.C. supports for one full year.
○	**STABLE**	**120.0.5**		A version that is feature-complete, fully tested, and is in widespread use.
○	**RELEASE** Recommended	**120.0.5**		A version that is feature-complete and well tested.
◉	**CURRENT**	**120.0.8**		A "release candidate" version that is tested but may not be feature-complete.
○	**EDGE**	**120.0.8**		A development version for testing **only** and **not** for production servers.

3.12.3 Staging Directory

cPanel is a large and complicated piece of software made up of a lot of different components. To improve updating your system, cPanel likes to have a directory on the filesystem it can use to stage files in. You will see a list of available locations where cPanel can stage files. Keep in mind that you are going to need several gigabytes.

Staging Directory

The staging directory stores update data before the system applies it. Make sure to select a directory with enough disk space.

Staging Directory:

Enter a directory path or select a partition from available partitions. This value defaults to the /usr/local/cpanel directory.

/usr/local/cpanel

Available Partitions:

	Staging Directory	Mount Point	Size	Used	Available	Percent Used	Device
◉	/usr/local/cpanel	/	141.92 GB	20.2 GB	121.72 GB	14%	/
○	/tmp	/tmp	3.87 GB	312 KB	3.67 GB	0%	/tmp
○	/var/tmp	/var/tmp	3.87 GB	312 KB	3.67 GB	0%	/var/tmp

Save

3.13 WHM Marketplace

You can use this interface to add and manage extensions as well as manage the license for your server. As the time of this writing, cPanel only offers cPanel and WHM, and WP Toolkit through the WHM Marketplace.

 WHM Marketplace

Home / Server Configuration / WHM Marketplace

This interface enables you to manage licenses on your server as well as install products with active licenses.

Manage Your Extensions

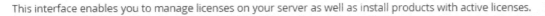

	Product	License Status	Expiration Date	
> cPanel & WHM	cPanel & WHM®	✔ Active	N/A	Manage
>	WP Toolkit	✔ Free	N/A	

4 Support

For VPS/Dedicated Servers

The information in this section applies to VPS and dedicated servers.

This chapter is going to cover the support section for cPanel and WHM as you would expect. This is how you will receive support for cPanel. If you are a reseller user, this chapter will not apply to you. If you are a reseller, you should contact your hosting provider for support.

Important About Support

cPanel has an interesting support policy that usually catches new users off guard. While every license holder of cPanel is entitled to support from cPanel, you must first attempt to receive support from your license provider. Most web hosting companies will gladly sell you a cPanel license with your server. However, you must contact them first, if that's where you got your license from, for support. If they cannot resolve the issue, you can contact cPanel for support.

4.1 Create Support Ticket

This will open a Support Ticket Wizard. You can make your selection based on the type of support you need.

Support Ticket Wizard

A support ticket is how you request help with our product. Select the option below that best describes your situation.

 **Info:** WHM will transmit your support request directly to cPanel, L.L.C.

I need help with an existing feature or technical issue.

If your issue is related to cPanel & WHM software or extensions, please open a Support Ticket for direct assistance.

Get Started

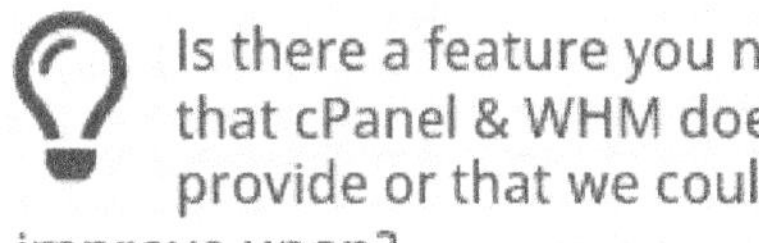

Is there a feature you need that cPanel & WHM does not provide or that we could improve upon?

cPanel L.L.C. loves to hear our customer's ideas about how to improve our product. You may suggest a feature or vote on features suggested by other users.

Visit our feature site

If you click on **Get Started** under the heading "I need help with an existing feature or technical issue.", you will then be taken to a cPanel ID login page. You will need to have a cPanel ID to continue. If you don't have one, click on "Create an account" to follow the process to create a cPanel ID. Otherwise, login with your cPanel ID.

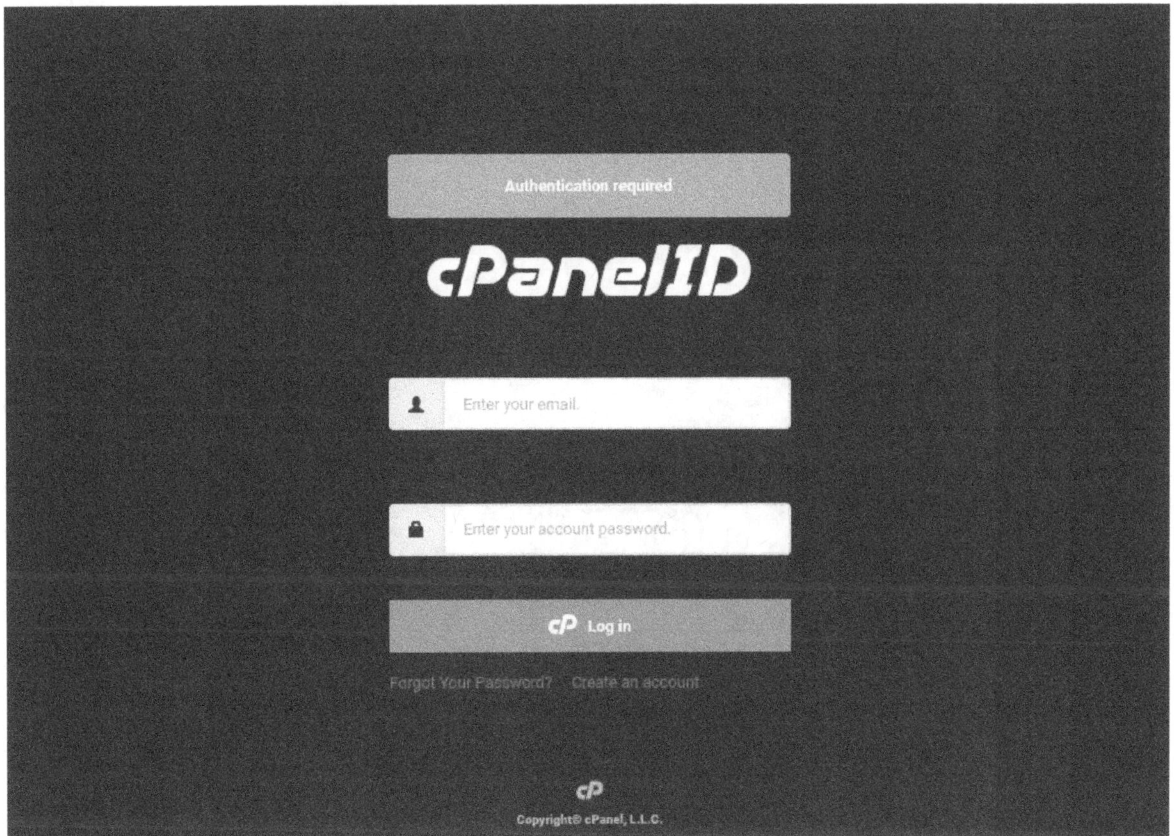

Once you are signed in, you will be at the main cPanel support page.

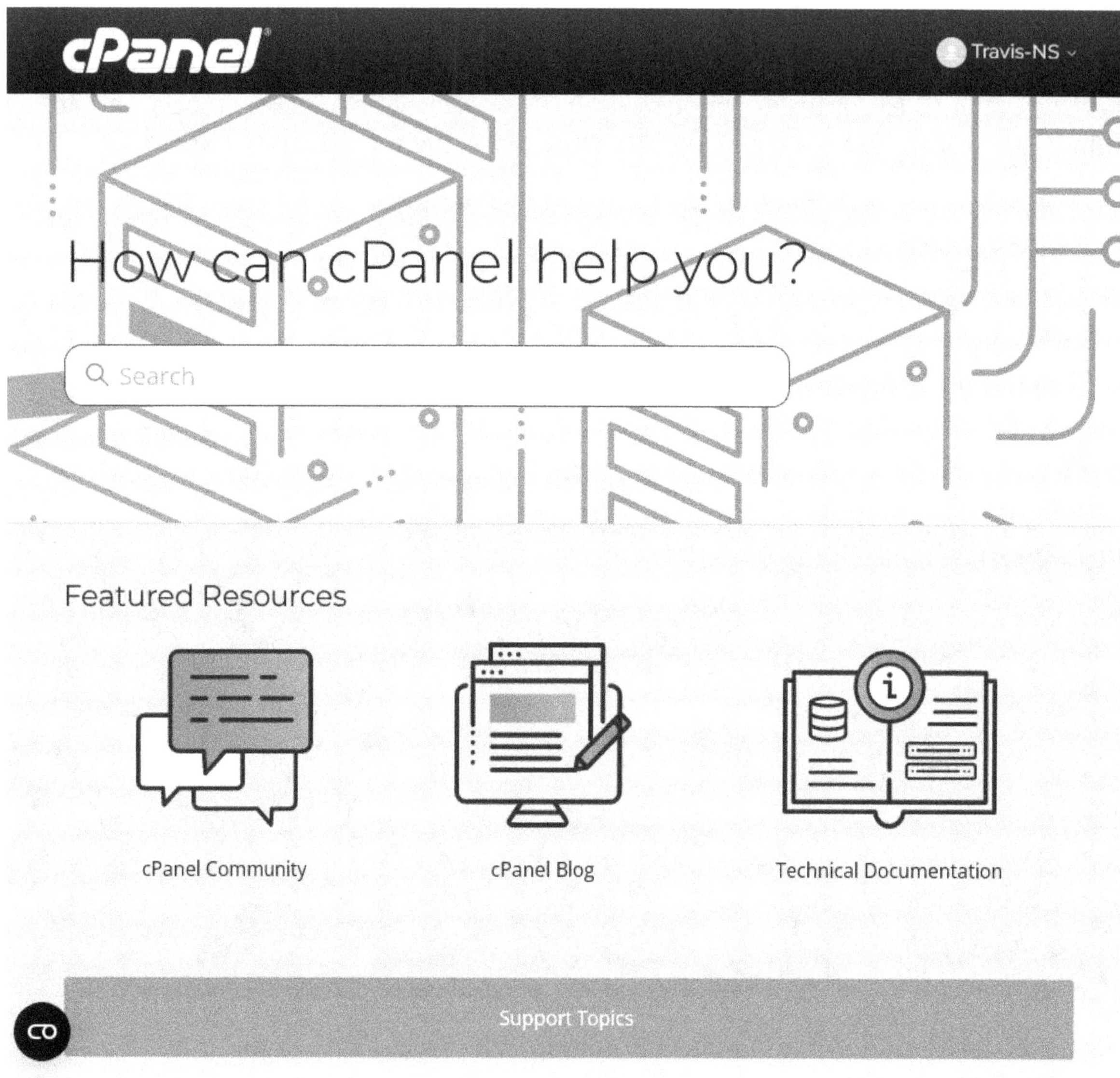

Obviously, cPanel's goal here is to prevent you from opening a ticket. They will encourage you to ask the community, check the blog, or review the technical documentation. If none of these resources work or you have a very serious problem, you can proceed with opening a ticket.

After you click on the big orange **Support Topics** button, if you look at the top menu, you'll notice that there is now a **Submit a Request** link. Click on this link.

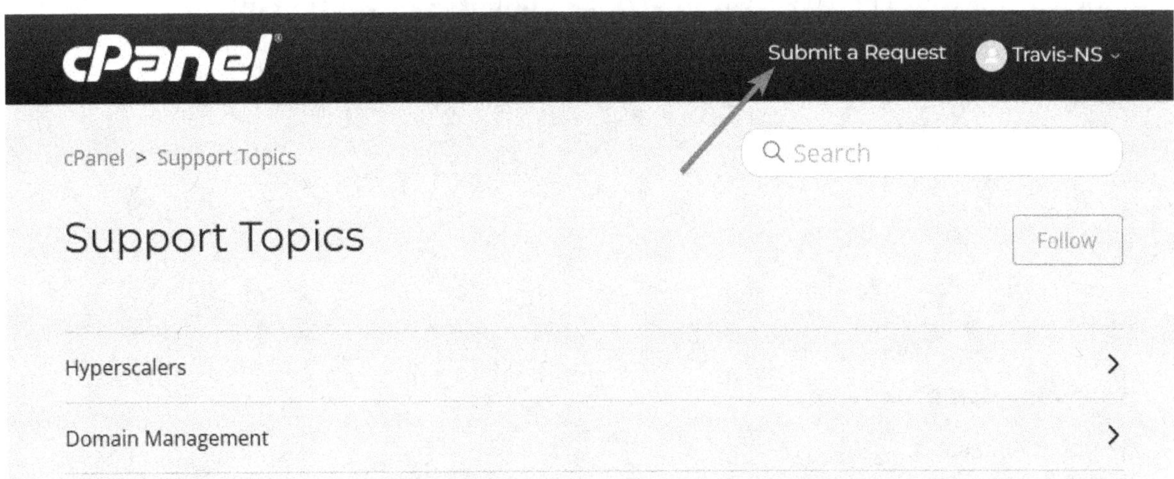

When you click on **Submit a Request**, you will need to select the request type. Here you will choose Technical Support Request. You will see additional fields added to the page. Enter any emails that should be CC'd on this request. You'll also need to enter your server's primary IP address that the cPanel license is tied to at this point.

cPanel > Submit a request

Search

Submit a request

Please select a request type

Technical Support Request

CC

Add emails

Licensed IP Address

How do I find my Licensed IP Address?

When you enter your IP address, cPanel will run a validation to make sure it is licensed. If all is good, another field will show up called **Support Access ID**. This is available from your cPanel server in WHM > Support > Support Center.

Additionally, this is where you can find your server's licensed IP address.

Once you provide the Support Access ID, you will then see the Subject and Description fields appear. Provide a brief description of the issue in the subject line and then in the Description field, provide as much information as possible.

If you want to deny cPanel access to the server, you can check the box requesting to deny server access. You typically do not want to do this.

If you have any attachments, such as screenshots or log files, you can add them to the attachments section.

Finally, agree to the Terms of Service and read the Technical Support Agreement.

At this point, your support ticket will be created. You'll be presented with a list of knowledge base articles that may help. If any of these articles help, you can self-resolve your ticket, otherwise, you can proceed with opening your ticket.

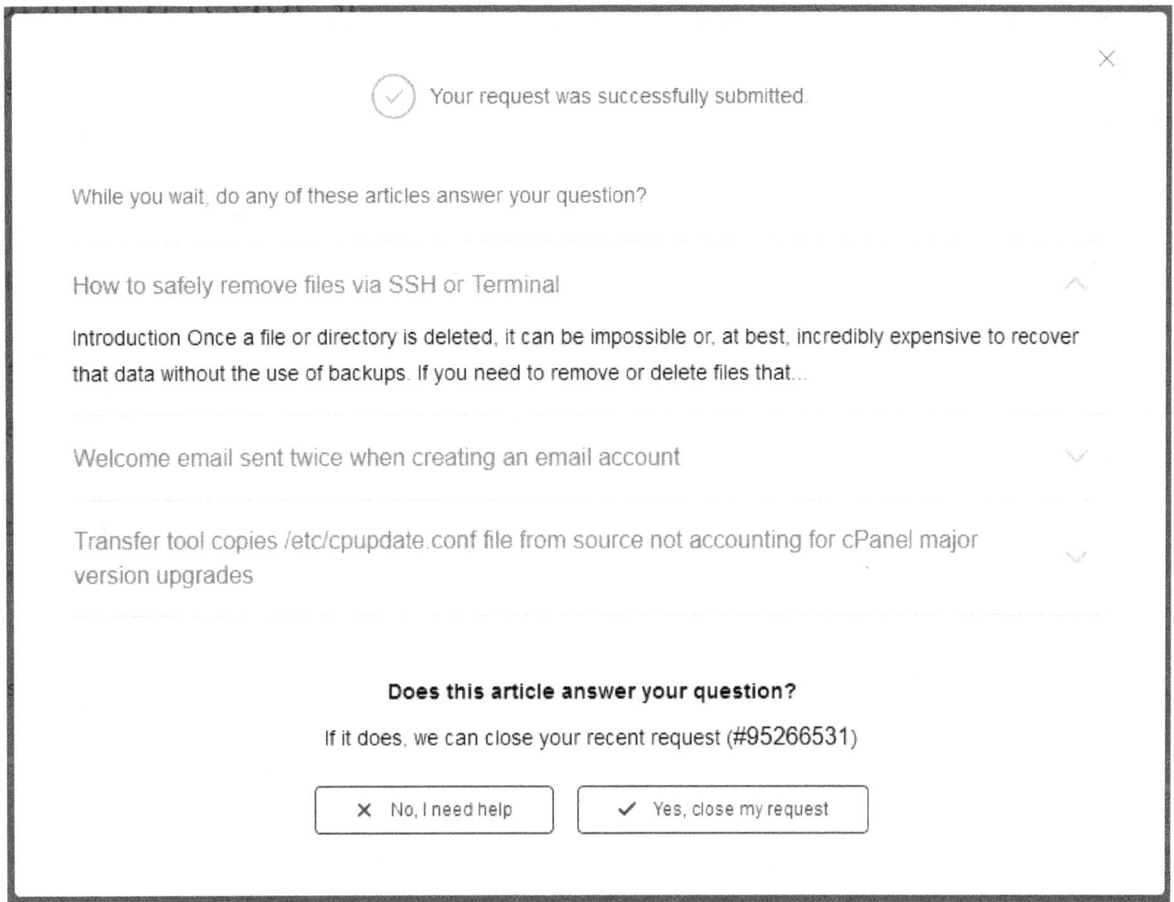

When the ticket is opened, you will then need to prepare your server for support. The support ticket will have the above window open up. It will ask for information about your server and then prepare your server so that cPanel Technical Support can access it. You should read through this carefully and follow the directions in order to ensure they can connect to your server.

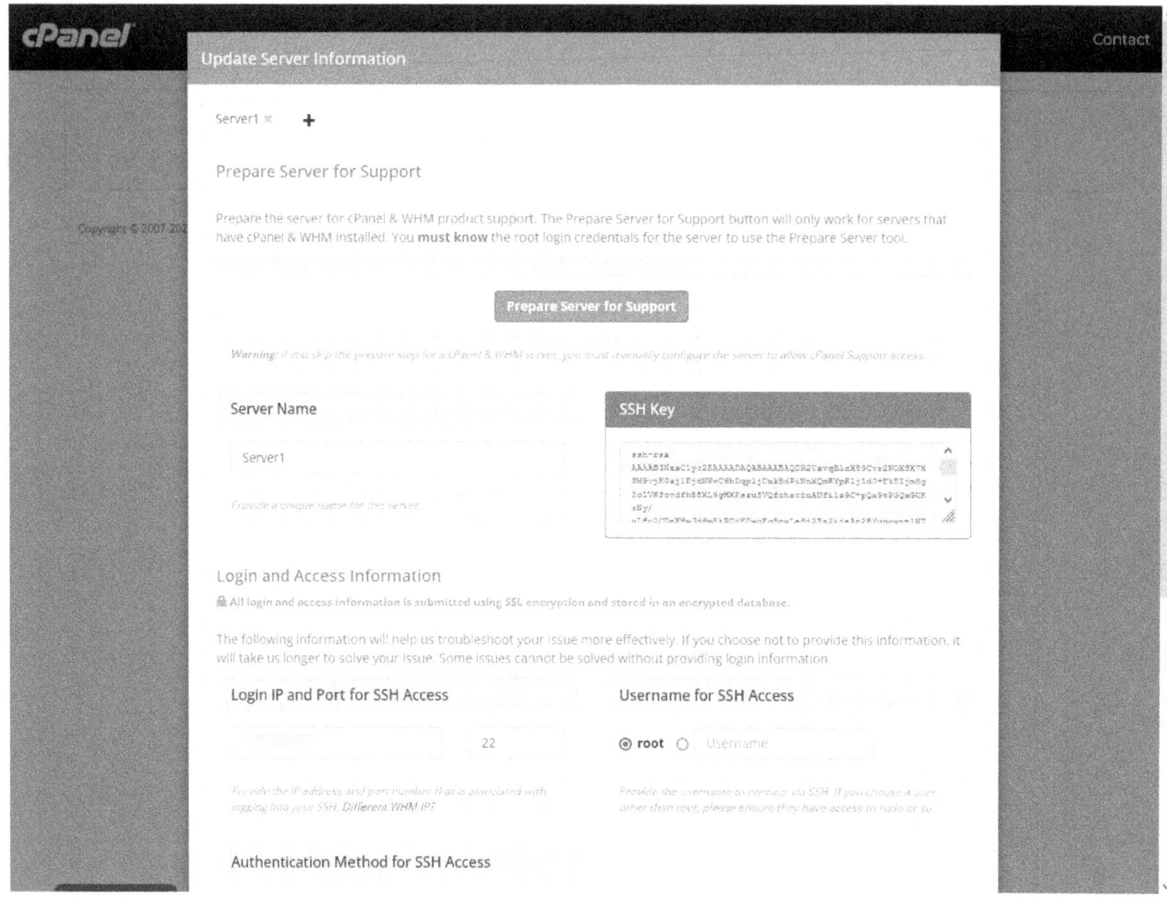

Now your ticket will be opened. Support can connect to your server and you'll receive a reply within a few hours.

4.2 Grant cPanel Support Access

This section will help you grant cPanel Support access to your server. Typically, you will need to have an active support ticket open (see the previous section).

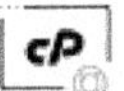

Grant cPanel Support Access - Login

Home / Support / Grant cPanel Support Access

To grant cPanel support access to your server, you **must** connect your server to the cPanel Customer Portal and transfer the necessary authentication details.

Click *Log in to cPanel Customer Portal* to establish a secure connection between your server and the cPanel Customer Portal.

Warning: If you suspect your server is root compromised, do not use this functionality. Contact cPanel support directly by using the cPanel Customer Portal.

Log in to cPanel Customer Portal

Info: If you need to remove cPanel support's access to your system, and you do not have a cPanel Customer Portal account, use WHM's Manage root's SSH Keys interface.

4.3 Support Center

The Support Center page contains some additional resources for getting support and information on cPanel.

Support Center

Home / Support / Support Center 

Resources

cPanel & WHM Knowledge Base

Access our library of information about cPanel & WHM.

Support Forums

Find and share solutions with cPanel & WHM users around the world.

WHM Documentation

Learn how to set up, use, and troubleshoot WHM.

cPanel Documentation

Learn how to set up, use, and troubleshoot cPanel.

cPanel Release Notifications

Learn when new versions of cPanel are propagating.

cPanel News

Get the latest news about upcoming releases.

cPanel University

Test your skills now, or develop your skills further with the cPanel University coursework.

Additionally, this is where you can find your server's IP address and Support Access ID.

5 Networking Setup

For VPS/Dedicated Servers

The information in this section applies to VPS and dedicated servers.

This chapter focuses on the networking aspects of your server. Don't worry, you don't have to be a network administrator to understand it!

5.1 Change Hostname

Your hostname is how the server identifies itself. It's a subdomain on your domain name. Since SSL is enabled by default, cPanel will be helpful and generate a subdomain using your server's IP address and the domain name cprapid.com. The cprapid.com domain is simply a temporary name and it cannot be used for a lot of things, including authoritative name servers.

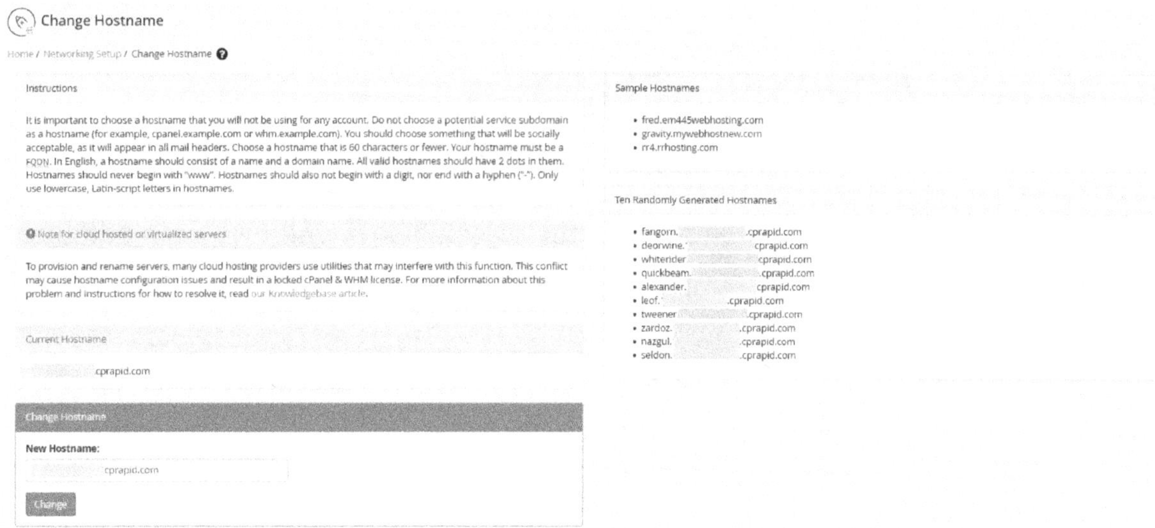

This page will help you pick a hostname by generating some random names that you can consider as well as some sample hostnames to help you better understand what a hostname is. As soon as you have a hostname, you can populate it in the Change Hostname field.

When you change your hostname, cPanel will update it in all the appropriate places and restart some services. You'll receive confirmation when this is complete.

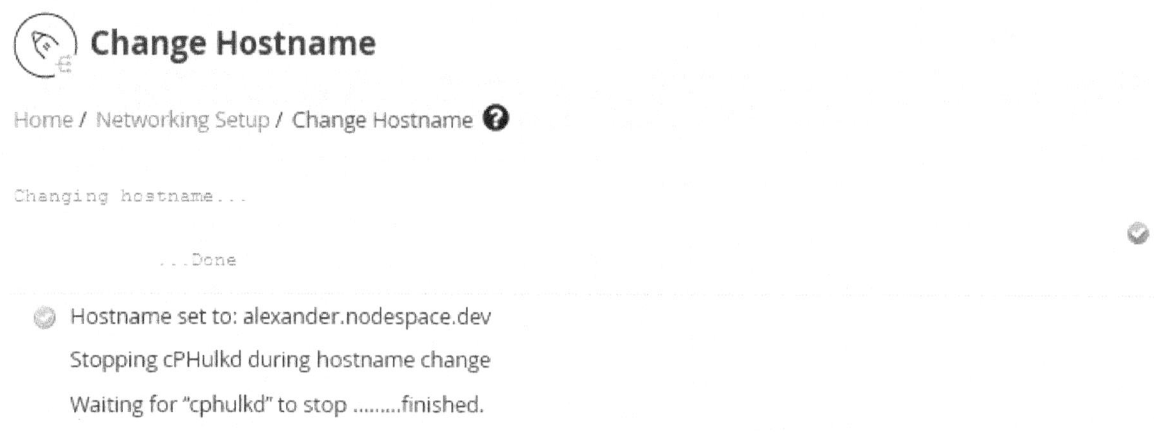

cPanel will also remind you that you should add an A entry for your hostname if you don't already have one. If you are hosting your DNS on this server, you can click the button provided.

You should probably Add an A entry for your hostname if you don't already have one.

If you click the button, you will be taken to the screen below where you can add the hostname directly to DNS.

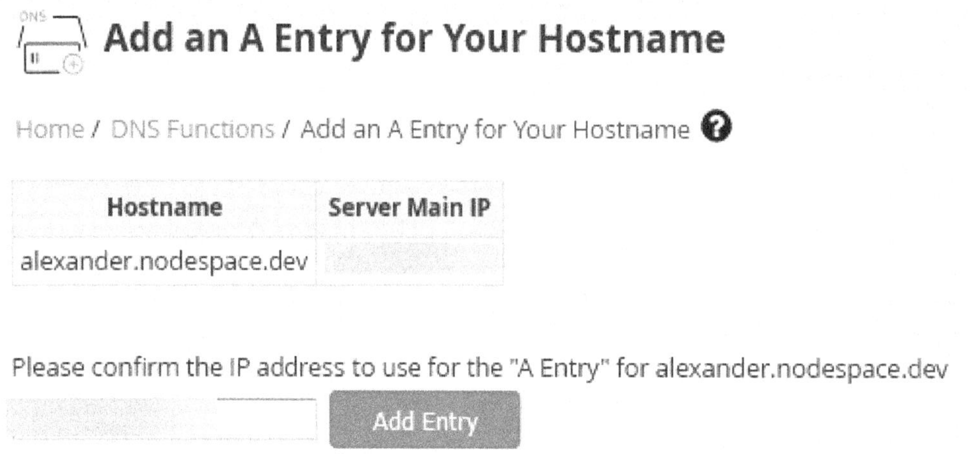

5.2 Resolver Configuration

DNS resolvers help your server resolve hostnames out on the internet. For example, it's very unlikely that your server knows how to reach other servers, so this is where DNS resolvers come in.

If you need to change your resolvers, this is also the place to do it.

To get started, click on the **Proceed** button.

Resolver Configuration

Home / Networking Setup / Resolver Configuration 

This wizard will guide you through setting up your resolver configuration (/etc/resolv.conf).

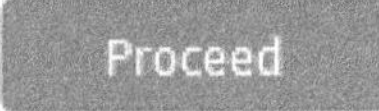

You will then need to put in the IP addresses of DNS resolvers. Some hosting providers run their own internal DNS servers. In which case, you would use your hosting provider's. Alternatively, the next safest ones to use are Google's public DNS servers at `8.8.8.8` and `8.8.4.4`. You may be tempted to use Cloudflare, but a lot of data center networks have issues with Cloudflare's `1.1.1.1` and `1.1.2.2`.

Resolver Configuration

Home / Networking Setup / Resolver Configuration 

Step 2

Enter the IP addresses of at least two nameservers that you will use for DNS resolution. Your datacenter should be able to provide you with at least one IP of a DNS server you can access. If you do not know the IP address of your provider's local resolvers, you should contact them. It is very important that these nameservers are correct, or your server will not function properly. If you do not know what to put in the boxes below and cannot contact your provider please close this window and go though this setup at a later time. Your server should still function normally; however, connections made to the server may be slower than normal.

Primary Resolver	8.8.8.8
Secondary Resolver	8.8.4.4
Tertiary Resolver (optional)	

Continue

Once you have the DNS resolvers entered, click on **Continue**.

You will then receive confirmation that your DNS resolvers have been updated.

6 Security Center

Security on a cPanel server is paramount. This section contains many tools to help you harden your server and keep your server safe from hackers and mischievous clients who will attempt you use your service for nefarious reasons.

Important Note

Security is always a cat and mouse game! The settings and recommendations in this chapter should be carefully reviewed. What is considered safe and secure today, may not be tomorrow. Especially since this is a book, this knowledge and information is the most that is likely to change and evolve a great deal. Major updates will always be posted on this book's website at https://www.nodespacebooks.com/whm.

6.1 Apache mod_userdir Tweak

For VPS/Dedicated Servers

The information in this section applies to VPS and dedicated servers.

This is a feature that is disabled on most systems by default. This is because cPanel will configure Apache to run web server processes as the user. cPanel provides instructions on the changes you need to make to your system to enable this feature.

The main purpose of this feature is to restrict mod_userdir to URLs whose users own the URL's domains so that malicious users cannot use one domain to drain the bandwidth of another on the system.

For example: if the server has the domain `example.com`, a user could go to `example.com/~michael` and this would load up the website under the "`michael`" account, but the bandwidth would be counted against the user who owns "`example.com`".

With this feature enabled, users must either use the DefaultHost (which is the server's hostname) or a domain on their account. You can either disable protection entirely by checking the "Exclude Protection" box next to the domain or subdomain or you can add additional users to a domain to use it with mod_userdir. For example, if "`michael`" was permitted to load through "`example.com`", then you could add the username "`michael`" next to the `example.com` entry.

Click on **Save** to save the settings and apply them.

6.2 SMTP Restrictions

For VPS/Dedicated Servers
The information in this section applies to VPS and dedicated servers.

This is a feature that will prevent users from bypassing the mail server to send mail. While this is commonly used by spammers, it may have some unintended consequences. For example, if you have a user who needs to send mail through their own mail server, if SMTP restriction is enabled, then any attempts to connect to that other mail server will be blocked. If this restriction is disabled, then the connection will be permitted.

If this setting is enabled, only the Mail Transfer Agent (MTA) software, mailman software, and root user will be permitted to connect to remote SMTP servers.

Generally, it is safer to keep this enabled, but I recommend disabling it if you receive support ticket requests from users saying they cannot connect to an external mail server.

6.3 Compiler Access

For VPS/Dedicated Servers
The information in this section applies to VPS and dedicated servers.

A lot of common Linux exploits need a working C compiler as they distribute payloads via source code and then compile this source code on the system. By default, this access is enabled. To harden your system, click on the **Disable Compilers** button.

If you find that you need to permit some unprivileged users access, you can then allow specific users access to use the compilers.

6.4 Configure Security Policies

For VPS/Dedicated Servers

The information in this section applies to VPS and dedicated servers.

Out of the box, cPanel offers standard Linux security. That is my way of saying that it's just very basic operating system level security. You will likely want to harden your system by configuring security policies.

Configure Security Policies

Home / Security Center / Configure Security Policies

This interface provides the configuration settings of the Security Policy that apply to cPanel, cPanel webmail, and WHM on your server.

Security Policy Items

- ☐ Limit logins to verified IP addresses.
- ☐ Two-Factor Authentication: Google Authenticator
- ☐ Password Strength
- ☐ Password Age

Security Policy Extensions

In addition to cPanel, cPanel webmail, and WHM interfaces, enable Security Policies for the following request types:

- ☐ API requests
- ☐ DNS Cluster Requests

Warning: When you enable the Security Policy Extensions for the remote APIs and DNS cluster requests, incompatibilities will become difficult to diagnose. We recommend you do not enable these extensions unless you have an in-depth understanding of your remote API usage and DNS cluster configuration.

You may need to reset your password or provide other information immediately after you click Save.

You can check the items that you want to enable.

- **Limit logins to verified IP addresses.** This option will require users to set and answer security questions. Once the answers to the questions are validated, their IP address will be added to the system's list of verified IP addresses. To edit or add security questions, see the Security Questions section in this chapter.

- **Two-factor Authentication: Google Authenticator.** This option will require that users setup and configure Google Authenticator (or another compatible app) for 2FA. When this is enabled, a Time-Based One-Time Password (TOTP) must be entered.
- **Password Strength.** This setting will enforce a minimum password strength for all system users. This ensures that your users are setting secure passwords.
- **Password Age.** This option can be enabled to enforce that passwords are regularly rotated out. You can enter the number of days that you want a password to be valid. Once the number of days has passed, the user will be forced to change their password.

It's strongly recommended that at a minimum, you enable the Password Strength security policy.

Before enabling either of the Security Policy Extensions, take note of the warning presented. It is not recommended you enable these options.

6.4.1 SSH without Security Questions

If you need to SSH to your server and you have security questions enabled, you are going to find that you will not be able to access the root user. To add your IP address to the system's trusted IPs, use SSH (or the Terminal) to login as the root user. You will then need to edit the file `var/cpanel/userhomes/cpanel/.cpanel/securitypolicy/iplist/root` in your preferred editor. Add the public IP address that will need to access the root user over SSH. Save and close the file. Now access will be permitted without needing to use the security questions.

6.5 cPHulk Brute Force Protection

For VPS/Dedicated Servers
The information in this section applies to VPS and dedicated servers.

cPanel includes a brute force protection tool called cPHulk. It's enabled by default on systems and should remain on. While it is a basic tool, it does provide more protection than you might think. You will find that there are several tabs: Configuration Settings, Whitelist Management, Blacklist Management, Countries Management, and History Reports.

6.5.1 Configuration Settings

This section contains all the configuration options for configuring cPHulk.

Username-based Protection

This section contains brute force protection settings by username. You can adjust these settings as you would like.

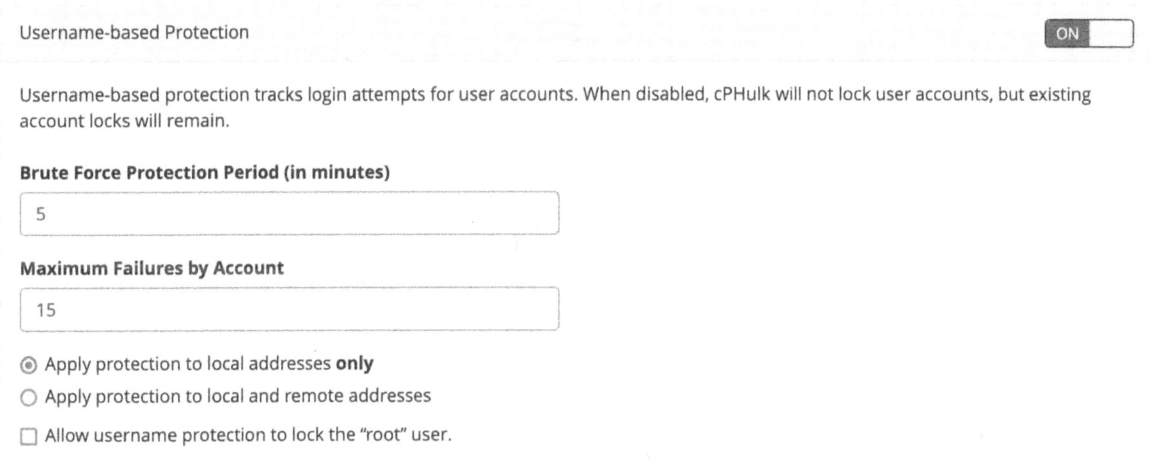

Use caution when enabling the option to allow username protection to lock the root user. When the root user is locked, then you will not be able to access your system, including from the console.

The settings shown here mean that if there are 15 failures of attempting to login to a user and they fail, then the account will be locked out for 5 minutes before unlocking again. The remote IP address will be blacklisted by the system. Think of this as "Stage One" on your 3-stage protection plan.

IP Address-based Protection

This section contains configuration details for IP Address-based protection. This "stage two". Once an account failure occurs (on the 16th attempt), then the IP Address-based protection counter starts.

IP Address-based Protection ON

IP Address-based protection tracks login attempts from specific IP addresses. When disabled, cPHulk will not block IP addresses, but existing blocks will remain.

IP Address-based Brute Force Protection Period (in minutes)

15

Maximum Failures per IP Address

5

Command to Run When an IP Address Triggers Brute Force Protection

Command Text

☐ Block IP addresses at the firewall level if they trigger brute force protection

In this case, after 5 failed attempts, an IP address will be blocked for 15 minutes. If an IP address triggers, you can also have cPHulk run a custom command – for example, reporting the IP address to your security desk for investigation. If you have a system firewall installed, you can also have the IP address blocked by the firewall.

One-day Blocks

This is "third stage" of protections – strike three, you're out!

One-day Blocks

Maximum Failures per IP Address before the IP Address is Blocked for One Day

30

Command to Run When an IP Address Triggers a One-Day Block

Command Text

☑ Block IP addresses at the firewall level if they trigger a one-day block

This option triggers after 30 failed attempts from an IP address and it is blocked for a full 24-hours. Additionally, it is added to the system firewall. You can also run a custom command when this triggers.

Login History

By default, the system will retain all failed logins for 360 minutes. You can change this value if you would like, but 360 minutes is a good value.

Notifications

The notifications section will allow you to have email alerts sent on several login conditions.

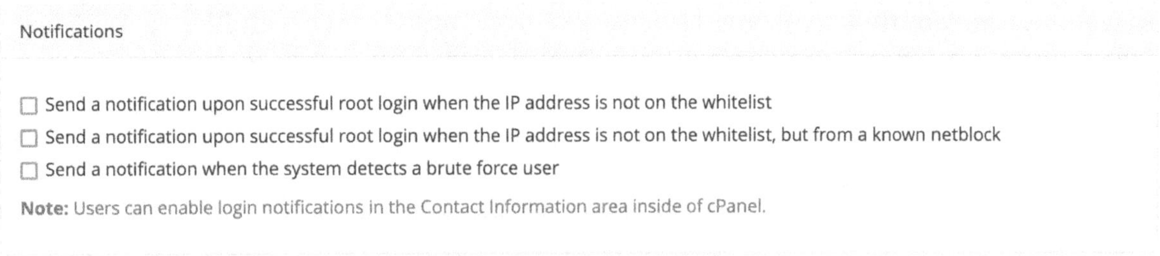

Notifications

- [ ] Send a notification upon successful root login when the IP address is not on the whitelist
- [ ] Send a notification upon successful root login when the IP address is not on the whitelist, but from a known netblock
- [ ] Send a notification when the system detects a brute force user

Note: Users can enable login notifications in the Contact Information area inside of cPanel.

For example, if you have a whitelist containing office IP addresses and root logs in from a location not on the list, cPHulk can send an alert about this. Same if there is a root login when the IP isn't on the whitelist, but from a known network. Finally, you can also choose to receive an alert when the system detects a brute force attempt.

It is a good idea to enable these alerts for visibility and security on your system.

6.5.2 Whitelist Management

You can use the Whitelist Management tab to add IP addresses and networks to the whitelist. IPs on this list can always login no matter what. It is strongly recommended to only add IP addresses from trusted locations (like a home or office) that are unlikely to change.

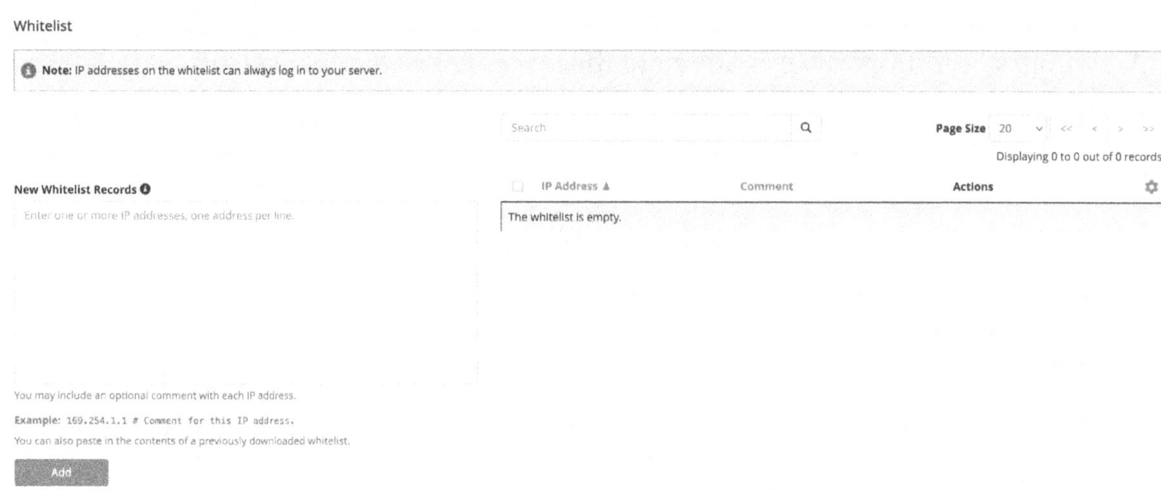

A helpful aspect of this tab is you can also enter a comment with an IP address. This way you can keep track of why it's there. For example, you might use the following format:

```
100.65.54.12 # Main Office
100.73.2.64 # Michael Scott Home
```

With this formatting, you'll see the IPs show up nicely in the list of IPs along with their comments.

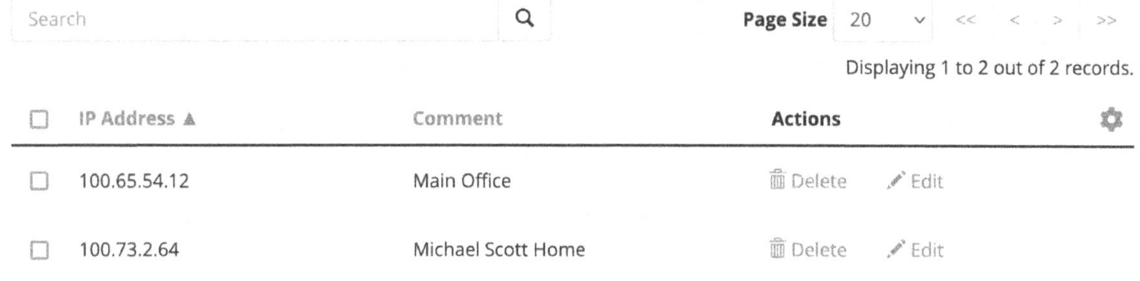

If you need to add or edit the comment on an entry, click the edit button.

IP Address

100.65.54.12

Comment

Main Office

Update Cancel

You cannot edit an IP address. Instead, you will need to delete and then re-add the IP address.

If the IP address you are currently logged into WHM with is not on the whitelist, you will receive an alert with a button that will allow you to add it.

6.5.3 Blacklist Management

If you go to the Blacklist Management, you can add IPs to the blacklist. Blackisted IPs are not permitted to login to the server at all.

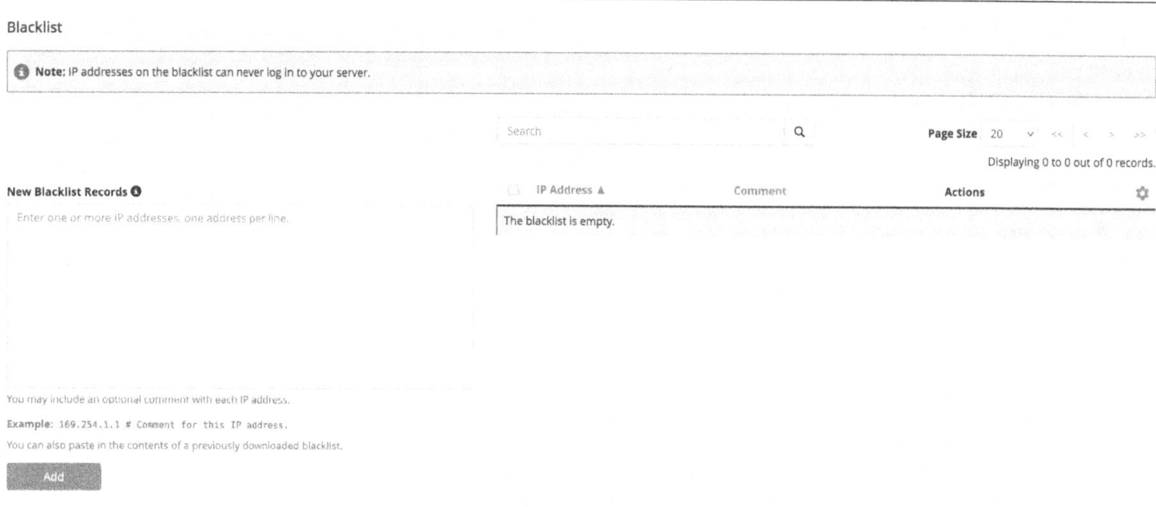

Just like with the whitelist, you can enter a comment with an IP address. This is helpful to keep track of why it's there. For example, you might use the following format:

```
100.65.54.12 # Hacker
100.73.2.64 # Toby Flenderson
```

With this formatting, you'll see the IPs show up nicely in the list, along with their comments.

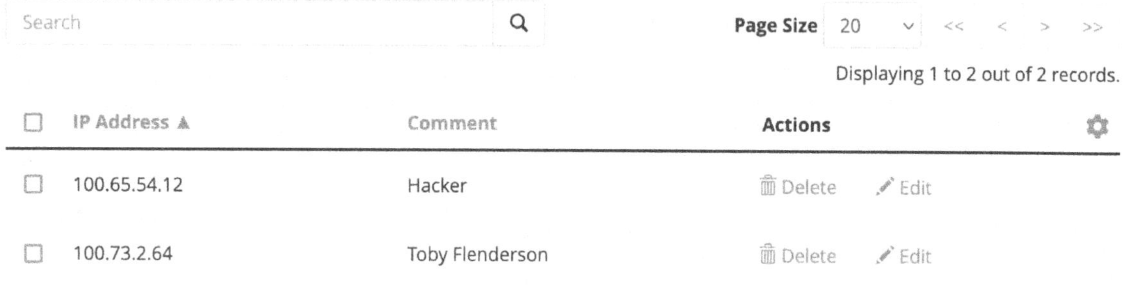

If you need to add or edit the comment for an entry, click the edit button.

IP Address

100.73.2.64

Comment

Toby Flenderson

Update Cancel

Again, you cannot edit an IP address. You need to delete and then re-add the IP address.

6.5.4 Countries Management

The countries management tab allows you to whitelist or blacklist entire countries. Any countries whitelisted will always be allowed to access your server. Blacklisted countries will never be allowed to access your server. This is useful if you only want certain countries to be able to access your server or there are some countries you never want to connect to your server. For example, if you're a business based in the United States and you only do business locally, you may want to block high risk countries.

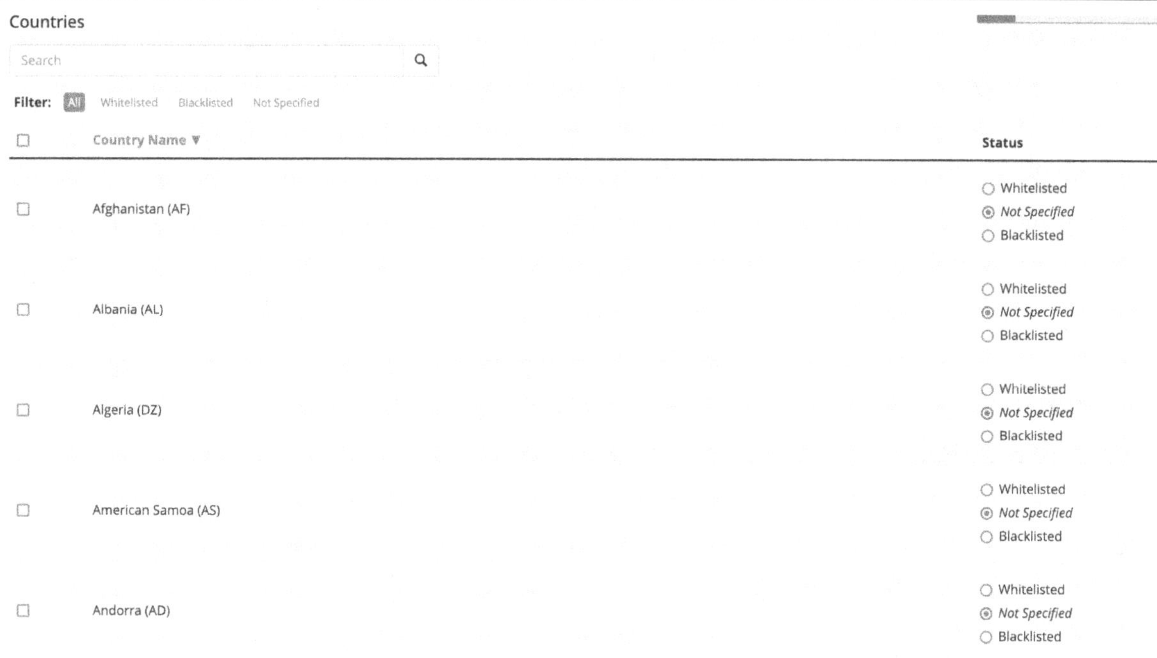

6.5.5 History Reports

The History Reports section will show you details about blocked users and IP addresses. There are several reports available that will show you failed logins, blocked users, blocked IP addresses, and one-day blocks.

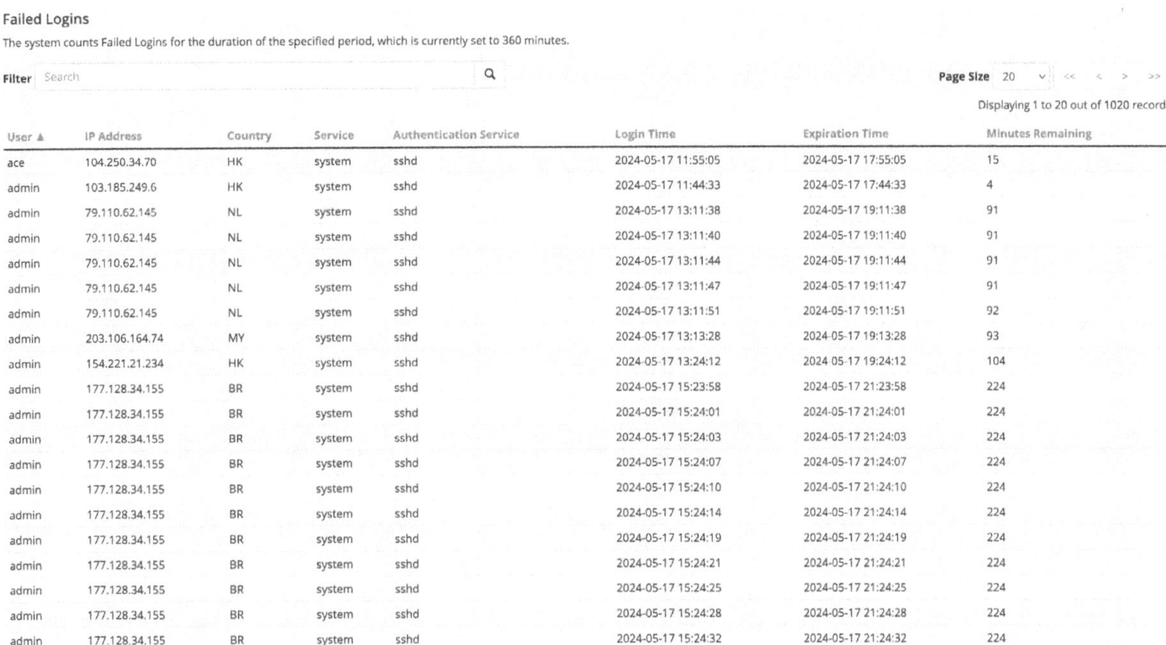

Failed Logins

The system counts Failed Logins for the duration of the specified period, which is currently set to 360 minutes.

Filter Search

Page Size 20

Displaying 1 to 20 out of 1020 records

User ▲	IP Address	Country	Service	Authentication Service	Login Time	Expiration Time	Minutes Remaining
ace	104.250.34.70	HK	system	sshd	2024-05-17 11:55:05	2024-05-17 17:55:05	15
admin	103.185.249.6	HK	system	sshd	2024-05-17 11:44:33	2024-05-17 17:44:33	4
admin	79.110.62.145	NL	system	sshd	2024-05-17 13:11:38	2024-05-17 19:11:38	91
admin	79.110.62.145	NL	system	sshd	2024-05-17 13:11:40	2024-05-17 19:11:40	91
admin	79.110.62.145	NL	system	sshd	2024-05-17 13:11:44	2024-05-17 19:11:44	91
admin	79.110.62.145	NL	system	sshd	2024-05-17 13:11:47	2024-05-17 19:11:47	91
admin	79.110.62.145	NL	system	sshd	2024-05-17 13:11:51	2024-05-17 19:11:51	92
admin	203.106.164.74	MY	system	sshd	2024-05-17 13:13:28	2024-05-17 19:13:28	93
admin	154.221.21.234	HK	system	sshd	2024-05-17 13:24:12	2024-05-17 19:24:12	104
admin	177.128.34.155	BR	system	sshd	2024-05-17 15:23:58	2024-05-17 21:23:58	224
admin	177.128.34.155	BR	system	sshd	2024-05-17 15:24:01	2024-05-17 21:24:01	224
admin	177.128.34.155	BR	system	sshd	2024-05-17 15:24:03	2024-05-17 21:24:03	224
admin	177.128.34.155	BR	system	sshd	2024-05-17 15:24:07	2024-05-17 21:24:07	224
admin	177.128.34.155	BR	system	sshd	2024-05-17 15:24:10	2024-05-17 21:24:10	224
admin	177.128.34.155	BR	system	sshd	2024-05-17 15:24:14	2024-05-17 21:24:14	224
admin	177.128.34.155	BR	system	sshd	2024-05-17 15:24:19	2024-05-17 21:24:19	224
admin	177.128.34.155	BR	system	sshd	2024-05-17 15:24:21	2024-05-17 21:24:21	224
admin	177.128.34.155	BR	system	sshd	2024-05-17 15:24:25	2024-05-17 21:24:25	224
admin	177.128.34.155	BR	system	sshd	2024-05-17 15:24:28	2024-05-17 21:24:28	224
admin	177.128.34.155	BR	system	sshd	2024-05-17 15:24:32	2024-05-17 21:24:32	224

If you need to unblock an IP address, you will find, on the reports, a **Remove Block** link you can select.

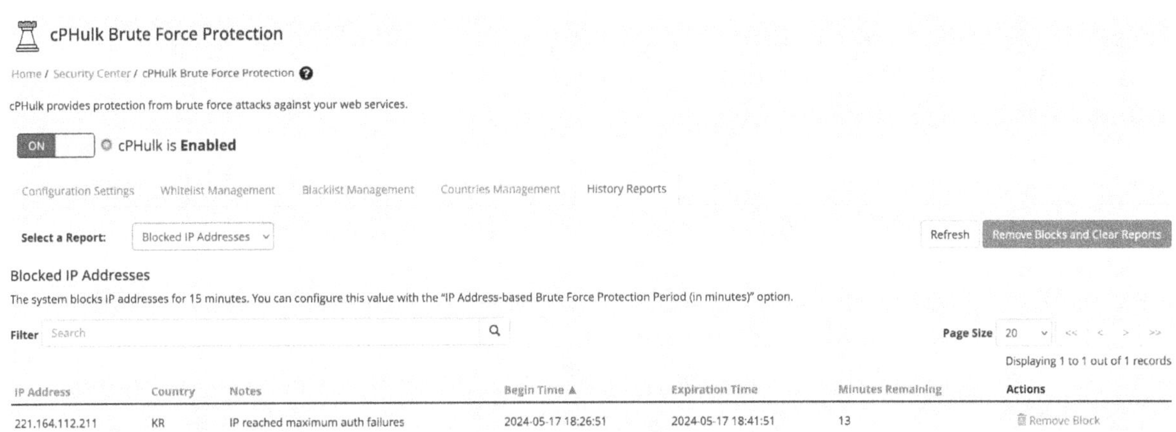

IP Address	Country	Notes	Begin Time ▲	Expiration Time	Minutes Remaining	Actions
221.164.112.211	KR	IP reached maximum auth failures	2024-05-17 18:26:51	2024-05-17 18:41:51	13	Remove Block

6.6 Host Access Control

For VPS/Dedicated Servers

The information in this section applies to VPS and dedicated servers.

The host access control feature works like a firewall. It will let you to allow or block connections on specified port numbers from certain IPs or networks.

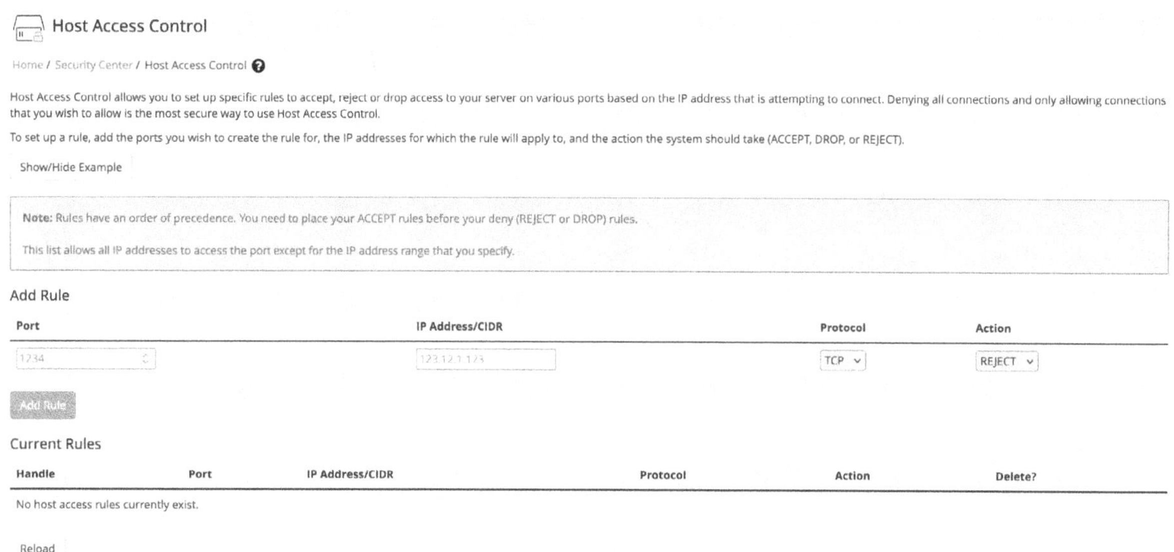

Since this works exactly like a firewall, it's important to remember that order of rules matters. Firewall rules are always processed from the top to the bottom and when the first rule matches, none of the other rules are evaluated. You also need to be extremely careful about the rules that you add as you can inadvertently block yourself from accessing the server.

When you go to craft rules, I suggest using a piece of paper (or a spreadsheet) and plan out your rules. When you add rules, start with your ALLOW rules first. Once rules are added, they cannot be reordered – only deleted.

As an example, the rules in the screenshot below, will never let anyone SSH into the server. Because the REJECT rule applies to ALL IPs, the firewall will never see the traffic from the 192.168.0.0/24 network and these users will never be able to connect.

Current Rules

Handle	Port	IP Address/CIDR	Protocol	Action	Delete?
9	22	ALL	tcp	REJECT	
10	22	192.168.0.0/24	tcp	ACCEPT	

Actions are also important as they define the action that the firewall should take when a rule matches.

- ACCEPT – The traffic will be allowed without any further inspection.
- DROP – The firewall will silently drop the packet.
- REJECT – The firewall will send a response to the sender that the connection was not allowed.

When crafting firewall rules, you may want to choose DROP rather than REJECT.

Host Access Control is a very basic firewall for your server. While you may choose to use it, there are more flexible and easier to use solutions.

6.7 Manage External Authentications

For VPS/Dedicated Servers

The information in this section applies to VPS and dedicated servers.

If you want to allow third-party logins from external OpenID Connect accounts, you can configure those from Manage External Authentications.

To use this feature, you need to make sure that SSL is enabled and configured properly. You should be able to access cPanel, WHM, and Webmail from a valid SSL certificate.

cPanel has several third-party account providers built-in and you can configure and enable these from the Configure tab.

Authentication Provider	Status (cpaneld)	Status (webmaild)	Status (whostmgrd)	
Log in via WHMCS *The provider is not configured. You cannot enable this provider until you configure it.*	Disabled	Disabled	Disabled	Configure
Log in via Slack *The provider is not configured. You cannot enable this provider until you configure it.*	Disabled	Disabled	Disabled	Configure
Log in via PayPal *The provider is not configured. You cannot enable this provider until you configure it.*	Disabled	Disabled	Disabled	Configure
Log in via Google *The provider is not configured. You cannot enable this provider until you configure it.*	Disabled	Disabled	Disabled	Configure
Log in via Facebook *The provider is not configured. You cannot enable this provider until you configure it.*	Disabled	Disabled	Disabled	Configure
Log in via cPanelID	Disabled	Disabled	Disabled	Configure
Log in via Amazon *The provider is not configured. You cannot enable this provider until you configure it.*	Disabled	Disabled	Disabled	Configure

You can enable any or all these providers if you want to be able to allow your users to link their local accounts with a third-party provider. You can also link one or more cPanel accounts, WHM accounts, or webmail accounts to one or more external authentication providers.

It is also important to know that if you have multi-factor authentication enabled on the cPanel server, you must authenticate at the third-party provider as well as any local multi-factor authentication that is configured.

You can configure any of the provided authentication providers by clicking on the **Configure** link in the row of that provider.

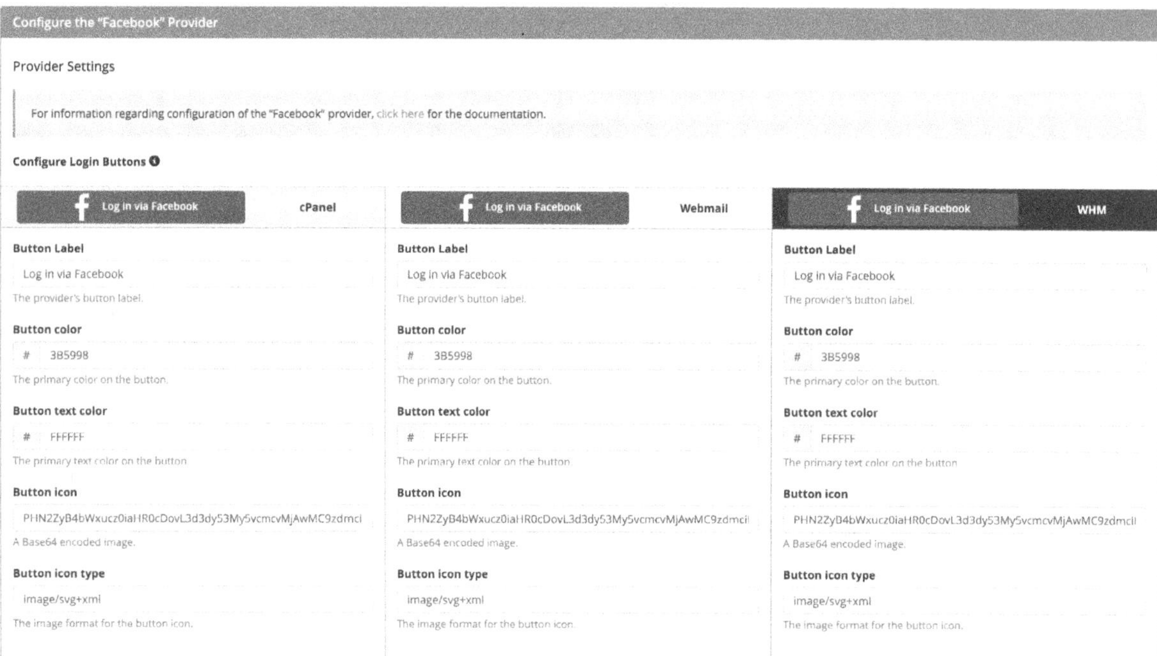

On the configuration page, you can customize the look of the login button that will be displayed on each of the login pages. You can change the button label, color, text color, button icon (encoded in Base64) and the icon type. You will also find the information that your identity provider requires to enable authentication. You will find your required redirect URLs as well as any secrets that need to be provided or to place IDs and secrets from your provider.

Do not use this feature on reseller shared hosting! If you are using this server as a server to host reseller clients, you should not enable this feature. There is no reseller access to this feature and logins will be associated with your company. Not a good idea if you're trying to provide private-label reseller hosting services.

For any users that have linked accounts, you can manage those users and their links from the Manage Users tab.

6.8 Manage root's SSH Keys

For VPS/Dedicated Servers

The information in this section applies to VPS and dedicated servers.

It's best practice to always use SSH keys, especially for your root user. From this interface, you can upload existing keys and manage private keys for the root user.

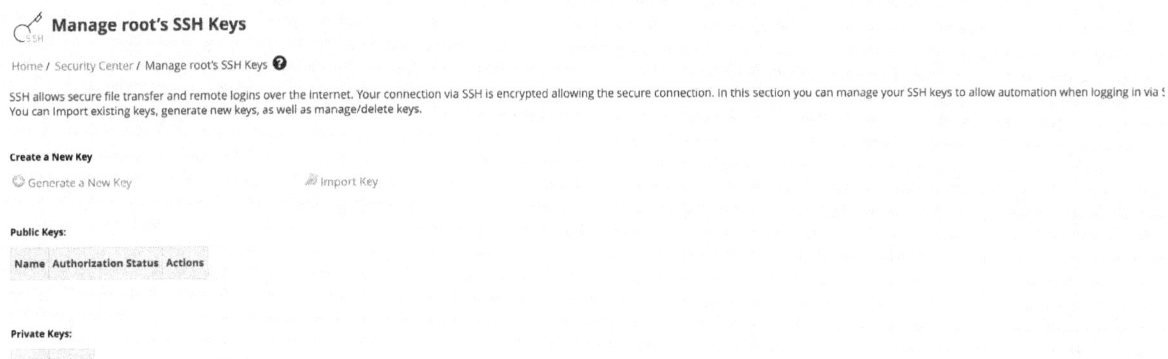

If you have an existing key you generated on your local system, you can import that key.

Manage root's SSH Keys

Home / Security Center / Manage root's SSH Keys

Choose a name for this key (defaults to id_dsa):

Private key passphrase (Needed for PPK import only):

Paste the Private Key in this box (you can also paste a PPK file as well):

Paste the Public Key in this box:

Import

Note: You don't have to import both keys. It is perfectly acceptable to just import a public OR private key if that is all you need on the server.

Return to SSH Manager

You don't have to provide both a public key and private key. As the note at the bottom of the page says, either one is acceptable. In most cases, you will want to provide your public key. It should be in RSA format, but WHM also accepts PPK (Putty) files.

Once you import the key, you will need to authorize the key otherwise authentication will not work. If you need to temporarily deactivate a key, you can deactivate it rather than deleting it. This essentially just comments out the key from the authorized_keys file for the root user.

6.9 Manage Wheel Group Users

For VPS/Dedicated Servers

The information in this section applies to VPS and dedicated servers.

On Enterprise Linux, the wheel group is a special group. The users in this group can run sudo or su commands from the terminal.

Manage Wheel Group Users

Home / Security Center / Manage Wheel Group Users

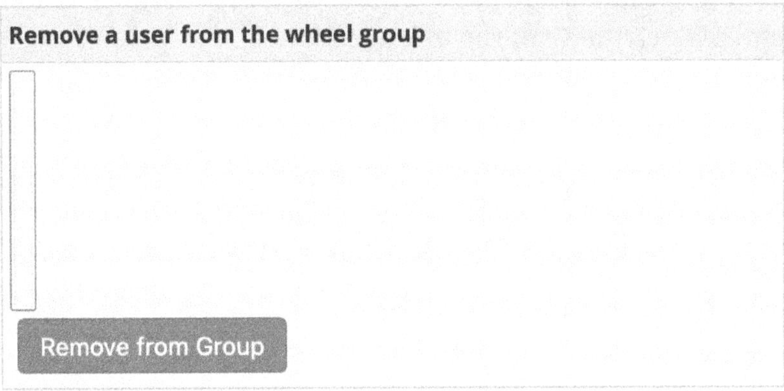

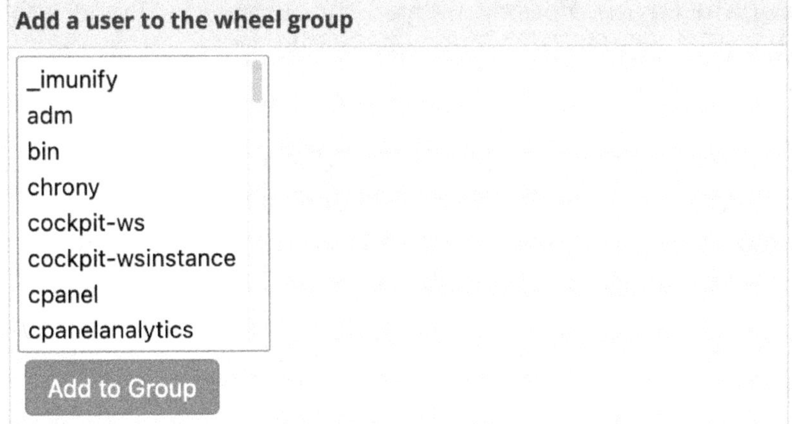

Note: This group controls which users can use the system's `su` utility.

Essentially, any users added here can easily perform actions on behalf of root or even switch to the root user. You should not add any users to the wheel group in normal web hosting operations without good reason. If you do need to, it's incredibly rare, and they should only be in the wheel group for a limited amount of time.

6.10 ModSecurity

ModSecurity is a security tool that helps protect websites on your server. When rules are loaded, it can prevent people from doing really bad things. It works like a web application firewall. It can help prevent XSS attacks, SQL injection attacks, path transversal, and more. It's a powerful tool!

Because it's powerful, it can also flag a lot of legitimate traffic as bad actors and even trigger the system to block the IP of the offender.

6.10.1 ModSecurity Configuration

This section will help you configure the global directives of ModSecurity.

Audit Log Level should remain at "Only log noteworthy transactions." This is best for performance and security. This will also make it easier for tracking down false positives.

Connections Engine can be set to "Process the rules". Otherwise, "Do not process the rules" will turn off the engine. For testing, you should enable "Process the rules in verbose mode, but do not execute disruptive actions." This will prevent ModSecurity from blocking connections while you validate rules for false-positives.

Rules Engine can be set to "Process the rules". Otherwise, "Do not process the rules" will turn off the engine. For testing, you should enable "Process the rules in verbose mode, but do not execute disruptive actions." This will prevent ModSecurity from blocking connections while you validate rules for false-positives.

Backend Compression should be set to Enabled unless you're experiencing a high server load.

Geolocation Database allows you to specify a path on the filesystem where a geolocation database can be set. MaxMind offers a free geolocation database as well as a more detailed database in a paid format. Refer to the ModSecurity documentation for assistance.

Google Safe Browsing Database allows you to specify a path on the filesystem where the Google Safe Browsing Database is located. Refer to the ModSecurity documentation for assistance.

Guardian Log allows you to specify an external program to pipe transaction log information. Refer to the ModSecurity documentation for assistance.

Project Honey Pot Http:BL API Key is where you can specify your Project Honey Pot API key. For more information and assistance, refer to Project Honey Pot and the ModSecurity documentation.

The values for **Perl Compatible Regular Expressions Library Match Limit** and **Perl Compatible Regular Expressions Library Match Limit Recursion** default to 1500 and don't need to be adjusted unless you have a reason to do so. Refer to the ModSecurity documentation for assistance with how you should change this value.

6.10.2 ModSecurity Tools

The ModSecurity Tools screen will allow you to add rules lists that ModSecurity will use to analyze traffic against. You will be taken to the Hits List first. If you have any enabled rules and there are hits, you will find these here. This is a useful list for troubleshooting or auditing. If you click on the **Add Rule** button, you can add your own custom ModSecurity Rule.

ModSecurity™ Tools

Home / Security Center / ModSecurity™ Tools » Edit Custom Rules

Use the text box to edit all of your custom ModSecurity™ rules.

Edit Custom ModSecurity™ Rules

Rules

References

ModSecurity™ Specification Reference
- SecRule Reference
- SecAction Reference
- Variables Reference
- Actions Reference
- Transformations Reference

ModSecurity™ FAQ

Do you want to deploy your rules and restart Apache?

☐ Deploy and Restart Apache

The system will deploy any other unpublished changes when you select this checkbox.

Save Cancel

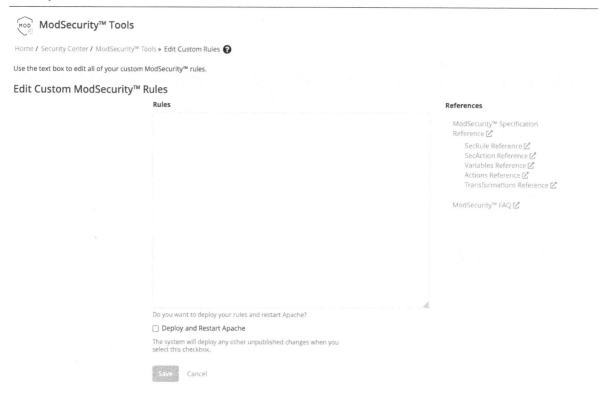

For assistance with writing a custom ModSecurity rule, refer to the ModSecurity product documentation for assistance. Rule writing is outside the scope of this book.

6.10.3 ModSecurity Vendors

ModSecurity is useless without rules and writing your own rules is time consuming. That's where the ModSecurity vendors comes in.

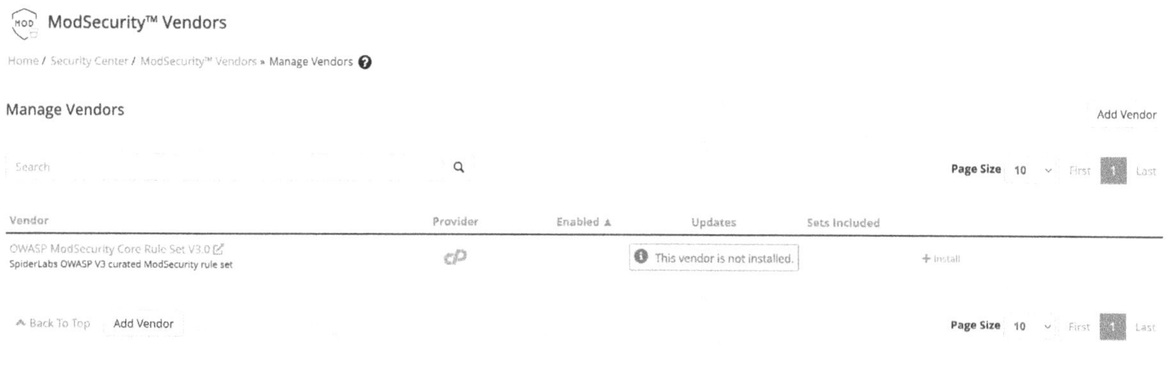

cPanel publishes their own rule set for ModSecurity and it is the default vendor to install. Since this is a curated list published by cPanel, I've found it to be a good balance between the right amount of protection and too many false-positives. No matter what ruleset you use, you will always have a few false-positives.

To get started with the cPanel ruleset, click on the **Install** button and then **Install and Restart Apache** to apply the rules.

Vendor	Provider	Enabled ▲	Updates	Sets Included		
OWASP ModSecurity Core Rule Set V3.0 SpiderLabs OWASP curated ModSecurity rule set	cP	On Off	On Off	22 / 22	Edit	Delete

With the vendor installed, you can enable or disable it as well as updates. Additionally, you can edit or delete the vendor.

If you click on **Add Vendor**, you can add a custom vendor. You will need to provide the URL to the metadata YAML file and this will load the appropriate data onto the server for you to install.

If you are technical, cPanel provides instructions for creating your own vendor.

6.10.4 Resolving False-Positives

When you encounter false-positives, it can be tricky to track down but with some patience, you can resolve false-positives. A *false-positive* occurs when ModSecurity blocks a legitimate request. Typically, this will be observed when you go to a page on a website or attempt to load a page in an application and you get a 403 Forbidden error when you know you should not.

Once you've tracked down what is causing the false-positive, you can then go to **ModSecurity Tools** and search in the Hits List for the hit.

Date ▼	Host	Source	Severity	Status	Rule ID	
2024-05-17 20:33:44	[illegible]	[illegible].177	CRITICAL	403	930130: Restricted File Access Attempt	More
2024-05-17 20:33:44	[illegible]	[illegible].177	CRITICAL	403	949110: Inbound Anomaly Score Exceeded (Total Score : 5)	More
2024-05-17 20:33:44	[illegible]	[illegible].177		403	980130: Inbound Anomaly Score Exceeded (Total Inbound Score: 5 - SQLI=0,XSS=0,RFI=0,LFI=5,RCE=0,PHPI=0,HTTP=0,SESS=0): Restricted File Access Attempt	More

If you can identify your IP address, you can then expand the entry and view the full details of the hit.

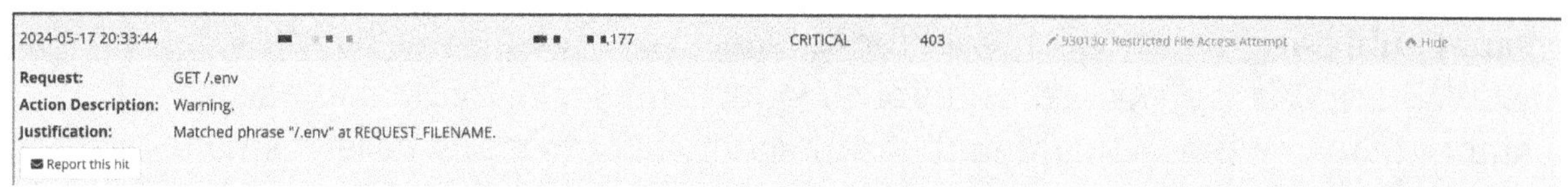
2024-05-17 20:33:44 CRITICAL 403
Request: GET /.env
Action Description: Warning.
Justification: Matched phrase "/.env" at REQUEST_FILENAME.

The example shown is a legitimate request and block. However, for the sake of an example, we will pretend it is a false-positive. If you click on the rule ID, you will be taken to the rule. While you cannot edit vendor provided rules, you can disable the individual rule.

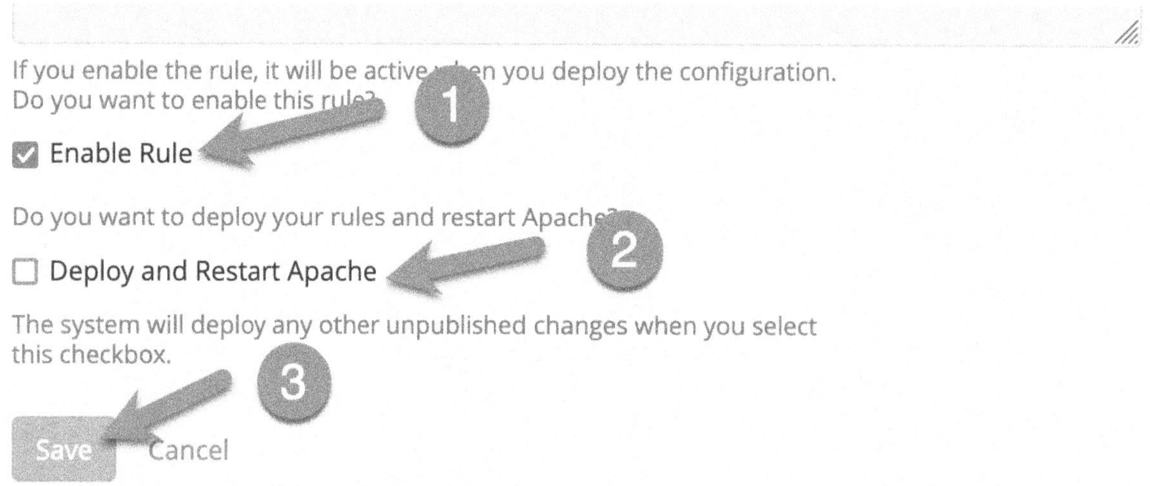

Uncheck the "Enable Rule" option, check the "Deploy and Restart Apache" option and then click Save. This rule would then be disabled and no longer affect all websites on the server.

6.10.5 Enabling Domain-Level Control of ModSecurity

By default, ModSecurity is either on or off for all websites on the server. In most cases, standard websites will be protected by ModSecurity and it should not be disabled. However, there are occasionally some users doing more advanced things and ModSecurity causes more harm than good and would prefer to have it disabled.

To enable domain-level control of ModSecurity, find **Feature Manager** in WHM. Edit the default feature list.

Manage feature list

default

Edit Delete

Check the ModSecurity Domain Manager tool to enable it.

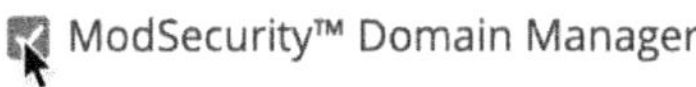

Click **Save**.

Now in the cPanel interface, users will see the ModSecurity icon in the Security toolbox.

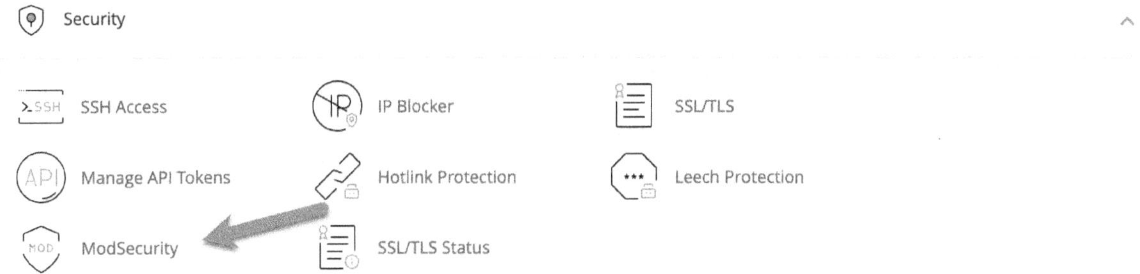

Users can then choose to disable ModSecurity across all domains and subdomains in their account as well and on an individual domain or subdomain basis.

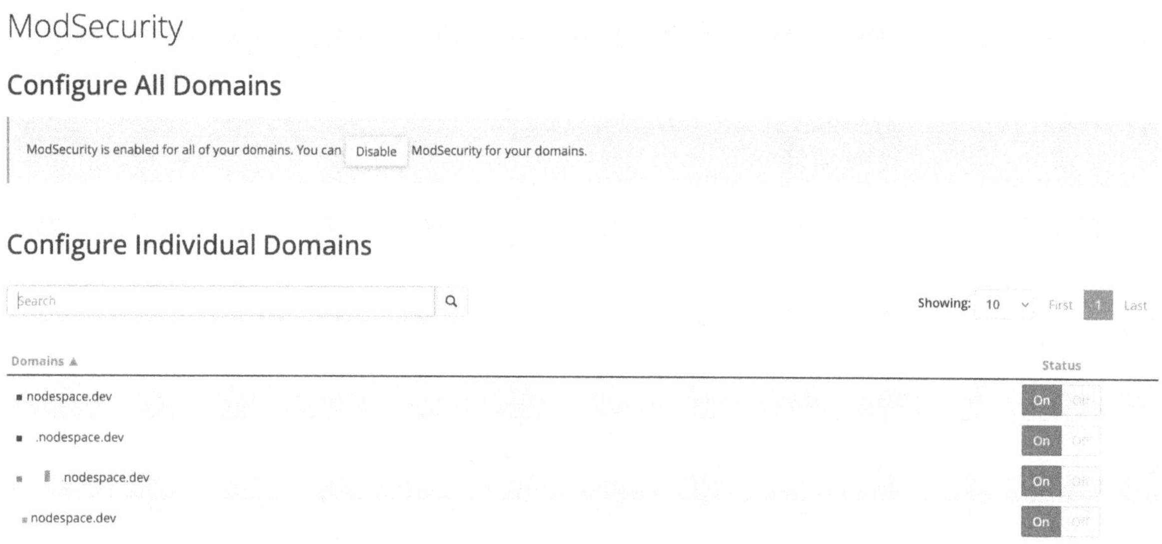

ModSecurity

Configure All Domains

ModSecurity is enabled for all of your domains. You can Disable ModSecurity for your domains.

Configure Individual Domains

Search

Showing: 10 First 1 Last

Domains ▲	Status
nodespace.dev	On Off
.nodespace.dev	On Off
nodespace.dev	On Off
nodespace.dev	On Off

6.11 Password Strength Configuration

For VPS/Dedicated Servers

The information in this section applies to VPS and dedicated servers.

Using strong passwords is critical on web servers as there are always attackers and other threats trying to gain access. With the Password Strength Configuration tool, you can ensure that passwords are set to an acceptable level.

The scale runs from 0 to 100 with 0 being the least secure password imaginable and 100 being an incredibly difficult password. The default password strength is 65. This means that all services must be at least 65. You can override this by adjusting the passwords requirements.

For example, you may require that since email accounts are under constant attack to make the required minimum 75. Since SSH keys are extremely crucial, you might set these to 90 while leaving the others at the defaults.

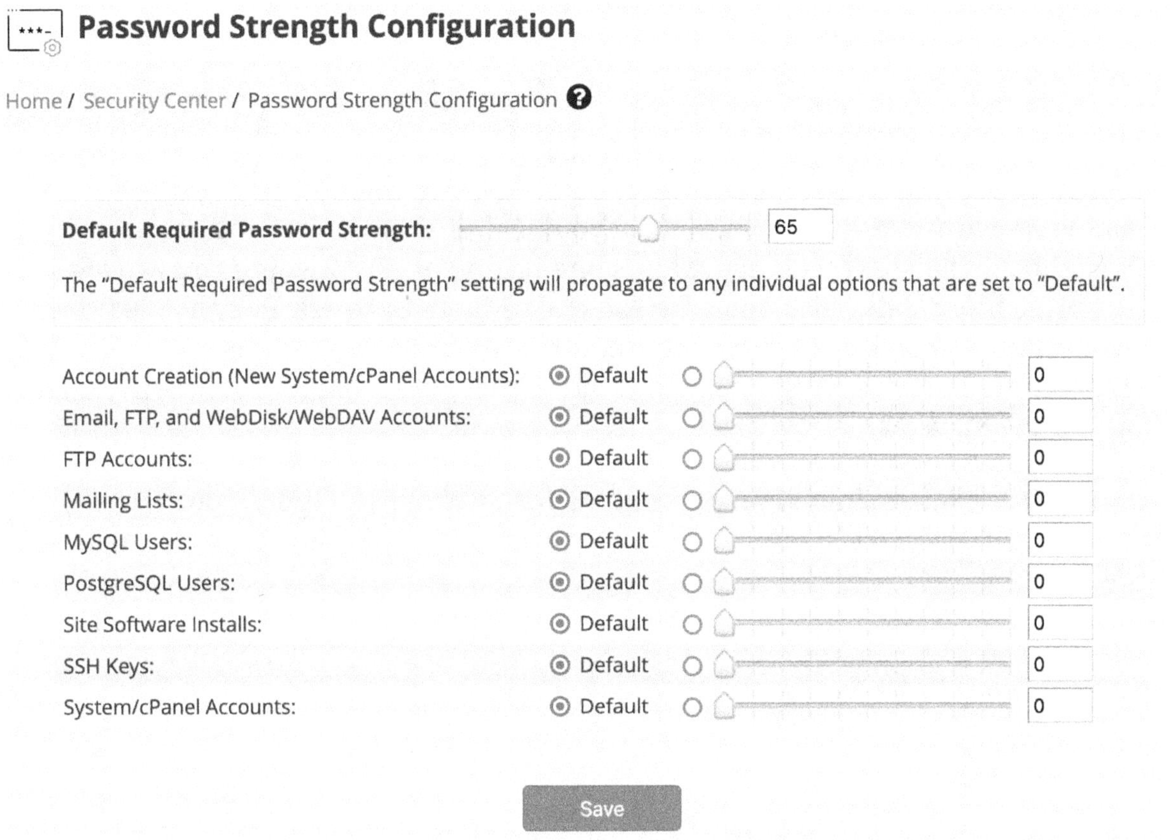

Password Strength Configuration

Home / Security Center / Password Strength Configuration

Default Required Password Strength: 65

The "Default Required Password Strength" setting will propagate to any individual options that are set to "Default".

Account Creation (New System/cPanel Accounts):	Default	0
Email, FTP, and WebDisk/WebDAV Accounts:	Default	0
FTP Accounts:	Default	0
Mailing Lists:	Default	0
MySQL Users:	Default	0
PostgreSQL Users:	Default	0
Site Software Installs:	Default	0
SSH Keys:	Default	0
System/cPanel Accounts:	Default	0

Save

There are some caveats with this tool to keep in mind.

- If you adjust the password strength requirement, it will not affect existing passwords.
- This requirement only applies to new accounts. If you want to make these requirements affect existing accounts, you must enable Security Policies (see "Configure Security Policies" earlier in this chapter).
- Users that have shell access can override these requirements by using the command line tools.

Remember, you should not set a minimum requirement below 65. This setting will generate fairly secure passwords.

6.12 Security Advisor

For VPS/Dedicated Servers

The information in this section applies to VPS and dedicated servers.

Keeping an eye on the overall security of your server is important and the Security Advisor tool will help you do that. This is one section of WHM where you will see cross-promotional advertisements for some of cPanel's partners. Imunify360 is one such partner and product. You are not required to purchase anything recommended here. I always recommend shopping this out as there are a handful of security tools that work with cPanel.

This tool is broken up into different sections with various levels of importance. This tool does make great recommendations so you should review and fix or tweak the issues.

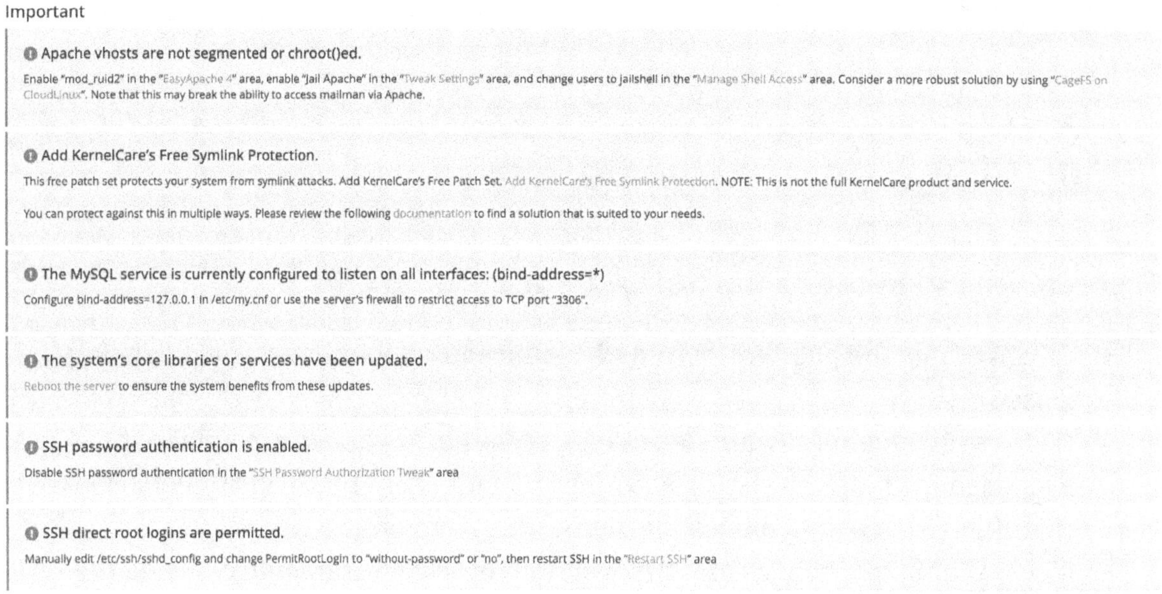

Important

Apache vhosts are not segmented or chroot()ed.

Enable "mod_ruid2" in the "EasyApache 4" area, enable "Jail Apache" in the "Tweak Settings" area, and change users to jailshell in the "Manage Shell Access" area. Consider a more robust solution by using "CageFS on CloudLinux". Note that this may break the ability to access mailman via Apache.

Add KernelCare's Free Symlink Protection.

This free patch set protects your system from symlink attacks. Add KernelCare's Free Patch Set. Add KernelCare's Free Symlink Protection. NOTE: This is not the full KernelCare product and service.

You can protect against this in multiple ways. Please review the following documentation to find a solution that is suited to your needs.

The MySQL service is currently configured to listen on all interfaces: (bind-address=*)

Configure bind-address=127.0.0.1 in /etc/my.cnf or use the server's firewall to restrict access to TCP port "3306".

The system's core libraries or services have been updated.

Reboot the server to ensure the system benefits from these updates.

SSH password authentication is enabled.

Disable SSH password authentication in the "SSH Password Authorization Tweak" area

SSH direct root logins are permitted.

Manually edit /etc/ssh/sshd_config and change PermitRootLogin to "without-password" or "no", then restart SSH in the "Restart SSH" area

One of the really nice things about Security Advisor is that if there is a critical issue, it tells you exactly what you need to do to fix it. For example, this is a freshly installed cPanel server. As such, SSH access is set to the default where root can login. cPanel walks you through what to do to solve it: manually edit `/etc/ssh/sshd_config` and change `PermitRootLogin` to "`no`" and restart SSH – even with a handy link to do it right from WHM.

If some of these tasks seem questionable or you're not sure how, ask your hosting provider. In most cases, they'll gladly take care of issues like this for you.

6.13 Security Questions

In the "Configure Security Policies" section of this chapter, I mentioned that if you enable the Security Questions policy, you would create and edit security questions in this section.

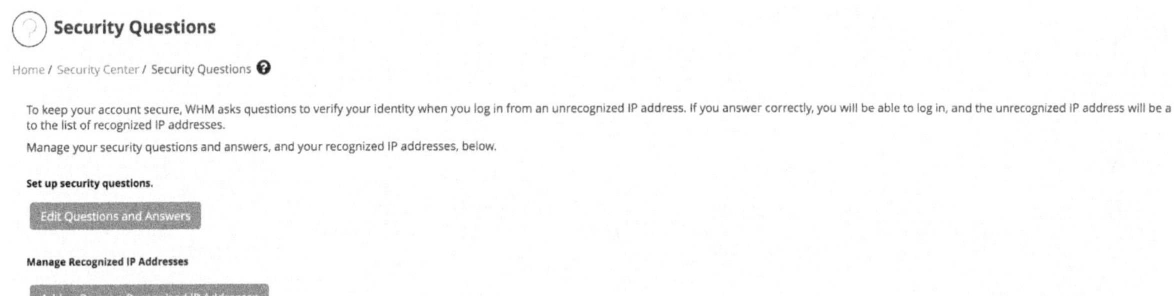

If you click on Edit Questions and Answers, you can pick or type your own questions and answers. Whenever you login to WHM, you will be prompted to answer these questions.

Edit Questions and Answers

Home / Security Center / Security Questions / Edit Questions and Answers

To keep your account secure, WHM will ask you 4 questions when you try to log in from an unrecognized IP address.
Please set your questions and answers below.

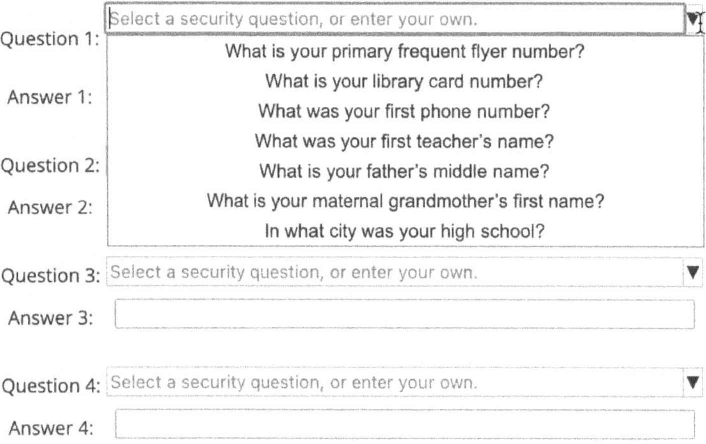

Question 1:
Select a security question, or enter your own.
What is your primary frequent flyer number?
What is your library card number?
What was your first phone number?
What was your first teacher's name?
What is your father's middle name?
What is your maternal grandmother's first name?
In what city was your high school?
Answer 1:
Question 2:
Answer 2:
Question 3:
Select a security question, or enter your own.
Answer 3:
Question 4:
Select a security question, or enter your own.
Answer 4:

Continue

You can also add and remove recognized IP addresses from this tool. If the system recognizes an IP address, it won't ask the security questions. Remember, you're only editing the recognized IPs for this account (root).

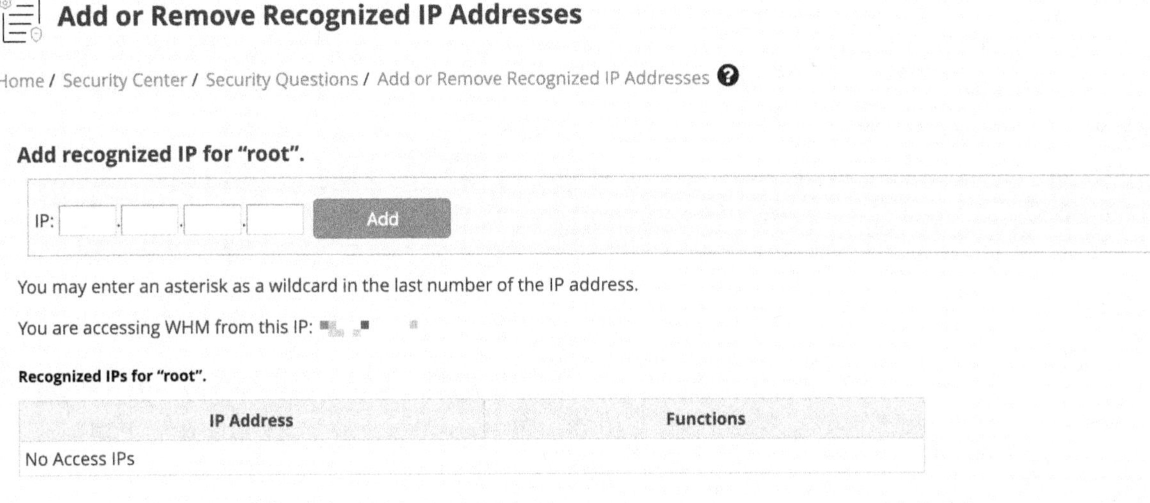
Add or Remove Recognized IP Addresses

Home / Security Center / Security Questions / Add or Remove Recognized IP Addresses

Add recognized IP for "root".

IP: [ ].[ ].[ ].[ ] Add

You may enter an asterisk as a wildcard in the last number of the IP address.

You are accessing WHM from this IP:

Recognized IPs for "root".

IP Address	Functions
No Access IPs	

[Go Back]

It is suggested to only add in trusted IP addresses to this list. For example you might want to add your office, and home.

6.14 Shell Fork Bomb Protection

If you don't know what a fork bomb is, it is when a process keeps forking itself into an endless loop until it consumes all the resources on a system. It is a type of Denial of Service (DoS) attack and it can either be self-inflicted or inflicted by a bad actor.

If you intend on allowing shell access to the server, you should enable this option. It will protect the server from novice users as well as malicious users.

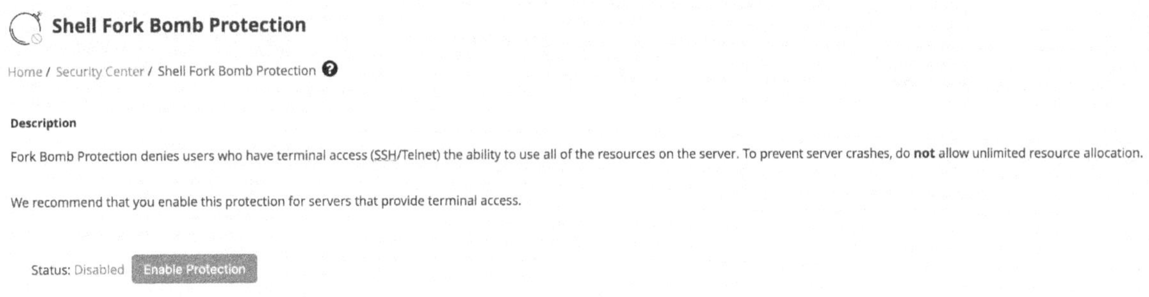

When you **Enable Protection**, the system uses the `ulimit` command to limit user actions. From the terminal, you can use `ulimit` with the following options to further improve security.

Limit	Option	Description
200000	`-c`	Limits the maximum size of core files that users can create.
200000	`-d`	Limits the maximum size of a processes data segment.
200000	`-m`	Limits the maximum resident set size.
100	`-n`	Limits the maximum number of open-file descriptors.
8192	`-s`	Limits the maximum stack size.
35	`-u`	Limits the maximum number of processes that are available to a single user.
Unlimited	`-v`	The amount of virtual memory available for the processes.

For more information about `ulimit`, please see https://ss64.com/bash/ulimit.html

6.15 SSH Password Authorization Tweak

For VPS/Dedicated Servers
The information in this section applies to VPS and dedicated servers.

This is a quick setting that will allow you to disable password authentication over SSH. When password authentication is disabled, you need to use "Manage root's SSH Keys" to provide keys that can SSH using the root user. This will also remove password authentication for users, although they should be using the terminal from within cPanel for security reasons.

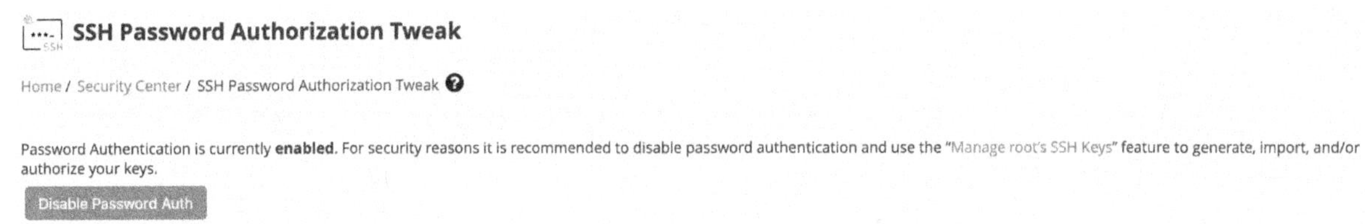

SSH Password Authorization Tweak
Home / Security Center / SSH Password Authorization Tweak
Password Authentication is currently enabled. For security reasons it is recommended to disable password authentication and use the "Manage root's SSH Keys" feature to generate, import, and/or authorize your keys.
Disable Password Auth

6.16 Traceroute Enable/Disable

For VPS/Dedicated Servers

The information in this section applies to VPS and dedicated servers.

This tool will allow you to either enable or disable the traceroute application. Traceroute is a very helpful tool for troubleshooting, however in a shared environment and when users can have access to the shell, there is a chance that it can be used to focus a hacking attack. I personally leave this on, but if you are worried about users mapping out the data center network, or other network routes, you can use this tool to disable it.

Traceroute Enable/Disable

Home / Security Center / Traceroute Enable/Disable

Traceroute displays the packet routing statistics from the server to another network host. It can be used to map the network's topology and subsequently be used as a tool to focus a hacking attack.

Traceroute Status

Traceroute is currently enabled.

Binary	Permissions
/usr/bin/traceroute	755

Disable

6.17 Two-Factor Authentication

This section allows you to configure Two-Factor Authentication on cPanel for user accounts (if you're root), and mange Two-Factor Authentication for your account.

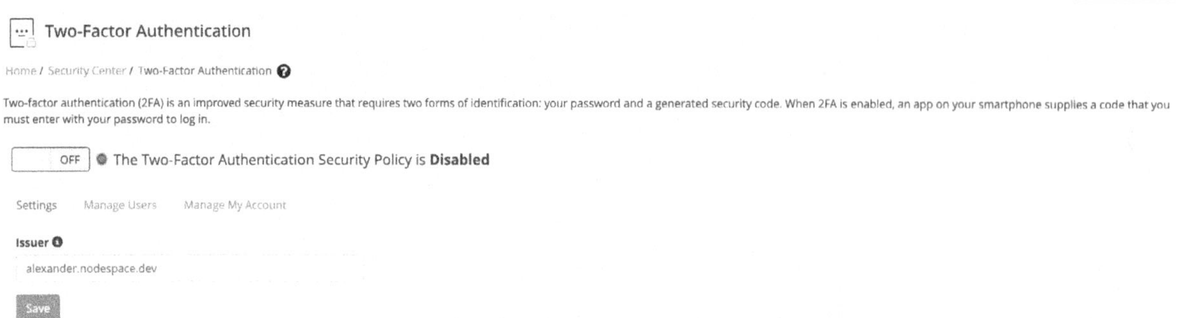

When setting up Two-Factor Authentication (2FA), make sure your hostname is set correctly.

If you are a root user, you can manage users with 2FA configured. This can be useful if a user forgets their 2FA authenticator, or needs to have it reset.

When you configure 2FA for your account, you will be presented with a two-step process. First, make sure you have a compatible app, such as Google Authenticator, Microsoft Authenticator, Bitwarden, or several other password managers, that also handle 2FA codes.

You will have a QR code to scan with your phone. If you're using a password manager app, you may have to copy/paste in the Account name and the Key. Keep the key secret as anyone with this key can generate valid 2FA codes!

Step 1

Scan the following QR code with a two-factor authentication app on your phone.

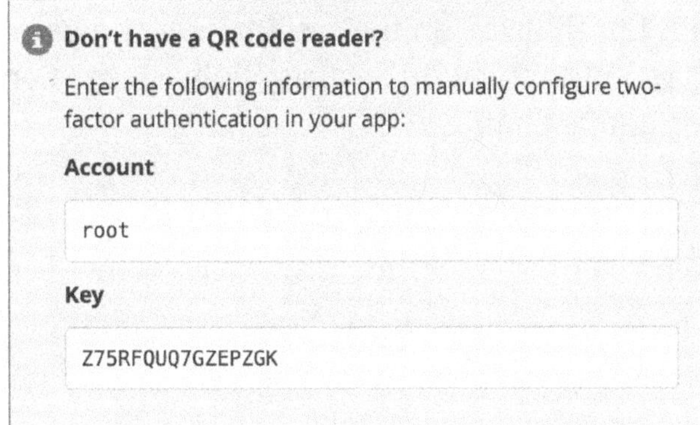

Don't have a QR code reader?
Enter the following information to manually configure two-factor authentication in your app:
Account
root
Key
Z75RFQUQ7GZEPZGK

Finally, to validate that 2FA is working properly, provide the 6-digit security code that your app provides. Keep in mind that this number rotates so you only have a limited amount of time to enter it.

Step 2

Enter the security code generated by your two-factor authentication app.

Security Code

six-digit code

Configure Two-Factor Authentication   Cancel

If the code is validated, you will then be able to enable 2FA and you will be prompted to provide the current code each time you login.

If you want to force 2FA for all users on the system, you can use the toggle at the top to enable the Two-Factor Authentication Security Policy (see "Configure Security Policies" section earlier in this chapter.

7 Server Contacts

For VPS/Dedicated Servers

The information in this section applies to VPS and dedicated servers.

Things don't always go right. If we were in a perfect world, nothing bad would ever happen. You'd launch your server, and it would sit in its rack slot or sit on its virtual host, humming away happily for years. But the truth is, we don't live in a perfect world. When issues occur, you need to know about them, sooner rather than later. And that's what this chapter is all about. Making sure your server can call you when it needs a human hand.

7.1 Contact Manager

The Contact Manager tool allows you to setup different notification channels for your server. cPanel includes several options.

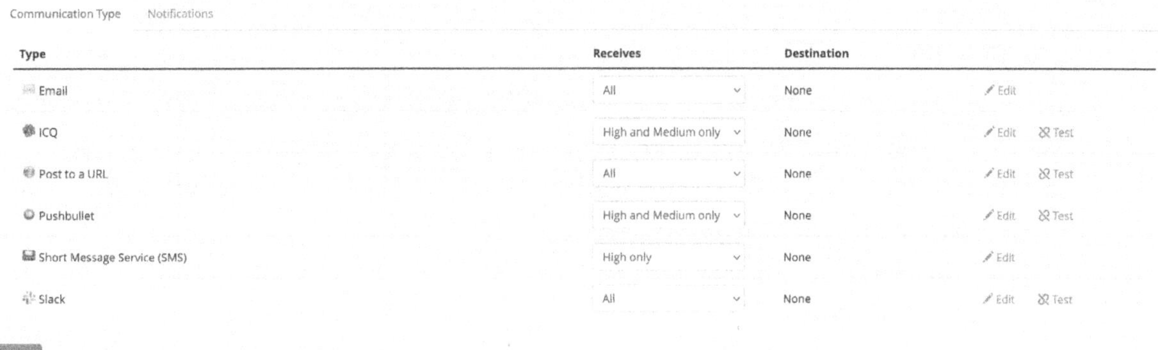

Each notification type also has what type of notifications it receives. For example, by default, Email is set to receive every notification from the server. SMS, on the other hand, is set, by default, to receive only high notifications.

When you configure any of the notification methods, you will be taken to the Basic WebHost Manager Setup > Contact Information tab (see 3.1.1.1). Once you have one or more of these setups, if there is a test option, clicking the test link will fire a test notification to the service.

The priority of the notification (High, Medium, Low) is set on the Notifications tab for each notification.

- **Email** – This will send an email from the cPanel server's root account to the email address or addresses you specify.
- **ICQ** – As I previously mentioned in Chapter 3 about ICQ, this service shut down on June 26, 2024, and is no longer functional. It should be removed from a future version of cPanel.
- **Post to a URL** – This is a fancy way of saying "Webhook". When cPanel triggers a notification, data will be sent to this URL for processing. It requires custom coding.
- **Pushbulle**t – This is a service that can notify several devices all at once. I have not used it so I cannot say how useful or reliable it is.
- **SMS** – This is text messaging. You might be wondering how cPanel can text you. It's through the magic of Email to SMS Gateways that every carrier operates. Here's how you can format your number to receive texts from emails (remember to replace "number" with your unformatted phone number, for example 5551234567). As carriers change, you might need to update these addresses, but the new carrier should keep the previous SMS gateway online for some time. E.g. a former Sprint number should work under either the Sprint gateway or T-Mobile gateway. Consult your carrier for details.
    - AT&T: `number@txt.att.net`
    - Boost Mobile: `number@sms.myboostmobile.com`
    - Cricket Wireless: `number@sms.cricketwireless.net`
    - Google Fi: `number@msg.fi.google.com`
    - MetroPCS: `number@mymetropcs.com`
    - Sprint: `number@messaging.sprintpcs.com`
    - T-Mobile: `number@tmomail.net`
    - US Cellular: `number@email.uscc.net`
    - Verizon: `number@vtext.com`
    - Virgin Mobile: `number@vmobl.com`
- **Slack** – This is an office messenger application. Slack is "freemium" SaaS. However, I like and use Mattermost, which is an open source, SaaS or self-hosted (meaning you can host it on your own server anywhere), Slack-

compatible messenger. Slack and Mattermost are the most modern notification services on this list.

7.1.1 Notifications

On the Notifications tab, you can re-prioritize notifications. For example, cPanel ranks an Account Creation notification as “Low” but you might consider this “Medium”. From the dropdown menu under the Importance column, you can switch this over to Medium.

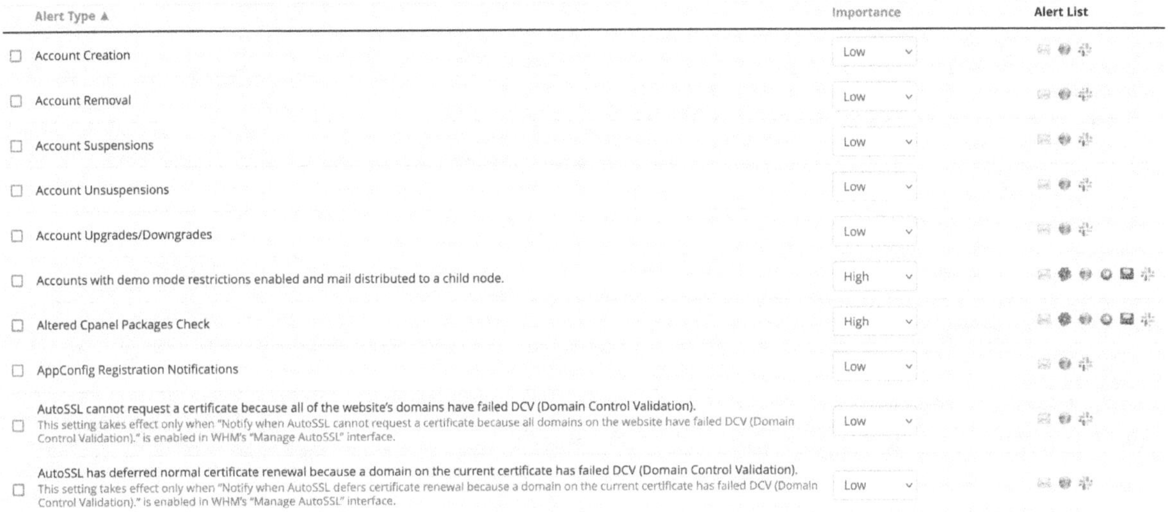

Alert Type ▲	Importance	Alert List
☐ Account Creation	Low	
☐ Account Removal	Low	
☐ Account Suspensions	Low	
☐ Account Unsuspensions	Low	
☐ Account Upgrades/Downgrades	Low	
☐ Accounts with demo mode restrictions enabled and mail distributed to a child node.	High	
☐ Altered Cpanel Packages Check	High	
☐ AppConfig Registration Notifications	Low	
☐ AutoSSL cannot request a certificate because all of the website’s domains have failed DCV (Domain Control Validation). This setting takes effect only when “Notify when AutoSSL cannot request a certificate because all domains on the website have failed DCV (Domain Control Validation).” is enabled in WHM’s “Manage AutoSSL” interface.	Low	
☐ AutoSSL has deferred normal certificate renewal because a domain on the current certificate has failed DCV (Domain Control Validation). This setting takes effect only when “Notify when AutoSSL defers certificate renewal because a domain on the current certificate has failed DCV (Domain Control Validation).” is enabled in WHM’s “Manage AutoSSL” interface.	Low	

You should review the list of notifications and re-prioritize the notifications based on you or your team’s preference. I personally put any type of “error” or “failure” as High.

I use this to “re-tune” notifications. Since we live in a connected world, my phone has Mattermost on it (Mattermost is an open source Slack-like messenger and the API is Slack-compatible). In one of our teams, I have a Monitoring Alerts channel. All high priority cPanel notifications are sent via email and to Mattermost (via the Slack integration). This way, I’m always aware of any major issues. Email receives all other notifications which are processed in a monitoring ticket queue.

The following table, from the WHM documentation, goes over the alert type and what event triggers the alert. You can also modify the alert template if you would like, but be warned that there is always a chance that a cPanel update could overwrite the changes you made to the template, so modify with caution.

Alert Type	Event that triggers	Notification Template
Account Creation	A system administrator or reseller creates an account.	`wwwacct/Notify.*.tmpl`
Account Removal	A system administrator or reseller removes an account.	• `killacct/Notify.*.tmpl` • `killacct/PostTerminateCleanup.*.tmpl`
Account Suspensions	A system administrator or reseller suspends an account.	`suspendacct/Notify.*.tmpl`
Account Unsuspensions	A system administrator or reseller unsuspends an account.	`unsuspendacct/Notify.*.tmpl`
Account Upgrades/ Downgrades	A user modifies the package for an account or uses WHM's Upgrade/Downgrade an Account interface.	`upacct/Notify.*.tmpl`
Accounts with demo mode restrictions enabled and mail distributed to a child node.	A demo account is distributing mail to a child node.	`DemoMode/MailChildNodeExists.*.tmpl`
Altered Cpanel Packages Check	The `/usr/local/cpanel/scripts/check_cpanel_pkgs` script finds altered packages.	`Check/CpanelPackages.*.tmpl`

Alert Type	Event that triggers	Notification Template
AppConfig Registration Notifications	The system registers an application with AppConfig.	`appconfig/Notify.*.tmpl`
AutoSSL cannot request a certificate because all of the website's domains have failed DCV (Domain Control Validation).	AutoSSL fails to request a certificate because all of the website's domains have failed DCV.	`AutoSSL/CertificateExpiring.*.tmpl`
AutoSSL has deferred normal certificate renewal because a domain on the current certificate has failed DCV (Domain Control	AutoSSL defers normal certificate renewal because a domain on the current certificate has failed DCV.	`AutoSSL/CertificateExpiringCoverage.*.tmpl`

Alert Type	Event that triggers	Notification Template
Validation).		
AutoSSL has installed a certificate successfully.	AutoSSL installs an SSL certificate. Note: This setting also requires you to enable the *Notify when AutoSSL has renewed a certificate successfully.* setting in WHM's Manage AutoSSL interface (*WHM » Home » SSL/TLS » Manage AutoSSL*).	`AutoSSL/CertificateInstalled.*.tmpl`
AutoSSL has provisioned a new certificate for a dynamic DNS domain.	AutoSSL provisions a new certificate for a specific dynamic DNS domain.	`AutoSSL/DynamicDNSNewCertificate.*.tmpl`
AutoSSL has renewed a certificate, but the new certificate lacks at least one domain that the previous certificate secured.	AutoSSL renews a certificate but the new certificate lacks at least one domain that the previous certificate secured. **Note**: This setting also requires you to enable the *Notify when AutoSSL has renewed a certificate and the new certificate lacks at least one domain that the previous certificate secured.* setting.	`AutoSSL/CertificateInstalledReducedCoverage.*.tmpl`

Alert Type	Event that triggers	Notification Template
AutoSSL has renewed a certificate, but the new certificate lacks one or more of the website's domains.	AutoSSL renews a certificate but the new certificate lacks one or more of the website's domains.	`AutoSSL/CertificateInstalledUncoveredDomains.*.tmpl`
AutoSSL will not secure new domains because a domain on the current certificate has failed DCV (Domain Control Validation), and the certificate is not yet in the renewal period.	AutoSSL **cannot** add any additional domains because domains that fail validation exist on the current certificate.	`AutoSSL/CertificateRenewalCoverage.*.tmpl`
Backup Delayed	The backup process continues to run after 16 hours.	`Backup/Delayed.*.tmpl`

Alert Type	Event that triggers	Notification Template
Backup Failed To Finish	The system fails to finish a backup.	`Backup/Failure.*.tmpl`
Backup Finished With Partial Failure	The backup process completed but experienced some errors.	`Backup/PartialFailure.*.tmpl`
Backup Successful	A backup succeeds.	`Backup/Success.*.tmpl`
Backup Transport Error	A backup encounters transport errors.	`Backup/Transport.*.tmpl`
Bandwidth Data Processing Timeout	The system times out while it attempts to process bandwidth data.	`Logd/Notify.*.tmpl`
Bandwidth File Conversion Disk Space Failure	The system does not have enough free disk space to upgrade bandwidth files.	`installbandwidth/Notify.*.tmpl`
Bandwidth Limits	An account exceeds its bandwidth limit.	`BandwidthUsageExceeded/Owner.*.tmpl`
CloudLinux License Detected	The system detects a CloudLinux™ license and provides installation instructions.	`CloudLinux/Update.*.tmpl`
Conversion of cpupdate.conf settings to	The system converts settings in the `cpupdate.conf` file to settings in the local.versions file.	`RPMVersions/Notify.*.tmpl`

Alert Type	Event that triggers	Notification Template
local.versions		
Conversion of cpupdate.conf Settings to local.versions (legacy notification)	The system converts settings in the `cpupdate.conf` file to settings in the `local.versions` file.	`RPMVersions/Notify.*.tmpl`
Convert Addon Domain to Account Notifications	A system administrator or reseller converts an addon domain into an account.	`ConvertAddon/ConversionCompleted.*.tmpl`
Corrupt Database Tables	The `/scripts/check*mysql` script finds corrupted database tables.	`Check/MySQL.*.tmpl`
cPanel & WHM End of Life Notice	The cPanel & WHM version that exists on the server will reach its End Of Life (EOL) soon.	`Update/EndOfLife.*.tmpl`
cPanel Account Password	A user changes their password.	`ChangePassword/User.*.tmpl`
cPanel Backup	WHM generates a backup. Note:This event does not apply to cPanel account backups that a cPanel user generates.	`Backup/Success.*.tmpl`

Alert Type	Event that triggers	Notification Template
cPanel Backup (legacy notification)	WHM generates a legacy backup. Note:This event does not apply to cPanel account backups that a cPanel user generates.	`Backup/Success.*.tmpl`
cPanel Backup Destination Disabled	A user disables a backup destination.	`Backup/Disabled.*.tmpl`
cPanel Backup Destination Disabled (legacy notification)	A user disables a legacy backup destination.	`Backup/Disabled.*.tmpl`
cPanel Configuration Checks	The system **cannot** find the `/var/cpanel/cpanel.config` file and also **cannot** find the `cpanel.config.cache` file.	`Config/CpConfGuard.*.tmpl`
cPanel service SSL certificate warnings	The usr/local/cpanel/bin/checkallssl script detected issues with the cPanel & WHM services' SSL certificates.	`SSL/CheckAllCertsWarnings.*.tmpl`
cPanel Update Failures	The cPanel & WHM system fails to update.	• `upcp/Killed.*.tmpl` • `upcp/MaintenanceFailed.*.tmpl` • `upcp/PostSyncCleanupFailed.*.tmpl` • `upcp/UpdateNowFailed.*.tmpl`

Alert Type	Event that triggers	Notification Template
cPHulk Configuration Issues	cPHulk experiences configuration issues.	`Install/FixcPHulkConf.*.tmpl`
cPHulk Database Integrity Notices	cPHulk detects database corruption issues.	`Install/CheckcPHulkDB.*.tmpl`
cPHulkd Brute Force	cPHulk detects a brute force attempt.	`cPHulk/BruteForce.*.tmpl`
cPHulkd Login Notifications	The system detects a login with the `root` account. Note: This option is **not** available if cPHulk is disabled.	`cPHulk/Login.*.tmpl`
cPHulkd Notifications	cPHulk generates an alert. Note: The system sends a notice only **once** in a 24-hour window for a specific username, service, and IP address combination.	`cPHulk/Login.*.tmpl`
dbindex Cache File Out Of Date	The `dbindex` cache file is out-of-date by more than four hours.	`dbindex/Warn.*.tmpl`
Digest Authentication Disabled Due to Account Rename	An account's domain name changes and the system notifies the system administrator that it has disabled Digest Authentication.	`DigestAuth/Disable.*.tmpl`

Alert Type	Event that triggers	Notification Template
Disk Integrity Check	The system checks the integrity of a hard disk.	`Check/Smart.*.tmpl`
Disk Usage Warnings	Disk usage notifications.	`chkservd/DiskUsage.*.tmpl`
DNS Cluster Error	The system encounters an error with the DNS cluster.	`DnsAdmin/ClusterError.*.tmpl`
DNS Resolver Performance Issues	The server's DNS resolvers respond slowly or do not respond at all.	`Check/Resolvers.*.tmpl`
DNSSEC key synchronization failure	DNSSEC keys don't sync properly. This means servers in a DNS cluster don't currently serve DNSSEC records for a DNS zone.	`DnsAdmin/DnssecError.*.tmpl`
Dovecot Solr maintenance task errors.	The `/usr/local/cpanel/3rdparty/scripts/cpanel_dovecot_solr_maintenance` script fails.	`Solr/Maintenance.*.tmpl`
EasyApache 4 conflict removed	EasyApache 4 attempts to resolve a package conflict.	`EasyApache/EA4_ConflictRemove.*.tmpl`
EasyApache 4 template updated	The system detects an updated EasyApache 4 template.	`EasyApache/EA4_TemplateCheckUpdated.*.tmpl`
EasyApache	EasyApache 4 encounters a missing handler.	`EasyApache/EA4_LangHandlerMissing.*.tmpl`

Alert Type	Event that triggers	Notification Template
Configuration		
Email Client Configuration	The system sends the mail client configuration file to a new mail user.	`Mail/ClientConfig.*.tmpl`
Exim Update Failures	Exim fails to update.	`Check/EximConfig.*.tmpl`
Filesystem quotas are currently broken.	The system cannot enable disk quotas automatically. Note: This notification only affects systems that run Ubuntu®.	`Quota/Broken.*.tmpl`
Filesystem Quotas Ready	The system successfully finishes the process to enable filesystem quotas. Note: Because the system automatically enables filesystem quotas for all new installations of cPanel & WHM, you will receive this notification during the installation process.	`Quota/SetupComplete.*.tmpl`
Forced Disable of Digest Auth	A user or the system disables the Web Disk feature.	`Accounts/DigestAuthResetNeeded.*.tmpl`
Generic Notifications	Any event that generates an alert and does not appear this list.	N/A
Greylist System Changes	An administrator or the system removes a mail provider from the Greylisting Common Mail Providers list.	`Greylist/CommonProviderRemoval.*.tmpl`

Alert Type	Event that triggers	Notification Template
Hostname conflicts with a cPanel user account	The server's hostname is identical to a cPanel user account's site.	Check/HostnameOwnedByUser.*.tmpl
Hostname's SSL certificate expiring on a linked node	The system will send a notice when a linked node's hostname SSL certificate soon expires.	SSL/LinkedNodeCertificateExpiring.*.tmpl
Hung Service Checks	The system detects a hung device and restarts it.	chkservd/Hang.*.tmpl
Initial Website Creation	Website setup notifications.	InitialWebsite/Creation.*.tmpl
Installation of purchased SSL certificates	The system installs SSL certificates that a user purchases through the cPanel Market.	Market/SSLWebInstall.*.tmpl
Installation of purchased WHM Plugins.	The system fails to install a WHM plugin that a user purchases through the cPanel Store.	Market/WHMPluginInstall.*.tmpl
Instant Message Failure	The system fails to send a notification via an instant message.	iContact/SendIMFailed.*.tmpl

Alert Type	Event that triggers	Notification Template
Invalid Domains	The system detects invalid domains.	`Check/InvalidDomains.*.tmpl`
Invalid Hostname For Main IP Address	The system cannot resolve the hostname to the correct IP address.	`Check/ValidServerHostname.*.tmpl`
IP Address DNS Check	The system runs the `/usr/local/cpanel/scripts/ipcheck` script.	`Check/IP.*.tmpl`
Kernel Crash Check	The system finds specific errors in the output of the `dmesg` command.	`Check/Oops.*.tmpl`
Large Amount of Outbound Email Detected	A mail user exceeds the preconfigured threshold of 500 unique outbound messages (excludes mailing lists). The system either takes no action, holds, or rejects additional messages.	`Mail/SpammersDetected.*.tmpl`
Local configuration template detected upon service upgrade	The system detected a local custom configuration template for a service during an upgrade (for example, Dovecot).	`Check/LocalConfTemplate.*.tmpl`
Lost Contact With DNS Cluster	The system could not contact a server in the DNS cluster.	`DnsAdmin/UnreachablePeer.*.tmpl`

Alert Type	Event that triggers	Notification Template
Mail Server Out of Memory	The mail server runs out of memory while it processes mail for an account.	`MailServer/OOM.*.tmpl`
Mailbox Usage Warning	Mailbox quota warning notifications for a single mailbox.	`Quota/MailboxWarning.*.tmpl`
Maximum Hourly Emails Exceeded	A domain exceeds the threshold for the maximum number of sent emails in an hour.	`Mail/HourlyLimitExceeded.*.tmpl`
Migrate PowerDNS configuration upon upgrade	The system upgraded PowerDNS, but it may contain configuration settings which require manual migration and adjustment.	`Check/PdnsConf.*.tmpl`
Notices concerning goods and services purchased via the cPanel Market	A user purchases an SSL certificate or other product through the cPanel Market.	`Market/SSLWebInstall.*.tmpl`
Notification of New Addon Domains	A user creates an addon domain.	`parkadmin/Notify.*.tmpl`
Notifications of Outdated Software	The system detects outdated software. Note: These notifications are for applications on your server. You can	`OutdatedSoftware/Notify.*.tmpl`

Alert Type	Event that triggers	Notification Template
	control notices for cPanel & WHM updates with the *System Update Failures* and *Update Failures* settings.	
Offload Functionality to a Child Node Failure	The system failed to offload functionality to a linked cPanel & WHM child server node.	`Accounts/ChildDistributionFailure.*.tmpl`
Offload Functionality to a Child Node Success	The system successfully offloaded functionality to a linked cPanel & WHM child server node.	`Accounts/ChildDistributionSuccess.*.tmpl`
Outgoing Email Threshold Exceeded	A domain exceeds the daily emails sent threshold defined by the *Number of emails a domain may send per day before the system sends a notification.* Option.	`Mail/SendLimitExceeded.*.tmpl`
Package Extension Name Conflicts	The system renames a package extension and updates all dependent package extensions to use the new filename due to a name conflict.	`Install/PackageExtension.*.tmpl`
PHP-FPM Account is over quota.	An over-quota account prevents PHP-FPM from starting on a server that runs in a Virtuozzo environment.	`PHPFPM/AccountOverquota.*.tmpl`
queueprocd Critical Errors	The Queue Processor daemon shuts down because of repeated critical errors.	`queueprocd/Notify.*.tmpl`
Reboot To Enable Filesystem	The system requires a reboot to enable filesystem quotas.	`Quota/RebootRequired.*.tmpl`

Alert Type	Event that triggers	Notification Template
Quotas Reminder		
Reconfigure CalDAV/CardDAV clients	The system sends a notification email to all users with Calendar and Contacts Server (CCS) data. The email tells them to reconfigure their calendars and contacts applications for the replacement of CCS by the cpdavd service.	`Mail/ReconfigureCalendars.*.tmpl`
Remote MySQL Connection Failure	The system encounters a remote MySQL connection issue.	`Check/MysqlConnection.*.tmpl`
Remote MySQL Server Notifications	The system does not support the version of MySQL® on a remote MySQL server.	`Install/CheckRemoteMySQLVersion.*.tmpl`
Root Compromise Checks	The system detects that your server's `root` account is compromised.	`Check/Hack.*.tmpl`
Scheduled Backup Will Start Soon	The system sends this notification before it runs a backup.	`Backup/PreBackupNotice.*.tmpl`
Script Terminated Due to Deprecated Call	The system performs a deprecated call within a script and terminates the script.	`Logger/Notify.*.tmpl`

Alert Type	Event that triggers	Notification Template
Security Advisor State Change	WHM's Security Advisor interface detects new issues with high importance.	`Check/SecurityAdvisorStateChange.*.tmpl`
Service failures (ChkServd)	cPanel & WHM detects that a service fails, recovers, or times out.	`chkservd/Notify.*.tmpl`
Service SSL Certificate Expiration	A service-level SSL certificate expires.	`Check/SSLCertExpired.*.tmpl`
Service SSL Certificate Expires Soon	A service-level SSL certificate will expire soon.	`Check/SSLCertExpiresSoon.*.tmpl`
SSHD Configuration Error	The system detects an attempt to change the `sshd_config` file.	`SSHD/ConfigError.*.tmpl`
SSL certificates expiring	An account's SSL certificate expires soon.	`SSL/CertificateExpiring.*.tmpl`
Stalled Process Notifications	A user's process stalls.	`OverLoad/CpuWatch.*.tmpl`
Stalled Statistics and Bandwidth Process Notifications	A process stalls while it processes a user's statistics and bandwidth data.	`OverLoad/LogRunner.*.tmpl`

Alert Type	Event that triggers	Notification Template
Stats and Bandwidth Processing Errors	A process experiences an error while it processes a user's statistics and bandwidth data.	`Stats/Lagging.*.tmpl`
Stuck Script	The system detects a stuck script.	`StuckScript/Notify.*.tmpl`
System Log Approache s 2GB	A log file currently approaches 2 GB in size.	`Check/Biglog.*.tmpl`
System Out Of Memory	The system terminates a process to avoid a crash due to low memory.	`chkservd/OOM.*.tmpl`
System Update Failures	The system fails to update.	`sysup/Notify.*.tmpl`
Transfer Offloaded Functional ity between Child Nodes Failure	A parent server node failed to offload functionality to a different linked cPanel & WHM child server node.	`Accounts/ChildRedistribut ionFailure.*.tmpl`
Transfer Offloaded Functional ity between Child Nodes Success	A parent server node successfully offloaded functionality to a different linked cPanel & WHM child server node.	`Accounts/ChildRedistribut ionSuccess.*.tmpl`
Transfer Offloaded Functional ity from a	A parent server node failed to restore a cPanel account's offloaded service functionality from a child server node.	`Accounts/ChildDedistribut ionFailure.*.tmpl`

Alert Type	Event that triggers	Notification Template
Child Node Failure		
Transfer Offloaded Functionality from a Child Node Success	A parent server node successfully restored a cPanel account's offloaded service functionality from a child server node.	`Accounts/ChildDedistributionSuccess.*.tmpl`
Uncategorized Notifications	A notification that an existing notification type and template does not already handle.	`Application/base.*.tmpl`
Unmonitored Services	Every two weeks, the system scans all active services and sends a notification that lists all of the unmonitored services.	`Check/UnmonitoredEnabledServices.*.tmpl`
Update Blocker - Service Deprecation Notice	The cPanel & WHM update fails because of a deprecated service.	`Update/ServiceDeprecated.*.tmpl`
Update Failure Due to Immutable Files	The system cannot update cPanel & WHM due to immutable files.	`Check/ImmutableFiles.*.tmpl`
Update Failures	Update failure notifications.	`Update/Now.*.tmpl`
Update Version Blocker	The system fails to update because of an `upgrade version blocker.`	`Update/Blocker.*.tmpl`

Alert Type	Event that triggers	Notification Template
Upgrade Required - Service Is Outdated	The system will automatically upgrade a service.	`Update/UpgradeRequired.*.tmpl`
User Disabled Two-Factor Authentication	A user disables two-factor authentication.	`TwoFactorAuth/UserDisable.*.tmpl`
User Disk Usage Warning	Users approach or reach their disk quota limits.	• `Quota/DiskWarning.*.tmpl` • `Quota/List.*.tmpl`
User Enabled Two-Factor Authentication	A user enables two-factor authentication.	`TwoFactorAuth/UserEnable.*.tmpl`

7.2 Edit System Mail Preferences

By default, the system has several special email accounts: “cpanel”, “nobody”, and “root”. On this page, you can configure where these special email accounts forward. For example, some users may decide to reply back to a system notification or an email system will send a NDR (“bounce”) email. You should add some email addresses in here to forward these system emails to. For example, you might put your support email address, so if someone emails cpanel@server.example.com, it will forward to your support user.

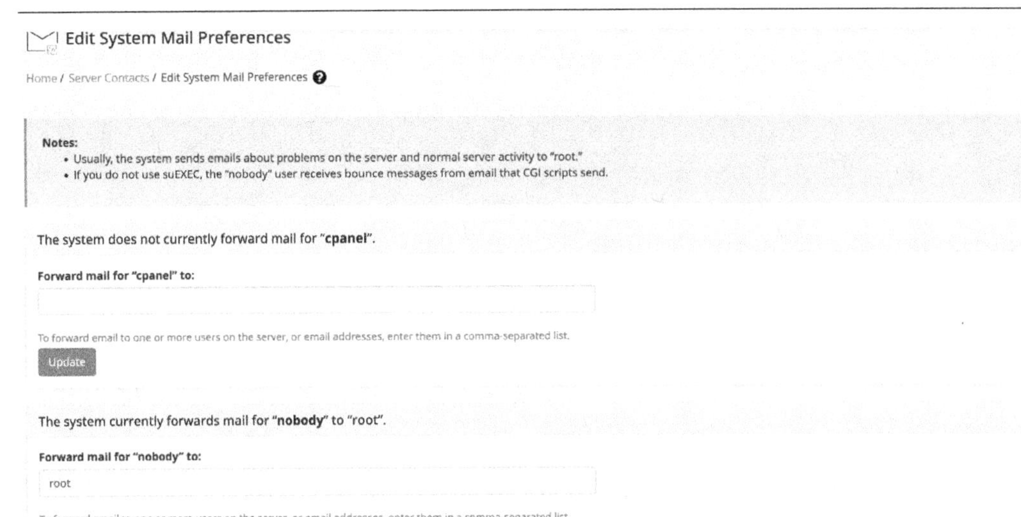
Edit System Mail Preferences
Home / Server Contacts / Edit System Mail Preferences
Notes:
Usually, the system sends emails about problems on the server and normal server activity to "root."
If you do not use suEXEC, the "nobody" user receives bounce messages from email that CGI scripts send.
The system does not currently forward mail for "cpanel".
Forward mail for "cpanel" to:
To forward email to one or more users on the server, or email addresses, enter them in a comma-separated list.
Update
The system currently forwards mail for "nobody" to "root".
Forward mail for "nobody" to:
root
To forward email to one or more users on the server, or email addresses, enter them in a comma-separated list.
Update
The system does not currently forward mail for "root".
Forward mail for "root" to:
To forward email to one or more users on the server, or email addresses, enter them in a comma-separated list.
Update

8 Resellers

For VPS/Dedicated Servers

The information in this section applies to VPS and dedicated servers.

If you plan on having **reseller accounts**, special accounts that will resell your hosting services as their own, then you will want to refer to this chapter quite a bit. The settings here will assign your users extra permissions to allow them access to WHM, but restrict their access to some of the more sensitive areas that they should not have access to.

8.1 Change Ownership of an Account

This is a deprecated feature and has been moved to Modify an Account. See Chapter 16.

8.2 Change Ownership of Multiple Accounts

Occasionally you may find that a transferred in account will belong to the root user or maybe there are other websites on the server that belong to one user, and you need to transfer ownership to another owner This tool will let you do that for multiple accounts at one time.

First, you will select the new reseller who will own the accounts. Then you will click on **Submit**. Then select the new account owner. Click on **Change Owner** to move the accounts to the new owner.

8.3 Edit Reseller Nameservers and Privileges

This is a special screen that lets you edit a specific reseller user's nameservers and privileges. If you have multiple resellers, you will be able to select the reseller you want to modify.

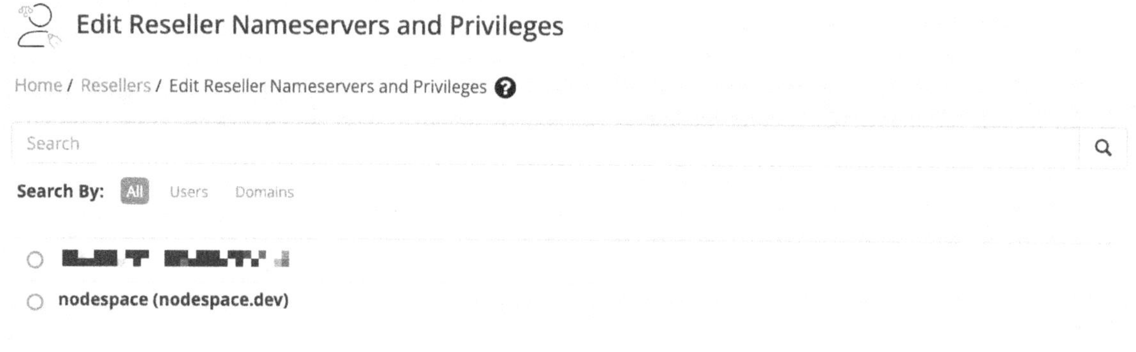

8.3.1 Account Creation Limits

Years ago, cPanel changed the way in which they license their software. It used to be that you could have an unlimited number of accounts on a server. Then cPanel moved to a license model that is based on the number of user accounts on the system. With this change, that meant reseller accounts were also bound by the same licensing constraints. So, many hosting companies created reseller plans that limit the number of accounts a reseller account can create. You can tweak those settings here.

Edit "nodespace"

Account Creation Limits

- [ ] Limit the total number of accounts nodespace can create
  Number of accounts
- [ ] Limit accounts that nodespace can create by Resource Usage.
- [ ] Specify which packages nodespace can use for account creation.
  - [ ] Limit the amount of accounts that nodespace can create per package.

Ideally, you should control these settings via the Packages options (see Chapter 20).

- Limit the total number of accounts: This is a hard limit. For example, if you set this to 5 and then the reseller user creates 5 users, they will not be able to create any more accounts.
- Limit accounts that <user> can create by Resource Usage: This requires creating a hosting package and assigning the reseller to that hosting package. With this option enabled, resellers will be bound by the number of resources assigned to their account from the reseller package.

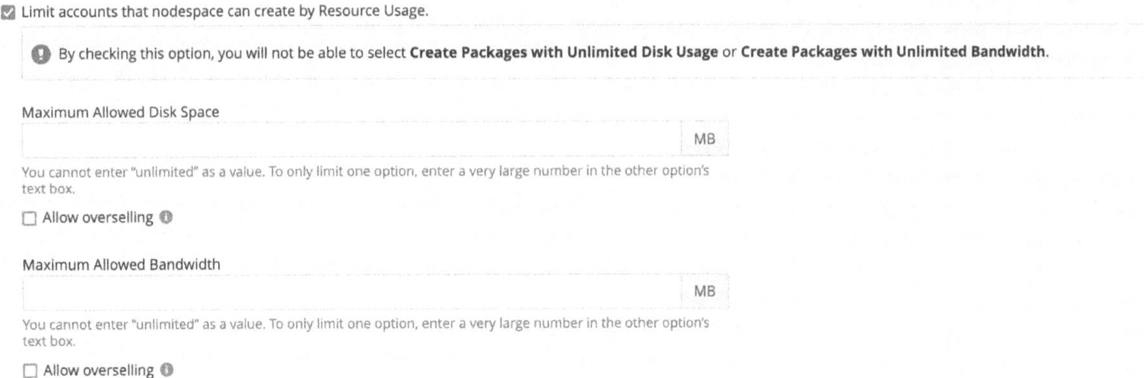

- Specify which packages <user> can use for account creation: Enabling this option will allow the user to be able to access selected packages already on the system. Resellers can always access the packages that they create.

- Limit the amount of accounts that <user> can create by package: Enabling this option will limit the number of accounts per package that the reseller user can create. For example if you have "package_a" and it's limited to 3 accounts and "package_b" and it's limited to 2 accounts. Once the reseller user creates 3 accounts on "package_a", they will not be able to create any more accounts with that package unless some are deleted.

8.3.2 Feature Limits (ACL Lists)

Yes, cPanel calls these "Access Control Lists Lists", but ignoring the redundancy, this is how you can limit the features that the reseller user will have access to in WHM.

While you might be tempted to not give users permissions, the fact of the matter is, most of these permissions are safe to give resellers. These are the permissions that allow them to do their job.

The Initial Privileges should all be enabled. These are the absolute bare minimum permissions that will allow resellers to do basic tasks.

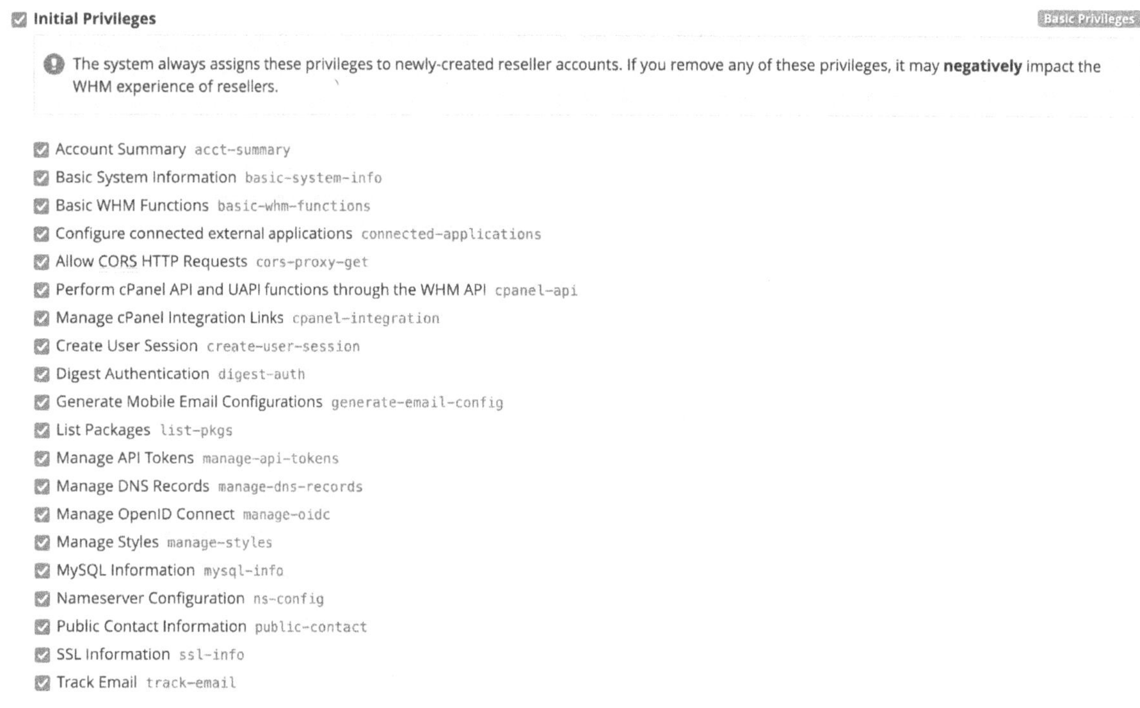

You should also enable the Account Information options. These allow resellers to view account details. Resellers can only view the accounts that they own. The root user can see all accounts on the system.

- [x] **Account Information** — Standard Privileges
  - [x] List Accounts `list-accts`
  - [x] View Account Bandwidth Usage `show-bandwidth`

Another group to enable is the Account Management group. This will allow your resellers to create accounts, terminate accounts, suspend and unsuspend accounts, manage SSL certificates for accounts, and more.

- [x] **Account Management** — Standard Privileges
  - [x] Create Accounts `create-acct`
  - [x] Terminate Accounts `kill-acct`
  - [x] Suspend/Unsuspend Accounts `suspend-acct`
  - [x] Upgrade/Downgrade Accounts `upgrade-account`
  - [x] SSL Site Management `ssl`
  - [x] Purchase SSL Certificates `ssl-buy`
  - [x] SSL CSR/Certificate Generator `ssl-gencrt`
  - [x] Edit MX Entries `edit-mx`
  - [x] Change Passwords `passwd`
  - [x] File and Directory Restoration `file-restore`

Another group to enable is the DNS group. This will allow the reseller to manage DNS settings for their users.

- [x] **DNS** — Standard Privileges
  - [x] Add DNS Zones `create-dns`
  - [x] Remove DNS Zones `kill-dns`
  - [x] Park DNS Zones `park-dns`
  - [x] Edit DNS Zones `edit-dns`

Unless you are creating packages and only allowing your resellers to resell those packages (which is not recommended, you should let your users create their own packages), you should enable the Packages group to allow resellers the option to create their own packages.

☑ **Packages** Standard Privileges

☑ Add/Remove Packages `add-pkg`

☑ Edit Packages `edit-pkg`

Another standard option, that is safe to enable, is to allow management of Third-Party Services.

☑ **Third-Party Services** Standard Privileges

☑ Manage Third-Party Services `thirdparty`

I personally believe you should give your resellers as much power as possible to support themselves and their users. You should also enable the Troubleshooting section which will enable the Troubleshoot Mail Delivery tool.

☑ **Troubleshooting** Standard Privileges

☑ Troubleshoot Mail Delivery `mailcheck`

Enabling the cPanel Management group will enable the News Modification tool. This allows resellers to post news directly into their user's cPanel accounts.

☑ **cPanel Management** Standard Privileges

☑ News Modification `news`

Another standard privilege to enable is the Account Enhancements. These can be used by third-party addons and applications so it is a good idea to enable them.

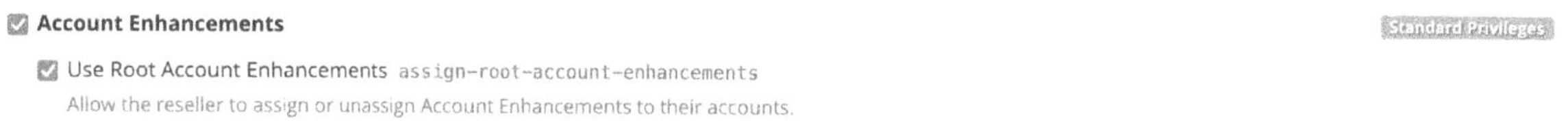

☑ **Account Enhancements** Standard Privileges

☑ Use Root Account Enhancements `assign-root-account-enhancements`

Allow the reseller to assign or unassign Account Enhancements to their accounts.

An option that you might want to weigh and decide if it's right for you is the option to allow your resellers the ability to create accounts with Shell Access. This will allow your resellers to give their users shell access to your server. You may need to enable this option or you can keep this disabled and have your reseller funnel shell access requests through your support desk.

Package Privileges

☑ **Accounts**

☑ Allow Creation of Accounts with Shell Access `allow-shell`

Another option to consider is allowing users access to root packages. This is one option that I do not enable on my servers. This can allow resellers access to my own reseller packages.

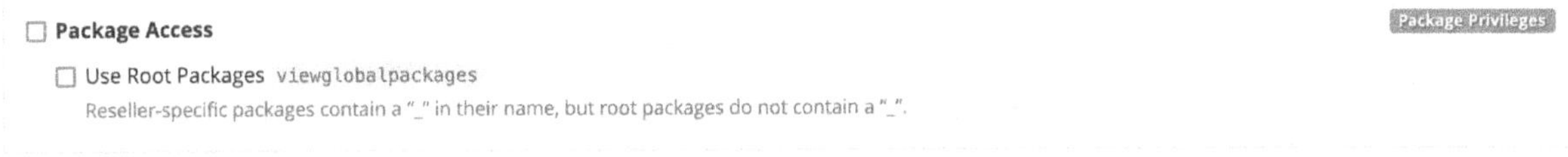

Package Privileges

☐ **Package Access**

☐ Use Root Packages `viewglobalpackages`

Reseller-specific packages contain a "_" in their name, but root packages do not contain a "_".

A group worth enabling (or enabling most of the options on) is the Package Creation group. This allows your resellers to create packages with the options selected. Adjust these selections based on what kind of packages you want your resellers to create and the resources available at your disposal.

Package Privileges

☑ **Package Creation**

☑ Create Packages with Addon Domains `allow-addoncreate`

☑ Create Packages with Parked (Alias) Domains `allow-parkedcreate`

☑ Create Packages with a Dedicated IP Address `add-pkg-ip`

☑ Create Packages with Shell Access `add-pkg-shell`

☑ Create Packages with Unlimited Features (for example, email accounts) `allow-unlimited-pkgs`

☑ Create Packages with Custom Email Limits `allow-emaillimits-pkgs`

☑ Create Packages with Unlimited Disk Usage `allow-unlimited-disk-pkgs`

☑ Create Packages with Unlimited Bandwidth `allow-unlimited-bw-pkgs`

If you have purchased a license for Imunify360 and want to make it available to your resellers, you can enable the Third-Party Services group with the Imunify360 plugin enabled.

Additional Software

☑ **Third-Party Services**

☑ Imunify360 plugin `software-imunify360`

WP Toolkit is available for free to cPanel license holders and so I like to also enable the WP Toolkit for my resellers. It allows them to create upselling opportunities by either adding value to their packages or selling it at an extra charge.

☑ **WP Toolkit** Additional Software

☑ Access to WP Toolkit `wp-toolkit`

Now we're getting into "Global Privilege" options, and these are the options you may not want to give to resellers. These options can reveal a lot of information about your server and can allow them to make changes that they should not make. So, enable these with extreme caution, or better yet, not at all.

In my quest to allow resellers to be self-sufficient, I usually allow them to view the Server Status, but I do not let them view server information.

⊟ **Server Information** Global Privileges

☑ View Server Status `status`

☐ View Server Information `stats`

Enabling the Restart Services option is very dangerous to give to resellers. This would allow them to restart services on the server such as Apache, SSH, MySQL, etc. You should not enable this.

☐ **Services** Global Privileges

☐ Restart Services `restart`

The option to resynchronize FTP passwords is generally a safe troubleshooting tool that you can enable.

☑ **Troubleshooting** Global Privileges

☑ Resynchronize FTP Passwords `resftp`

Next, we're getting into Super Privileges, and these are the ones you should really ask yourself, "is this a good idea?" before you enable them.

The account management features should be unchecked. They allow resellers to easily bypass any limits that you set on them. You also don't want to enable the "Demo Account" as this won't let the user do anything as it functions as a demo.

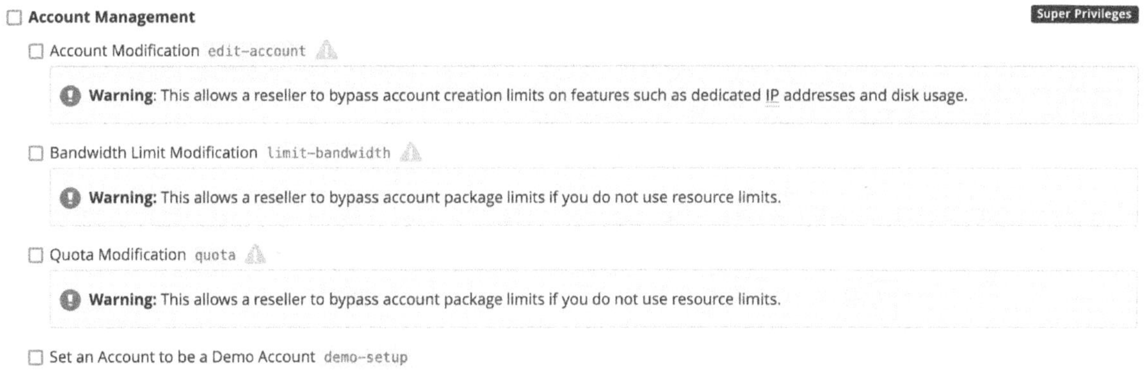

☐ **Account Management** Super Privileges

☐ Account Modification `edit-account` ⚠

Warning: This allows a reseller to bypass account creation limits on features such as dedicated IP addresses and disk usage.

☐ Bandwidth Limit Modification `limit-bandwidth` ⚠

Warning: This allows a reseller to bypass account package limits if you do not use resource limits.

☐ Quota Modification `quota` ⚠

Warning: This allows a reseller to bypass account package limits if you do not use resource limits.

☐ Set an Account to be a Demo Account `demo-setup`

If the system has multiple drives, the Rearrange Accounts function allows resellers to optimize disk usage by moving accounts across drives. This should not be enabled.

☐ **Advanced Account Management** Super Privileges

☐ Rearrange Accounts `rearrange-accts`
Use this to optimize disk usage across disk drives.

DNS Clustering would allow resellers to create and manage a cPanel DNS cluster. This is something that you, as the server administrator, should control and manage, not your resellers. Best practice is to keep this disabled.

☐ **Clustering** Super Privileges

☐ DNS Clustering `clustering` ⚠

You can enable the Locales if you have some resellers that speak a different language. This will allow them to manage those language translations. However, this allows resellers to add HTML to all cPanel interface so enable this with caution.

☐ **Locales** Super Privileges

☐ Modify & Create Locales `locale-edit` ⚠

Something that you should **NEVER** enable for any standard reseller account is “Everything”. This is basically turning the reseller account into a root account. They will have access to everything. **There is never a good reason to enable this for a standard reseller account.**

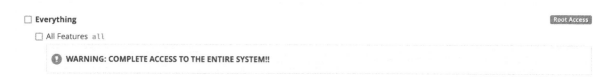

Finally, once you're happy with your selections, you can save them or, better yet, save the list as a standard reseller permissions ACL that can be applied to other reseller accounts. I like to do this, so I can apply this ACL via packages.

8.3.3 Nameservers

This is where you can specify the nameservers the reseller account will use and the system will use when setting up accounts. If you're using the server's temporary hostname that uses the cprapid.com domain, you'll receive a warning that these nameservers won't work. Instead, you'll need to change the server's default name servers (see Chapter 3 > Basic WebHost Manager Config > Nameserves).

Nameservers

Set the default nameservers that the system uses when this reseller creates an account.

Inherit Nameservers from root

Nameserver 1: "ns1.[illegible]cprapid.com"

Nameserver 2: "ns2.[illegible].cprapid.com"

Explicitly Set the Nameservers

Nameservers that you explicitly set will transfer with the user to the new servers upon migration.

Default nameservers of the type .cprapid.com are not compatible with .com domain registrations. Learn More

Save All Settings

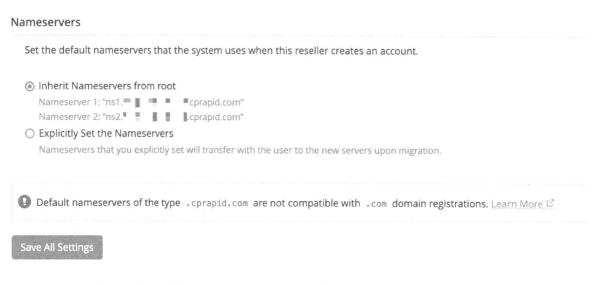

To save all your settings, click on the **Save All Settings** button.

8.4 Email All Resellers

This is a tool that does exactly what it sounds like: allows you to email all resellers directly from cPanel. While you should instead be using your billing software to email your resellers, this tool allows you to do just that. Enter the Sender Name, for example "Your Hosting Company", the sender email (for example support@example.com), the subject of the message, and then the message body. This message is sent in plain text to the email address on the cPanel account for all reseller accounts.

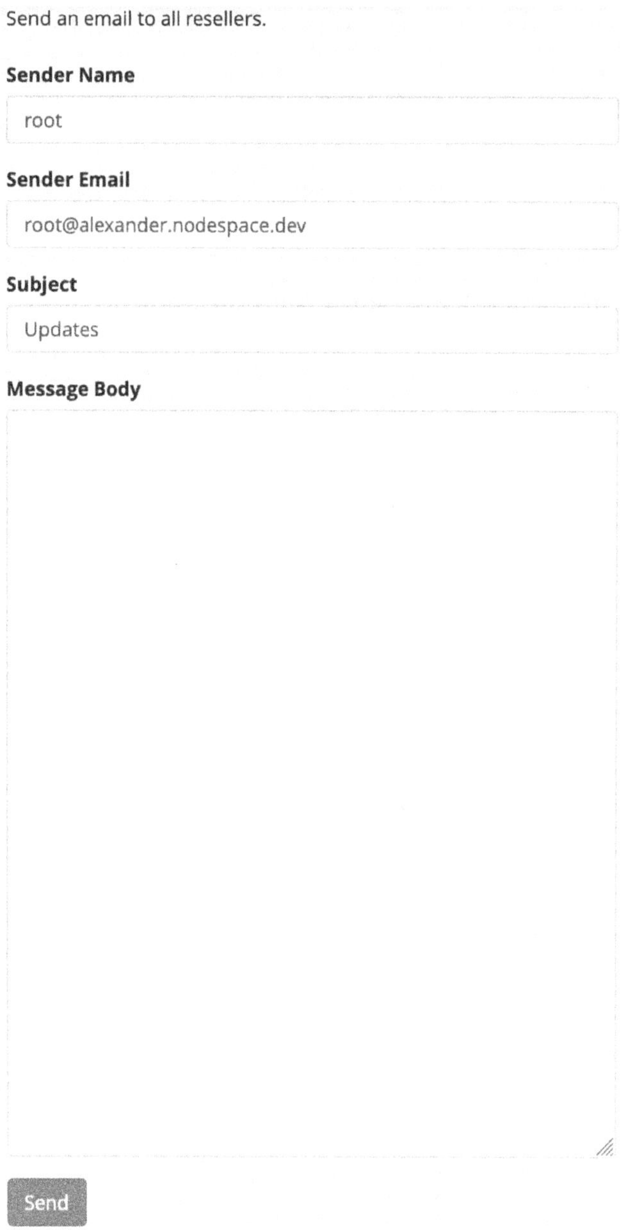

Send an email to all resellers.

Sender Name

root

Sender Email

root@alexander.nodespace.dev

Subject

Updates

Message Body

Send

8.5 Manage Reseller's IP Delegation

If you have multiple IP addresses on your system or have a reseller that has their own netblock of IPs routed to your server, you can use this tool to allow resellers to use these IPs or to reserve these IPs for use by a particular reseller.

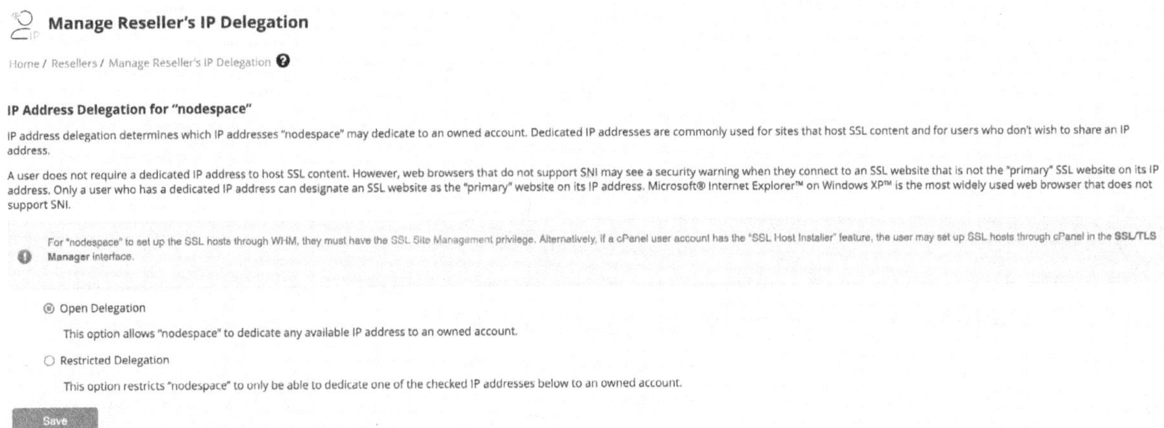

Manage Reseller's IP Delegation
Home / Resellers / Manage Reseller's IP Delegation
IP Address Delegation for "nodespace"
IP address delegation determines which IP addresses "nodespace" may dedicate to an owned account. Dedicated IP addresses are commonly used for sites that host SSL content and for users who don't wish to share an IP address.
A user does not require a dedicated IP address to host SSL content. However, web browsers that do not support SNI may see a security warning when they connect to an SSL website that is not the "primary" SSL website on its IP address. Only a user who has a dedicated IP address can designate an SSL website as the "primary" website on its IP address. Microsoft® Internet Explorer™ on Windows XP™ is the most widely used web browser that does not support SNI.
For "nodespace" to set up the SSL hosts through WHM, they must have the SSL Site Management privilege. Alternatively, if a cPanel user account has the "SSL Host Installer" feature, the user may set up SSL hosts through cPanel in the SSL/TLS Manager interface.
Open Delegation
This option allows "nodespace" to dedicate any available IP address to an owned account.
Restricted Delegation
This option restricts "nodespace" to only be able to dedicate one of the checked IP addresses below to an owned account.
Save

To restrict the IP addresses a reseller can use, set the delegation to restricted.

Keep in mind this tool may not be used now with most systems typically only having a single IP address.

8.6 Manage Reseller's Shared IP Address

This interface allows you to manage the shared IP addresses on the system for resellers. For example, if you have multiple IP addresses on a system, you can use this to allot an IP address to a single reseller and then that IP address is shared with the reseller's users versus all the other users on the system.

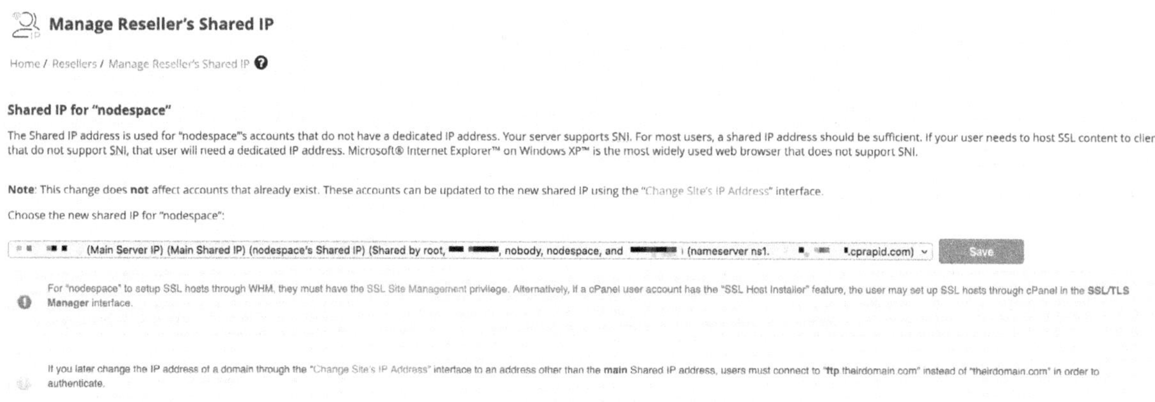

Manage Reseller's Shared IP
Home / Resellers / Manage Reseller's Shared IP
Shared IP for "nodespace"
The Shared IP address is used for "nodespace"'s accounts that do not have a dedicated IP address. Your server supports SNI. For most users, a shared IP address should be sufficient. If your user needs to host SSL content to clients that do not support SNI, that user will need a dedicated IP address. Microsoft® Internet Explorer™ on Windows XP™ is the most widely used web browser that does not support SNI.
Note: This change does not affect accounts that already exist. These accounts can be updated to the new shared IP using the "Change Site's IP Address" interface.
Choose the new shared IP for "nodespace":
(Main Server IP) (Main Shared IP) (nodespace's Shared IP) (Shared by root, nobody, nodespace, and (nameserver ns1. .cprapid.com)
Save
For "nodespace" to setup SSL hosts through WHM, they must have the SSL Site Management privilege. Alternatively, if a cPanel user account has the "SSL Host Installer" feature, the user may set up SSL hosts through cPanel in the SSL/TLS Manager interface.
If you later change the IP address of a domain through the "Change Site's IP Address" interface to an address other than the main Shared IP address, users must connect to "ftp.theirdomain.com" instead of "theirdomain.com" in order to authenticate.

8.7 Reseller Center

This is typically the main interface for controlling and managing reseller accounts. This will give you the shortcuts for accessing all these sections quickly and for a specific reseller account. You can use this screen to promote a regular account to a reseller account, remove reseller permissions from a reseller turning their account into a standard user account (no access to WHM).

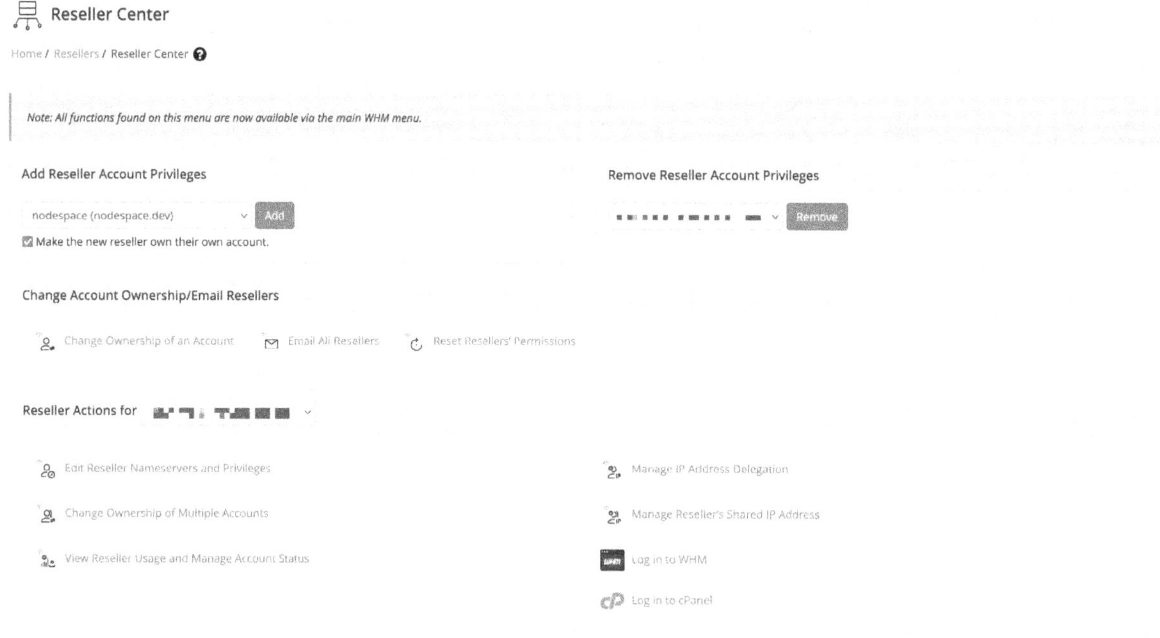

Keep in mind that the Reseller Center seems to soon be a deprecated feature as there is a notice saying all these functions are available via the main WHM menu which is on the left-hand side of the screen. Additionally, we've covered most of these option in this chapter.

Reseller Center is still useful for some options. Under the Reseller Actions, select the reseller account you want to work with. You will have some options that haven't been migrated to the main menu yet:

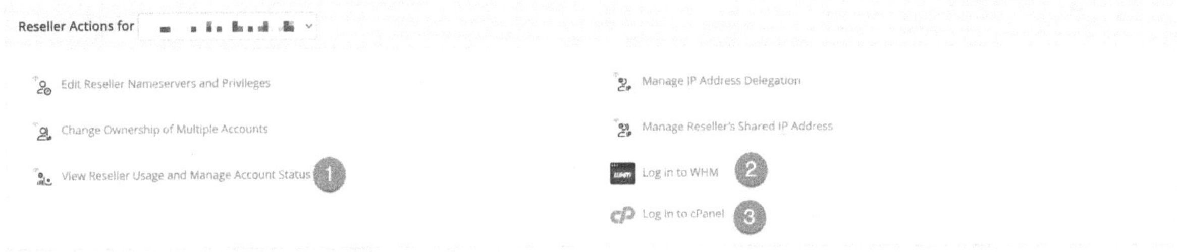

8.7.1 View Reseller Usage and Manage Account Status

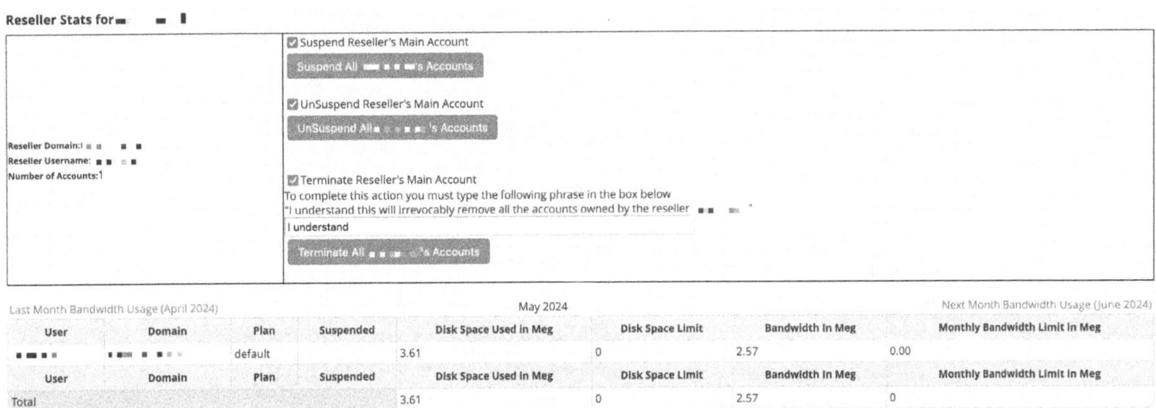

User	Domain	Plan	Suspended	Disk Space Used in Meg	Disk Space Limit	Bandwidth in Meg	Monthly Bandwidth Limit in Meg
		default		3.61	0	2.57	0.00
User	**Domain**	**Plan**	**Suspended**	**Disk Space Used in Meg**	**Disk Space Limit**	**Bandwidth in Meg**	**Monthly Bandwidth Limit in Meg**
Total				3.61	0	2.57	0

This will give you an overview of a particular reseller user. You will see all the accounts they own, and details about their account and their users. You can see the domain names, plan, if the account is suspended, disk space used, and bandwidth used. You also can suspend/unsuspend the reseller's main account as well as terminate the reseller's main account.

8.7.2 Login to WHM

This option lets you impersonate the reseller and login to WHM as the reseller. This allows you to see what your reseller sees and is a great way to double check ACLs and permissions.

8.7.3 Login to cPanel

This option allows you to impersonate the reseller's standard user account and access their cPanel account.

8.8 Reset Resellers

The reset resellers tool allows you to reset the package permissions on a reseller and force them to only use packages that they own. If they have any users that are using different packages, those accounts will continue to have access to that package except the reseller will not be able to assign the packages again.

Home / Resellers / Reset Resellers 

Reset package permissions to default

Here you can force a reseller to only use packages they own This will override any other packages they current have access to but will not change any packages that are currently being used on their accounts.

Select Reseller(s) to reset:

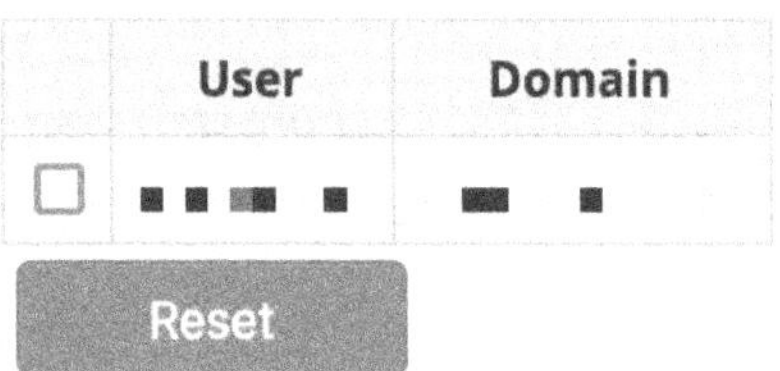

8.9 Show Reseller Accounts

This tool will show a report of all the reseller users on the server, and it will show a list of all the accounts they own. It will show you the reseller user, the main user, their domain, and the package to which they are assigned. This is a helpful reporting tool.

8.10 View Reseller Usage and Manage Account Statistics

See Reseller Center, "View Reseller Usage and Manage Account Status."

9 Service Configuration

For VPS/Dedicated Servers

The information in this section applies to VPS and dedicated servers.

This chapter gets into configuring and tweaking the services that make up a cPanel server from Apache, Log Rotation, Web Disk, Exim, and more. We'll explore each of these services and the different ways to configure and tweak them for the best performance and for providing a secure hosting environment.

9.1 Apache Configuration

Apache is the primary web server software that comes with cPanel servers. Apache is a very easy to use web server and is one of the oldest web servers still in active development on the Internet. cPanel provides a lot of useful tools for managing and configuring Apache.

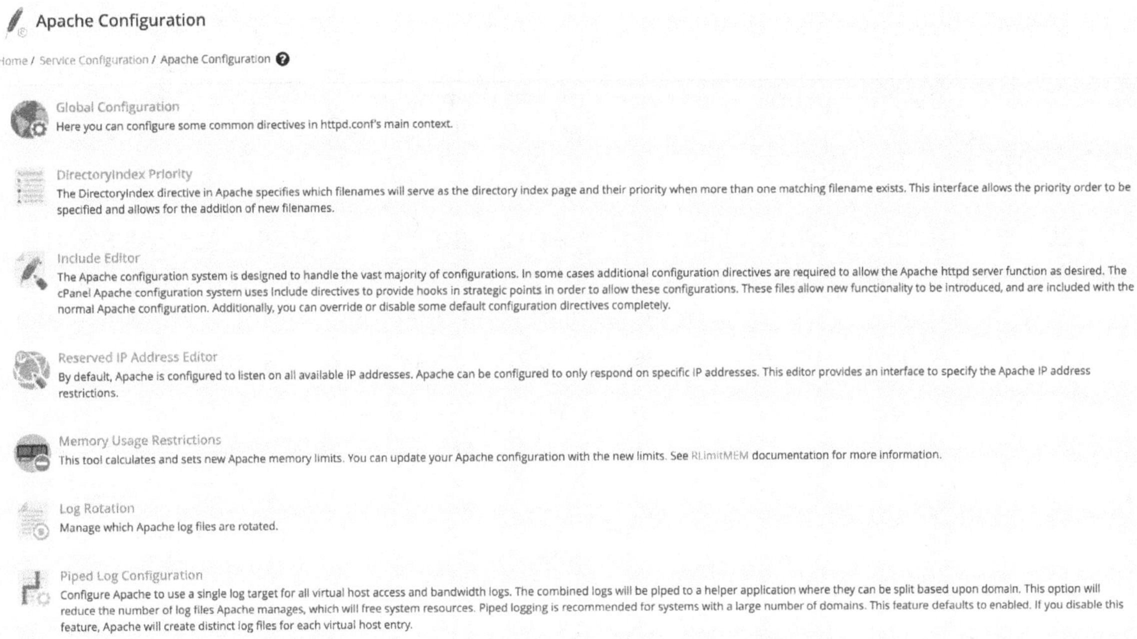

Apache Configuration
Home / Service Configuration / Apache Configuration
Global Configuration
Here you can configure some common directives in httpd.conf's main context.
DirectoryIndex Priority
The DirectoryIndex directive in Apache specifies which filenames will serve as the directory index page and their priority when more than one matching filename exists. This interface allows the priority order to be specified and allows for the addition of new filenames.
Include Editor
The Apache configuration system is designed to handle the vast majority of configurations. In some cases additional configuration directives are required to allow the Apache httpd server function as desired. The cPanel Apache configuration system uses Include directives to provide hooks in strategic points in order to allow these configurations. These files allow new functionality to be introduced, and are included with the normal Apache configuration. Additionally, you can override or disable some default configuration directives completely.
Reserved IP Address Editor
By default, Apache is configured to listen on all available IP addresses. Apache can be configured to only respond on specific IP addresses. This editor provides an interface to specify the Apache IP address restrictions.
Memory Usage Restrictions
This tool calculates and sets new Apache memory limits. You can update your Apache configuration with the new limits. See RLimitMEM documentation for more information.
Log Rotation
Manage which Apache log files are rotated.
Piped Log Configuration
Configure Apache to use a single log target for all virtual host access and bandwidth logs. The combined logs will be piped to a helper application where they can be split based upon domain. This option will reduce the number of log files Apache manages, which will free system resources. Piped logging is recommended for systems with a large number of domains. This feature defaults to enabled. If you disable this feature, Apache will create distinct log files for each virtual host entry.

9.1.1 Global Configuration

The settings in the Global Configuration are applied at the server level for Apache. Any changes to settings made here will not take effect until the mail Apache configuration file is rebuilt and Apache is restarted.

9.1.1.1 SSL

The first main section of the Apache Global Configuration is regarding how the server handles SSL.

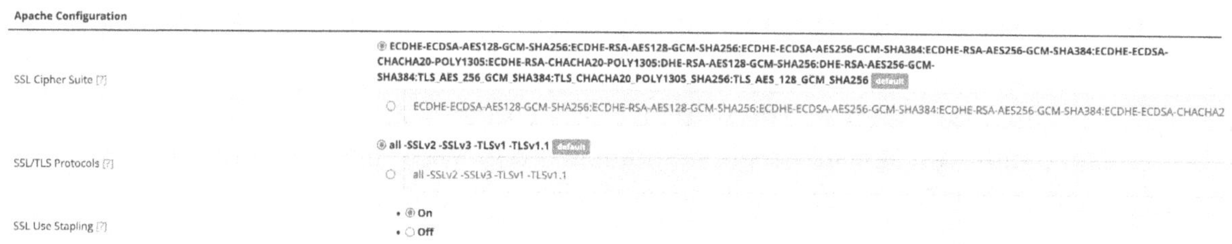

These options should not be changed unless you know what you are doing. By modifying the Cipher Suite, you may inadvertently break SSL on your server, causing certificates to not work properly or you may weaken security on your server.

9.1.1.2 Status & Logging

This section contains options for providing extra information on the Apache Status page about incoming requests and then configuring the information in the Apache log files. You should not need to change any of the LogFormat options otherwise you could potentially break things with system logging and analytics applications.

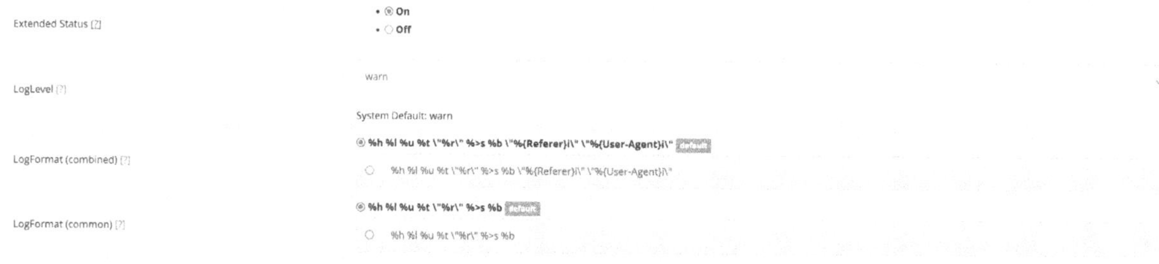

9.1.1.3 Trace, Server Signature, Server Tokens

These options are all restricted by default. The system default is defaulting for the sake of PCI compliance. Whether or not you care, the defaults are acceptable here.

The TraceEnable is part of Apache. From the Apache documentation:

This directive overrides the behavior of `TRACE` for both the core server and `mod_proxy`. The default `TraceEnable on` permits `TRACE` requests per RFC 2616, which disallows any request body to accompany the request. `TraceEnable off` causes the core server and `mod_proxy` to return a `405` (Method not allowed) error to the client.

The server signature option will have Apache display some additional details for the server, which is not recommended to be enabled.

The server token option can cause Apache to display additional details about the version being ran so it's best to leave this to product only. Product only will display simply "Apache".

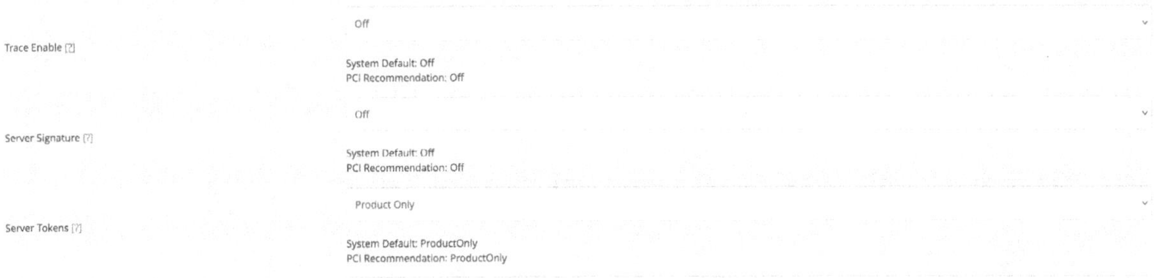

Trace Enable [?]	Off System Default: Off PCI Recommendation: Off
Server Signature [?]	Off System Default: Off PCI Recommendation: Off
Server Tokens [?]	Product Only System Default: ProductOnly PCI Recommendation: ProductOnly

The following settings are good at being left as the defaults. However on more busy servers, you may find that you need to tweak the number of Start Servers, Minimum Spare Servers, Maximum Space Servers, Server Limit, Max Request Workers, and Max Connections Per Child.

In most cases, the default settings are fine. On busy shared servers, you may find that you need to increase the number of start servers, spare servers, etc. These values need to be carefully balanced between how much RAM and CPU your server has, otherwise if you set these values too high, you may inadvertently DoS yourself.

If you find that Apache is needing more resources, I recommend testing these values by increasing in increments of 5. For example, for Start Servers which defaults to 5, increase to 10 and increase the Spare Servers to 10.

The key for tweaking performance is to do it slowly and incrementally.

The next group of options is related to the Apache Keep-Alive settings and Timeout along with Symlink protection. The Keep-Alive timeouts are generally fine and do not need adjustments in normal use. These settings really are fine as-is and do not need adjustments unless you absolutely require it.

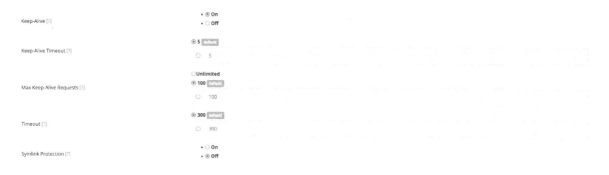

9.1.2 DirectoryIndex Priority

The DirectoryIndex Priority is the priority of index files in websites. For example, if you have an index.html and an index.php file, which file wins? Well, according to the default settings, index.php will take priority over index.htm. You can use this tool to adjust the priority of index files or add additional index files as needed. Files at the top of the list have higher priority than files lower down. So according to the default list, index.php has higher priority than index.shtml but index.shtml has higher priority than index.htm.

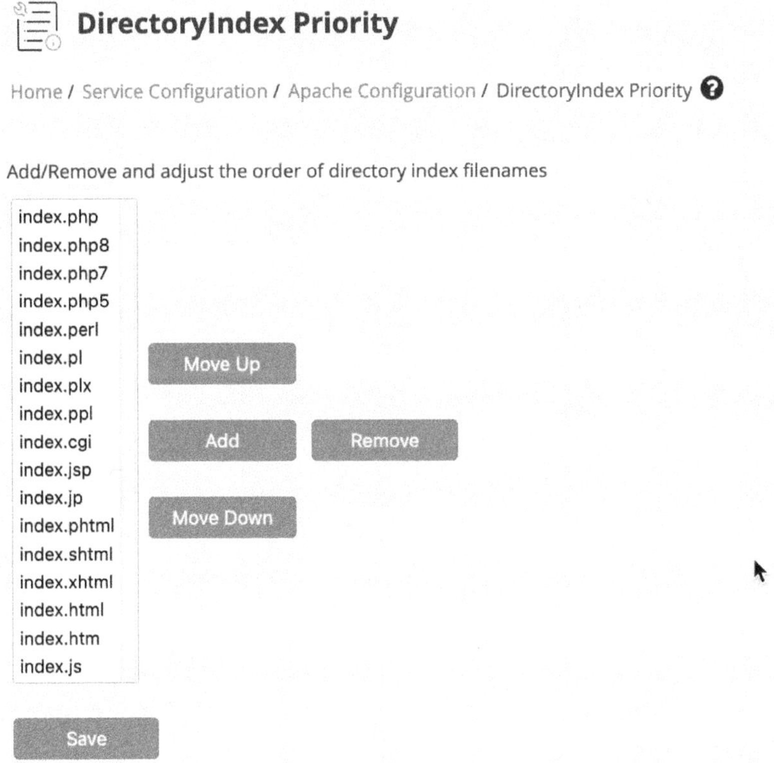

9.1.3 Include Editor

The Include Editor will allow you to insert custom Apache configurations into specific include points (or "hooks"). cPanel offers 3 include points: Pre Main Include, Pre VirtualHost Include, and Post VirtualHost Include.

9.1.3.1 Editing an Include

To edit an include, go to the include section that you want to edit. From the **Select an Apache Version** drop-down menu, select the **All Versions** option.

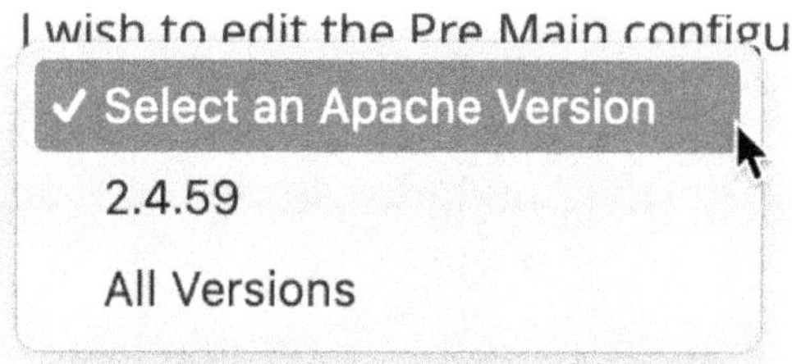

Next, enter your Apache configuration.

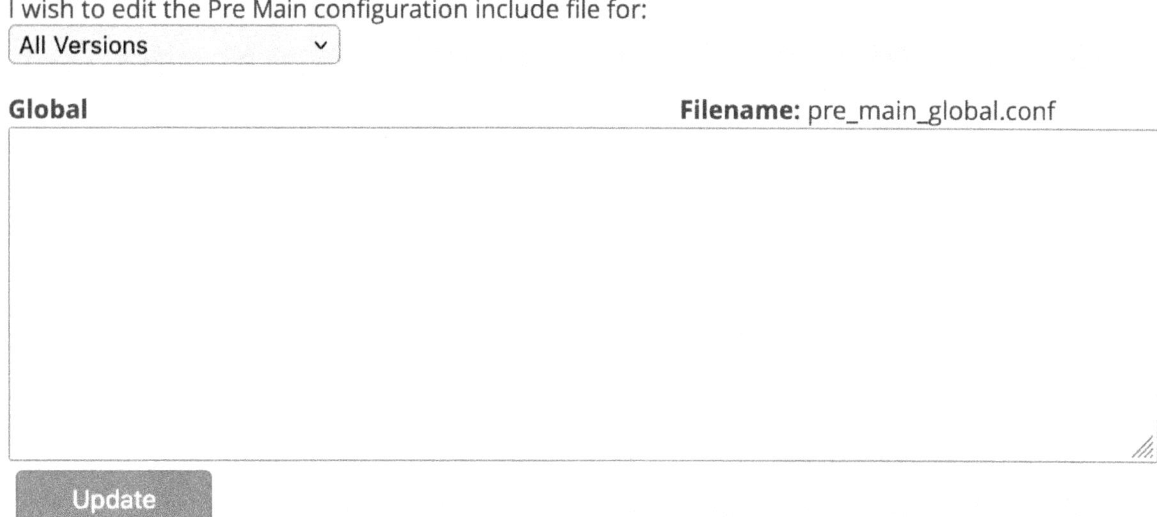

Click on **Update** to save the file. You will then need to restart Apache in order for the configuration to take effect.

Check Your Syntax
Check your Apache syntax. If you enter invalid syntax, Apache will not restart and may be stuck in a failed state.

9.1.4 Reserved IP Address Editor

By default, Apache will listen on every IP address added to your server. However, if you want to configure Apache to only listen on specific IP addresses, you can use this interface to specify IP addresses that Apache *will not* listen on.

By selecting **Reserved** next to an IP address, Apache will not listen on that IP address.

9.1.5 Memory Usage Restrictions

This tool will allow you to specify Apache memory limits. By default, Apache can use all the memory available on the system, but this tool will help you calculate the recommended memory limit for Apache. This can improve system stability, but it may slightly reduce performance.

9.1.6 Log Rotation

This tool will allow you to configure the Apache log files that are in rotation. If you unselect a log file, cPanel will *not* rotate it when it reaches the threshold size.

9.1.7 Piped Log Configuration

This option will allow configuring Apache to use a common target for logging. Then, cPanel will split up the log files to appropriate domains. This option defaults to on.

9.2 cPanel Log Rotation Configuration

This screen will let you configure which log files are in log rotation. If you're not familiar, log rotation ensures that log files do not take up a lot of space on the system by occasionally rotating them out when they reach a certain size. Old log files are available as compressed entries on the filesystem. By default, all the files listed should be in rotation. It's a good idea to make sure that all files are being rotated out.

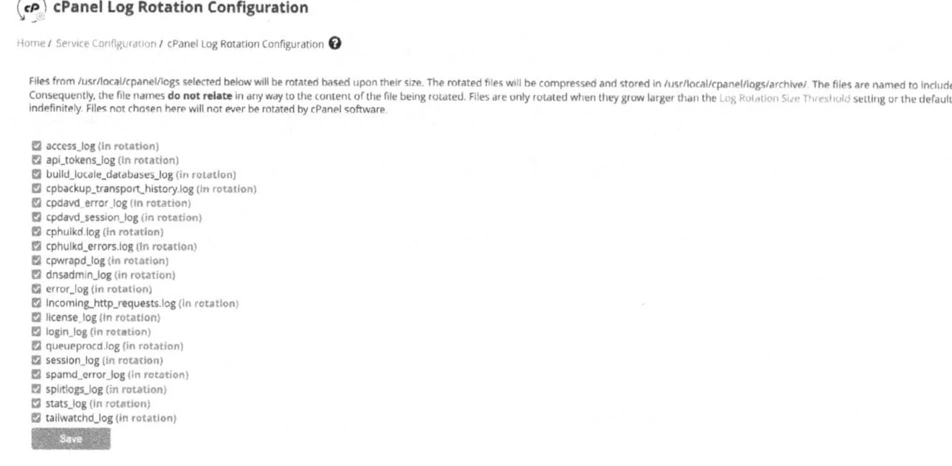

9.3 cPanel Web Disk Configuration

The settings here are related to the SSL configuration for DAVFS, WebDisk, CalDAV, and CardDAV services. These settings generally do not need to be adjusted unless you are sure of what you're doing. Misconfiguration here can break the SSL configuration for these services.

cPanel Web Disk Configuration

Home / Service Configuration / cPanel Web Disk Configuration 

The cPanel Web Service provides DAVFS, WebDisk, CalDAV, and CardDAV services over the HTTPS protocol.

TLS/SSL Cipher Suite

ECDHE-ECDSA-AES128-GCM-SHA256:ECDHE-RSA-AES128-GCM-SI

This complex directive uses a colon-separated "cipher-spec" string consisting of OpenSSL cipher specifications to configure the cipher suite that the client negotiates in the SSL handshake phase.

TLS/SSL Protocols

SSLv23:!SSLv2:!SSLv3:!TLSv1:!TLSv1_1

This complex directive uses a space-separated string consisting of protocol specifications to configure the SSL and TLS protocols that the client and server negotiate in the SSL/TLS handshake phase.

9.4 cPanel Web Services Configuration

These settings are related to the SSL configuration for cPanel, WHM, and Webmail services. These settings do not need to be modified unless you are sure of what you're doing.

cPanel Web Services Configuration

Home / Service Configuration / cPanel Web Services Configuration 

cPanel Web Services provide cPanel, WHM, and Webmail services over HTTP and HTTPS

This interface allows you to configure various aspects of cPanel Web Services' behavior.

TLS/SSL Cipher List

ECDHE-ECDSA-AES128-GCM

This is a standard format list of the TLS/SSL ciphers cPanel Web Services should use. Typically this will only need to be adjusted for PCI compliance.

TLS/SSL Protocols

SSLv23:!SSLv2:!SSLv3:!TLSv

This is a standard format list of the TLS/SSL protocols cPanel Web Services should use. Typically this will only need to be adjusted for PCI compliance.

Save

9.5 Exim Configuration Manager

Exim is the Mail Transfer Agent (MTA) that cPanel uses. Exim is the SMTP server that is used to transfer mail. The Exim Configuration Manage will allow you to adjust settings and configure the Exim server. By default, cPanel's settings will work just fine but you may find that on occasion you will need to adjust your Exim configuration, such as if you are going to be using a SMTP service such as MailChannels to send email.

Email is a complicated and very technical component of the Internet. Adjusting settings here against recommendation or to improper values can result in your server not being able to receive email from other servers on the Internet. Use caution and if you are unsure, consult Exim documentation as well as your web hosting provider.

This section is quite extensive as Exim is a very extensive piece of software. You will find that when loading up the Exim Configuration Manager, you will find a **Basic Editor, Advanced Editor** and options to **Backup, Restore,** and **Reset.**

Most settings can be changed from the Basic Editor and in the basic editor, you'll find a simple interface for changing these options based on categories.

9.5.1 Basic Editor

9.5.1.1 ACL Options

These settings limit who can send mail to your server.

9.5.1.1.1 Apache SpamAssassin Reject Spam Score Threshhold

The Apache SpamAssassin Reject Spam Score Threshold can be a positive or negative number which can contain a single decimal point. The default setting is No Reject Rule which means that no spam will be rejected by the system. Entering a value here will cause the system to reject messages with a spam score greater than or equal to the value entered. **Use this with caution as many emails that are legitimate may have a high spam score.** It is best to leave this at the default value and then let each of the domain users specify the value. Otherwise, set this value to something high, greater than 20 as no legitimate email should ever be this high (though, you might be surprised).

Keep in mind too that if you enter a value that contains an integer greater than or less than `0` and a decimal point, Apache SpamAssassin multiplies the value that you enter by a measure of ten. For example, if you enter a spam score threshold of `1.6`, Apache SpamAssassin sets the threshold to `16`.

9.5.1.1.2 Dictionary Attack Protection

This is a setting that will help prevent dictionary attacks when attackers try to guess email addresses or passwords on a system. A dictionary attack is when an attacker will use dictionary words to guess email addresses and passwords. This setting should remain on.

9.5.1.1.3 Reject Remote Mail Sent to the Server's Hostname

In most cases, your server's hostname should not be receiving email. This is a common spammer target. This setting defaults to Off but you should enable it. Keep in mind that this is specifically for your server's hostname, not the domain name. With this setting enabled, it will reject mail sent to user@server.example.com but not user@example.com.

9.5.1.1.4 Enable Apache SpamAssassin for Secondary MX Domains

This setting is specifically for rate limiting SMTP connections that violate RFCs. Real mail servers always follow RFC specifications. This setting is On by default.

9.5.1.1.5 Apache SpamAssassin Ratelimit Spam Score Threshold

This is a setting that helps controls a server that may be sending your server a lot of spam. When the remote system violates one or several conditions, it can be rate limited by this value. For example, if you enter a spam score of 20, if a remote system begins sending multiple emails with a spam score at or above 20, the remote mail server will begin to be reatelimited. Condition 1: A host reaches or exceeds the score entered in this space. Condition 2: The host exceeds the number of emails the rate-limit formula specifies. Exim averages rate limits over time. The default formula is:

```
ratelimit 1.2 / 1h / strict / per_conn / noupdate
```

The default value is No ratelimiting by spam score.

9.5.1.1.6 Ratelimit Incoming Connections With Only Failed Recipients

When a remote SMTP server sends email only to failed recipients during 5 separate connection times per the past hour, then connections to your server will be rate limited. The default setting is On and should remain on.

9.5.1.1.7 Require HELO Before MAIL

This is a setting that requires that the sending SMTP server send a HELO command before they send a MAIL command. This setting defaults to On.

9.5.1.1.8 Introduce a Delay Into the SMTP Transaction for Unknown Hosts and Messages Detected as Spam

This is a setting that configures the SMTP receiver to wait a few additional seconds for a connection when your server detects spam messages. The purpose of this is to try and make sure the sender is legitimate. Typically legitimate mail servers will wait the additional time where spammers will not.

This setting will exclude some remote hosts from the delay:

- Neighbor IP addresses in the same netblock.
- Loopback addresses.
- Trusted Hosts.
- Relay Hosts.
- Backup MX Hosts.
- Skip SMTP Check Hosts.
- Sender Verify Bypass Hosts.

It's also important to note that if you use third party sites to diagnose mail server issues, this setting may falsely detect spam messages. If you use an external monitoring system, allow 45 seconds timeout for connections on port 25. If you encounter issues with this setting, you should add your monitoring system's IP to the system's Trusted SMTP IP Addresses section.

9.5.1.1.9 Do Not Delay the SMTP Connections for Hosts in the Greylisting "Trusted Hosts" List

This setting will configure the SMTP receiver to not delay any hosts that you have added in the Trusted Hosts tab of the WHM Greylisting interface. This setting is defaulted to On. It's generally okay to leave this setting on but continue to review and monitor any trusted host to ensure that it remains trusted.

9.5.1.1.10 Do Not Delay the SMTP Connections for Host in the Greylisting "Common Mail Providers" List

This list is of the common email providers (for example, Gmail, Microsoft, AOL, etc.) and these hosts are inherently trusted. Although these mail platforms are commonly used by spammers, the SMTP connections from these providers generally do not need to be delayed but it is a good idea to keep this setting Off. This setting defaults to Off.

9.5.1.1.11 Require Remote (Hostname/IP Address) HELO

This setting requires that incoming SMTP connections send a HELO command that does not match the primary hostname or a local IP address. This helps prevent spoofed emails. You should leave this setting on. It defaults to On.

9.5.1.1.12 Require Remote (Domain) HELO

This requires that any incoming SMTP connections send a HELO command that does not match any of the server's local domains. This helps prevent spoofed emails. Keep in mind that if your users are sending emails from other systems, they could potentially be blocked as Exim will block any remote connections providing a local domain in the HELO. This defaults to Off. Enable with care.

9.5.1.1.13 Require RFC-Compliant HELO

This will require that incoming SMTP connections send a RFC 2821 4.1.1.1 compliant HELO. If this setting is on, it will override entries in /etc/alwaysrelay and /etc/relayhosts files. This setting defaults to On.

9.5.1.1.14 Allow DKIM Verification for Incoming Messages

This setting will allow you to use DKIM verification to verify incoming messages. This can help prevent spam. While cPanel warns that enabling this can slow your server's performance, modern server hardware should not have a noticeable increase in load. This setting defaults to Off. You should consider enabling it.

9.5.1.1.15 Reject DKIM Failures

This will allow you to reject messages at SMTP time if the sender fails DKIM key validation. While this can cut down on spam, it may prevent legitimate email that is misconfigured from reaching users on your sever. This setting defaults to Off. Enable with care.

Note: This setting requires "Allow DKIM Verification for Incoming Messages" to be enabled.

9.5.1.1.16 Maximum Message Recipients (Soft Limit)

This setting will allow you to determine the number of recipient addresses your server accepts in a single message. Keep in mind that RFCs specify that SMTP servers are required to accept at least 100 RCPT commands for a single message. While this setting can help prevent spam, it's not recommended to enable. This setting defaults to No Rejection.

9.5.1.1.17 Maximum Message Recipients Before Disconnect (Hard Limit)

This setting will allow you to determine the number of recipient addresses your server accepts in a single message before it disconnects and rate-limits a connection. Keep in mind that RFCs specify that SMTP servers are required to accept at least 100 RCPT commands for a single message. While this setting can help prevent spam, it's not recommended to enable. This setting defaults to No Rejection.

9.5.1.2 Access Lists

These settings further limit who sends mail to your server]

9.5.1.2.1 Blacklisted SMTP IP Addresses

This setting allows you to edit the list of blacklisted SMTP IP addresses. The system does not allow these IPs to connect to the SMTP server and instead drops the connections with a 550 error.

9.5.1.2.2 Sender Verification Bypass IP Addresses

This setting will allow you to edit the list of IP addresses that the system excludes from SMTP sender verification checks.

9.5.1.2.3 Only-Verify-Recipient

This setting allows you to edit the list of hosts or IP addresses that the system excludes from all spam checks at SMTP connection time, except recipient verification checks. Any hosts or IP addresses entered here will be added to the /etc/trustedmailhosts file.

9.5.1.2.4 Trusted SMTP IP Addresses

This setting allows you to edit the list of hosts or IP addresses that the system excludes from the following checks at SMTP connection time:

- Recipient verification checks
- Sender checks (note: these senders must still use an RFC-compliant HELO name if the Require RFC-compliant HELO setting is enabled)
- Spam checks
- Relay checks

Note: The system adds any hosts' IP addresses that you enter her to the /etc/skipsmtpcheckhosts file.

9.5.1.2.5 Backup MX Hosts

This setting allows you to edit the list of hosts from which the system permits SMTP connections regardless of rate limits. Make certain that you properly configure reverse DNS records for any hosts which you enter here.

9.5.1.2.6 Trusted Mail Users

The Trusted Mail Users setting allows system administrators to designate certain users as trusted mail users. his setting affects the *EXPERIMENTAL: Rewrite From: header to match actual sender* setting in the *Mail* tab. Trusted users can bypass the *EXPERIMENTAL: Rewrite From: header to match actual sender* setting. The *Trusted mail users* setting allows the listed users to modify their *From:* header, and the *EXPERIMENTAL: Rewrite From: header to match actual sender* setting does not override these changes. Enter the trusted mail usernames or their email addresses, one per line.

9.5.1.2.7 Blocked Domains

This setting allows you to filter your server's incoming email by domain. When you click on Manage, a new browser tab will open with WHM's Filter Incoming Emails By Domain interface.

9.5.1.2.8 Blocked Countries

This setting allows you to filter your server's incoming email by region or country. When you click Manage, a new browser tab will open with WHM's Filter Incoming Emails by Country interface.

[DOMAINS AND IPS – These settings change the IP address from which Exim sends mail]

9.5.1.2.9 Send Mail From the Account's IP Address

This configuration enables the automatic routing of email for users without a dedicated IP address through a reseller's primary shared IP address, rather than the server's main shared IP address. Additionally, the system uses the server's hostname for reseller accounts that share an IP address. If you wish to alter this behavior, a custom configuration is required.

It's crucial to ensure that the reverse DNS entries for your hosting provider are correctly configured, as incorrect entries can lead to mail servers rejecting your emails. This setting is specific to IPv4 addresses. When activated, the script located at `/usr/local/cpanel/scripts/updateuserdomains` will automatically update the `/etc/mailhelo` and `/etc/mailips` files, overwriting any manual modifications in these files. Furthermore, this setting disables the options to reference `/etc/mailhelo` for custom outgoing SMTP HELO and `/etc/mailips` for custom IP on outgoing SMTP connections.

9.5.1.2.10 Use the Reverse DNS Entry for the Mail HELO/EHLO if Available

The system will use the server's IP address as the reverse DNS for all outgoing SMTP connections. This only applies during the HELO/EHLO request. The setting defaults to On.

9.5.1.2.11 Rebuild Reverse DNS Cache and Update Mail HELO

This setting updates the reverse DNS cache and user domains for mail HELO. This setting only appears when you enable the *Use the reverse DNS entry for the mail HELO/EHLO if available* setting.

9.5.1.2.12 Reference /etc/mailhelo for Custom Outgoing SMTP HELO

This setting allows you to send a HELO command based on the domain name in the `/etc/mailhelo` file. For more information, you should reference cPanel's How to Configure the Exim Outgoing IP Address documentation: https://docs.cpanel.net/knowledge-base/email/how-to-configure-the-exim-outgoing-ip-address/

9.5.1.2.13 Reference /etc/mailips for Custom IP on Outgoing SMTP Connections

This setting allows you to send outgoing mail from the IP address that matches the domain name in the `/etc/mailips` file. For more information, you should reference cPanel's How to Configure the Exim Outgoing IP Address documentation: https://docs.cpanel.net/knowledge-base/email/how-to-configure-the-exim-outgoing-ip-address/

9.5.1.3 Filters

These settings allow you to select and configure filters that can block spam and potentially dangerous attachments.

9.5.1.3.1 System Filter File

Use this setting to enable or disable Exim's system filter file, which the system stores in the `/etc/cpanel_exim_system_filter` file. You can also choose to specify and customize another Exim system filter file. Regardless of the setting you select, the Exim configuration includes all of the files in the `/usr/local/cpanel/etc/exim/sysfilter/options/` directory. This setting defaults to */etc/cpanel_exim_system_filter*.

9.5.1.3.2 Attachments: Filter Messages with Dangerous Attachments

Select this setting to filter email messages that contain potentially dangerous attachments. The system filters the following file extensions:

• .ade • .adp • .bas • .bat • .chm • .cmd • .com • .cpl • .crt • .eml	• .exe • .hlp • .hta • .inf • .ins • .isp • .js • .jse • .lnk • .mdb • .mde • .msc	• .msi • .msp • .mst • .pcd • .pif • .reg • .scr • .sct • .shs • .url • .vbs • .vbe • .wsf • .wsh • .wsc

9.5.1.3.3 Apache SpamAssassin: Global Subject Rewrite

Select this setting to prefix the Subject header with information from the X-Spam-Subject header and omit the X-Spam-Subject header. This setting defaults to On.

9.5.1.3.4 Apache SpamAssassin: Bounce Spam Score Threshhold

Select this setting to define the spam score that Apache SpamAssassin uses to bounce incoming messages. Enter a positive or negative number, which may contain a single decimal point. For more information, read the Apache SpamAssasin documentation at: http://spamassassin.apache.org/doc.html

9.5.1.3.5 Apache SpamAssassin: X-Spam-Subject/Subject Header Prefix for Spam Emails

Select this setting to use the default X-Spam-Subject header prefix for spam email or to enter a custom prefix. This setting defaults to ***SPAM***.

9.5.1.4 Mail

Use these settings to configure specific mail settings

9.5.1.4.1 Log Sender Rates in the Exim mainlog

This can be helpful for tracking problems and spammers. This setting allows you to log sender rates in the Exim mail log. This setting defaults to Off but you may consider enabling it.

9.5.1.4.2 Sender Verification Callouts

This setting allows Exim to connect to the mail exchanger for an address. This allows Exim to verify that the address exists before Exim accepts the message. This setting defaults to Off. You may want to consider enabling this setting.

9.5.1.4.3 Smarthost Support

To set up a smarthost for sending outbound emails, you need to input a proper route_list value in the Smarthost support text box. When specifying IPv6 addresses, ensure they are enclosed in quotes and the list starts with `</` to make Exim recognize slashes as separators. This prevents Exim from misinterpreting the colons within IPv6 addresses as separators, which would mistakenly treat each address segment as a separate host. Also, remember to precede the IP addresses with an asterisk (*) for the smarthost to function correctly.

For example, to set up a smarthost with a single IP address, you would enter:

```
192.168.0.1
"</ 2001:0db8:85a3:0042:1000:8a2e:0370:7334"
```

To configure a smarthost using multiple IP addresses, you would enter:

```
192.188.0.20:192.188.0.21:192.188.0.22
"</ [2001:0db8:85a3:0042:1000:8a2e:0370:7334]:1225 / [::1]:1226 /
192.168.0.1"
```

If you need to specify smarthosts for specific domains, replace the asterisk with the respective domain name and separate multiple domains with a semicolon. For example, for IPv4 domains, you would enter:

```
example.com 192.188.0.20:192.188.0.21:192.188.0.22; exampletwo.com
192.168.0.1
```

And for IPv6 domains, you would input:

```
example.com "</ [2001:0db8:85a3:0042:1000:8a2e:0370:7334]:1225 /
[::1]:1226 / 192.168.0.1"; exampletwo.com "</
2001:0db8:85a3:0042:1000:8a2e:0370:7334"
```

9.5.1.4.4 Smarthost Requires SMTP Authentication

You can use the *Basic Editor* to manage smarthost configuration for domains that use the same credentials. If you used the *Advanced Editor* tab to modify the default configuration of Exim for smarthosts, you may be able to use the *Basic Editor* function now.

Use this setting to provide a username and a password for Exim to use when connecting to the smarthost servers. You must enter a valid route_list value in the Smarthost support text box in order to use this setting.

When you select the *On* button for the *Smarthost requires SMTP authentication* function, Exim will use SMTP authentication for all servers listed in the `route_list`.

9.5.1.4.5 Smarthost Username

You **must** set the *Smarthost requires SMTP authentication* setting to *On* to enable this setting. Due to limitations with Exim, the username and password **cannot** start or end with spaces or start with a caret character (^). You cannot use this interface if multiple smarthosts require different login credentials. Use the Advanced Editor tab instead. Use this setting to provide the username that Exim will use to connect to the smarthost servers.

9.5.1.4.6 Smarthost Password

You **must** set the *Smarthost requires SMTP authentication* setting to *On* to enable this setting. Due to limitations with Exim, the username and password **cannot** start or end with spaces or start with a caret character (^). You cannot use this interface if multiple smarthosts require different login credentials. Use the Advanced Editor tab instead. Use this setting to provide the password that Exim will use to connect to the smarthost servers.

9.5.1.4.7 Autodiscovery SPF Include Host from the Smarthost Route List

This setting allows the system to check the smarthost route list labels for SPF entries and insert an include entry to the SPF records. For example, `example.com` has an SPF record and the `* outbound.example.com` smarthost routelist setting. The system adds an include entry for all SPF-enabled domains. This setting defaults to On.

9.5.1.4.8 SPF Include Hosts for all Domains on this System

This setting allows you to enter hosts that the system will add as SPF include entries for all SPF enabled-domains. Use commas (,) to separate multiple host entries. This feature is useful if you need to include specific SPF includes on all hosted websites. This defaults to None.

9.5.1.4.9 EXPERIMENTAL: Rewrite From: Header to Match Actual Sender

To maintain originality and clarity while explaining the purpose and function of this email setting, the following rewritten paragraph retains the key details:

This configuration adjusts the From header in emails to display the true identity of the sender for all messages dispatched from your server. Recipients can view the original From header through the `X-From-Rewrite` header along with the modified From header. This is particularly useful for identifying the actual sender of an email. Malicious users might manipulate the From header to deceive recipients, such as by logging in as `user@example.com` and sending emails as `account@forged.example.com`. Enabling this setting ensures Exim modifies the From header to reflect the authenticated sender (e.g., `user@example.com`).

Activating this setting guarantees that the From header in emails sent from your servers aligns with one of these methods:

- The actual sender: If you authenticate as user@example.com, the From header will always show `user@example.com`.
- An address forwarded to the actual sender: If user@example.com forwards mail to `account@domain.org`, then account@domain.org may use either address in the From header.
- An address accessible by the sender: If authenticated as user, the From header can be set to any email account controlled by user.

This setting only affects emails sent from the local server and does not alter the From header of incoming emails from remote hosts, as it's not feasible to verify the sender's identity from these machines. Trusted users can bypass this setting.

The available options for this setting include:

- remote: Uses SMTP to align the From header in outgoing emails with the actual sender. This adjustment applies when a local user sends an email to a remote host but not when receiving from a remote host or during local deliveries.
- all: Adjusts the From header in all outgoing emails to match the actual sender, including local deliveries and remote hosts.
- disable: Leaves the From header unchanged in all emails, which is the default behavior.

This configuration ensures the integrity and authenticity of email senders within the system, providing better transparency and security.

9.5.1.4.10 Allow Mail Delivery if Malware Scanner Fails

This configuration determines how the system handles email delivery when the malware scanner is not functioning. If set to "**On**," the server will continue to deliver all emails as usual, even if the malware scanner fails. Conversely, if set to "**Off**," no new messages will be delivered to users until the malware scanner is fixed. By default, this setting is enabled ("**On**") and it is highly recommended to keep it that way to ensure continuous email delivery.

9.5.1.4.11 Sender Verification

This setting allows you to verify the origin of mail senders. The default setting is On.

9.5.1.4.12 Set SMTP Sender: Headers

This option allows you to configure the Sender: header as the `-f` flag passed to `sendmail` whenever the mail sender changes. When this setting is turned off, Microsoft Outlook will not include an "On Behalf Of" header, which could restrict your ability to monitor and track email system abuse. By default, this setting is turned off.

9.5.1.4.13 Allow Mail Delivery if Spam Scanner Fails

This option lets you disable the spam scanner if it encounters a failure. If set to "**On**," the system will continue to deliver all emails as usual despite the spam scanner failure. If set to "**Off**," users will not receive any new messages until the spam scanner is fixed. The default setting is "On."

9.5.1.4.14 Enable Sender Rewriting Scheme (SRS) Support

This setting rewrites sender addresses so that the email appears to come from the forwarding mail server. This allows forwarded email to pass an SPF check on the receiving server. This setting uses the default configuration for SRS. If you wish to customize the SRS configuration., use the Advance Editor interface. This setting defaults to Off, but it might be helpful to enable this feature.

9.5.1.4.15 Trust X-PHP-Script Headers to Determine the Sender of Email Sent from Processes Running as Nobody

This setting allows Exim to trust messages that the `nobody` user sends with *X-PHP-Script* headers. This setting also enables the mail server to determine the true sender. This provides a faster delivery process than a query to the Apache server to determine the sender. Advanced users may forge this header. If your users may misuse this function, disable this setting and send a query to the Apache server to determine the sender of `nobody` messages. This setting defaults to On. It should not be disabled.

9.5.1.4.16 Hosts to Which to Advertise the SMTP DSN Option

This setting allows you to specify a list of hostnames to which to advertise SMTP Delivery Status Notification (DSN) support. Enter a list of hostnames to which to advertise the SMTP DSN extension in the text box, or an asterisk (`*`) to advertise to all of the hosts on the internet. Refer to RFC 3461 documentation. This setting defaults to Disabled for All Hosts.

9.5.1.4.17 Hosts to Which to Advertise the SMTPUTF8 SMTP Option

This setting allows you to specify a list of hostnames to which to advertise SMTP support for international email addresses that contain UTF-8 characters. Enter a list of hostnames to which to advertise the SMTP UTF-8 support in the text box, or an asterisk (`*`) to advertise to all of the hosts on the internet. Refer to RFC 6531 documentation. This setting defaults to Disabled for All Hosts.

9.5.1.4.18 Delivery Behavior for Suspended cPanel Accounts

This setting configures what action the server should perform when an email message is sent to a suspended account. Delivering email to a suspended account requires the evaluation of filters, redirection lists, and other data that can be abused to retain access to the server. This setting defaults to Accept and Queue Messages.

9.5.1.4.19 Maximum Line Length for SMTP Transports

This setting allows you to set the maximum line length for SMTP transports in bytes. The system will refuse to send (bounce) any messages longer than the maximum line length. On bouncing a message, the system will attempt to return a failure message to the sender. You may need to increase this value if you receive reports of Microsoft Outlook users receiving bounce messages referencing maximum line length errors. This setting defaults to 2048, but it may need to be increased to 4096 or larger if you receive lots of errors.

9.5.1.4.20 Disable Pipelining

This setting tells Exim not to use pipelining when it delivers to remote hosts. Pipelining cuts down on Exim's synchronization time but can cause delivery problems on some servers. This setting defaults to Off.

9.5.1.4.21 Mailbox Quota Query Timeout

This setting defines how long Exim spends checking mailbox quotas. We recommend that you increase this interval if Exim times out while checking quotas for large mailboxes. Enter a number followed by `s` for seconds or `m` for minutes. This setting defaults to 45s.

9.5.1.5 RBLs

These settings allow you to configure your mail server to check incoming mail against available RBLs.

9.5.1.5.1 Manage Custom RBLs

To manage your server's RBLs, click on the **Manage** button. This action opens a new interface where you can see and handle the current RBLs. The table displayed provides the following details for each RBL:

- Origin: This indicates where the RBL comes from.
- Custom: Shows that you have added the RBL yourself.
- System: Shows RBLs that come included with cPanel.
- RBL name: The name of the RBL.
- DNS list: The DNS list associated with the RBL.
- Info URL: A URL where you can find more information about the RBL.
- Action: For custom RBLs, there is an option to delete them by clicking the **Delete** button.

Note that RBLs included with cPanel cannot be deleted.

9.5.1.5.2 RBL: bl.spamcop.net

This setting allows you to reject mail at SMTP-time if the sender's host is in the `bl.spamcop.net` RBL. Defaults to Off, recommended to enable.

9.5.1.5.3 RBL: zen.spamhaus.org

This setting allows you to reject mail at SMTP-time if the sender's host is in the `zen.spamhaus.org` RBL. Defaults to Off, recommended to enable.

9.5.1.5.4 Exempt Servers in the Same Netblock as this one from RBL Checks

This setting allows you to disable RBL checks of mail from servers in the same IANA netblock. Defaults to On, recommended to disable.

9.5.1.5.5 Exempt Servers in the Greylisting "Common Mail Providers" List from RBL Checks

This setting allows you to disable RBL checks of mail from an IP address block that you include in the *Common Mail Providers* list in WHM's Greylisting interface. Defaults to On. You should not disable this as it may have unintended consequences and random blocking of legitimate email.

9.5.1.5.6 Exempt Servers in the Greylisting "Trusted Hosts" List from RBL Checks

This setting allows you to disable RBL checks of mail from an IP address block that you include in the *Trusted Hosts* list in WHM's Greylisting interface. Defaults to off.

9.5.1.5.7 Whitelist: IP Addresses that should not be Checked Against RBLs

This setting allows you to choose a list of IP addresses to whitelist. Exim does **not** RBL-check these addresses. Enter one IP address per line.

9.5.1.6 SECURITY

These settings allow you to configure security settings for your mail server

9.5.1.6.1 Allow Weak SSL/TLS Ciphers

This setting allows you to use weak SSL/TLS encryption ciphers. This option defaults to Off.

Weak SSL/TLS encryption ciphers violate PCI compliance. cPanel & WHM only supports TLSv1.2 or later. The system enables TLSv1.2 by default. Not all clients will support TLSv1.3, which requires OpenSSL 1.1.1 or higher.

9.5.1.6.2 Require Clients to Connect with SSL or Issue the STARTTLS Command Before they are Allowed to Authenticate with the Server

This setting allows you to specify whether clients must connect with SSL or issue the `STARTTLS` command before they authenticate. This setting defaults to On.

9.5.1.6.3 Scan Messages for Malware from Authenticated Senders

This setting configures the ClamAVconnector plugin to scan all outbound messages for malware. The system rejects any mail that tests positive for malware. This setting requires that you have ClamAV installed on your server. This setting defaults to Off.

9.5.1.6.4 Scan Outgoing Messages for Malware

This setting configures the ClamAVconnector plugin to scan mail from non-whitelisted domains for malware. The system rejects any mail from non-whitelisted domains that tests positive for malware. This setting requires that you have ClamAV installed on your server. This setting defaults to Off.

9.5.1.6.5 Options for OpenSSL

This setting configures SSL and TLS protocols in OpenSSL that Exim will use to securely communicate with client software. Either select the default setting or enter a space-separated list of protocols that you wish to disallow in the text box.

9.5.1.6.6 SSL/TLS Cipher Suite List

This setting allows you to configure the cipher suites in OpenSSL that Exim uses to securely communicate with client software. Either select the default setting or enter a cipher suite that you wish to use.

9.5.1.7 Apache SpamAssassin Options

These settings allow you to configure Apache SpamAssassin to suite your server's needs.

9.5.1.7.1 Apache SpamAssassin: Forced Global ON

This setting allows you to turn on Apache SpamAssassin for all accounts on the server without a setting for the users to disable it. This setting defaults to Off.

9.5.1.7.2 Apache SpamAssassin: Message Size Threshold to Scan

This setting allows you to set the maximum size, in Kilobytes (KB), for messages that Apache SpamAssassin scans. It is generally inefficient to scan large messages because spam messages are typically small (`4` KB or smaller). This setting defaults to *1000 KB*.

9.5.1.7.3 Scan Outgoing Messages for Spam and Reject Based on the Apache SpamAssassin Internal spam_score Setting

This setting allows Apache SpamAssassin to scan and reject messages to non-local domains with a higher spam score than Apache SpamAssassin's internal `spam_score` setting of `5`. This setting does not affect outbound forwarded mail. Forwards use the

Do Not Forward Mail to External Recipients if it Matches The Apache SpamAssassin Internal spam_score Setting setting. Enabling this setting disables the Scan Outgoing Messages for Spam and Reject Based on Definied Apache SpamAssassin Score setting.

9.5.1.7.4 Scan Outgoing Messages for Spam and Reject Based on Defined Apache SpamAssassin Score

This configuration lets you establish the spam score threshold that Apache SpamAssassin employs to decide when to reject emails sent to non-local domains. To activate this setting, input a numerical value in the provided text box, which will serve as the minimum spam score.

- The acceptable range for this value is from 0.1 to 99.9.
- The number can only have one decimal place.

It's important to note that this setting does not influence outbound forwarded emails. For forwards, the system relies on the "Do Not Forward Mail to External Recipients if it Matches The Apache SpamAssassin Internal spam_score Setting" option.

9.5.1.7.5 Do Not Forward Mail to External Recipients if it Matches the Apache SpamAssassin Internal spam_score Setting

This setting allows Apache SpamAssassin to scan and reject messages in the forwarder queue with a higher spam score than Apache SpamAssassin's internal `spam_score` setting of `5`. The system disables this setting by default. To use this setting, each user must have enabled Apache SpamAssassin. You can also enable the Apache SpamAssassin: Forced Global ON setting to ensure that Apache SpamAssassin has access to each user.

9.5.1.7.6 Enables BAYES_POISON_DEFENSE Apache SpamAssassin Ruleset

This setting increases the scoring thresholds that the Bayes Poison Defense module needs to learn SPAM and HAM (not spam). This helps Apache SpamAssassin to better protect the system against spammers who use Bayes poisoning. This setting defaults to On and is recommended to not be disabled.

9.5.1.7.7 Enable Passive OS Fingerprinting for Apache SpamAssassin

This setting allows Apache SpamAssassin to use Passive OS Fingerprinting. You must enable the Passive OS Fingerprinting setting in the Service Manager interface for this setting to function. This setting defaults to On.

9.5.1.7.8 Enable KAM Apache SpamAssassin Ruleset

This setting allows Apache SpamAssassin to use the Kevin A. McGrail's KAM ruleset, with significant contributions from Joe Quinn. For more information about the KAM ruleset, read the module's documentation at https://www.pccc.com/downloads/SpamAssassin/contrib/KAM.cf.

9.5.1.7.9 Enable the Apache SpamAssassin Ruleset that cPanel uses on cpanel.net

This setting allows Apache SpamAssassin to use the ruleset that WebPros International, LLC uses on the `cpanel.net` servers. This setting defaults to On.

9.5.2 Advanced Editor

This feature is for advanced users. Exercise extreme caution when you use this feature. Changes that you make to the default configuration can significantly impact Exim's performance and may render Exim nonfunctional. Exim does **not** update your configuration changes across Exim updates and reinstallation. If you manually change any of these directives, you may break Mail SNI integration in cPanel & WHM:

- `tls_privatekey`
- `tls_certificate`
- `tls_verify_certificates`

Only make changes to sections in the Advance Editor if you know what you're doing or by consulting the Exim documentation at https://www.exim.org.

9.5.3 Backup

The backup tab allows you to backup your Exim configuration. This is strongly recommended before making any major changes. You can backup by downloading the configuration or by saving on the server. Saving on the server allows you to quickly restore this backup.

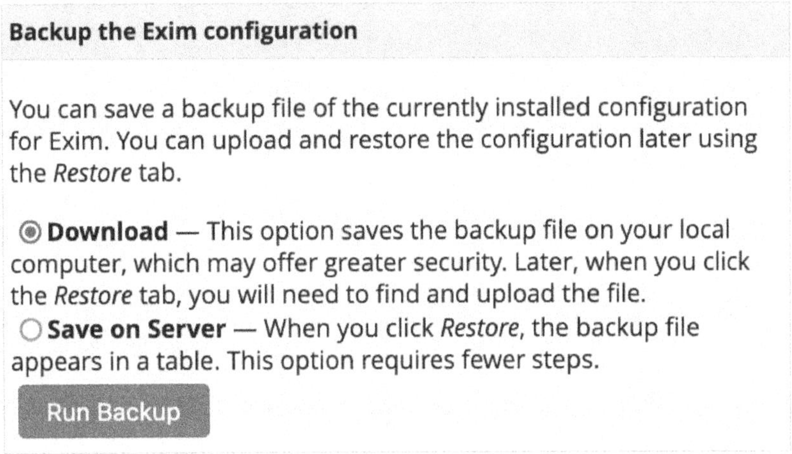

Backup the Exim configuration

You can save a backup file of the currently installed configuration for Exim. You can upload and restore the configuration later using the *Restore* tab.

◉ **Download** — This option saves the backup file on your local computer, which may offer greater security. Later, when you click the *Restore* tab, you will need to find and upload the file.
○ **Save on Server** — When you click *Restore*, the backup file appears in a table. This option requires fewer steps.

Run Backup

9.5.4 Restore

If you have a backup configuration to restore from, you can select this option. Take note that you need to make sure your backup matches the current Exim version. You can backup from your local computer or from the server.

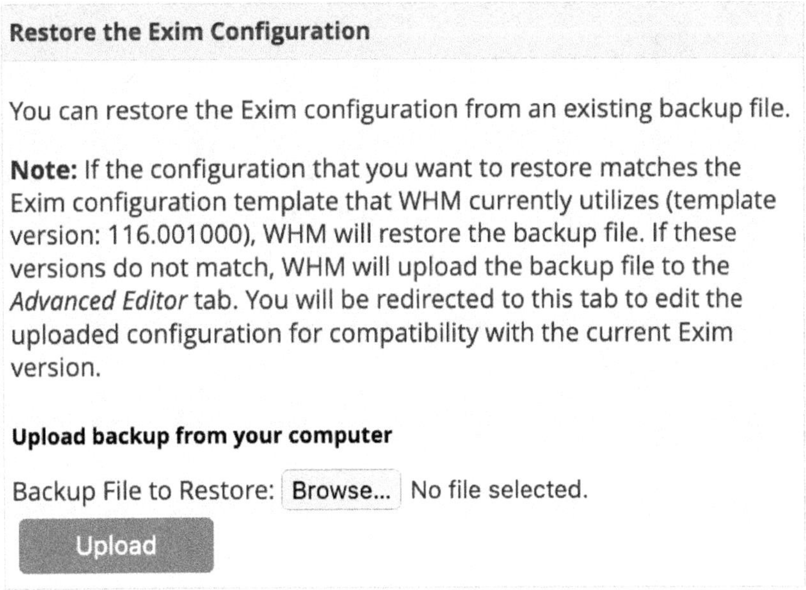

Restore the Exim Configuration

You can restore the Exim configuration from an existing backup file.

Note: If the configuration that you want to restore matches the Exim configuration template that WHM currently utilizes (template version: 116.001000), WHM will restore the backup file. If these versions do not match, WHM will upload the backup file to the *Advanced Editor* tab. You will be redirected to this tab to edit the uploaded configuration for compatibility with the current Exim version.

Upload backup from your computer

Backup File to Restore: Browse... No file selected.

Upload

9.5.5 Reset

If you really need to reset Exim, the reset tab will allow you to reset all of Exim or portions of Exim. There are various reset configuration options available based on the level of "messed up" things are.

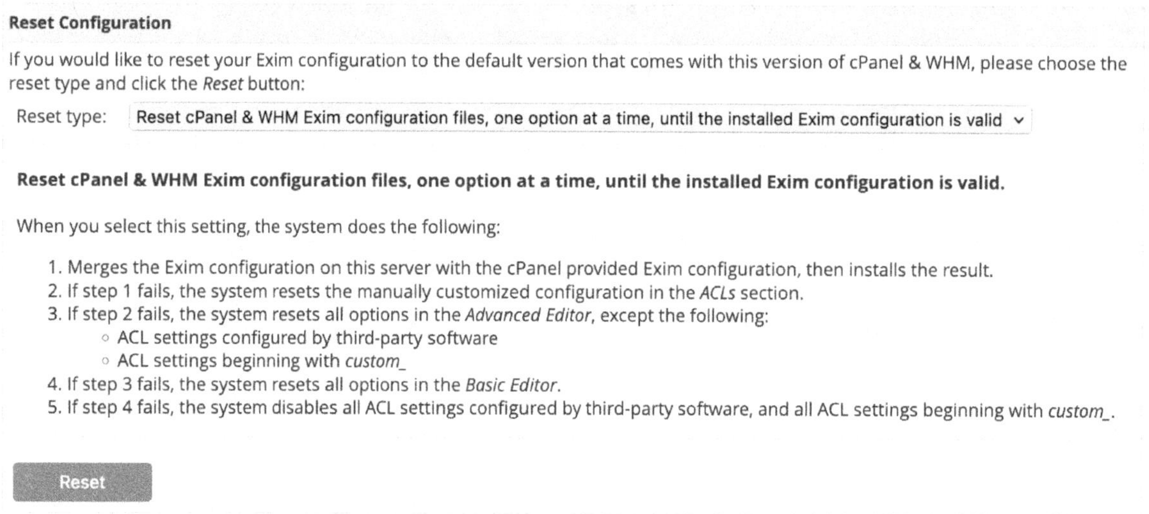

Reset Configuration

If you would like to reset your Exim configuration to the default version that comes with this version of cPanel & WHM, please choose the reset type and click the *Reset* button:

Reset type: Reset cPanel & WHM Exim configuration files, one option at a time, until the installed Exim configuration is valid

Reset cPanel & WHM Exim configuration files, one option at a time, until the installed Exim configuration is valid.

When you select this setting, the system does the following:

1. Merges the Exim configuration on this server with the cPanel provided Exim configuration, then installs the result.
2. If step 1 fails, the system resets the manually customized configuration in the *ACLs* section.
3. If step 2 fails, the system resets all options in the *Advanced Editor*, except the following:
   - ACL settings configured by third-party software
   - ACL settings beginning with *custom_*
4. If step 3 fails, the system resets all options in the *Basic Editor*.
5. If step 4 fails, the system disables all ACL settings configured by third-party software, and all ACL settings beginning with *custom_*.

Reset

9.6 FTP Server Selection

If you read *The Ultimate cPanel Guide*, I mentioned that cPanel has discontinued installing an FTP server in favor of SFTP. In the event you decide you want to install an FTP server for your users – which is discouraged as you should get used to supporting and using SFTP – you can select an FTP server to install from this screen. cPanel offers two FTP servers: ProFTPD and Pure-FTPd. If you absolutely need to have an FTP server, ProFTPD is the best option.

Select **ProFTPD** and click on Save.

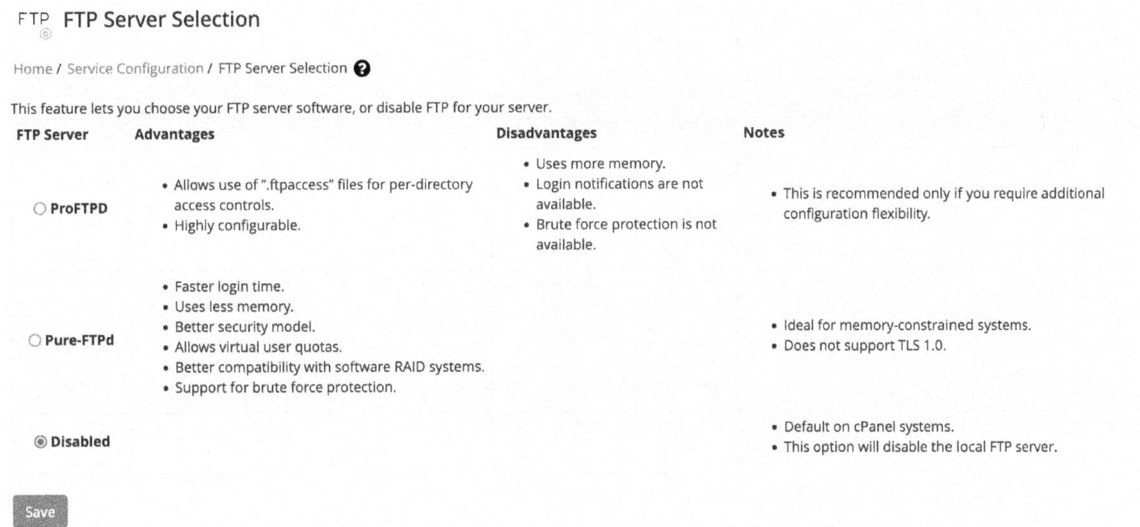

FTP Server Selection
Home / Service Configuration / FTP Server Selection
This feature lets you choose your FTP server software, or disable FTP for your server.
FTP Server
Advantages
Disadvantages
Notes
ProFTPD
Allows use of ".ftpaccess" files for per-directory access controls.
Highly configurable.
Uses more memory.
Login notifications are not available.
Brute force protection is not available.
This is recommended only if you require additional configuration flexibility.
Pure-FTPd
Faster login time.
Uses less memory.
Better security model.
Allows virtual user quotas.
Better compatibility with software RAID systems.
Support for brute force protection.
Ideal for memory-constrained systems.
Does not support TLS 1.0.
Disabled
Default on cPanel systems.
This option will disable the local FTP server.
Save

If ProFTPD is not installed, clicking **Save** will cause cPanel to install and configure ProFTPD.

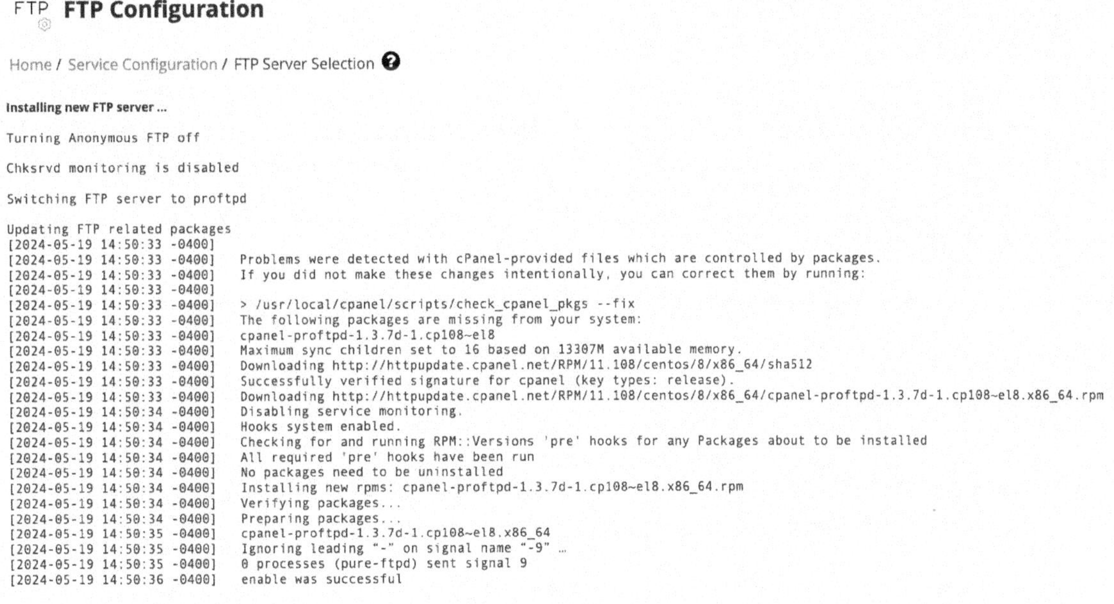

FTP Configuration
Home / Service Configuration / FTP Server Selection
Installing new FTP server ...
Turning Anonymous FTP off
Chksrvd monitoring is disabled
Switching FTP server to proftpd
Updating FTP related packages
[2024-05-19 14:50:33 -0400]
[2024-05-19 14:50:33 -0400] Problems were detected with cPanel-provided files which are controlled by packages.
[2024-05-19 14:50:33 -0400] If you did not make these changes intentionally, you can correct them by running:
[2024-05-19 14:50:33 -0400]
[2024-05-19 14:50:33 -0400] > /usr/local/cpanel/scripts/check_cpanel_pkgs --fix
[2024-05-19 14:50:33 -0400] The following packages are missing from your system:
[2024-05-19 14:50:33 -0400] cpanel-proftpd-1.3.7d-1.cp108~el8
[2024-05-19 14:50:33 -0400] Maximum sync children set to 16 based on 13307M available memory.
[2024-05-19 14:50:33 -0400] Downloading http://httpupdate.cpanel.net/RPM/11.108/centos/8/x86_64/sha512
[2024-05-19 14:50:33 -0400] Successfully verified signature for cpanel (key types: release).
[2024-05-19 14:50:33 -0400] Downloading http://httpupdate.cpanel.net/RPM/11.108/centos/8/x86_64/cpanel-proftpd-1.3.7d-1.cp108~el8.x86_64.rpm
[2024-05-19 14:50:34 -0400] Disabling service monitoring.
[2024-05-19 14:50:34 -0400] Hooks system enabled.
[2024-05-19 14:50:34 -0400] Checking for and running RPM::Versions 'pre' hooks for any Packages about to be installed
[2024-05-19 14:50:34 -0400] All required 'pre' hooks have been run
[2024-05-19 14:50:34 -0400] No packages need to be uninstalled
[2024-05-19 14:50:34 -0400] Installing new rpms: cpanel-proftpd-1.3.7d-1.cp108~el8.x86_64.rpm
[2024-05-19 14:50:34 -0400] Verifying packages...
[2024-05-19 14:50:34 -0400] Preparing packages...
[2024-05-19 14:50:35 -0400] cpanel-proftpd-1.3.7d-1.cp108~el8.x86_64
[2024-05-19 14:50:35 -0400] Ignoring leading "-" on signal name "-9" ...
[2024-05-19 14:50:35 -0400] 0 processes (pure-ftpd) sent signal 9
[2024-05-19 14:50:36 -0400] enable was successful

This will then enable the FTP Server Configuration interface.

9.7 FTP Server Configuration

Note

This interface will not be available if your server does not have a FTP server installed. Refer to "FTP Server Selection" to choose and install a FTP server. Please also note that this book only covers the settings for ProFTPD.

FTP is inherently insecure as it passes credentials in plain text and encryption is more of an afterthought than implemented from the start. For these reasons alone, you should strongly consider using SFTP. However, we understand that you may have some users that still need FTP or want to provide FTP.

9.7.1 TLS Encryption Support

This setting controls whether TLS encryption is optional or required for all connections to the FTP server. Users should always use encryption, if possible, but many older FTP clients are incapable of secure FTP sessions. The 'Optional' setting is recommended for best compatibility.

9.7.2 TLS Options

To relax the requirement that the SSL session from the control connection be reused for data connections, set this to 'NoSessionReuseRequired' for best compatibility.

9.7.3 TLS Cipher Suite

This is a standard format list of the SSL/TLS ciphers ProFTPD should use. Typically, this will only need to be adjusted for PCI compliance.

9.7.4 TLS Protocol

This is a space-delimited list of the SSL/TLS protocols ProFTPD should use. Again, typically, this will only need to be adjusted for PCI compliance.

9.7.5 Allow Anonymous Logins

Allowing anonymous FTP logins is generally considered to weaken the security of the server. Setting this option to "No" is recommended. There is no reason to allow anonymous FTP on the modern internet.

9.7.6 Maximum Idle Time in Seconds

Maximum amount of time in seconds that an FTP connection may spend idle before it is disconnected by the server. Setting this value to 0 disables the idle connection timer completely and is not recommended.

9.7.7 Maximum Number of FTP Processes

Maximum number of processes ProFTPD may create. Each client connection to ProFTPD is handled by a different process, so this value will limit the total number of simultaneous connections allowed. Setting this to 'none' disables any limits on process creation.

9.7.8 Show Symlinks

This option causes ProFTPD to display symlinks as symlinks, and not as plain files or directories. It's recommended to leave this option on.

9.7.9 Symlink Compatibility

Enabling this setting allows some FTP clients to display symlinks to directories correctly. You must also enable the Show Symlinks setting to use this setting.

9.8 Mail Server Configuration

The mail server configuration will help you configure the Dovecot mail server. This screen will help you configure Dovecot based on your preferences.

9.8.1 Protocols Enabled

Select the protocols you want Dovecot to listen on. You can select between IMAP and POP3, but LMTP cannot be disabled. cPanel's Webmail system requires IMAP to function. If you do not select any option, then the system will operate in authentication-only mode.

9.8.2 IPv6 Enabled

This option allows you to enable Dovecot to listen on IPv6 addresses. You must select a protocol before the system will listen on IPv6 addresses.

9.8.3 Allow Plaintext Authentication (from remote clients)

This setting will allow remote email clients to authenticate using unencrypted connections. When set to “no”, only connections originating on the local server will be allowed to authenticate without encryption. Selecting “no” is preferable to disabling IMAP in the *Protocols Enabled* section since it will force remote users to use encryption while still allowing webmail to function correctly.

9.8.4 SSL Cipher List

This is a standard format list of the SSL ciphers Dovecot should use. Typically, this will only need to be adjusted for PCI compliance.

9.8.5 SSL Minimum Protocol

This value represents the minimum SSL protocol that Dovecot clients may use to connect. Typically, you will only need to adjust this value for PCI compliance.

9.8.6 Maximum Number of Mail Processes

Specifies the maximum number of mail (IMAP and POP3 servers) processes that may be running at one time.

9.8.7 Process Memory Limit for Mail (MB)

The maximum memory usage of the IMAP and POP3 processes, in MB. These processes read mostly memory-mapped files, so setting a high limit should not affect your server’s performance.

9.8.8 Maximum IMAP Connections Per IP Address

Specifies the number of simultaneous IMAP connections that a single user (IP address) may make from each IP address. It is not recommended to change this value unless necessary.

9.8.9 Interval Between IMAP IDLE "OK Still here" Messages

Specifies the number of minutes between IMAP IDLE "OK Still here" messages. Increasing this may help increase battery life for some mobile clients.

9.8.10 Maximum POP3 Connections per IP Address

Specifies the number of simultaneous POP3 connections that a single user (IP address) may make from each IP address.

9.8.11 Number of Spare Authentication Processes

This specifies how many spare authentication processes should be kept running to listen for new connections. If your server is busy, you may need to increase this value.

9.8.12 Maximum Number of Authentication Processes

Specifies the maximum number of authentication processes that may be running at one time. If your server is busy, you may need to increase this value.

9.8.13 Process Memory Limit for Authentication

The maximum memory usage of the IMAP and POP3 login processes, in MB. This value probably does not need to be changed.

9.8.14 Idle Hibernate Timeout

The number of seconds to delay before moving users to the IMAP hibernate process. This will help save system memory. A value of "0" disables this option.

9.8.15 Size of Authentication Cache

The master authentication process keeps a cache of validated logins so that it does not need to recheck the login credentials each time mail is retrieved. This specifies the amount of memory used for the cache, in MB. You may not need to change this value except on large servers.

9.8.16 Time to Cache Successful Logins

The time, in seconds, that successful logins will be stored in the authentication cache. A lower value may cause more work for the authentication server but decrease the likelihood of problems when passwords are updated.

9.8.17 Time to Cache Failed Logins

The time in seconds that failed logins will be stored in the authentication cache. Lowering this value may cause more work for the authentication server but decrease the likelihood of problems when passwords are updated.

9.8.18 Use New Authentication Process for Each Connection

Specifies whether to use a new login process for each new POP3 or IMAP connection. Setting this to yes may improve the security of the Dovecot authentication processes, but doing so imposes a significant performance penalty on heavily loaded servers. The default is “No”.

9.8.19 Process Memory Limit Config

The maximum memory usage (in MB) of Dovecot’s internal “config” service. Each SSL/TLS certificate that Dovecot tracks require additional memory. Servers with many domains may need to increase this value to ensure that Dovecot operates correctly.

9.8.20 Idle Check Interval

The time in seconds between updates to idle IMAP connections. Lowering this value will cause idle clients to see new messages faster, however lower values may also increase server load slightly. The default setting of 30 is recommended.

9.8.21 Include Trash in Quota

When this option is enabled, the system will count email messages in the Trash folder against the user’s quota. To recalculate existing quotas, you must run the `/usr/local/cpanel/scripts/generate_maildirsize --allaccounts --confirm` command in a root shell after you modify this option.

9.8.22 Compress Messages

When you enable this option, the system will compress recently created and delivered messages.

9.8.23 Compression Level

The compression level to save messages in when you enable “Compress Messages”.

9.8.24 Auto Expunge Trash

When this option is enabled, the system will remove messages in the Trash and Deleted Messages folders based on the expiration time configured below.

9.8.25 Trash Expire Time

The number of days to keep messages before the *Auto Expunge Trash* function removes them. This function only works if the *Auto Expunge Trash* function is enabled.

9.8.26 Auto Expunge Spam

When this option is enabled, the system will remove messages in the Spam folder based on the expiration time configured below.

9.8.27 Spam Expire Time

The number of days to keep messages before the *Auto Expunge Spam* function removes them. This function only works if the *Auto Expunge Spam* function is enabled.

9.8.28 MDBOX Rotation Size

The maximum size to which a MDBOX mailbox file may grow before the system rotates it.

9.8.29 MDBOX Rotation Interval

The maximum time that an MDBOX mailbox file may exist before the system rotates it. This value is in weeks or days.

9.8.30 Disk Quota Delivery Failure Response

How Dovecot will respond when a system disk quota or mailbox disk quota prevents delivery:

- Reject the message permanently.
- Defer delivery temporarily.

9.8.31 Minimum Available LMTP Processes

The minimum number of processes that the system will attempt to reserve to accept more client connections. A setting of 0 will only start the LMTP server when needed and will conserve memory.

9.8.32 LMTP Process Limit

The maximum number of LMTP server processes.

9.8.33 LMTP User Concurrency Limit

The maximum number of concurrent LMTP deliveries per user. A value of "0" disables the per-user limit.

9.9 Manage Service SSL Certificates

This tool will allow you to manage the SSL certificates on the system for the system daemons - SMTP server, FTP server (if installed), Calendar, cPanel, WebDisk, Webmail, WHM, and Dovecot and the iOS Mail Push Notifications (APN) certificate.

By default, these certificates will use Let's Encrypt so these certificates will automatically renew every 90 days (certificates should renew around once every 60 days assuming that everything with the domain is working).

If you prefer to not use Let's Encrypt SSL certificates, you can use this screen to install a certificate from a different CA.

9.10 Nameserver Selection

cPanel will allow you to select a nameserver software for your server. There are two packages available: PowerDNS and BIND. Each server has their advantages and disadvantages, but the recommended option is **PowerDNS**. PowerDNS will allow you to have DNS clustering and it also supports DNSSEC.

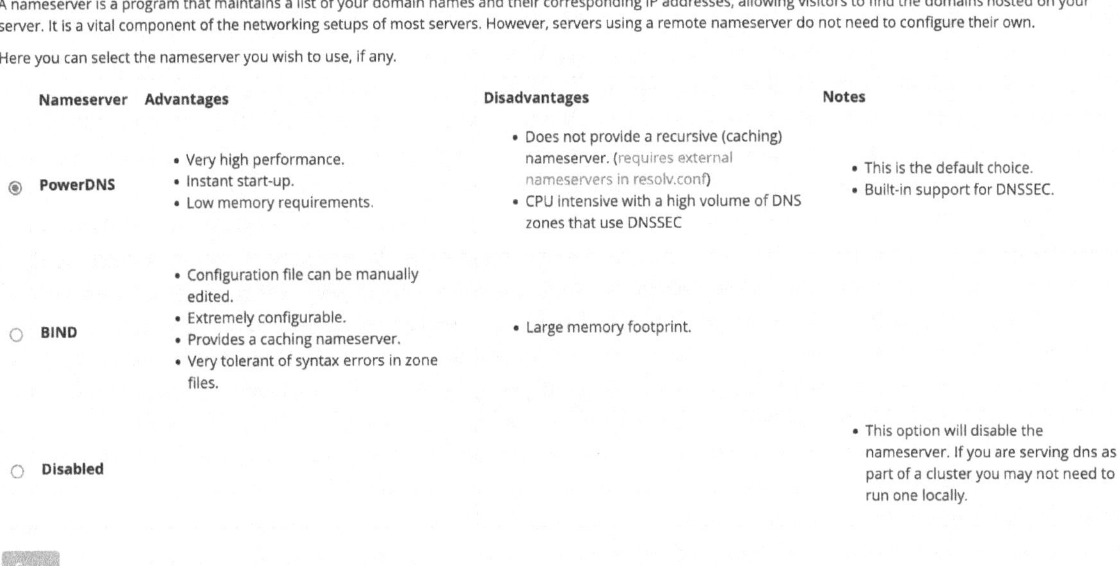

If none of your websites are going to use DNS, you can disable DNS completely by selecting the Disabled option. Do not select Disabled if there is a chance users will be using external DNS services. In most cases, you want to have a DNS server.

9.11 Service Manager

The Service Manager will list all the server's services and allows you to enable and monitor them.

9.11.1TailWatch Drivers in the tailwatchd Module

Driver	Description
APNSPush	This driver notifies iOS® devices when new mail arrives.
ChkServd	This driver monitors the services that you configure in the *Service Manager* interface. • The *ChkServd* driver attempts to restart a service when it detects that the service fails. • The *ChkServd* driver sends alerts about service failure, recovery, and timeouts to the contact information that you provide in Basic WebHost Manager Setup.
Eximstats	This driver tracks Exim mail statistics. The *Eximstats* driver maintains the email bandwidth logs, limits email usage, and populates data for the *Mail Delivery Reports* system.
JailManager	This driver manages the jailshells that the *EXPERIMENTAL: Jail Apache Virtual Hosts using mod_ruid2 and cPanel® jailshell* setting in Tweak Settings uses. The *JailManager* driver updates each user's jailshell with the `root` filesystem. **Note:**If the *EXPERIMENTAL: Jail Apache Virtual Hosts using mod_ruid2 and cPanel® jailshell* setting is disabled, the system disables the *JailManager* option.
MailHealth	This driver monitors the mail log for the Dovecot mail services' memory status. The system administrator receives a message if Dovecot is out of memory.
ModSecLog	This driver parses the ModSecurity® audit log and stores the information in the `modsec` database.
RecentAuthedMailIpTracker	This driver tracks the IP addresses for recently-authenticated IMAP and POP3 sessions.

Driver	Description
cPBandwd	This driver generates the bandwidth logs for the IMAP and POP3 mail services.

Table source: https://docs.cpanel.net/whm/service-configuration/service-manager/

9.11.2Service Daemons

The server's installed services and the server's profile determine which daemons this interface displays.

Daemon	Description
ClamAV Daemon (`clamd`)	This daemon scans your server for malicious programs. Note: This service **only** appears if you install the *ClamAV for cPanel* plugin in WHM's Manage Plugins interface.
`cpanel-dovecot-solr`	This daemon enables IMAP Full-Text Search (FTS) Indexing. Note: This service **only** appears if you install the *Full Text Search Indexing for IMAP powered by Apache Solr™* plugin in WHM's Manage Plugins interface. The *Database* and *DNS* server profiles **disable** this daemon.
PHP-FPM service for cPanel Daemons (`cpanel_php_fpm`)	This daemon improves the performance of PHP-based internal applications that ship with cPanel & WHM, such as: • phpMyAdmin • phpPgAdmin • Webmail applications • Any third-party PHP application that the user installs. Note: This daemon will accelerate a maximum of ten concurrent processes per user.

Daemon	Description
cPanel DAV Daemon (`cpdavd`)	This daemon enables a set of extensions that allow users to manage their websites, calendars, and contacts remotely. Important: If you plan to host other people's websites or email on your web server, do **not** disable this daemon. Note: The *Database* and *DNS* server profiles **disable** this daemon.
cPanel Greylisting Daemon (`cpgreylistd`)	This daemon manages Greylisting, a service that protects your server against spam from sources that your server does not recognize. Note: The *Database* and *DNS* server profiles **disable** this daemon.
cPHulk Daemon (`cphulkd`)	This daemon manages cPHulk Brute Force Protection, a service that provides protection for your server against brute force attacks.
Cron Daemon (`crond`)	This daemon manages cron job scheduling.
cPanel DNS Admin Cache (`dnsadmin`)	This daemon runs as a standalone daemon. This improves speed but increases it memory usage. Deselect this option if you wish to use multiple `dnsadmin` processes for zone-related actions.
Exim Mail Server (`exim`)	This daemon is the part of your mail server that sends and receives mail. We recommend that you monitor and enable this daemon for most servers.
Exim Mail Server (on another port) (`exim-altport`)	This daemon allows you to configure Exim to listen to an additional port. By default, Exim listens to the following ports:

Daemon	Description
	• `25` • `465` • `587` Note: In the text box, enter the additional port number on which you wish to allow Exim to run.
FTP Server (`ftpd`)	This daemon runs your FTP server. Important: We **strongly** recommend that you monitor this daemon. Note: The *Database*, *DNS*, and *Mail* server profiles **disable** this daemon.
Apache Web Server (`httpd`)	This daemon processes HTTP requests from visitors. Enable this feature to host websites on your web server. Note: The *Database*, *DNS*, and *Mail* server profiles **disable** this daemon.
IMAP Server (`imap`)	This daemon for Dovecot processes how your users download their mail. For more information, read our IMAP vs. POP3 documentation. Important: We **strongly** recommend that you monitor this daemon. Note: The *Database* and *DNS* server profiles **disable** this daemon.

Daemon	Description
IP Aliases (`ipaliases`)	This daemon allows you to add more than one IP address to your network adapter. The system stores IP addresses that you add in WHM's Add a New IP Address interface in the `/etc/ips` file. The `ipaliases` service activates those IP addresses when the server starts. Use this configuration to run multiple connections on a single network, where each connection serves an additional purpose.
LMTP Server (`lmtp`)	This daemon allows Exim to connect to the Dovecot mail server.
Mailman (`mailman`)	This daemon allows your users to create a single email address to send mail to multiple email addresses. Note: The *Database* and *DNS* server profiles **disable** this daemon. The system does **not** start the Mailman service until the server hosts at least one mailing list.
MySQL Server (`mysql`)	This daemon processes database queries. If you plan to host any content management systems or applications that require a database, enable this daemon or the *PostgreSQL Server* daemon. Important: We recommend that you monitor this daemon. The system does **not** monitor this daemon by default. Note: The *Mail* server profile **disables** this daemon.
DNS Server (`named`)	This daemon runs the nameservers. Note: The *Database* server profile **disables** this daemon.
Name Service Cache Daemon (`nscd`)	This daemon manages a cache for name service requests.

Daemon	Description
	Important: We **strongly** recommend that you **only** enable this service on servers with **at least** 1,000 MB of available memory.
Passive OS Fingerprinting Daemon (`p0f`)	This daemon reports the visitor's operating system and other information for email notifications that the system administrator requests in WHM's Contact Manager interface. This information helps a system administrator quickly identify visitors that trigger events that cause alerts. The spam prevention and cPHulk systems use this information to identify potential spammers and brute force attacks. For example, if a user logs in to a server from multiple locations and uses multiple operating systems, this may indicate that someone has compromised the user's account. Note: If you disable this daemon, the notification footers will no longer contain the visitor information.
POP3 Server (`pop`)	This daemon processes how your users will download their mail. Warning: We **strongly** recommend that you monitor this daemon. The system does **not** monitor this daemon by default. Note: The *Database* and *DNS* server profiles **disable** this daemon.
PostgreSQL Server (`postgresql`)	This daemon processes database queries. If you plan to host any content management systems or applications that require a database, enable this feature or the *MySQL Server* daemon.

Daemon	Description
	Note: The *DNS* and *Mail* server profiles **disable** this daemon.
Apache SpamAssassin™ (`spamd`)	This daemon attempts to filter spam messages. If you disable this daemon, make sure that you also disable it in WHM's Tweak Settings interface. Note: The *Database* and *DNS* server profile **disables** this daemon.
SSH Daemon (`sshd`)	This daemon allows users to connect to your server in a terminal session via SSH.
rsyslog System Logger Daemon (`rsyslogd`)	This daemon monitors your web server and logs the system activity. Important: We **strongly** recommend that you enable this daemon.

Table source: https://docs.cpanel.net/whm/service-configuration/service-manager/#service-daemons

10 Locales

For VPS/Dedicated Servers

The information in this section applies to VPS and dedicated servers.

Locales are a way for you to offer additional languages for cPanel, WHM, and Webmail other than English. Working with additional locales is easy within WHM. It is not common to work with locales as cPanel provides a lot of common languages, but they are made available for further translations if required.

10.1 Configure Application Locales

This tool will let you configure the locale for each stats program language based on the main language. Not all applications have the main locale available so they will default to a similar language (such as another language in the region) or English.

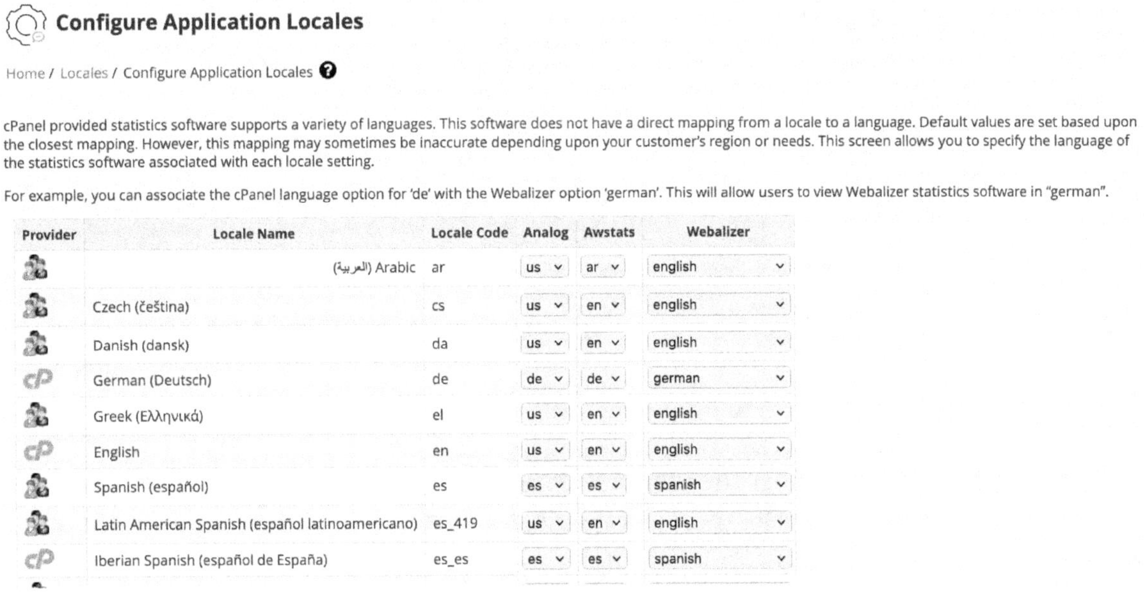

Configure Application Locales

Home / Locales / Configure Application Locales

cPanel provided statistics software supports a variety of languages. This software does not have a direct mapping from a locale to a language. Default values are set based upon the closest mapping. However, this mapping may sometimes be inaccurate depending upon your customer's region or needs. This screen allows you to specify the language of the statistics software associated with each locale setting.

For example, you can associate the cPanel language option for 'de' with the Webalizer option 'german'. This will allow users to view Webalizer statistics software in "german".

Provider	Locale Name	Locale Code	Analog	Awstats	Webalizer
	(العربية) Arabic	ar	us	ar	english
	Czech (čeština)	cs	us	en	english
	Danish (dansk)	da	us	en	english
cP	German (Deutsch)	de	de	de	german
	Greek (Ελληνικά)	el	us	en	english
cP	English	en	us	en	english
	Spanish (español)	es	es	es	spanish
	Latin American Spanish (español latinoamericano)	es_419	us	en	english
cP	Iberian Spanish (español de España)	es_es	es	es	spanish

As you will notice, Webalizer's locales are limited, but Analog and Awstats have a larger range of locale support. The icon will also tell you where the language came from. If you see the cPanel logo, then it's an official language pack. If you see the icon of people, that means it is community provided so it may contain some errors or may not be fully complete.

10.2 Copy a Locale

The Copy a Locale tool will let you duplicate a locale into another locale, either in standard or non-standard mode. A standard locale is a language with the data in the Unicode CLDR. A non-standard local is a language with no data in the CLDR.

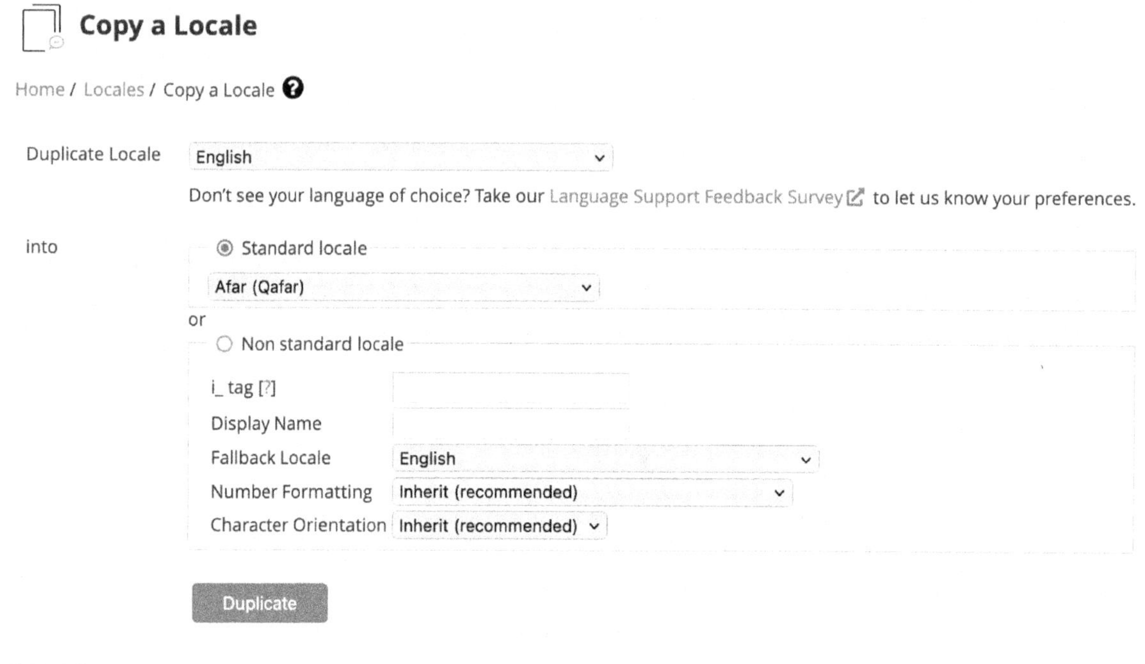

10.2.1Standard Locale

When you copy a locale, select the original from the **Duplicate Locale** dropdown menu. Select **Standard Locale** and select a locale from the dropdown menu. If you don't see your language, you can let cPanel know directly at: https://cpanel.typeform.com/changeLng.When you click on **Duplicate**, the system will redirect you to a new screen where you can then download the duplicate in XML format.

10.2.2 Non-Standard Locale

When you copy a locale, select the original from the Duplicate Locale dropdown menu. Select Non-Standard Locale and enter a name for the copy, prefixed with the `i_` tag, in the appropriate boxes. An `i_` tag is a standard way to create, identify, and work with a non-standard locale. It consists of a code prefixed with the letter `i`, followed by an underscore (_). Select the options from the Fallback Locale, Number Formatting, and Character Orientation menus. When an `i_` tag's lexicon does not have a phrase, the tag will reference the locale that is set to *Fallback* to find the phrase there. Click on **Duplicate** and you'll be redirected. Click to download the duplicate in XML format.

10.3 Delete a Locale

If you want to delete a locale from the system, you can do so from this interface. Keep in mind that you can only remove locales that are not provided by cPanel.

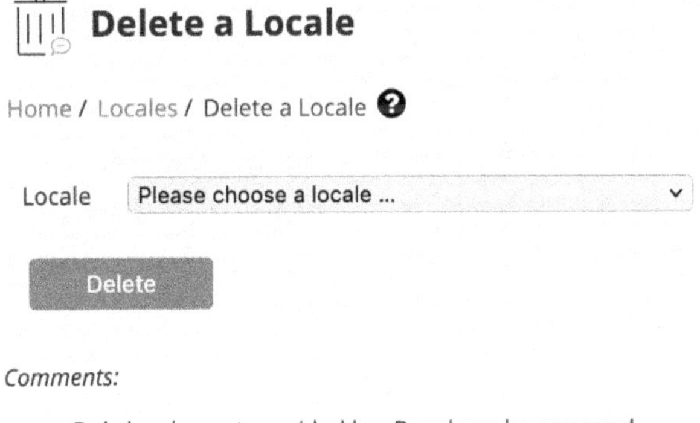

Select the locale you want to delete from the dropdown menu and then click on the Delete button.

10.4 Edit a Locale

You can edit a locale from this interface. After you use this interface, you must run the `/usr/local/cpanel/bin/build_locale_databases` script from the command line. If you do not run this script, your changes will not appear in the cPanel interface until the next time that the `upcp` script runs. To edit a locale offline, download the locale file from Locale XML Download interface and make the desired changes, upload the file in the Locale XML Upload Interface.

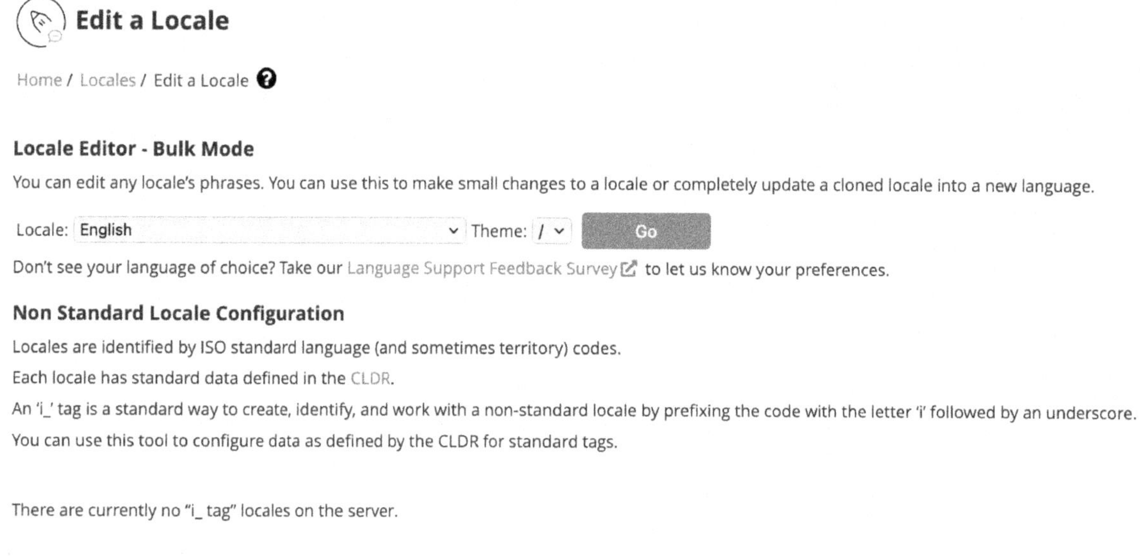

Edit a Locale
Home / Locales / Edit a Locale
Locale Editor - Bulk Mode
You can edit any locale's phrases. You can use this to make small changes to a locale or completely update a cloned locale into a new language.
Locale: English
Theme: /
Go
Don't see your language of choice? Take our Language Support Feedback Survey to let us know your preferences.
Non Standard Locale Configuration
Locales are identified by ISO standard language (and sometimes territory) codes.
Each locale has standard data defined in the CLDR.
An 'i_' tag is a standard way to create, identify, and work with a non-standard locale by prefixing the code with the letter 'i' followed by an underscore.
You can use this tool to configure data as defined by the CLDR for standard tags.
There are currently no "i_ tag" locales on the server.

10.4.1 Locale Editor – Bulk Mode

The *Bulk Mode* editor allows you to edit any of a locale's phrases. Select the desired locale from the dropdown menu. Then select a theme from the Theme dropdown menu. Click on Go. A new interface will display. Click on Edit under the phrase you wish to edit.

Home / Locales / Edit a Locale / Locale Editor

Editing the "en" locale in "/".

Local edits will be saved to /var/cpanel/locale.local/en.yaml

The compiled database file is at /var/cpanel/locale/en.cdb

Key: ... and [numf,_1] more
English Value: ... and [numf,_1] more
Value: ... and [numf,_1] more
Edit

Key: ... done.
English Value: ... done.
Value: ... done.
Edit

Edit the phrase in the Value box. Then click on Save Changes to save your changes. Click on Revert to Default Value to undo changes or edits to a specific phrase.

10.4.2 Non-Standard Locale Configuration

This tool allows you to configure data for a non-standard locale. A non-standard locale is a language with no data in the CLDR. The system adds the prefix `i_` to the names of these locales. These tags are standard ways to create, identify, and work with non-standard locales. To configure a non-standard locale, select a locale from the dropdown menu and click **Go**. Enter a display name. Select the fallback locale, number formatting, and character orientation. When a non-standard locale's lexicon does not have a phrase, the system displays the fallback locale's phrase. Click on **Save**.

10.5 Locale XML Download

You can use the Locale XML Download to download the XML file of the locale for offline editing. The download will include any local edits made. Select the locale from the dropdown menu and click on **Download XML.**

XML Locale XML Download

Home / Locales / Locale XML Download

You can download a locale in XML or XLF format for offline editing. It includes entries for all files in root, including addons, and in all themes. The download will include any local edits.

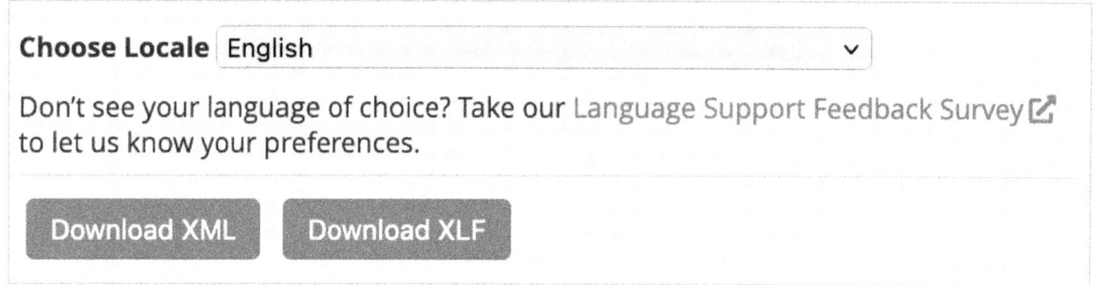

You can upload the edited XML file via the Locale XML Upload feature or via the command line script `/scripts/locale_import --import=path/to/your/file.xlf` (pass it --help for more information).

Note:

If a locale seems to be missing you may need to rebuild the locale databases in order to bring it into the system.

You can then edit the file locally.

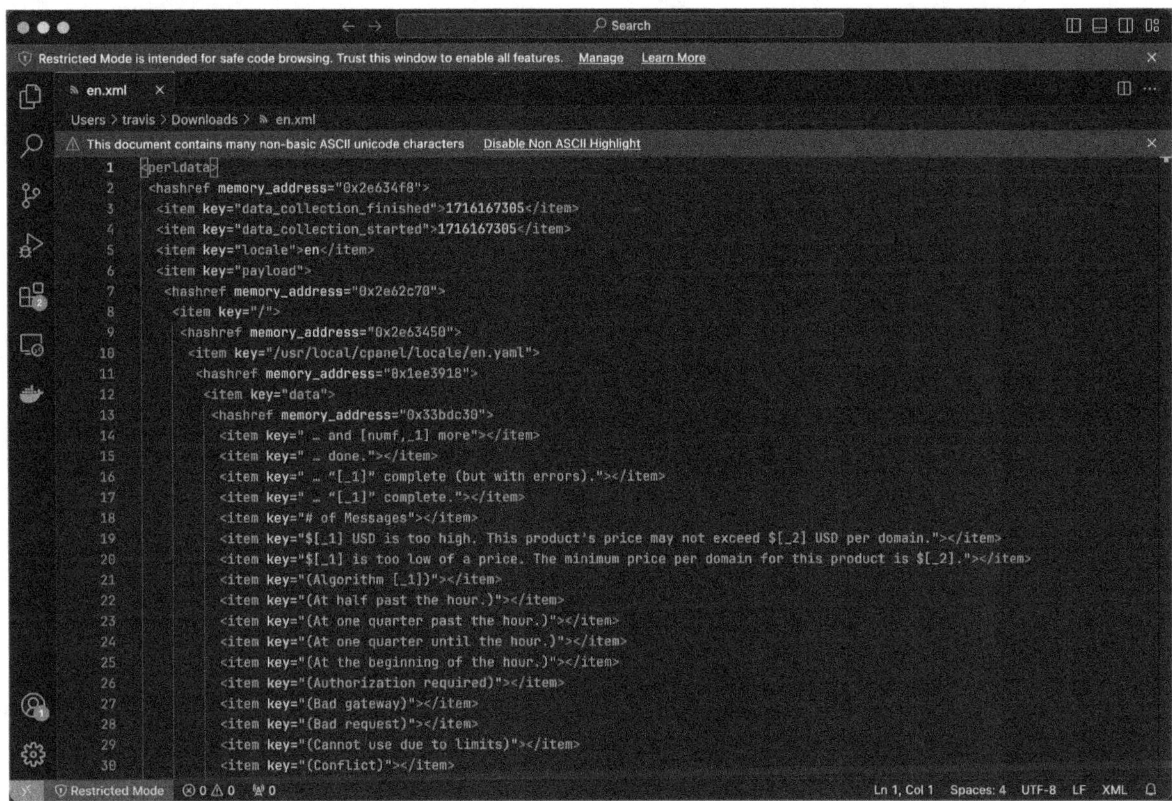

When you're done with your changes, save the XML file and you can then upload it to the server.

10.6 Locale XML Upload

When you have downloaded a cPanel XML locale and made edits, you use the Locale XML Upload interface to upload the file. From the interface, click on the **Browse** button to locate the XML file on your local computer then click on the Upload button to upload the locale to the server and update (or add) the locale.

XML Locale XML Upload

Home / Locales / Locale XML Upload 

You can upload a locale in XML format via the Locale XML Download feature or via the command line script `/scripts/locale_export --locale=locale_tag_here` (pass it --help for more information).

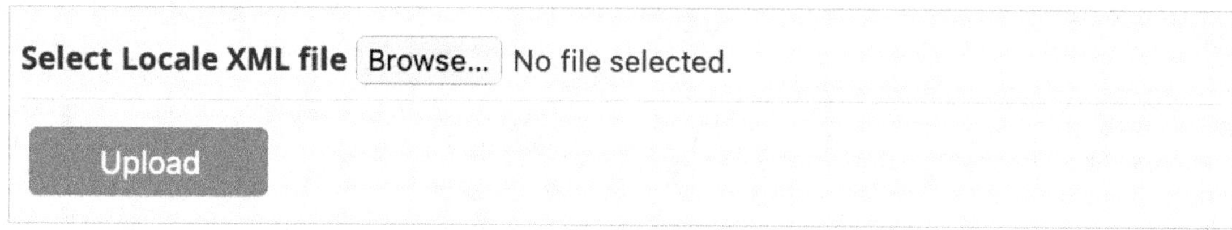

If the locale does not exist on the server, all files are created.

If the locale already exists, the following happens:

- Core files: Only keys that are in the XML data that do not exist in the file system's files are added.
- Local edit files: All keys that are in the XML data are added to or overwritten in the file system's files.

10.7 View Available Locales

This screen will show you the locales that are currently available on the system along with the themes it's available in. The "/" is the main cPanel, WHM, and Webmail and "Jupiter" is the current main cPanel theme.

View Available Locales

Home / Locales / View Available Locales 

Provider	Name	Locale	/	jupiter
	(العربية) Arabic	ar		
	Czech (čeština)	cs		
	Danish (dansk)	da		
	German (Deutsch)	de		
	Greek (Ελληνικά)	el		
	English	en		
	Spanish (español)	es		
	Latin American Spanish (español latinoamericano)	es_419		

You can use this interface to determine if the system has processed a custom locale.

11 Backup

For VPS/Dedicated Servers

The information in this section applies to VPS and dedicated servers.

Backups are like insurance – you hope you never need it but when you do, you're sure glad you have it! This is one of the most important chapters in this book. If you don't read any other chapter in this book, please read this chapter!

Backups Work! My personal story…

If you don't think backups are important, let me tell you why they are. Many years ago, I was migrating an old cPanel server to a new cPanel server. I migrated my personal website to test out the new server. I deleted it from my old server. I never configured backups on the new server. A few days after migrating, my website stopped working. I checked out the server only to find out that the hard drive failed! I had no backups of my site. I deleted my site from the old cPanel server so I couldn't even transfer it again. It was gone! Years of work all gone in an instant! ***Configure backups!***

11.1 Backup Configuration

The main Backup Configuration interface will help you configure backup jobs. This is also one of the interfaces that advertises third-party services. You are under no obligation to purchase any of the advertised third-party services. cPanel thinks you'll like JetBackup, and I like it and use it. I cover Jetbackup in *The Ultimate cPanel Guide* from an end-user experience, but I won't be covering it in this book as it is a third-party service.

You'll find under the **Backup Settings** tab all the general settings for managing backups.

11.1.1Global Settings

First and foremost, the Backup Status section has one option: **Enable Backups**. If this is unchecked, you will not have any backups on your system. Backup jobs will not run.

Backup Status

☐ **Enable Backups**

Toggle backup activity.

Under Global Settings, you'll find the backup type. There are several options here:

- **Compressed** – These backups will use less disk space, but it will take more time to complete a backup and you'll notice your server's CPU usage will be elevated during the backup process.
- **Uncompressed** – This will use a lot more disk space, but it'll take less time to complete. Your server's CPU won't be as strained.
- **Incremental** – This will start with an initial backup and then only backup information that has been changed since the last backup.

When using incremental backups, you will only be able to use rsync destinations. But if you change from compressed or uncompressed to incremental, your other backups will not be changed or altered.

Next, you will check the available disk space. It's strongly recommended to keep this checked as the system will need some local disk space to stage backups. You can adjust the disk space check, but 5% is a good base depending on the number of accounts on your system. If there is less disk space available than this percentage, the system will not run backups.

You can also change this setting to a specific size of free space in megabytes.

☑ **Check the Available Disk Space**

If you enable this option and the available disk space is less than the amount that you specified, the system will not run the backup.

5 | %

The **Maximum Destination Backup Timeout** is a timeout for the backup destination. If it does not respond within the timeout, the system will cancel the backup job. Adjust this only if you happen to be using a slow backup system that takes some time to respond. The default 7200 seconds is good enough for most systems.

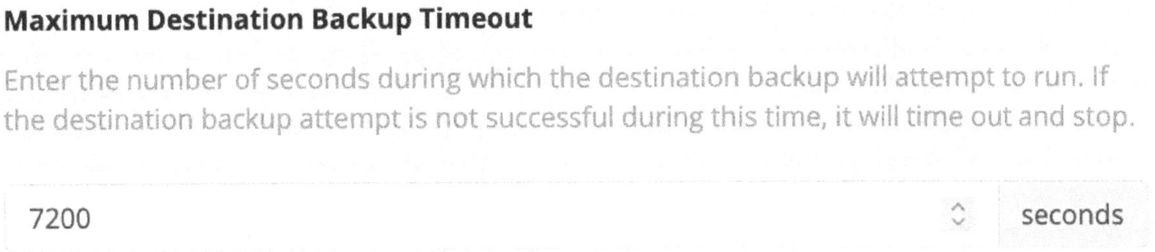

Maximum Destination Backup Timeout

Enter the number of seconds during which the destination backup will attempt to run. If the destination backup attempt is not successful during this time, it will time out and stop.

7200 seconds

The next section, **Maximum Backup Restoration Timeout**, is for restoring backups. This is the number of seconds cPanel will wait while trying to restore a backup job before cancelling the job. The default of 21600 seconds is decent and doesn't need to be changed unless you're working with a slow destination.

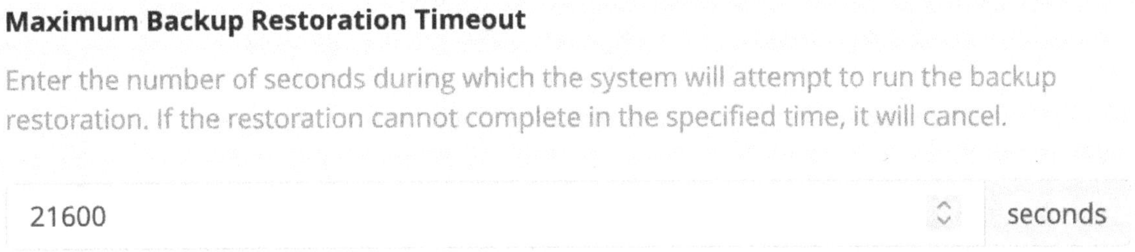

Maximum Backup Restoration Timeout

Enter the number of seconds during which the system will attempt to run the backup restoration. If the restoration cannot complete in the specified time, it will cancel.

21600 seconds

11.1.2Scheduling and Retention

Backups work on a schedule and will also retain a certain number of backups for restoration. cPanel's default schedule is a daily backup on Sunday, Tuesday, Thursday, and Saturday, while retaining the last 5 backups. You have the option to also enable Weekly and Monthly backups.

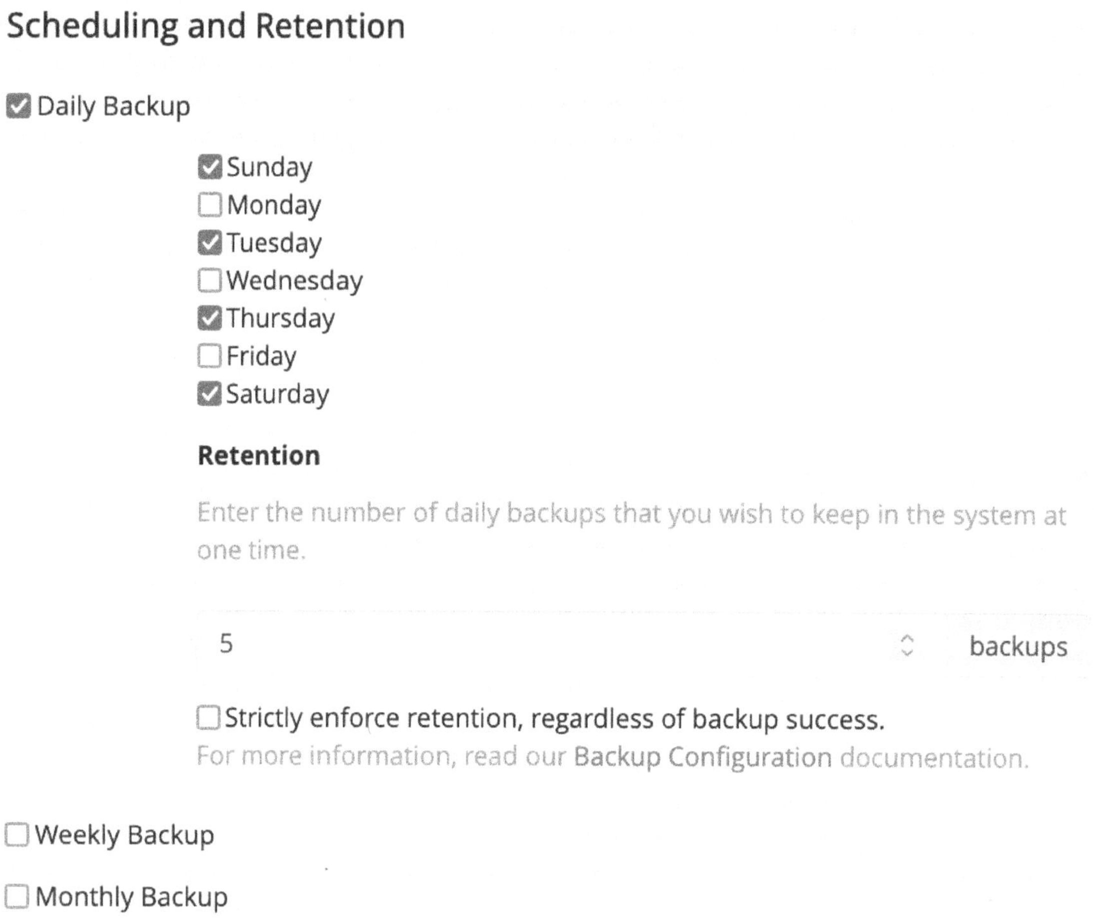

Scheduling and Retention

- [x] Daily Backup
    - [x] Sunday
    - [ ] Monday
    - [x] Tuesday
    - [ ] Wednesday
    - [x] Thursday
    - [ ] Friday
    - [x] Saturday

    Retention

    Enter the number of daily backups that you wish to keep in the system at one time.

    5 backups

    - [ ] Strictly enforce retention, regardless of backup success.

    For more information, read our Backup Configuration documentation.

- [ ] Weekly Backup
- [ ] Monthly Backup

When you check weekly backups, you will have the option of the backup running any day of the week and a weekly backup on the same day only one backup will run if you have the weekly backup run on a day you do not have a corresponding daily backup you will have a backup run. When you enable a monthly backup, cPanel will give you the options of taking a backup on the 1st or the 15th of the month. Likewise, if a weekly and/or daily backup is enabled for that day, cPanel will run just one backup on that day.

You shouldn't check the "Strictly enforce retention" box unless you absolutely want to rotate out good backups even if a failed backup occurs. With this box unchecked, the system will not delete or rotate out backups until there is a successful backup completed.

11.1.3 Files

This section lets you provide some control over the files that cPanel will be backing up. By default, all users on the system will be backed up. If for some reason you don't want to backup a particular user, you can go to the **Select Users** button and then **disable** backups on an individual account basis. You can also choose whether you want to backup suspended accounts. I always recommend it as people can forget about bills, their site gets suspended, and if/when they get unsuspended, it turns out they need to restore a backup because something was corrupted. It always seems to occur on suspended accounts. If you don't backup suspended accounts, their accounts could be rotated out. I don't backup access logs as these can get quite large and it's generally not something that people care about. The only other option I enable is a backup of bandwidth data. This way if the account is restored, bandwidth data is available. You will also find that Backup System Files is enabled. This will help you restore the entire server if the server fails. It's strongly recommended to keep this enabled.

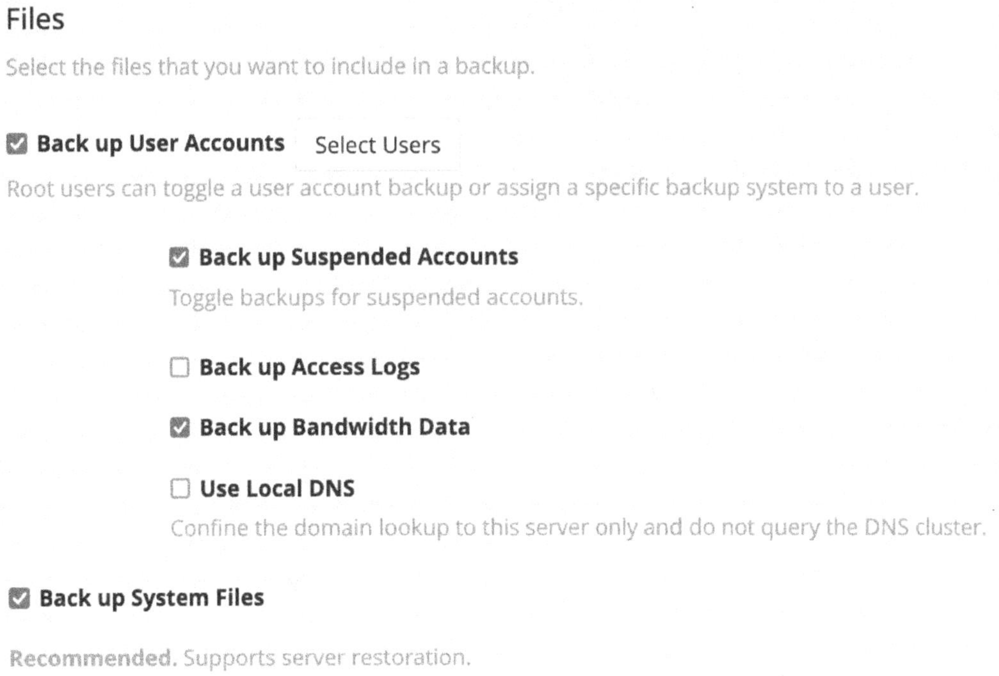

Files

Select the files that you want to include in a backup.

☑ **Back up User Accounts** Select Users

Root users can toggle a user account backup or assign a specific backup system to a user.

☑ **Back up Suspended Accounts**

Toggle backups for suspended accounts.

☐ **Back up Access Logs**

☑ **Back up Bandwidth Data**

☐ **Use Local DNS**

Confine the domain lookup to this server only and do not query the DNS cluster.

☑ **Back up System Files**

Recommended. Supports server restoration.

11.1.4 Databases

This section is how you want to handle backing up databases. There are a few options and I like to use the default option of Per Account Only. This will use the `mysqldump` command to create backup databases for each account. Per Account and Entire Data Directory is another good option to select if you want to protect a little more than just user data.

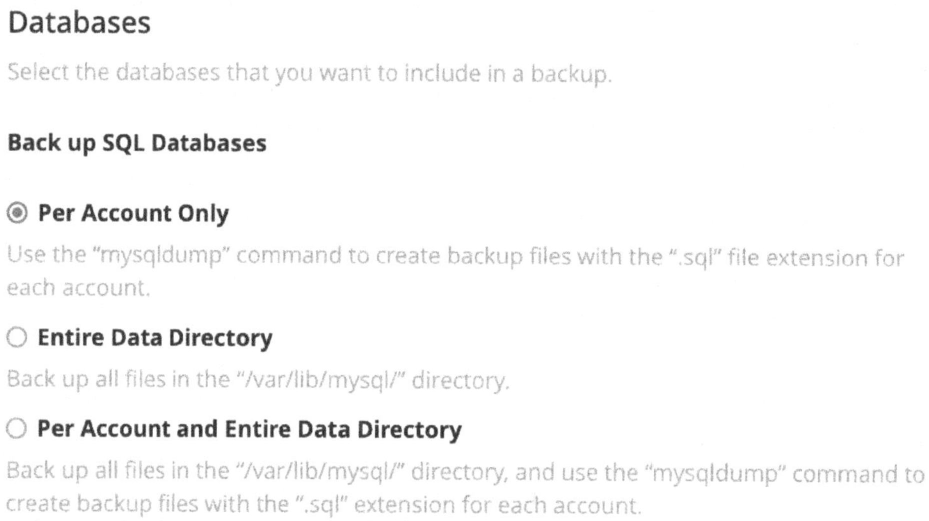

Databases

Select the databases that you want to include in a backup.

Back up SQL Databases

◉ **Per Account Only**

Use the "mysqldump" command to create backup files with the ".sql" file extension for each account.

○ **Entire Data Directory**

Back up all files in the "/var/lib/mysql/" directory.

○ **Per Account and Entire Data Directory**

Back up all files in the "/var/lib/mysql/" directory, and use the "mysqldump" command to create backup files with the ".sql" extension for each account.

11.1.5 Configure Backup Directory

The default backup directory is where the system will store backups. Keep in mind that this is a local backup. If the server fails, the backups generally go down with the server.

Configure the Backup Directory

Default Backup Directory

You must enter an absolute path to the local backup directory.

/backup

> The system does not apply quota limits to the default backup directory, /backup. To avoid performance degradation, we recommend that you store backups in a quota-disabled filesystem.

Additionally, the server will use this directory for staging backup files. That is why it is important to make sure this is on a drive that has enough disk space just larger than the largest account on the server. If your largest account is 25 GB, you should have just over 25 GB of disk space in this location.

Backup Staging Directory

You must enter an absolute path. The backup staging directory temporarily stores a remote backup's files and directories during a backup restoration. The directory empties once the system restores the backup.

/backup

> The system restores backups one at a time. The backup staging directory must be large enough to contain the largest remote backup file that you wish to restore.

Other options are to retain backups in the default backup directory. I highly recommend you uncheck this as a common issue will be that you will notice your backup location running out of disk space (or your main server disk) despite having an external location set. In most cases, it's because this box was left checked. Additionally, if your backups are on a separate drive, you can enable the option to mount the backup drive as needed. This is a good option to enable to help protect backups from any potential malware.

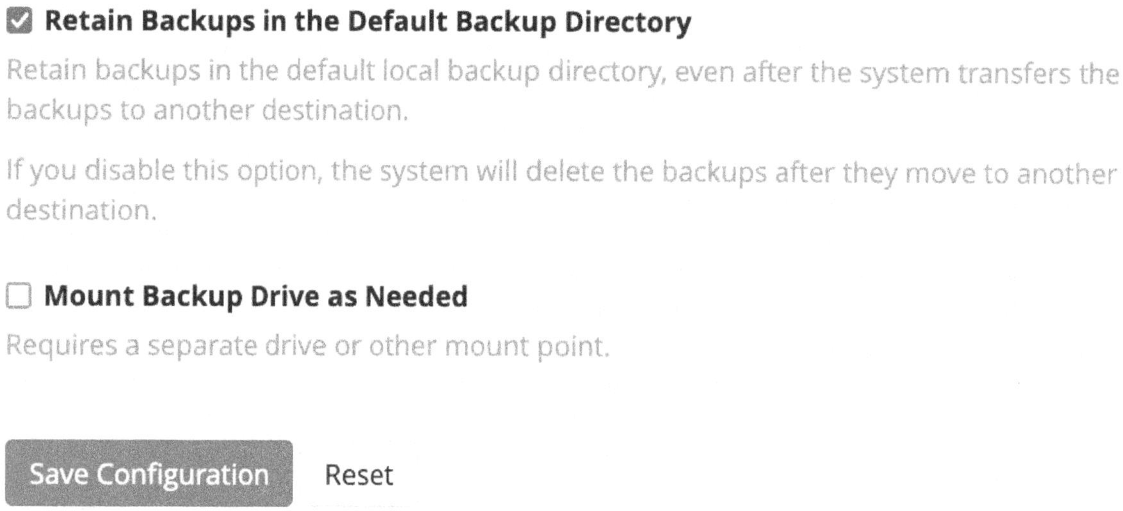

☑ **Retain Backups in the Default Backup Directory**

Retain backups in the default local backup directory, even after the system transfers the backups to another destination.

If you disable this option, the system will delete the backups after they move to another destination.

☐ **Mount Backup Drive as Needed**

Requires a separate drive or other mount point.

Save Configuration   Reset

11.2 Additional Destinations

The additional destinations tab is how you can configure other storage locations for backups. If you follow the 3-2-1 backup rule, you will want to make use of this section. After all, by default backups will be retained on the server which is not best practice.

To add a destination, under Destination Type dropdown menu, select the destination and then click on **Create New Destination** to configure the destination.

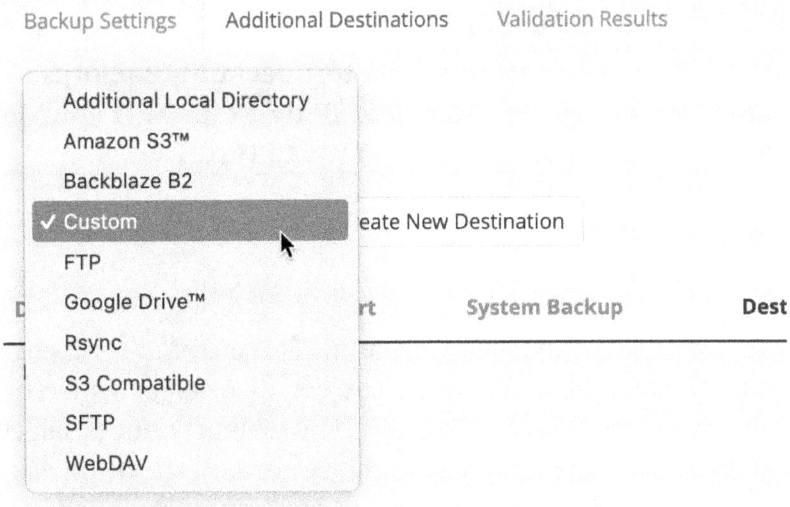

You can setup as many destinations as you would like. Keep in mind that transferring to locations outside of your data center may incur extra bandwidth charges. If you're backing up 100 GB of data on a daily basis, your sever will consume 100 GB of outbound bandwidth or data transfer daily.

Select the backup service or location you would like to use and then follow the directions in the interface to configure it. Due to the massive number of possible combinations, we cannot provide specific configuration details. Just remember if you want to use incremental backups and you will need storage with rsync ability.

External services may have additional charges for data and bandwidth. Consult with any external service you are considering for pricing details.

When you have a destination setup, the validation results will help you monitor to make sure the backup destination is working, not necessarily that the backups are good.

11.3 Backup Restoration

Backups are great, but restoring them is even better. If you find that you need to perform a restoration, the backup restoration interface will help you out. You will be able to select the destination where your backups are located (on the local server in the `/backups` directory or another local location if you changed it).

Note

You should always test restoration with a test account. Backups are no good if you A) don't know how to get to them, and B) don't know if your backups are even good. Do not use live customer accounts to test.

11.3.1 Restore by Account

The main restore option is to restore by account. The interface will check the backup location and list all the available accounts. You can also select a specific date and then an account if there was a backup on that date. Once an account is selected, you will add it to the restoration queue and process the restore. Restoration can take several minutes to complete depending on the size and location of the backup.

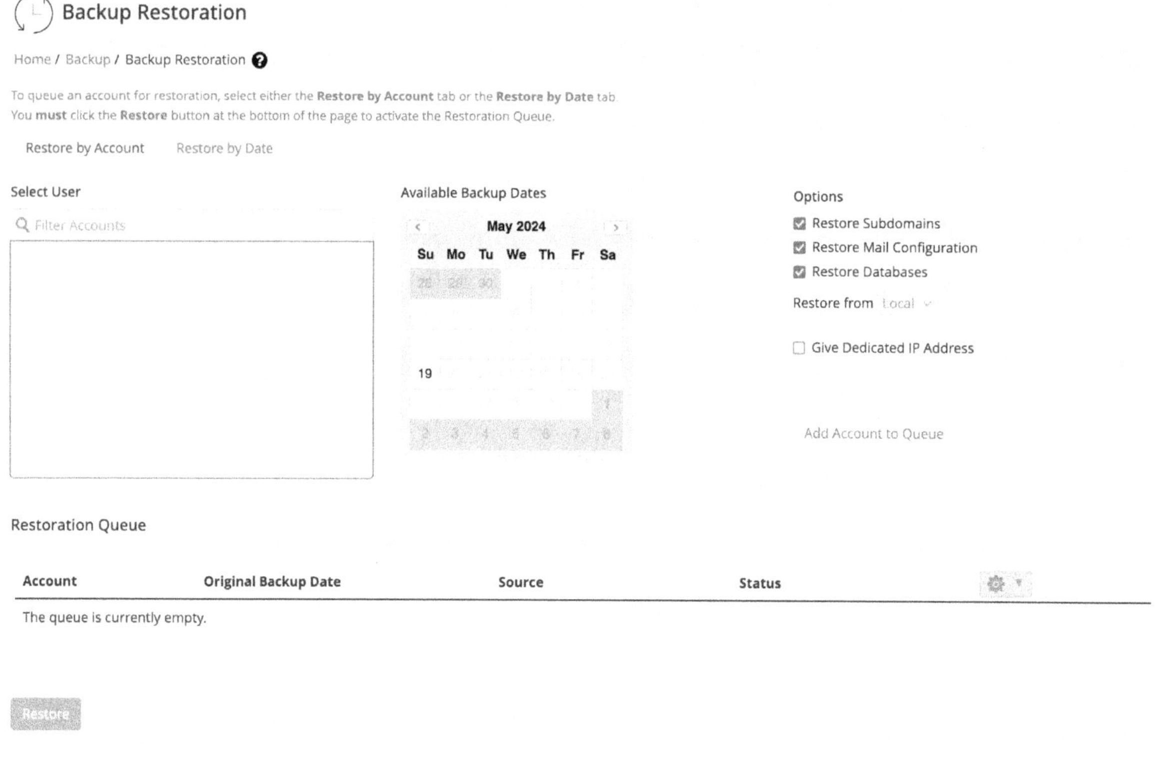

11.3.2 Restore by Date

This feature works in reverse to Restore by Account. See Restore By Account for full details.

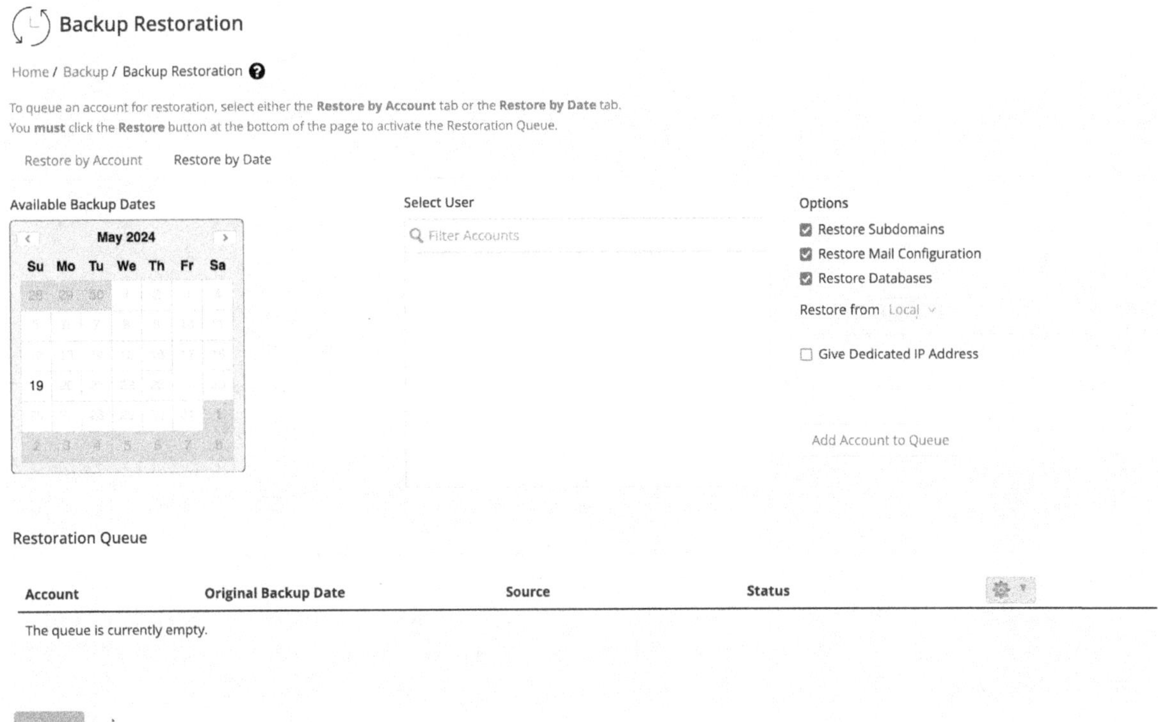

11.4 Backup User Selection

This interface will list all the users on the server. You can select or deselect accounts that you do not want to backup by moving the toggle between enable and disable.

Backup User Selection

Home / Backup / Backup User Selection

This interface allows you to enable or disable user account backups.
To enable or disable all users, click *Account Actions*.

Filter Users/Domain

Page Size 10

Account Actions

Displaying 1 to 3 out of 3 items

User	Domain	Backups
		Enable
nodespace	nodespace.dev	Enable
		Enable

11.5 File and Directory Restoration

This interface is used for restoring individual files and directories. The only drawback to this feature is that you must be using local backups in order to use this feature. If you want to use this feature but you use remote backups, you must transfer a full backup file from the external location to the local server. This interface also will not allow you to restore an account's `.cpanel` and mail directories. Instead, you will need to perform a full account restore.

To begin, select a cPanel account name from the list and click **View Backups**. The next interface contains two sections, **Files and Directories** and **Backups**. The **Files and Directories** section shows the files and directories that contain backups. The backups will appear in the **Backups** section. You can access backups from this interface in two ways. You can enter a direct path to the file or directory, or you can browse through files and directories to find the file that you wish to restore.

11.5.1 Enter a direct path to restore a file or directory

To browse a directory's contents, select "**Browse files and directories**." If you choose "Enter a path," the system will not display the directory's contents.

To restore a file or directory using a direct path within your cPanel account's home directory, follow these steps:

In the "Files and Directories" section, select "Enter a path."

Type the direct path to the file or directory into the text box. The path should be relative to the cPanel account user's home directory. For instance, to restore the `/home/user/public_html` directory, simply enter `public_html` in the text box, where "user" is the cPanel account's username.

Click "**Show Backups**" to display the available backups for that file or directory. The backups will be listed in the "Backups" section of the interface.

In the "Backups" section, select the desired backup and click "**Restore.**"

The system will prompt you to confirm the restoration. Click "Restore" again to confirm. A message indicating success or failure will then appear.

11.5.2 Browse your home directory to restore a file or directory

To locate and restore a specific file or directory within the home directory, follow these steps:

1. In the "Files and Directories" section, select "Browse files and directories." This action will display the contents of the cPanel account user's home directory.
    - To view the contents of a particular directory, simply click on its name.
2. Click "**Show Backups**" to list the available backups for the selected file or directory. These backups will be displayed in the "Backups" section of the interface.
3. In the "Backups" section, select the backup you want to restore and click "Restore."
4. The system will prompt you to confirm the restoration. Click "**Restore**" again to confirm. A message will appear indicating whether the restoration was successful or failed.

Files and directories that have been successfully restored will now be visible in the cPanel account user's home directory.

12 Clusters

For VPS/Dedicated Servers

The information in this section applies to VPS and dedicated servers.

Clustering allows you to link and join multiple cPanel servers together. They can work together and share data back and forth. Within this chapter, we're going to look at the two types of clusters that cPanel offers: Configuration Clusters and DNS Clusters.

12.1 Configuration Cluster

If you have a significant number of cPanel/WHM servers, you may consider setting up a configuration cluster. A configuration cluster will link together a bunch of secondary servers to a primary server. That primary server will then send its configuration to the secondary servers.

The benefit from this is that you only have to deal with a single server when making configuration changes. If your operation grows and you add a new cPanel server, you can join it to your configuration cluster and then push out all your configuration options and get the server ready to go for new customers right away.

Another benefit is consistency. All servers will have the exact same options and configuration.

Home / Clusters / Configuration Cluster

Use this interface to link this server to other servers in a configuration cluster. You can then copy this server's configuration settings to the cluster's servers in WHM's Update Preferences interface. When you update a setting, you can choose to copy this server's changes out to all of its cluster servers.

To import a configuration from a remote server, you must use the Transfer Tool interface. You can transfer the following: "Database Server", "Exim", "AutoSSL Options", "cPanel & WHM", "ModSecurity", "Backups", "Easy Apache", "Hulk", "GreyList", and "User Interface Themes"

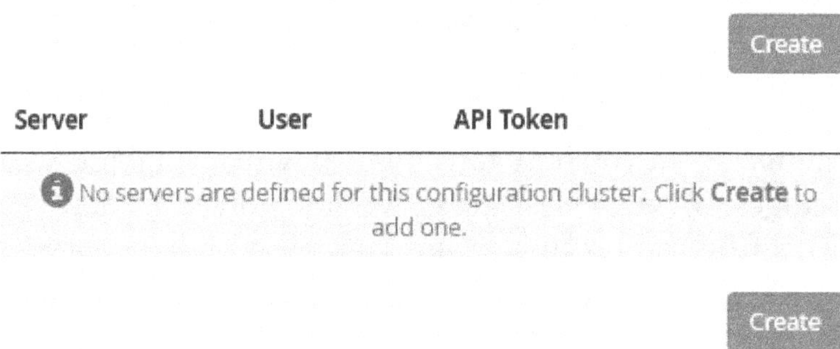

To create a Configuration Cluster, you will need to have at least two servers running the same version of cPanel.

On the server that will be the primary server, go to the Configuration Cluster interface and then click on the **Create** button. This will provide you a form with some details you will need from the other server.

Switch to the other server and login with the root or a user with root-like privileges. You will need to navigate to the Manage API Tokens interface and create an API token. It's important to note that an API token for a configuration cluster requires **Everything** ACL permission. If you don't give it Everything, then the configuration will not work.

Note

Avoid using Remote Access Keys. This is a legacy authentication measure that cPanel has officially deprecated and is not as secure as API tokens. You should not use Remote Access Keys.

Once you have the API Token, go back to your primary server. In the box, enter the server name in the Server box. Then enter the root username or the username of the user with root-like privileges in the User box. Then paste in your API Token into the API Token or Remote Access Key box and click on **Save**. You will now see the server in the configuration clusters server table.

12.1.1 Edit Configuration Cluster Server

Once a server is created, you can edit the user and API token if needed. For example, if you originally set it up with a Remote Access Key and are upgrading to an API Token.

12.1.2 Delete Configuration Cluster Server

From the list of the configuration cluster servers, you can click the trash can icon next to the server in the list. Confirm that you want to delete the server from the cluster and click on **Continue**.

Note

When you delete a secondary server from a configuration cluster, the settings that you have applied will remain on that server. The primary server will not relay any new changes and will not overwrite any changes you made on the previously linked server.

12.1.3 Making Changes

It is important that any changes you make are done on the primary cPanel server. These changes will then be filtered down to secondary servers that are part of the configuration cluster. While you can login to secondary servers like normal, changes made will be overwritten whenever the primary server synchronizes its changes down to secondary servers.

Always make sure you are making important changes on the primary server in the cluster otherwise you may find that those changes don't exist on the server you need them to.

12.2 DNS Cluster

A DNS cluster is what it sounds like – it's a cluster of DNS servers with cPanel. Rather than hosting DNS on a single cPanel server, the DNS cluster option allows you to use multiple external cPanel servers running a special version of cPanel called DNSONLY, and syncing DNS records to those member servers.

DNS clustering is easy and it's one that I recommend. This way, your clients DNS will always work, even if your main cPanel server is down. While they can't make changes to their DNS in that case, if they're hosting some services externally such as email, they will continue to function, as DNS will be available.

DNS clustering also has some other advantages. One big advantage is if you migrate a cPanel account from one server to another and both servers are in the DNS cluster, DNS changes are made automatically, and your client doesn't need to adjust their DNS settings at all.

12.2.1Planning Your DNS Cluster

Plan out your DNS cluster for cost efficiency as well as for maximum uptime. The best way to do this is to diagram your infrastructure. In this example, suppose you have 2 cPanel servers – **server1.examplehost.com** and **server2.examplehost.com**.

Both servers should then be joined in a cluster with **dns1.examplehost.com** (which will use the registered nameserver **ns1.examplehost.com**) and **dns2.examplehost.com** (which will use the registered nameserver **ns2.examplehost.com**).

As mentioned, doing this will make it easier to rebalance accounts between servers as clients will not need to adjust their nameservers at their registrar.

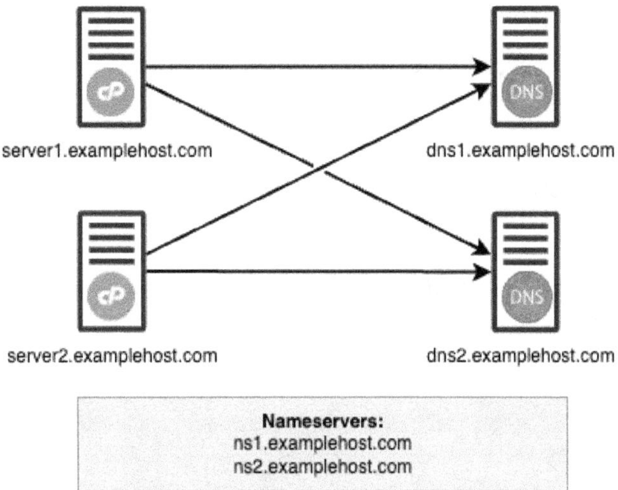

In the future, if your hosting operation expands, you can add a third cPanel server to this DNS cluster.

You can also use the same DNS cluster with resellers, and this will allow your resellers to benefit from the DNS cluster.

12.2.2 Creating a DNS Cluster

First, you are going to need at least one other cPanel server, this server should be running the special version of cPanel called **cPanel DNSONLY**. DNSONLY is currently offered for free, and it will install and configure cPanel only to operate as a DNS server. This can be installed on bare metal or, more recommended, a VPS or virtual machine. Bonus points for installing DNSONLY in a big cloud provider as it will have some extra redundancies built in.

You should use AlmaLinux 8 or 9 (or another supported version of Linux) and at the very least, you will need around 20 GB of disk space and a minimum of 1 GB of RAM.

The only other requirement is if you are using or planning on using/supporting DNSSEC, then all servers in the cluster must be running PowerDNS as their DNS server software. You can make this change by adjusting the Nameserver Selection (see chapter 9).

Once installed, you will find that WHM on DNSONLY is a very light version and lacks a lot of features. Don't worry, the only thing you need to do in here is to generate an API Token for the root user.

When you create the API token on the DNSONLY servers, the absolute minimum privilege required is the DNS Clustering privilege.

On your main cPanel server, you will find that, by default, the clustering option is disabled. Click on the button **Enable DNS Clustering** to enable it.

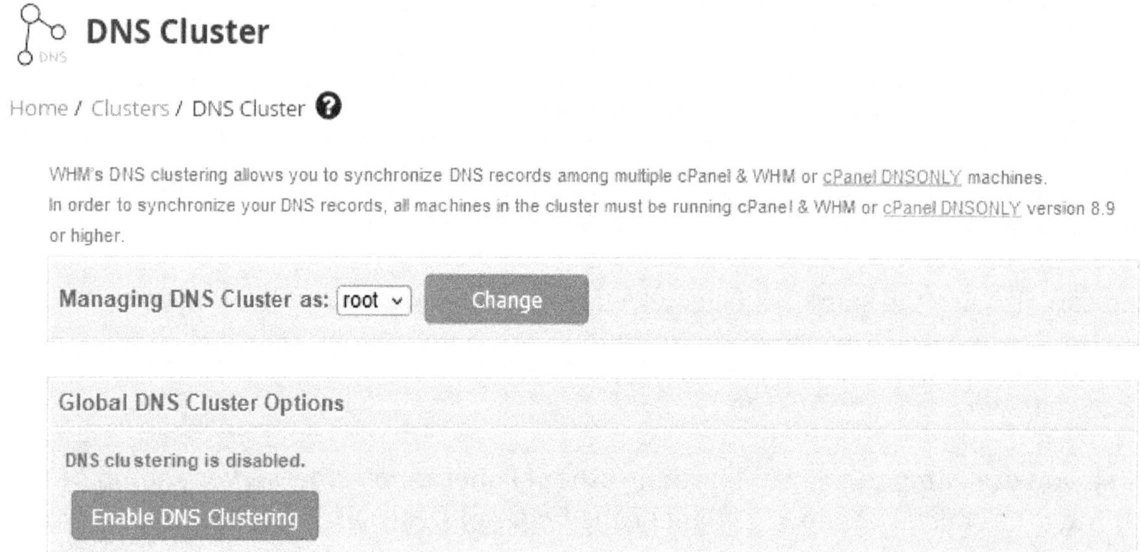

Once enabled, you will find that there is an option for a failure threshold. This is the number of DNSadmin commands that may fail before WHM will disable a member in the cluster. 10 is the default and is what I would recommend.

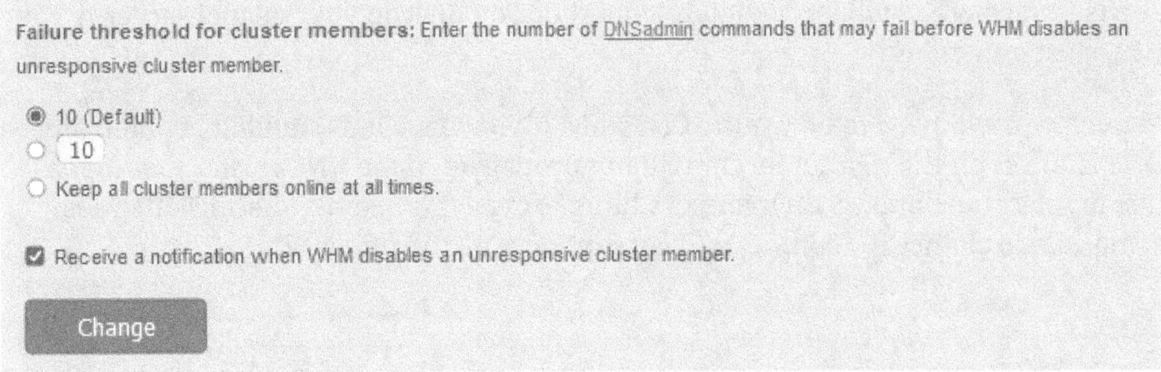

Below that, you'll find the option "Servers in your DNS Cluster". This is where you will add the secondary servers to the cluster. Currently, cPanel only allows you to add cPanel servers. Since DNSONLY servers are cPanel, you're all set. Click on the **Configure** button.

Servers In Your DNS Cluster

Making direct links between servers can decrease CPU load, improving the performance of your servers. The more steps that exist between a web server and a nameserver, the slower the servers will perform. When you add a server and set it to synchronize, the DNS path diagram below will update. Try to minimize the width of the diagram as much as possible.

Read more at our DNS Clustering Quick-Start Guide.

Add a new server to the cluster

Backend Type: cPanel (Show All)

Configure

When you add a new DNS server to the cluster, you will need to have several pieces of information. First, you'll need the remote host – this can be the IP address or the DNS hostname of the server. You will need the remote server username – this will be or should be root. Then you will need the remote API token. If you don't have one, this interface will take you to the other server in a new tab where you can setup the API token.

You will also find two options checked: Setup Reverse Trust Relationship and Synchronize Zones Immediately. Both options should remain checked. The Setup Reverse Trust will allow two-way communication between the servers. Synchronize

Zones Immediately will immediately send the zone files on your cPanel server to the DNS cluster member.

Finally, you will need to adjust the DNS Role. If you leave it as standalone, then any DNS changes on this cPanel server will not propagate to the DNS cluster members. I like to select the option **Synchronize Changes** over "Write-only" because there is sometimes a chance for conflict and corruption with "Write-only".

Remote cPanel & WHM DNS host:

Remote server username:

Remote server API token:

- [x] Setup Reverse Trust Relationship
- [x] Synchronize Zones Immediately
- [ ] Debug mode

DNS Role: Standalone

DNS Role Notes:

Synchronize Changes: All changes made on this server will propagate to any server in the cluster that is linked to this server. Synchronization is one-way: changes made on another server will not propagate to this server unless ***Synchronize changes*** is selected on the other server as well.

Standalone: No changes made on this server will propagate to any other servers.

Write-only: This server will write changes to the remote server. Changes to the remote server will not propagate back to this server. **Warning:** Two ***Write-only*** servers that attempt to write changes to a matching record on the same remote server will cause a conflict and may corrupt data.

Submit Cancel

You can add multiple cPanel servers to a single DNS cluster and use the same DNS cluster members to serve those DNS records. The only thing that you need to make sure is that the domains only exist on one of the cPanel servers. For example, if you have "example.com" on cpanel1 and "example.com" on cpanel2 and both cpanel1 and cpanel2 are in the same DNS cluster, then there will be issues with the example.com zone.

I prefer to put multiple cPanel servers in the same DNS cluster because it permits some cost reduction. DNS servers don't use many resources, so it makes sense to combine resources when necessary. The other benefit is that if you need to do some rebalancing within your cPanel servers, it reduces the risk for clients to find their website not working because they failed to update some DNS settings.

12.2.3 Remove a Server from a DNS Cluster

The procedure to remove a server is easy. Login to the server that you want to remove from the cluster. Go to the DNS Cluster interface and in the Modify Cluster Status box, select Disable DNS Clustering and then click on Change. Login to the cPanel servers in the cluster and then find the server that you want to delete. Click on the X icon under the Actions heading. This will remove the server from the cluster.

13 System Reboot

For VPS/Dedicated Servers

The information in this section applies to VPS and dedicated servers.

The System Reboot section will allow you to reboot your server. You may have to reboot your server for several reasons: updates such as kernel updates, reloading libraries, etc. Remember, rebooting a system will cause some temporary downtime while the system reboots. If you're on a virtual server, system reboots usually happen quickly. Bare metal dedicated servers can take upwards of 5-10 minutes to reboot, even on high quality hardware.

13.1 Forceful Server Reboot

This option will forcefully reboot the server. It will not wait for processes to slowly end. With this option, there is a risk to data loss. This option is like pulling the power cord out of your server. You should only try this option if a graceful reboot does not work.

13.2 Graceful Server Reboot

This is the preferred option to reboot your server. It will send the shutdown signal to the server, which will cause processes to exit cleanly. This means there is a lower risk for data loss. For example, it will let MySQL finish writing any items to the database and then end the MySQL process. Once processes have cleanly exited, the server will reboot.

13.3 Technical Support Reboot

This isn't an option in WHM, but I just wanted to put it here. If you have trouble rebooting your server from WHM, your data center or web hosting provider can generally help force a reboot to your server. Keep in mind that most data center providers won't gracefully reboot your server – they'll generally issue a hard reboot from the PDU or IPMI interface.

14 Server Status

For VPS/Dedicated Servers

The information in this section applies to VPS and dedicated servers.

Keeping an eye on your server is important to make sure that everything is working smoothly. The Server Status section will help you to that by keeping an eye on Apache, processes, your server information, service status, and task queues.

14.1 Apache Status

The Apache Status page will show you what is going on with Apache on your server. This will show you traffic requests that are currently happening and it can help you keep an eye on things. It has several sections, and we'll talk about these here.

14.1.1Heading Information

Apache server status for alexander.nodespace.dev

Server Version: Apache/2.4.59 (cPanel) OpenSSL/1.1.1k mod_bwlimited/1.4
Server MPM: prefork
Server Built: May 15 2024 04:00:53

Current Time: Monday, 20-May-2024 10:40:31 EDT
Restart Time: Friday, 17-May-2024 15:54:50 EDT
Parent Server Config. Generation: 8
Parent Server MPM Generation: 7
Server uptime: 2 days 18 hours 45 minutes 41 seconds
Server load: 0.01 0.03 0.00
Total accesses: 3593 - Total Traffic: 21.3 MB - Total Duration: 304770
CPU Usage: u4.93 s5.86 cu12.79 cs5.41 - .0121% CPU load
.0149 requests/sec - 92 B/second - 6.1 kB/request - 84.8233 ms/request
1 requests currently being processed, 0 workers gracefully restarting, 8 idle workers

```
__W______.............................................................
......................................................................
```

At the top, you'll find some helpful information about your server. The server version shows you the full version information of Apache that is currently running on your server. The server built is when this version of Apache was installed on your server. Most of these other values are self-explanatory.

“Total accesses” are the total number of requests to your server from when the Apache process was last restarted. Total traffic is the total amount of traffic to your server in megabytes. You can use this to help track inbound bandwidth usage to Apache.

“CPU usage” will show you the current CPU usage and current load percentage of the CPU. It will also show you the number of requests per second, bytes per second, and kilobytes per second. You will also see the number of Apache sub-servers (workers or children) that serve requests as well as the number of idle workers.

14.1.2 Scoreboard

The scoreboard displays information about the Apache workers on your system. This is a live look at what requests workers are handling. If you refresh the page, you will see this information update. Keep in mind the status page is rather old school and simple, so it lacks automatic updates.

```
__W_______..........................................................
....................................................................
......................
```

Scoreboard Key:
"_" Waiting for Connection, "S" Starting up, "R" Reading Request,
"W" Sending Reply, "K" Keepalive (read), "D" DNS Lookup,
"C" Closing connection, "L" Logging, "G" Gracefully finishing,
"I" Idle cleanup of worker, "." Open slot with no current process

Srv	PID	Acc	M	CPU	SS	Req	Dur	Conn	Child	Slot	Client	Protocol	VHost
0-7	1736939	0/39/402	_	0.09	12	292	33653	0.0	0.09	2.44		http/1.1	
1-7	1738736	0/8/328	_	0.04	72	0	42543	0.0	0.04	2.85		http/1.1	
2-7	1736942	0/13/335	**W**	0.05	0	0	41434	0.0	0.04	2.26		http/1.1	alexander.nodespace.dev:80
3-7	1736943	0/13/328	_	0.04	14	310	28359	0.0	0.06	1.65		http/1.1	
4-7	1736940	0/13/324	_	0.05	29	0	31810	0.0	0.07	1.56		http/1.1	alexander.nodespace.dev:80
5-7	1736941	0/11/279	_	0.05	26	1	27660	0.0	0.06	1.37		http/1.1	
6-7	1741345	0/9/300	_	0.03	79	0	22017	0.0	0.05	1.47		http/1.1	
7-7	1749088	0/2/66	_	0.00	19	0	5150	0.0	0.01	0.27		http/1.1	
8-7	1749089	0/5/273	_	0.01	74	0	16238	0.0	0.03	1.88		http/1.1	
9-6	-	0/0/238	.	0.00	7318	3	15578	0.0	0.00	1.17		http/1.1	alexander.nodespace.dev:80
10-6	-	0/0/307	.	0.00	50723	0	14132	0.0	0.00	2.26		http/1.1	alexander.nodespace.dev:80
11-6	-	0/0/130	.	0.00	7318	1	8057	0.0	0.00	0.56		http/1.1	
12-6	-	0/0/66	.	0.00	70340	0	4173	0.0	0.00	0.34	::1	http/1.1	alexander.nodespace.dev:80
13-6	-	0/0/55	.	0.00	70337	0	1769	0.0	0.00	0.23	::1	http/1.1	alexander.nodespace.dev:80
14-5	-	0/0/14	.	0.00	81118	0	110	0.0	0.00	0.08	::1	http/1.1	alexander.nodespace.dev:80
15-0	-	0/0/1	.	0.00	240260	0	0	0.0	0.00	0.00	::1	http/1.1	alexander.nodespace.dev:80
16-1	-	0/0/43	.	0.00	210674	0	1966	0.0	0.00	0.29	::1	http/1.1	alexander.nodespace.dev:80
17-4	-	0/0/100	.	0.00	157116	0	10108	0.0	0.00	0.57	::1	http/1.1	alexander.nodespace.dev:80
18-0	-	0/0/3	.	0.00	240237	0	3	0.0	0.00	0.02	::1	http/1.1	alexander.nodespace.dev:80
19-0	-	0/0/1	.	0.00	240259	0	0	0.0	0.00	0.00	::1	http/1.1	alexander.nodespace.dev:80

Srv	Child Server number - generation
PID	OS process ID
Acc	Number of accesses this connection / this child / this slot
M	Mode of operation
CPU	CPU usage, number of seconds
SS	Seconds since beginning of most recent request
Req	Milliseconds required to process most recent request
Dur	Sum of milliseconds required to process all requests
Conn	Kilobytes transferred this connection
Child	Megabytes transferred this child
Slot	Total megabytes transferred this slot

- *Srv* — The worker's server number.
- *PID* — The operating system's process ID number.

- *Acc* — The number of requests that this worker has served for this connection, this child, and this slot, separated by forward slashes (/). For example, *0/2055/7670* indicates the following request data:
    - 0 requests for this connection.
    - 2055 requests for this child.
    - 7670 requests for this slot.
- *M* — The mode of operation. This column displays the following modes:
    - _ — The server is waiting for the connection.
    - *S* — The server is starting.
    - *R* — The server is reading the request.
    - *W* — The server is sending a reply.
    - *K* — The server is in keep alive (read) mode.
    - *D* — The server received a DNS request.
    - *C* — The server is closing the connection.
    - *I* — Idle worker cleanup.
    - . — Idle worker.
- *CPU* — The worker's CPU usage.
- *SS* — The number of seconds since the start of the most recent request.
- *Req* — The amount of time that the worker required to process the most recent request, in milliseconds.
- *Conn* — The amount of information that the worker transferred to the visitor, in kilobytes (KB).
- *Child* — The total amount of information that the worker transferred, in kilobytes (KB).

- *Slot* — The total amount of information that the slot transferred, in megabytes (MB).
- *Client* — The IP address of the user who requested the data.
- *VHost* — The domain name of the server that requested the data.
- *Request* — The type of request that the server received.
    - *GET* — indicates that Apache downloaded data.
    - *POST* — indicates that Apache sent information to the server.

14.1.3 Apache Dummy Requests

Apache uses dummy requests to wake processes that listen for new connections. A dummy request is an HTTP request that Apache sends to itself. These requests, when Apache uses them without SSL, appear in access log files with the remote address set to the local host (`127.0.0.1` for IPv4 or `::1` for IPv6). These dummy requests are a normal part of Apache's functionality, which you can safely ignore.

14.2 Daily Process Log

This is a feature that will display information about your server's consumption of processing power and memory. This is a historical log that shows you what processes ran on a day and the resources used. This can also be useful for tracking down users who end up using a lot of system resources. This tool only tracks resources that are used by cPanel users.

<< 05-18-2024 05-19-2024 05-20-2024 >>

Note: These figures are averages since 0000 hours today.
Note: This script will only track CGI CPU/memory usage if the processes run as the cPanel user.

You have 8 CPUs; therefore, these CPU percentages are divided by 8 to indicate the true percentage of all CPU power used.

User	Domain	% CPU	% MEM	Database Processes
cpanelconnecttrack		0.01	0.00	0.0
[illegible]	[illegible]	0.01	0.00	0.0
nodespace	nodespace.dev	0.00	0.00	0.0
nobody		0.00	1.00	0.0
wp-toolkit		0.00	0.70	0.0
polkitd		0.00	0.10	0.0
chrony		0.00	0.00	0.0
cpanelphpmyadmin		0.00	0.00	0.0
dovenull		0.00	0.00	0.0
libstoragemgmt		0.00	0.00	0.0
mailman		0.00	0.00	0.0
event_scheduler		0.00	0.00	1.0
root		0.00	0.00	1.0

You can select the day you want to view and then view the resources by user. The *Usage by User* table displays usage for each user on the server. This allows you to check which users use the most resources on your server. The %CPU, %MEM, and Database Processes are the daily averages of each of these values. These values are collected every 5 minutes by the system starting at midnight and then averaged out.

Under the tasks by users table, you will find the Top Processes table. The Top Processes table shows the individual processes that consumed the most CPU that day. This table displays processes that have at one time, used many resources (top processes). Top process may only run for a few seconds, or for much longer. As a result, a top process may not actually consume a significant percentage of the resources on the server for a specified day.

Top Processes

User	Domain	% CPU	Process
		14.5	php-fpm: pool
nodespace	nodespace.dev	10.1	php-fpm: pool ce_nodespace_dev
cpanelconnecttrack		0.1	/usr/local/cpanel/3rdparty/sbin/p0f -i any -u cpanelconnecttrack -d -s /var/cpanel/userhomes/ cpanelconnecttrack/p0f.socket less 400 and not dst port 80 and not dst port 443 and tcp[13] & 80

14.3 Server Information

The server information page will tell you more than you have ever wanted to know about your server and its hardware (or virtual hardware). You will find the information about the processors – including the number of total processors (which will be the number of physical cores), the speed, type, and cache size.

You will find information about the memory, showing an output from the Linux command line. The memory will be listed in kilobytes, the first value being the amount of RAM used and the amount of RAM available.

The system information will show you your server's hostname and kernel information.

The Physical disks information will show you information about the physical disks in your server, such as how many and what kind of disks are installed in the system.

Current memory usage will show you the memory configuration of your system. You'll see how much memory you have, how much is used, how much is free, and how much is shared. This will also show you your SWAP usage and then finally the total amount.

Finally, the disk usage section will show you the partitioning on your system and the usage of those partitions.

14.4 Service Status

This page will show you the status of monitored services. You can change the statuses that are monitored through the Service Manager (see Chapter 9). This table will list the services and show you the version information and then the status of the service. If the service is working normally, the status should be "up" with a checkmark.

Service	Version	Status	
cpanel_php_fpm		up	✔
cpanellogd		up	✔
cpdavd		up	✔
cphulkd		up	✔
cpsrvd		up	✔
crond	1.5.2-8	up	✔
dnsadmin		up	✔
exim	4.97.1-1.cp118~el8	up	✔
httpd	2.4	up	✔
imap	2.3.19	up	✔
ipaliases		up	✔
lmtp	2.3.19	up	✔
mailman	2.1.39-1.cp108~el8	up	✔
mysql	8.0	up	✔
nscd	2.28-236	up	✔
p0f	0	up	✔
pop	2.3.19	up	✔
powerdns	4.7.3-1.cp110~el8	up	✔
proftpd	1.3	up	✔
queueprocd		up	✔
rsyslogd	8.2102.0-15	up	✔
spamd	3.4	up	✔
sshd	8.0p1-19	up	✔

Below the services, you will find more information about the server. This will show the server load, memory used, and swap used. If these values are within range, you will see a checkmark in the status column.

System Information

System Item	Details	Status
Server Load	0.001953 (8 CPUs)	✔
Memory Used	15.5% (2,500,116 of 16,126,132)	✔
Swap Used	0% (0 of 8,388,604)	✔

Finally, you'll see a status of the disk information. The partitions on your system and their current disk usage will be shown.

Disk Information

Device	Mount Point	Usage	Status
/var/tmp	/var/tmp	0% (312 of 4,054,752)	✔
/	/	14% (21,176,936 of 148,817,924)	✔
/tmp	/tmp	0% (312 of 4,054,752)	✔

14.5 Task Queue Monitor

When WHM/cPanel has tasks that need to be done, they are added into a Task Queue. The Task Queue monitor allows you to see the tasks that are queued up. If there are no tasks, the queue will show as empty. This page is updated in real-time.

15 Account Information

The Account Information section will allow you to manage the accounts on your server, as well as view information about the accounts on your server. The tools in this section are the tools you will probably use the most frequently in your day-to-day operations.

15.1 List Accounts

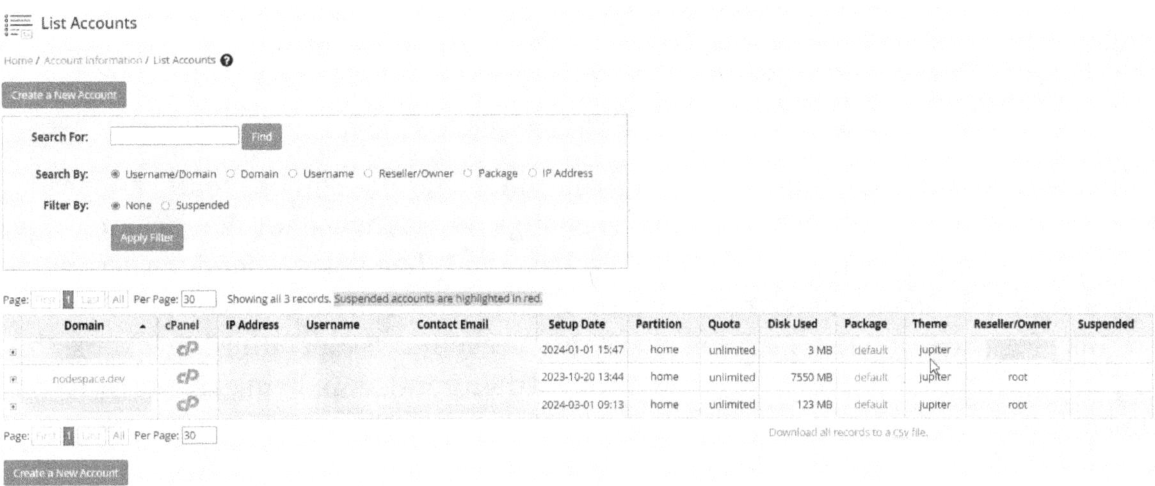

The list accounts screen allows you to sort and filter all the accounts on your server and displays a lot of helpful information at a glance. You can click the + icon to view available actions for the associated account. You can click on the domain name to go right to that website in your browser. If you click on the cPanel logo, this will log you into cPanel as that account with the root or reseller account. The IP Address column shows the IP address assigned to that website. The Setup Date will show you when the account was setup. This may not be the date the account was created on your server if the account was transferred in from another server. Partition lists the place on the filesystem where the account lives. Typically, this will be home, but if the system has a home2 or another location for accounts, you'll see it listed. Quota will show you the disk quota (in megabytes) assigned to the account either manually or by the package. Disk used is the amount of disk space that the entire account is currently using. Package is the assigned package for the account. This is the hosting package in most cases. Theme is the theme assigned to the account. Reseller/Owner shows you who owns the account. Finally, the suspended column will list a date when the account is suspended. Suspended accounts are also highlighted in red to be highly visible.

15.1.1 Modify Account Actions

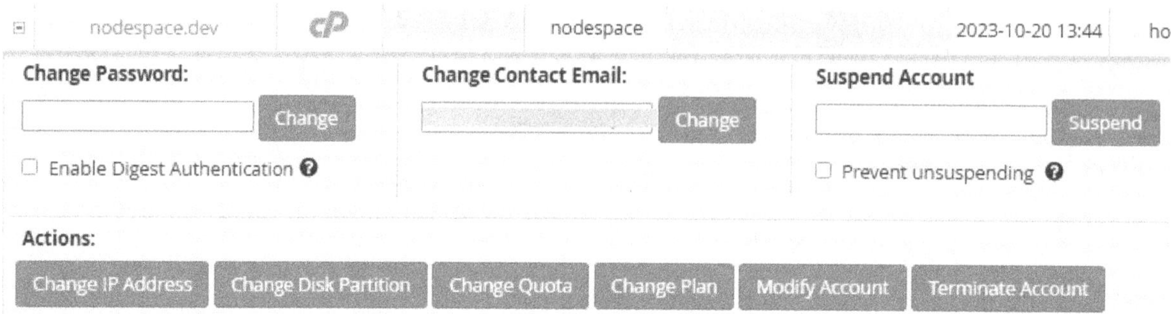

When you expand an account in the list, you can make some quick modifications to an account. For example, you can quickly change the password for the account, change the contact email, and suspend the account. When you suspend the account, you can enter a note as to why the account is being suspended such as "spam" or "terms of service violations". If you check the "Prevent Unsuspending" checkbox, this will prevent the account owner/reseller (other than root) from being able to unsuspend the account.

Under actions, you can do a little more with the account quickly. Clicking on **Change IP Address** will let you change the account's IP address. You can use this to assign a dedicated IP address or to switch to a shared IP.

Change Disk Partition will allow you to move the account's files to another location on the server. For example, if this is a large sever and you have a /home and /home2 partitions, you can move an account from /home2 to /home and vice versa.

Change Quota will allow you to manually change the quota on the fly. By clicking this button, you'll be taken to the quota modification interface. See chapter 16.

Clicking the **Change Plan** button will take you to the Upgrade/Downgrade Account interface where you can select a new plan for the account. See chapter 16 for more details.

15.2 List Parked Domains

The List Parked Domains interface will show you a list of Parked Domains (domain aliases) and the associated primary domain and user that to which they are assigned to.

15.3 List Subdomains

The List Subdomains interface will show you a list of all subdomains on the system along with the primary domain and user to which it is assigned to. This interface will also let you remove a subdomain by clicking **Remove**. Keep in mind that removing a subdomain will not remove any data associated with the subdomain, just the Virtual Host entries for the subdomain itself.

15.4 List Suspended Accounts

This interface is like the List Accounts interface only it will show you details about suspended accounts. You will see the domain, user, the account owner/reseller, the date it was suspended, the reason, and if it's locked. You can also choose to unsuspend an account listed here or terminate it. If the account is locked, then only the root user will be able to remove the suspension for that account.

Terminating account will remove all data on the server for that account so terminate accounts with caution.

15.5 Show Accounts Over Quota

This interface will show you any accounts that are over their disk space quota. This is a handy reporting tool that you can use to reach out to account owners and suggest they upgrade or clean up their accounts of old data that is no longer required. The list will show you the username, the space used, and the quota amount.

15.6 View Bandwidth Usage

The View Bandwidth Usage tool will let you view bandwidth usage of accounts on your server. You will be able to see accounts approaching bandwidth limits and those who have exceeded their bandwidth. For resellers, you can show all the accounts associated with a reseller and track their bandwidth usage. Additionally, the tool will show the total bandwidth usage for the server.

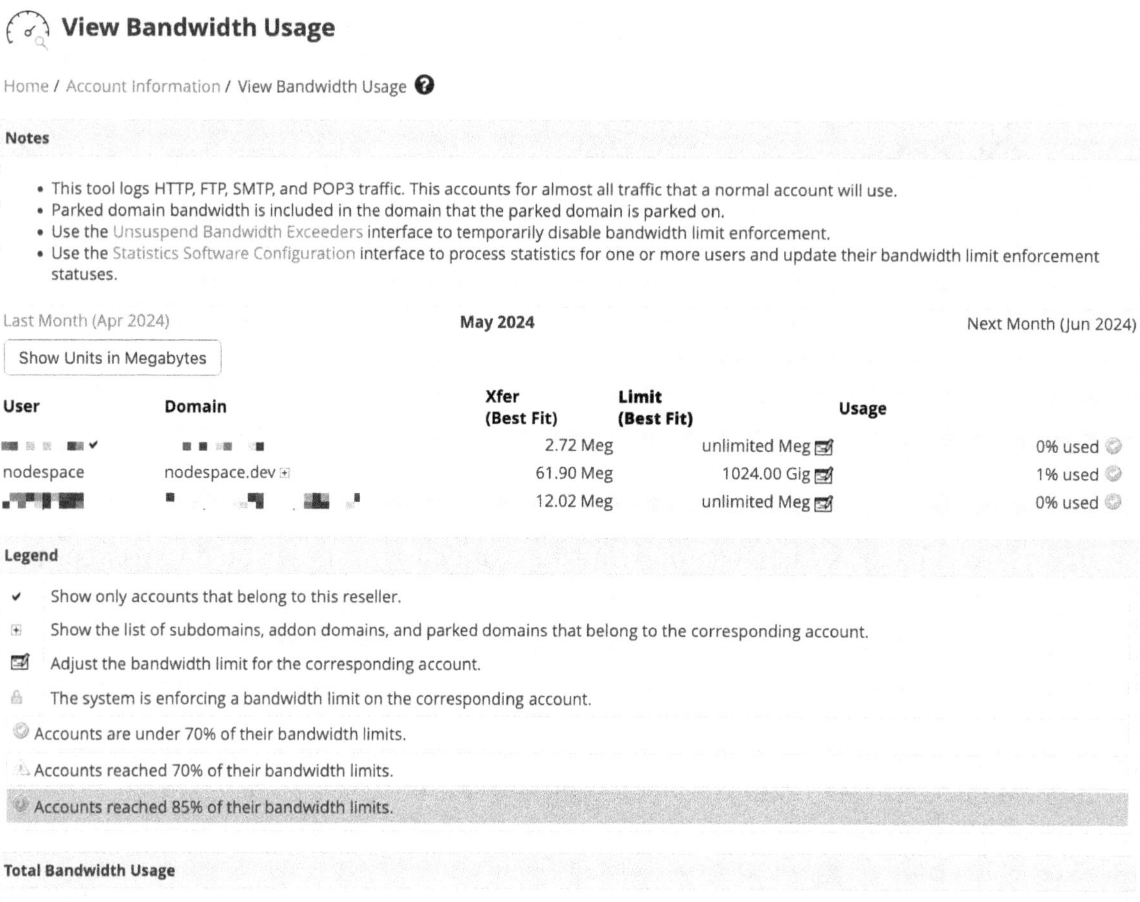

View Bandwidth Usage
Home / Account Information / View Bandwidth Usage
Notes
This tool logs HTTP, FTP, SMTP, and POP3 traffic. This accounts for almost all traffic that a normal account will use.
Parked domain bandwidth is included in the domain that the parked domain is parked on.
Use the Unsuspend Bandwidth Exceeders interface to temporarily disable bandwidth limit enforcement.
Use the Statistics Software Configuration interface to process statistics for one or more users and update their bandwidth limit enforcement statuses.
Last Month (Apr 2024)
May 2024
Next Month (Jun 2024)
Show Units in Megabytes
User
Domain
Xfer (Best Fit)
Limit (Best Fit)
Usage
2.72 Meg
unlimited Meg
0% used
nodespace
nodespace.dev
61.90 Meg
1024.00 Gig
1% used
12.02 Meg
unlimited Meg
0% used
Legend
Show only accounts that belong to this reseller.
Show the list of subdomains, addon domains, and parked domains that belong to the corresponding account.
Adjust the bandwidth limit for the corresponding account.
The system is enforcing a bandwidth limit on the corresponding account.
Accounts are under 70% of their bandwidth limits.
Accounts reached 70% of their bandwidth limits.
Accounts reached 85% of their bandwidth limits.
Total Bandwidth Usage
76.65 Meg

16 Account Functions

In the previous chapter, we looked at the tools that let you view information about an account. In this chapter, you'll find the tools that let you change details about an account or multiple accounts.

16.1 Change Site's IP Address

This tool can be used to change the IP address of a website. Select the account you want to change the IP address of and then on the next screen, select an available IP address on the system you want to assign to the account.

When you change an account's IP address, it will stop working from the previously assigned IP address. This may cause some temporary downtime while DNS propagates.

16.2 Create a New Account

This screen will let you manually create a new account on your cPanel server. You will provide information about the domain and assign a username and password as well as a notification email.

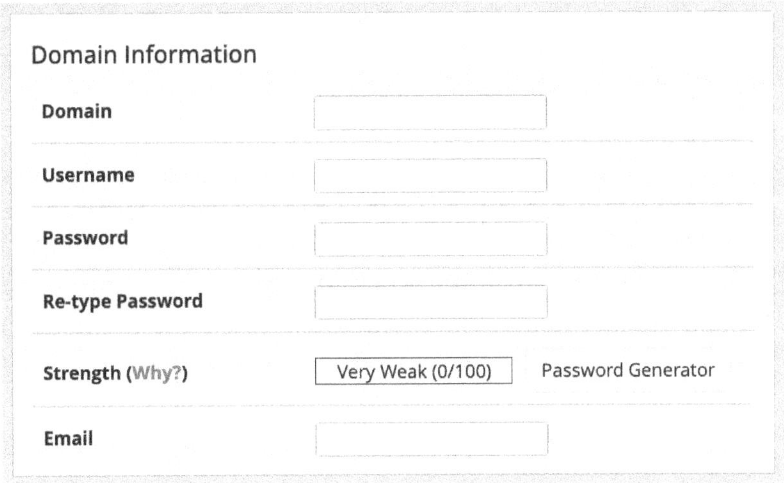

Domain Information

Domain

Username

Password

Re-type Password

Strength (Why?) Very Weak (0/100) Password Generator

Email

In the next section, you will need to choose a hosting package or set options manually. It is recommended to provide a hosting package. A green background means that the package can be assigned without any issues.

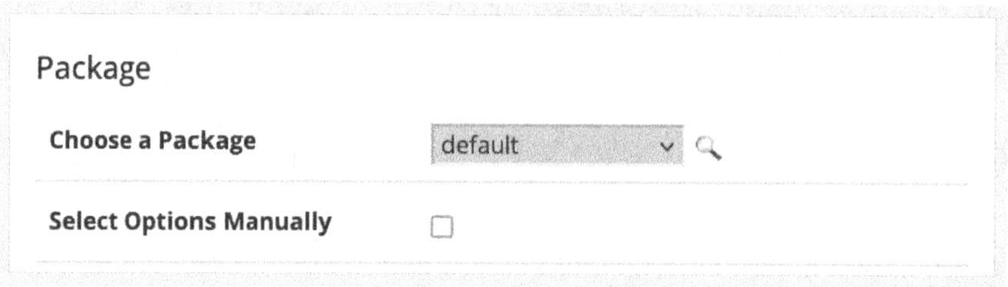

Next, there will be some additional options for enabling CGI access, setting a cPanel theme, setting the account language, enabling SpamAssassin and enabling the Spam Box. CGI Access must be enabled to allow the user to be able to run CGI and Perl scripts.

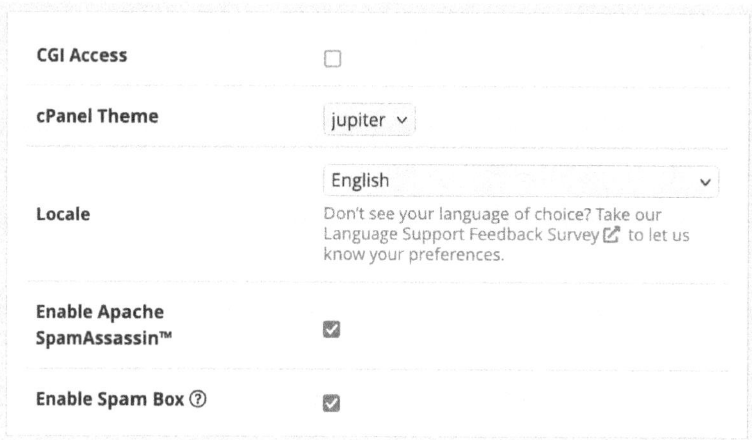

Optionally, you can set Mail Routing Settings. By default, this will default the domain to Local Mail Exchanger, although cPanel recommends using Automatically Detect Configuration.

Mail Routing Settings (optional)

- ○ Automatically Detect Configuration (recommended) more »
- ◉ Local Mail Exchanger more »
- ○ Backup Mail Exchanger more »
- ○ Remote Mail Exchanger more »
- ○ Mail Child Node more »

If this will be a reseller account, you can enable the options to make the account a reseller. If you allow the account to own itself, the account user can make changes to the account, potentially bypassing any restrictions set.

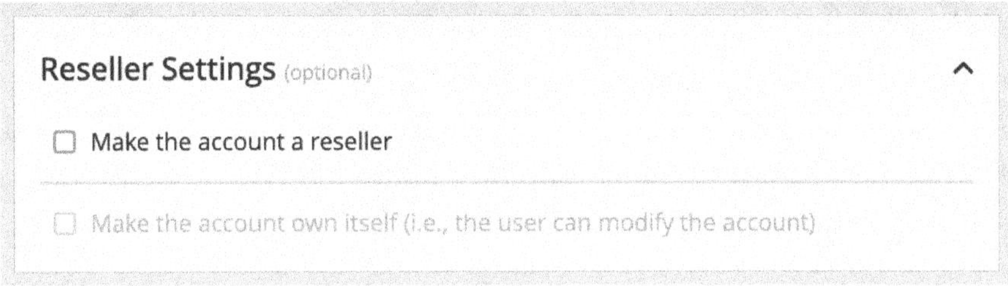

Finally, you will have the DNS settings. This will enable items like DKIM and SPF. You can optionally choose to use the nameservers specified at the domain which means this server won't be an authoritative server for the domain's DNS. You can choose to overwrite any existing DNS zones for the domain. Finally, you will see the name servers you should use for the domain.

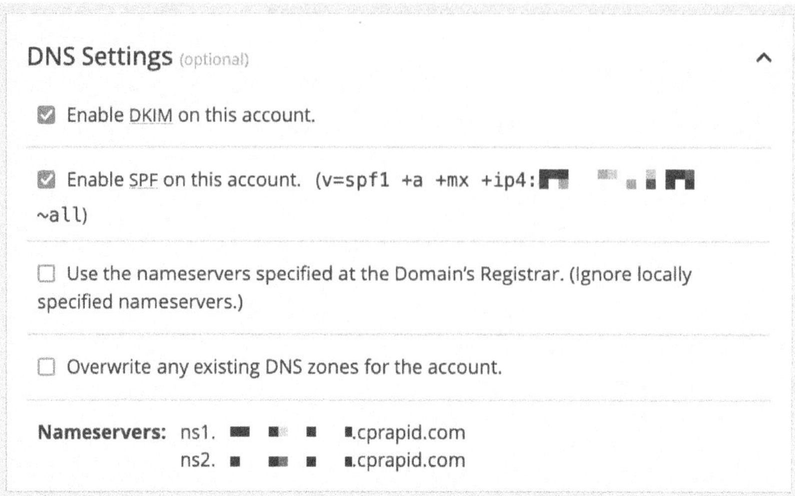

When you click on **Create**, a new account will be created using the details provided. You can then immediately start using the cPanel account.

Note

If you are manually creating accounts for web hosting, you should instead use business automation software like ClientExec and WHMCS that will handle the automatic creation and management of cPanel accounts as well as other business aspects like billing, support, and more.

16.3 Email All Users

This feature will allow you to email all users on the system. This feature is similar to the function for resellers to email their users, but this feature will apply only to accounts owned by root. Optionally, the box can be set to send emails to any resellers customers as well. It's not recommended to do this as you will also be contacting your reseller's customers. Ideally, you should be using a business automation software to send notifications to users.

Email All Users

Home / Account Functions / Email All Users

Send an email to all registered users.

Sender Name

root

Sender Email

root@alexander.nodespace.dev

Subject

Updates

Message Body

☐ **Send Email to Resellers' Customers as well.**

Send

16.4 Force Password Change

If you suspect or have been informed that a user account has been compromised, or just for good security hygiene like implementing a password policy, you can use the force password change interface to force selected users to change their password.

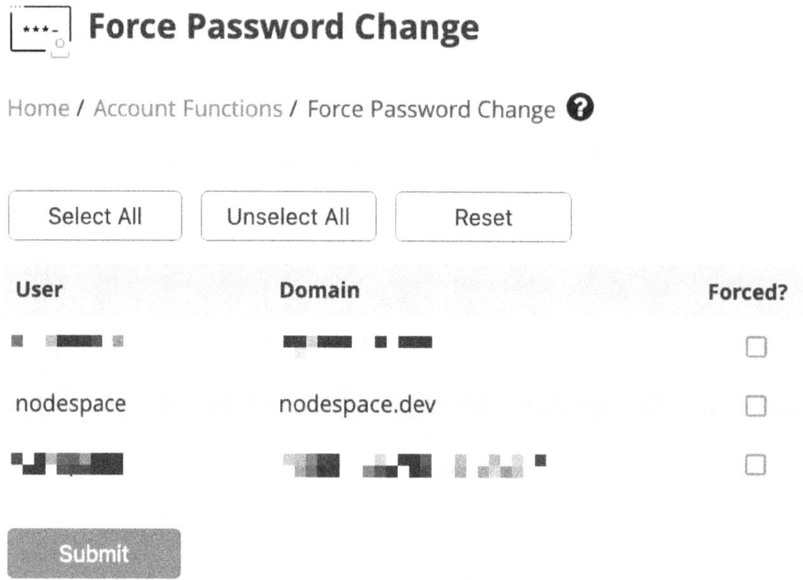

16.5 Limit Bandwidth Usage

This is like quota modification, but, instead of modifying the disk quota for an account, it allows you to modify the bandwidth limit for the account. You can choose to remove the bandwidth limit or update the bandwidth limit (in megabytes). Keep in mind that if you lower the limit beyond what the account has already used, you may cause the site to stop working and deny users' access.

 **Limit Bandwidth Usage**

Home / Account Functions / Limit Bandwidth Usage 

Please note that these limits only apply to http bandwidth usage and not the total bandwidth usage for an account.

Bandwidth Limiter			
User	Bandwidth Used	Bandwidth Limit	
nodespace (nodespace.dev)	61 MB	○ Unlimited ◉ 1048576 MB	Change

16.6 Manage Account Suspension

The manage account suspension interface will allow you to select an account by domain or by username and to suspend or unsuspend the account. Bandwidth limited sites are not actually suspended. If you're trying to fix a site that is bandwidth limited, see Limit Bandwidth Usage and modify the bandwidth limit.

16.7 Manage Demo Mode

Demo Mode is a special account mode that you can use to allow users to access cPanel but not actually cause any changes to the account. It is not recommended to enable demo mode but if you had users who would like to see cPanel and test it out, you should send them to cPanel's website and use the demo there[4].

This will not put your entire server into demo mode, just the account.

16.8 Manage Shell Access

This interface will allow you to provide shell access in a manner that allows you to modify multiple accounts at once. You have the option to set normal shell, jailshell, or no shell access. Before enabling shell access, make sure you understand the security risks associated with it. In most cases, you should provide jailshell access as this will

[4] https://recap.cpanel.com/demo/

prevent the user from running some commands on the server that they shouldn't. The normal shell does not have these restrictions.

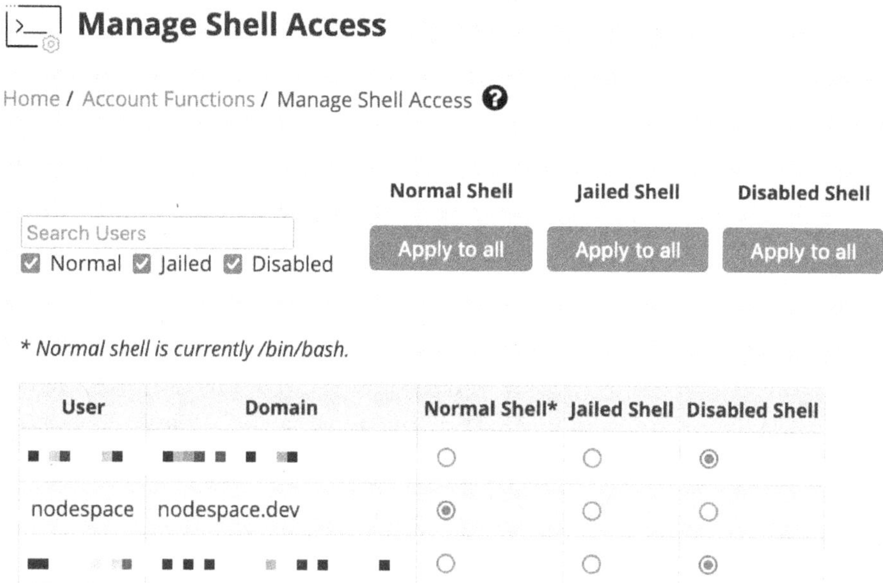

16.9 Modify an Account

Modifying an account is like creating a new account and you'll notice that this interface is actually very similar to creating a new account.

Basic Information

Primary Domain	nodespace.dev
Username	nodespace Rename prefixed databases and database users.
Account Owner	root [Current Owner]
Contact Email:	
Default Locale	English Don't see your language of choice? Take our Language Support Feedback Survey to let us know your preferences.
cPanel Theme	jupiter
Enable Apache SpamAssassin™	

The basic information will let you change the default domain name on the account, the account username (change this with caution! It can have many unintended consequences), change the account owner, change the contact email, update the language on the account, change the cPanel theme, and enable Apache SpamAssassin.

Most of these options can be changed from within other sections of the WHM interface as well.

Resource Limits

Package	"default" (Change)		
Disk Space Quota (MB) Currently using 6.26 GB	○		◉ Unlimited
Monthly Bandwidth Limit (MB) 61.9 MB transferred this month.	◉	1048576	○ Unlimited
Max FTP Accounts	○		◉ Unlimited
Max Email Accounts	○		◉ Unlimited
Max Mailing Lists	○		◉ Unlimited
Max SQL Databases	○		◉ Unlimited
Max Sub Domains	○		◉ Unlimited
Max Parked Domains	◉	0	○ Unlimited
Max Addon Domains	◉	0	○ Unlimited
Max Passenger Applications	○		◉ Unlimited
Maximum Hourly Email by Domain Relayed	○		◉ Unlimited (default)
Maximum percentage of failed or deferred messages a domain may send per hour.	◉	100	○ Unlimited (default)
Max Quota per Email Address (MB)	○		◉ Unlimited
	☐ Update all existing email accounts		
Max Team Users with Roles ⓘ	7		

You can also manually update resource limits on the account. However, the recommended method is to apply a hosting plan and then update the resource values from the plan instead. However, you can always "override" plan defaults. But if you're doing that, you should instead create a new plan.

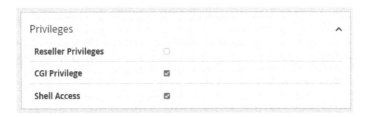

Under the privileges section, you can then enable specific privleges for the account. For example, checking Reseller Privleges will make the account a reseller. CGI allows the account to run CGI scripts, and Shell Access enables the account to be able to use the terminal in their account. These items can also be controlled by packages or enabled individually.

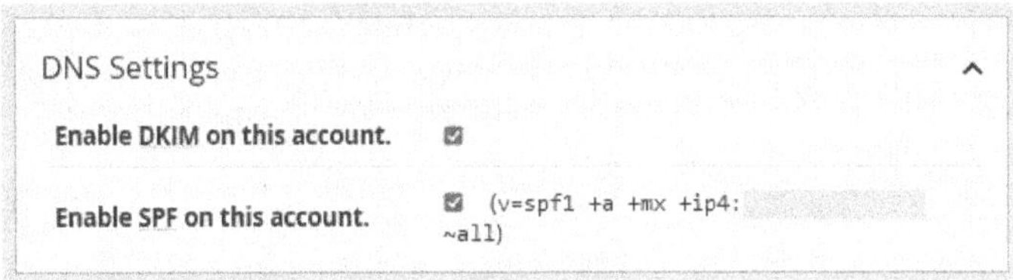

The DNS settings will help you enable DKIM and SPF automatically. By enabling these options (which should be enabled), the associated DNS records and keys will be generated and added by the system.

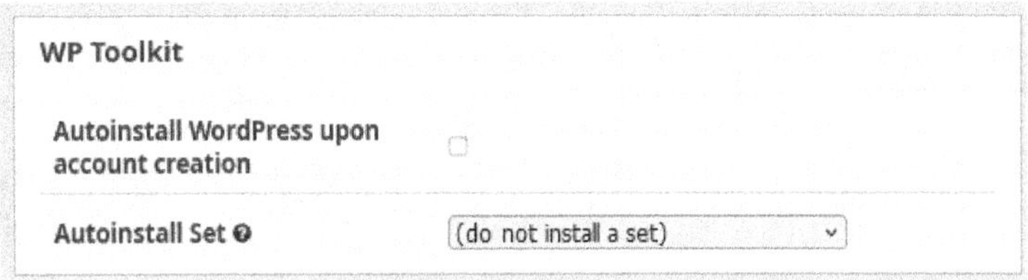

Finally, the last section will allow you to use WP Toolkit to automatically install WordPress on the account and an associated plugin set. These can also be managed by packages.

When you click on **Save**, then the associated changes will go into effect for the account.

16.10 Password Modification

This is an interface that allows you to change the password for an account. Select the account from the list and then enter the new password or use the password generator to generate a secure password. You can then click on **Change Password** to update the password for the user account.

16.11 Quota Modification

This interface will allow you to update the disk quota of an account. You can select the account you want to change the quota on and then click on **next**. If you change the quota to a value lower than what the account is currently using, the account will be over quota and the account will more than likely have issues uploading files, etc. Only modify the quota with caution. You should probably use packages instead.

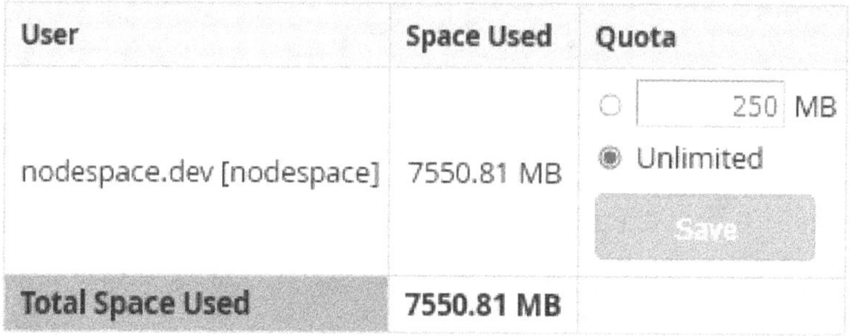

User	Space Used	Quota
nodespace.dev [nodespace]	7550.81 MB	250 MB Unlimited Save
Total Space Used	**7550.81 MB**	

16.12 Raw Apache Log Download

This interface will allow you to download the Raw Apache Log for the selected domain. This will download the log to your computer that you can use in a statistics program to analyze.

This file can be very large, especially on busy websites.

16.13 Raw FTP Log Download

This interface will allow you to download the Raw FTP Log for the selected domain. This will download the log to your computer that you can use in a statistics program to analyze.

This file can be very large.

16.14 Raw NGINX Log Download

This interface will allow you to download the Raw NGINX Log for the selected domain. This will download the log to your computer that you can use in a statistics program to analyze.

This file can be very large, especially on busy websites. Your server must also be using NGINX to use this feature.

16.15 Rearrange an Account

The Rearrange an Account interface allows you to move an account to another partition on the drive. For example, if you have `/home2` where there is more storage, you can use this tool to move the account to the additional storage.

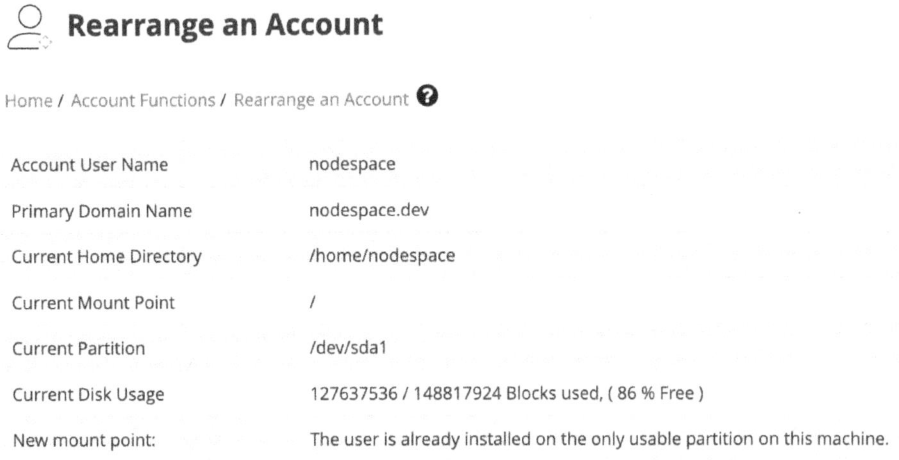

Rearrange an Account

Home / Account Functions / Rearrange an Account

Account User Name	nodespace
Primary Domain Name	nodespace.dev
Current Home Directory	/home/nodespace
Current Mount Point	/
Current Partition	/dev/sda1
Current Disk Usage	127637536 / 148817924 Blocks used, (86 % Free)
New mount point:	The user is already installed on the only usable partition on this machine.

16.16 Reset Account Bandwidth Limit

If you have changed an account's bandwidth limit, you can quickly reset it back to the package limit using this interface. Click the button to quickly reset the account's bandwidth limit.

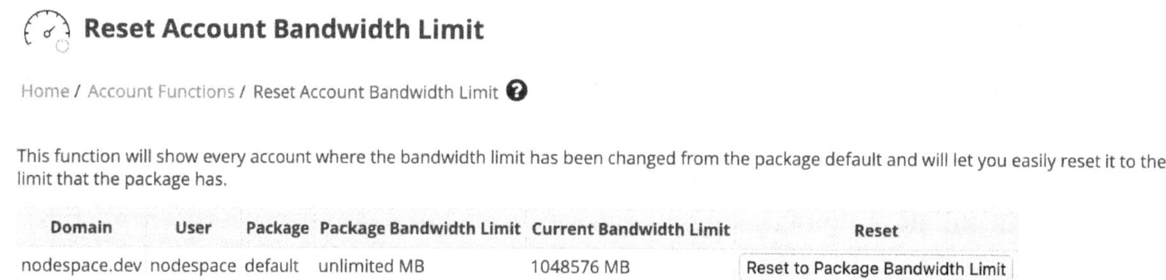

Reset Account Bandwidth Limit
Home / Account Functions / Reset Account Bandwidth Limit
This function will show every account where the bandwidth limit has been changed from the package default and will let you easily reset it to the limit that the package has.
Domain
User
Package
Package Bandwidth Limit
Current Bandwidth Limit
Reset
nodespace.dev
nodespace
default
unlimited MB
1048576 MB
Reset to Package Bandwidth Limit

16.17 Terminate Accounts

This interface will allow you to terminate one or more accounts on the system. Remember, terminating an account will remove it and its data from the server. If you need to restore the account, you will need to have an available backup.

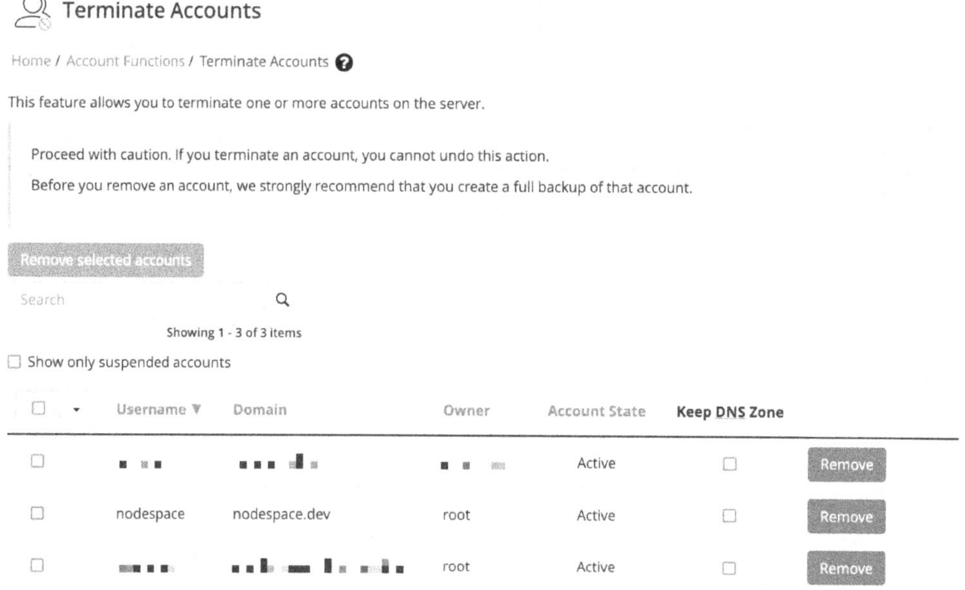

16.18 Unsuspend Bandwidth Exceeders

If you have one or more accounts that are receiving a message about exceeding bandwidth, this tool will allow you to temporarily remove the restriction until the next bandwidth check which is usually at the beginning of the next day.

16.19 Upgrade/Downgrade an Account

This will allow you to quickly change features and quotas on the account. Select your account and then click on the **Modify** button.

Upgrade/Downgrade an Account

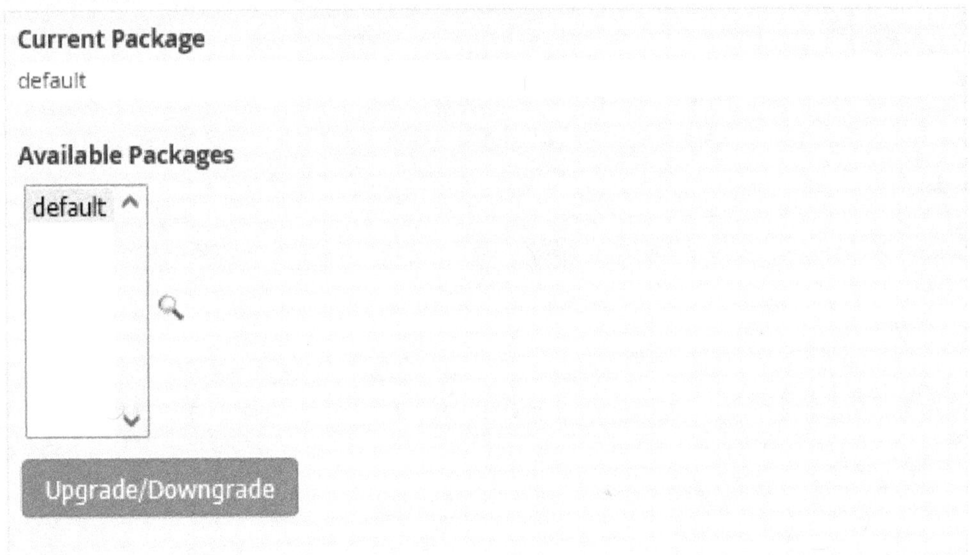

Select a new package and then **Upgrade/Downgrade** button to apply the new package and limits to the account.

16.20 Web Template Editor

cPanel includes some default pages for various functions. For example, a Default Website Template that is viewed if someone reaches a site that has not been configured or it was deleted but still points to the server, or is a suspended account. You can use the tools here to modify these templates to fit your branding, if you would like.

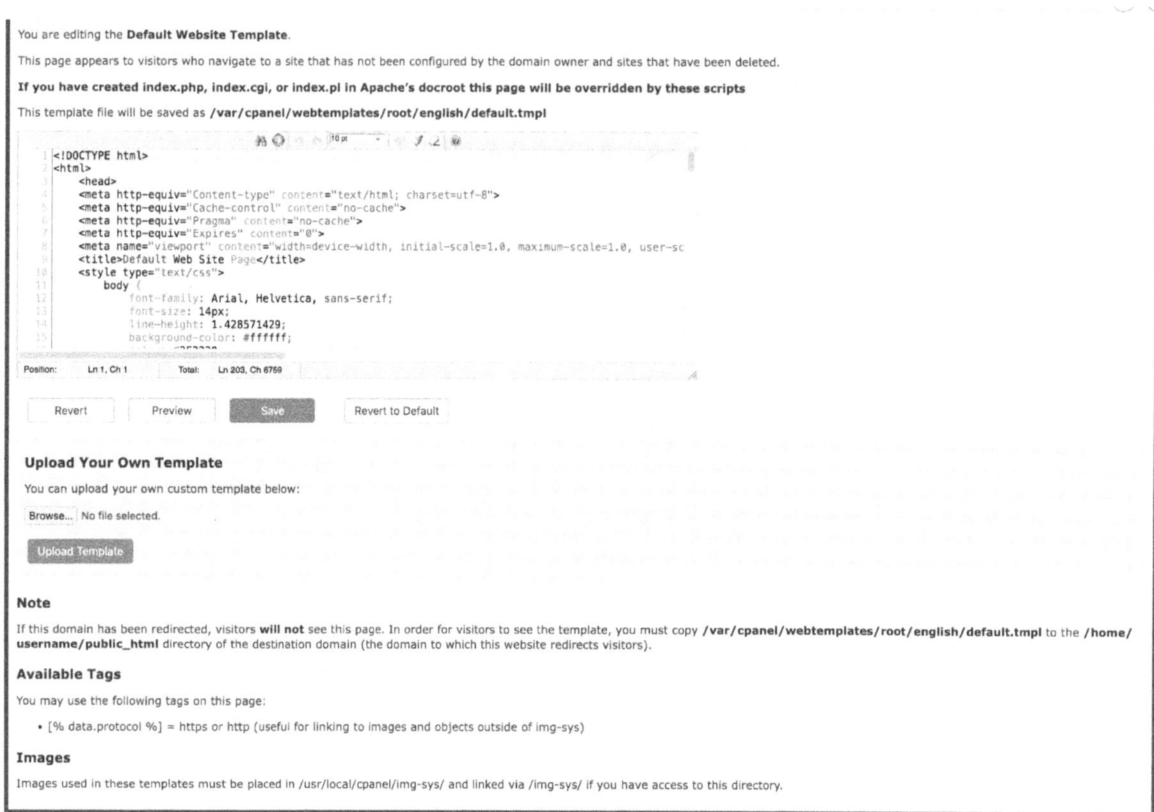

17 Multi Account Functions

The multi account function tools allow you to change multiple sites IP addresses at one time as well as the ability to upgrade/downgrade multiple accounts at the same time.

These functions work the same as previously explained in Chapter 16. However, instead of selecting one account at a time, you select multiple. Please refer to Chapter 16 for more information.

18 Transfers

For VPS/Dedicated Servers

The information in this section applies to VPS and dedicated servers.

The transfer tools will allow you to transfer accounts from other cPanel servers as well as internal type of transfers.

18.1 Convert Addon Domain to Account

If you've read *The Ultimate cPanel Guide*, then you know that addon domains are essentially separate websites. The only difference is that they live within an account. One of the issues with addon domains is that they can be a security risk. If they get compromised, they can compromise other domains on the same account. If you have a customer that wants to move an addon domain to its own account, this tool will let you do it.

There are a few things to consider with this process:

- The addon domain's data remains on the source account after this process completes. Due to this, converting an addon domain to a full cPanel account requires a large amount of disk space.
- After the process completes, you **must** remove the data from the source account. This reduces your account's data usage.
- We **strongly** recommend you perform a backup of the original account that owns the addon domain before you begin the conversion.
- You **must** delete the subdomains of the addon domain before you convert it to a cPanel account. If you do **not** perform this action, the conversion process will fail.

To convert an addon domain into an account, click **Convert** in the Action column for that domain. A new interface will appear with the following sections:

18.1.1Account Settings

This section of the interface lets you set up the basic details for a new account.

- **Username**: The username for the new account. By default, the system creates a username based on the addon domain name.
- **Contact Email (optional)**: The primary contact email address for the new account, which will receive system notifications.
- **Package (optional)**: The package assigned to the new account.
- **Preserve Account Ownership**: Check this box to ensure that the reseller account that owned the addon domain continues to own the new account.

18.1.2 Website Configuration

These settings enable you to duplicate the contents of the addon domain's document root and VirtualHost include files to the new account. To copy the website configuration settings, follow these steps:

1. Click on "Configure" in the Website Configuration section heading.
2. Select the checkboxes for the items you wish to copy:
1. **Copy contents of document root directory**: This option copies all contents from the addon domain's document root.
2. **Copy custom VirtualHost include files**: This option duplicates the custom VirtualHost include files.
3. **Copy the installed SSL certificate**: This option transfers the addon domain's SSL certificate.

18.1.3 Custom DNS Records

This option enables you to transfer the addon domain's custom DNS records to the new account. To copy these custom DNS records, simply follow these instructions:

1. Click on "**Configure**" within the Custom DNS Records section.
2. Check the "**Move custom DNS records**" option.
3. Click on "**Save Selections**" to finalize the configuration.

18.1.4 Email

These settings enable you to transfer the addon domain's email accounts, forwarders, and autoresponders to the new account. To perform this transfer, follow these steps:

1. Click on "**Configure**" under the Email section heading.
2. Select the checkboxes for the features you want to transfer:

- **Copy email accounts**: This option transfers all email accounts associated with the addon domain.
- **Move email forwarders**: This option transfers the email forwarders with the addon domain.
- **Copy autoresponders**: This option copies the autoresponders from the addon domain.
- **Copy webmail data**: This option transfers all Webmail data from the addon domain's email accounts.

3. Click "**Save Selections**" to confirm.

Note that each checkbox applies to all items of that type, meaning you cannot selectively transfer only some email accounts. The conversion process will automatically transfer the addon domain's mailing lists and Roundcube webmail data, even if you choose not to copy any email data. The new account for the addon domain will also inherit the mailbox storage format of the original account. For instance, if the parent account uses the maildir format, the new account will also use the maildir format.

18.1.5 Databases

This setting allows you to either copy or move the addon domain's databases to a new account. If you opt to copy the MySQL databases, make sure there is sufficient disk space available in the new location. To copy the addon domain's MySQL databases to the new account, start by clicking "**Configure**" in the MySQL Database section. Then, select "**Copy**" under the section asking how you want to transfer your MySQL databases. Choose the checkbox next to each database you wish to copy or select the checkbox in the table heading to choose all of them. You will need to enter a new name for each selected database. If the server has prefixing enabled, the new database name will automatically begin with the username prefix.

MySQL imposes a limit of 16 characters for the database username, including the database prefix, which is the first eight characters of the cPanel account's username followed by an underscore (_). For example, a MySQL database with a "db_" prefix allows usernames up to 13 characters long, while one with an "example_" prefix allows usernames up to eight characters. MariaDB, on the other hand, allows up to 47 characters for the database username, with the same inclusion of the database prefix in the character count. For instance, a MariaDB database with a "db_" prefix permits usernames up to 44 characters long, and one with an "example_" prefix allows usernames up to 39 characters. After making your selections, click "**Save Selection**."

To move the addon domain's MySQL databases to the new account, begin by clicking "**Configure**" in the MySQL Database section. Then, select "**Move**" under the section asking how you want to transfer your MySQL databases. Choose the checkbox next to each database you want to move or select the checkbox in the table heading to select all of them. When moving a database, be aware that the addon domain owner will lose access to the database, while the newly created cPanel account will gain full access. You will also need to select the checkbox next to each database user you want to move or select the checkbox in the table heading to select all users. Note that if you move a database user without moving the associated database, the user will lose all access to that database. Once you have made your selections, click "Save Selection."

18.1.6Subaccounts

This setting allows you to transfer the addon domain's subaccounts to the new account, with the system selecting these options by default. To copy the subaccounts, start by clicking "**Configure**" in the Subaccounts section. Then, choose the checkboxes for the items you wish to transfer. You can opt to copy the FTP accounts associated with the subaccounts and the Web Disk accounts for the subaccounts. These checkboxes are selected by default. After making your selections, click "**Save Selections**" to finalize the process.

18.1.7Start Conversion

After these settings are configured, you can click on **Start Conversion** to begin the process and view the Conversion History table.

18.2 Review Transfers and Restores

If you perform a transfer or restore, you'll find the full history log of the transfer or restore within this interface. If the transfer or restore had warnings, errors, or failed, you'll be able to review it in this interface to try and fix the issue. This log will remain for 30 days, after which the system will rotate the log out.

18.3 Transfer or Restore a cPanel Account

This is a tool that will help you move a cPanel account from another server or restore a full account backup provided by a client that they have uploaded to the server. This is one of my favorite interfaces to use to move and restore files. This is one of the newer tools that will probably eventually replace the Transfer Tool (which I'll cover next) but for the time being, both tools coexist. I just find this tool easier to use as it is more flexible.

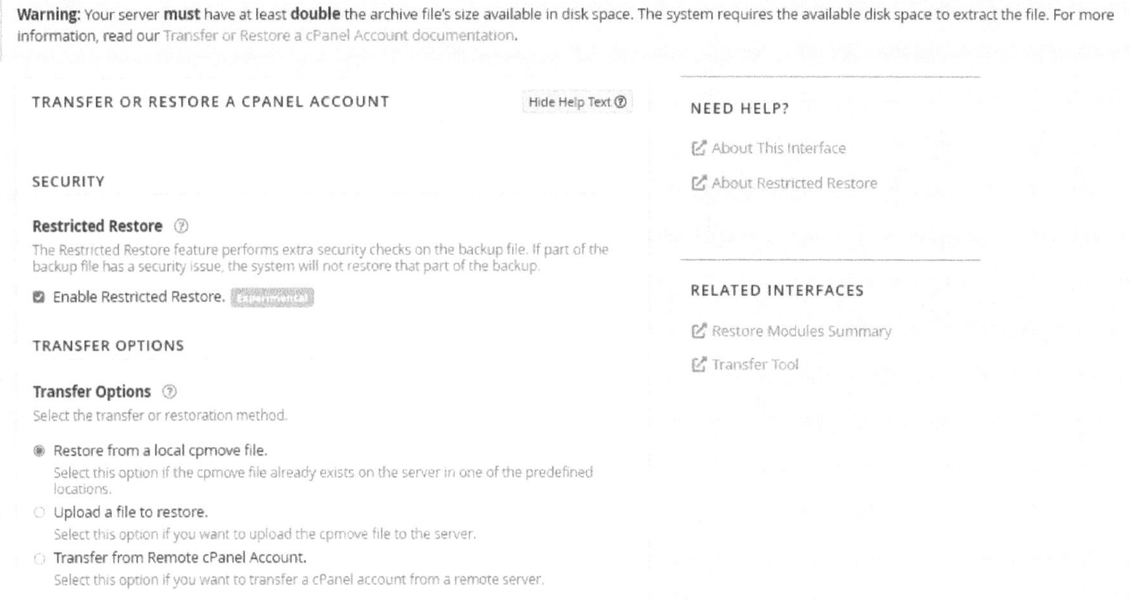

Warning: Your server must have at least double the archive file's size available in disk space. The system requires the available disk space to extract the file. For more information, read our Transfer or Restore a cPanel Account documentation.
TRANSFER OR RESTORE A CPANEL ACCOUNT
Hide Help Text
SECURITY
Restricted Restore
The Restricted Restore feature performs extra security checks on the backup file. If part of the backup file has a security issue, the system will not restore that part of the backup.
Enable Restricted Restore.
TRANSFER OPTIONS
Transfer Options
Select the transfer or restoration method.
Restore from a local cpmove file.
Select this option if the cpmove file already exists on the server in one of the predefined locations.
Upload a file to restore.
Select this option if you want to upload the cpmove file to the server.
Transfer from Remote cPanel Account.
Select this option if you want to transfer a cPanel account from a remote server.
NEED HELP?
About This Interface
About Restricted Restore
RELATED INTERFACES
Restore Modules Summary
Transfer Tool

When you start a transfer or restore, an experimental feature is the Restricted Restore option. The Restricted Restore feature performs extra security checks on the backup file. If part of the backup file has a security issue, the system will not restore that part of the backup. In all the restores I've done both with and without this option, I've never had a problem so it's alright to leave enabled. You can also just uncheck it.

Next, select the transfer option. You can choose to restore a cpmove file that is on the server or upload one (if it's a small account). A cpmove file is simply an archive of the user account. Typically, it is generated directly from cPanel to be valid. If you transfer or restore an account from an archive file, the file must meet certain criteria. The archive filename must use one of the following formats:

- `cpmove-{USER}`
- `cpmove-{USER}.tar`
- `cpmove-{USER}.tar.gz`
- `{USER}.tar`
- `{USER}.tar.gz`
- `backup-{MM.DD.YYYY}{HH-MM-SS}{USER}.tar`
- `backup-{MM.DD.YYYY}{HH-MM-SS}{USER}.tar.gz`
- `backup-{MM.DD.YYYY}_{HH-MM-SS}_{USER}.tar`
- `backup-{MM.DD.YYYY}_{HH-MM-SS}_{USER}.tar.gz`

The file must **also** reside in one of the following directories:

- `/home`
- `/home2`
- `/home3`
- `/root`
- `/usr`
- `/usr/home`
- `/web`

When transferring from a remote server, select the option Transfer from Remote cPanel Account. From here, you can enter the IP address or DNS name of the remote server and then the cPanel authentication.

TRANSFER OPTIONS

Transfer Options ⓘ

Select the transfer or restoration method.

○ Restore from a local cpmove file.

Select this option if the cpmove file already exists on the server in one of the predefined locations.

○ Upload a file to restore.

Select this option if you want to upload the cpmove file to the server.

◉ Transfer from Remote cPanel Account.

Select this option if you want to transfer a cPanel account from a remote server.

Remote Server: ⓘ

If the site is not reachable and the server is online, this should be the address of the server that contains the account.

192.0.2.100 or host.example.com

Remote username: ⓘ

The username of the cPanel account to transfer.

Remote password: ⓘ

The password of the cPanel account to transfer.

IP ADDRESS

Dedicated IP Address ⓘ

Assign a dedicated IP address to the new cPanel account.

☐ Dedicated IP Address

Transfer

Click on Transfer to start. A transfer can take a few minutes to several hours depending on how big the account is and the connection speed of the servers.

18.4 Transfer Tool

The transfer tool is another way to move accounts from a remote server. Unlike the Transfer or Restore a cPanel Account, this tool can handle multiple accounts at one time. If you're moving accounts from one server to another (such as in a business acquisition) or moving accounts from an old cPanel server to a new cPanel server, this is the tool you want to use. It will make the process seamless. This tool can also be used to transfer accounts from cPanel servers, DirectAdmin servers, and Plesk servers.

This tool does require that you have remote SSH access to the server. If you do not have SSH access or the old hosting provider won't work with you, then you will need to use the Transfer or Restore a cPanel Account interface.

Before using this tool, there are several important points to keep in mind. Do not shut down or restart any processes on either server during the transfer and restoration process. Also, avoid initiating a transfer during a system update (upcp) or starting a system update during a transfer, as the update will fail. The Transfer Tool feature replaces the source server's files with the target server's zone files under specific conditions: the target server must be in the same DNS cluster as the source server, and both the source server and the DNS nodes must use the Synchronized Changes DNS role. More details about DNS clusters can be found in the DNS Cluster documentation.

The Transfer Tool does not transfer DNS zone templates. If there are custom DNS zone templates on the remote server, the system ignores them when recreating the account on the destination server. For more details, refer to the transfer process section. Account transfers handle AAAA records differently than A records. The target server will not change AAAA records that point to servers other than the source server or related servers. If the target server does not have IPv6 enabled, it will strip locally managed AAAA records that pointed to the source server. If IPv6 is enabled, any source-related AAAA records will point to the account's shared IPv6 address in the domain's locally managed zone file.

During server transfers, the Restrict document roots to `public_html` Tweak Setting is disregarded. The transfer tool maintains any pre-transfer `public_html/` directory structures, even if they place addon and subdomain document roots outside the primary website's document root. However, after the transfer, addon and subdomains created by the restored user will follow this setting. Avoid using the skip-name-resolve setting in your server's MySQL configuration as it can cause problems, particularly on remote MySQL servers during account transfers.

It is strongly recommended that your source and target servers can communicate over port 2087. For more information on the ports used by cPanel & WHM, refer to the How to Configure Your Firewall for cPanel & WHM Services documentation. Due to networking requirements, an IPv6-only cPanel & WHM server cannot be run; at least one IPv4 address is required. This feature does not transfer Two-Factor Authentication (2FA) configuration information for an account, so users will need to reconfigure 2FA on the new server. If session timeouts are an issue, increase the inactivity timeout setting for SSH connections related to account transfers in WHM's Tweak Settings interface.

If one of the accounts to be transferred uses Microsoft FrontPage on the remote server, it is advisable to disable FrontPage for that account before transferring it. cPanel & WHM does not support FrontPage, and the restoration process does not restore FrontPage-specific files and directories. If you only have user credentials without root access or privileges, use WHM's Transfer or Restore a cPanel Account interface. Additionally, transferring accounts with calendars or contacts data from a server running cPanel & WHM version 120 or later to a server running version 118 or earlier is not recommended. In such cases, manually copy and import the accounts' calendars and contacts data after the transfer is complete.

Remote Server Information

Remote Server Address:

Remote SSH Port:

22

Authentication

Login:

- Root (default)
- User

Authentication Method:

- Password (default)
- SSH Public Key

You have no SSH keys registered on your server. Click here if you need to add an SSH key.

Root Password:

Security

- Restricted Restore

Note: Restricted Restore performs additional security checks on the backup file. If a component of the backup file has a security issue, the system will not restore that portion

Restricted Restore is experimental and should not be considered an effective security control at this time. It is intended to allow restoring backups from untrusted sources in a fu trust with root access to the server.

To display a sortable and searchable list of all modules and whether they are available in Restricted Restore, click Restore Modules Summary. This includes any custom modules I

For all other information, see: https://go.cpanel.net/insecurerestoreaccount

Advanced Show

Scan Remote Server

First, put in the remote server address. This can be the IP address or the DNS hostname of the server. Enter the remote SSH port. The default is 22. For authentication, you will want to use the root user (ideally) and then the root password, or better yet, the root's SSH key.

There are some optional items you can set.

To configure the advanced settings for the transfer, first, select the appropriate web control panel for the remote server from the Remote Server Type menu. The available options include Auto Detect, cPanel & WHM, DirectAdmin, Ensim (Parallels Pro), and Plesk. Next, choose the Unencrypted option to transfer files without encryption. You can also select Compressed Transfers to compress files during the rsync process, which helps in transferring files between the remote and destination servers. Note that this setting does not affect the package account function, which creates a gzip archive of the user's account on the remote server.

Opt for Low Priority if you want to reduce the CPU and input/output (I/O) usage on the remote server, although this will extend the duration of the transfer session. You can also select Use Incremental Backups speed-up to decrease the time taken to package the account on the remote server. If a daily incremental backup exists, WHM uses it as a starting point and updates the package before transfer. For using custom account packaging modules, select the Use custom account packaging modules from `/var/cpanel/lib/Whostmgr/Pkgacct` option. Ensure that the `/var/cpanel/lib/Whostmgr/Pkgacct` directory exists before selecting this setting.

Specify the number of CPU processes (threads) for the transfer session in the Number of Transfer Threads text box. This setting defaults to a number based on available memory and CPUs, with a maximum value of five, though the system may adjust it based on resources. Similarly, specify the number of CPU processes (threads) for the restore session in the Number of Restore Threads text box. Again, this setting defaults based on memory and CPU availability, with a maximum of five threads.

Enter the number of seconds the transfer session should remain open before timing out in the Transfer Session Timeout text box. Note that changes to this default setting only apply to the current session and must be re-entered each time you run a transfer. For a permanent change, adjust this value in WHM's Tweak Settings interface.

After making these selections, click Scan Remote Server to connect and scan the remote server for accounts to transfer. If no available IP addresses exist on the target server, accounts on the source server that use a dedicated IP address will not transfer. To copy accounts, select the checkbox for each cPanel account you wish to transfer. You can select all accounts currently displayed by selecting the checkbox at the top of the column in the table header. Use the Search text box to filter accounts and click a column header to sort them.

By default, the system adopts the username from the source server. To specify a new username, enter it in the User text box. User text boxes display warning indicators: a red highlight indicates an existing username or domain on the server, which will cause the transfer to fail unless changed or overwritten, while a green checkmark indicates the account does not already exist.

Assign dedicated IP addresses under the Dedicated IP Address heading. The interface selects the Dedicated IP checkbox for accounts currently using a dedicated IP address. Note that you can only assign available dedicated IP addresses from your server, and insufficient IP addresses will cause the transfer to fail.

Click Default to show the What to Transfer section, where you can choose to transfer the account's home directory, reseller privileges, databases, and bandwidth data. The system uses rsync for the home directory if no errors are found. Click Default again to show the Live Transfer section, and if your server uses a linked node, click Default to show the Linked Node Options section. You can choose to transfer locally or to a specific linked node for mail services.

Click Apply to save the What to Transfer and Linked Node Options settings for this account. To apply these settings to all selected accounts, click Apply to other selected accounts. To apply the default settings for this account, click Reset. The Overwrite column menu allows you to choose whether to overwrite local data: Do Not Overwrite, Overwrite, or Overwrite with Delete. Note that Overwrite with Delete will erase all files on the destination server that do not exist on the source server, and this action is irreversible, so it is recommended to create a backup first.

Click Copy to proceed to the Account Transfer interface. If the Home Directory setting is not selected, the system will not add the necessary SNI information to Dovecot's configuration files. To manually configure SNI information after an alternative transfer of home directories, run the specified command:

```
/usr/local/cpanel/scripts/build_mail_sni --rebuild_dovecot_sni_conf
--restartsrvs
```

Accounts will retain their mailbox format settings from the source server, such as the maildir format if used on the source server.

19 Themes

For VPS/Dedicated Servers

The information in this section applies to VPS and dedicated servers.

Themes are how everything within cPanel and Webmail looks and feels. Some of the larger web hosting companies will customize the cPanel themes to fit their brands. You can customize cPanel themes the same way.

19.1 Theme Manager

The theme manager will allow you to manage the themes that are installed with cPanel or customize existing themes.

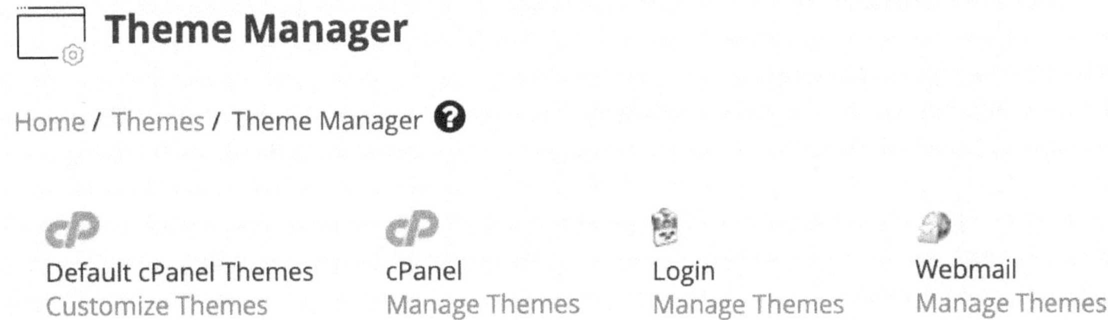

19.1.1 Customize Default cPanel Themes

This feature is in cPanel > Customization in section 27.2.

19.1.2 cPanel Manage Themes

From the Manage Themes section, you can install a theme ball file which will install the theme for cPanel.

Home / Themes / Theme Manager

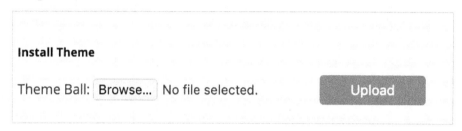

Manage "cPanel" Themes

Install Theme

Theme Ball: Browse... No file selected. Upload

"cPanel" Themes

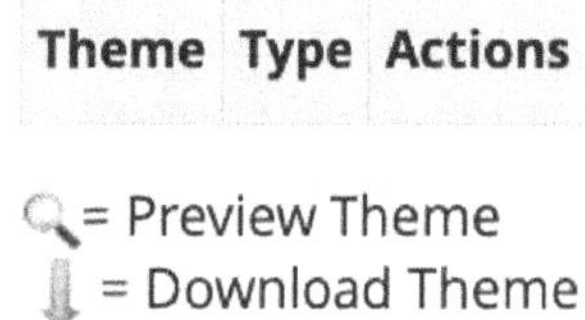

Addon cPanel Themes

Rather than create your own cPanel theme, which is quite difficult, you should instead customize the default theme. See Chapter 27.

19.1.3 Manage Login Themes

The login themes are the themes that are used for the login page. Currently, cPanel ships two versions: cpanel and cpanel-legacy.

cpanel-legacy is an old theme from the mid 2000s and it is not recommended to be used.

To build a custom login theme, you can clone the existing cpanel theme and then give it a new name.

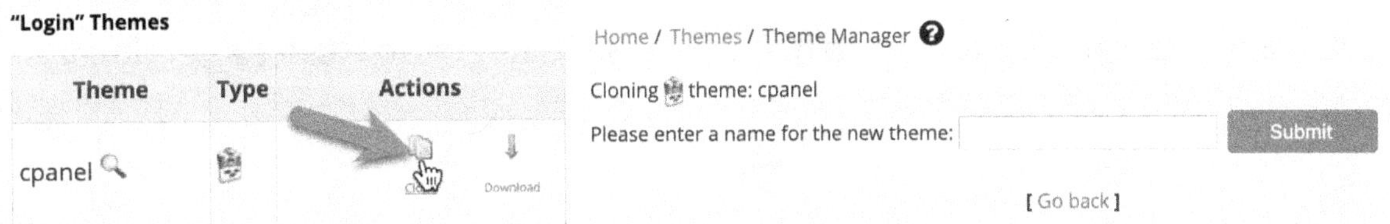

Once the theme has been cloned, you can then download the theme to your computer for editing.

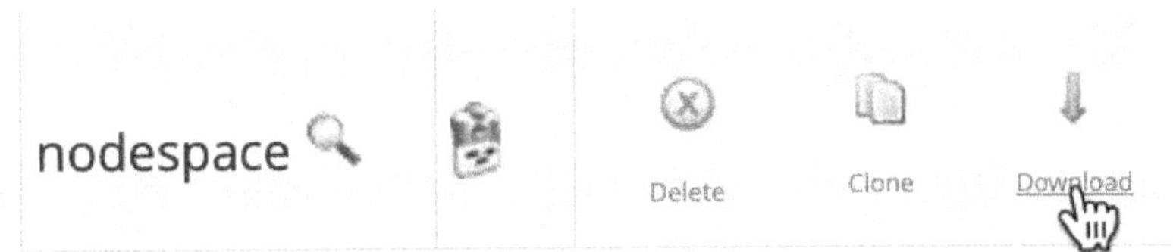

Once downloaded, extract the files. You can then modify and edit the theme as required.

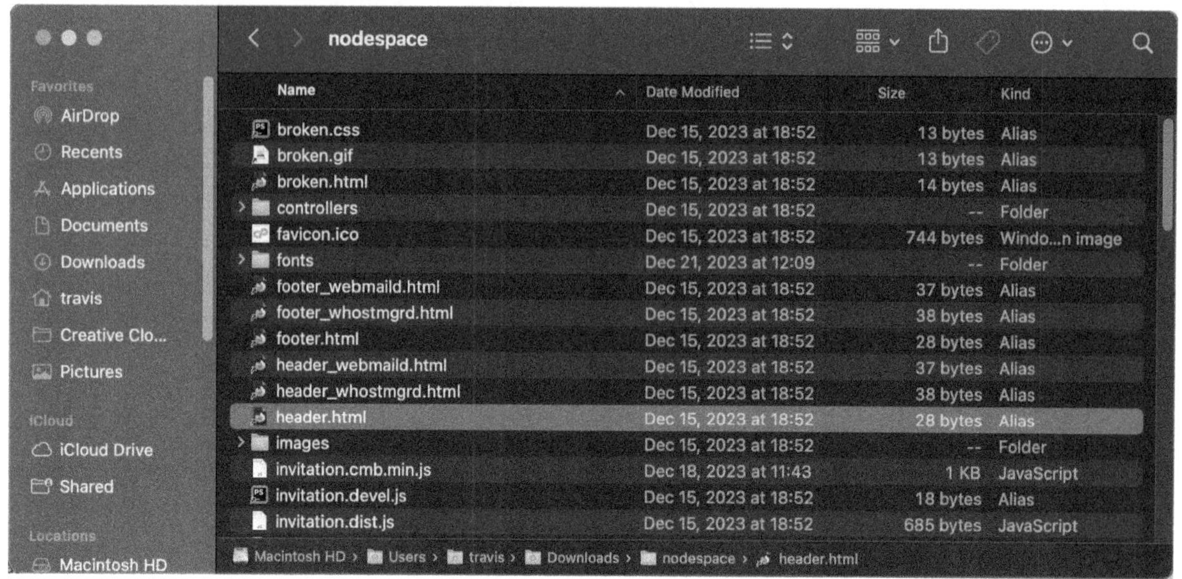

Once edited, re-package the theme and you can then upload it to the Manage Login Themes page.

If you want to create a custom login theme, you should refer to cPanel's Developer Documentation[5].

19.1.4 Webmail Themes

Webmail themes are also quite difficult to create. Instead, the customization feature (Chapter 27) should be used.

[5] https://api.docs.cpanel.net/guides/quickstart-development-guide/tutorial-create-custom-branded-login-pages/

20 Packages

In this chapter, we are going to cover creating and managing packages for your clients. We're also going to go over the Feature Manager which is how you can assign features to packages and clients. While this chapter will go into creating packages, it will not go into the logistics of what kind of hosting packages you should create. Disk space, bandwidth, features, and pricing are all going to be up to you to come up with.

This chapter will work for both resellers and those with their own VPS or dedicated server.

20.1 Add a Package

The Add a Package interface will allow you to create a new hosting package. Hosting packages are what allow you to sell pre-defined bundles of resources. When a hosting account is created, it is assigned a package which will allow your customers to access and use their resources.

Every package must have a unique name. Package names should be all one word and avoid including details, like pricing, because packages cannot be renamed once created.

For example, `starter`, `basics`, `advanced`, etc.

Package Name

Reseller packages will be prefixed with their username followed by an underscore and then their package name. For example, username_plan1 would belong to the reseller "username". Resellers are only able to view their own packages. The root user can see all packages on the system.

You can edit the resource values by the plan. If you are a reseller, you may be limited on the amount of resources you're allowed to create plans for by your hosting company. When you're logged in as a root user, you can create plans with "unlimited" resources.

Resources

Disk Space Quota (MB)	○ 10240	◉ Unlimited
Monthly Bandwidth Limit (MB)	○ 1048576	◉ Unlimited
Max FTP Accounts	○ 0	◉ Unlimited
Max Email Accounts	○ 0	◉ Unlimited
Max Mailing Lists	○ 0	◉ Unlimited
Max SQL Databases	○ 0	◉ Unlimited
Max Sub Domains	○ 0	◉ Unlimited
Max Parked Domains	◉ 0	○ Unlimited
Max Addon Domains	◉ 0	○ Unlimited
Max Passenger Applications	◉ 4	○ Unlimited
Maximum Hourly Email by Domain Relayed	○ 0	◉ Unlimited
Maximum percentage of failed or deferred messages a domain may send per hour	100	
Max Quota per Email Address (MB)	○ 1024	◉ Unlimited
Max Team Users with Roles ?	7	

You can adjust the default settings for the hosting package such as if it should have shell access enabled by default, CGI access, and digest authentication. If you have another cPanel theme, you can set it here. The Feature List will determine what features are made available to users on this plan.

Settings

Options	☐ Dedicated IP ☐ Shell Access ☑ CGI Access ☐ Digest Authentication at account creation.
cPanel Theme	jupiter
Feature List	default View
Locale	English Don't see your language of choice? Take our Language Support Feedback Survey to let us know your preferences.

Finally, if there are any extensions installed on the system that modify plans you can enable them here, such as making WP Toolkit available.

Package Extensions

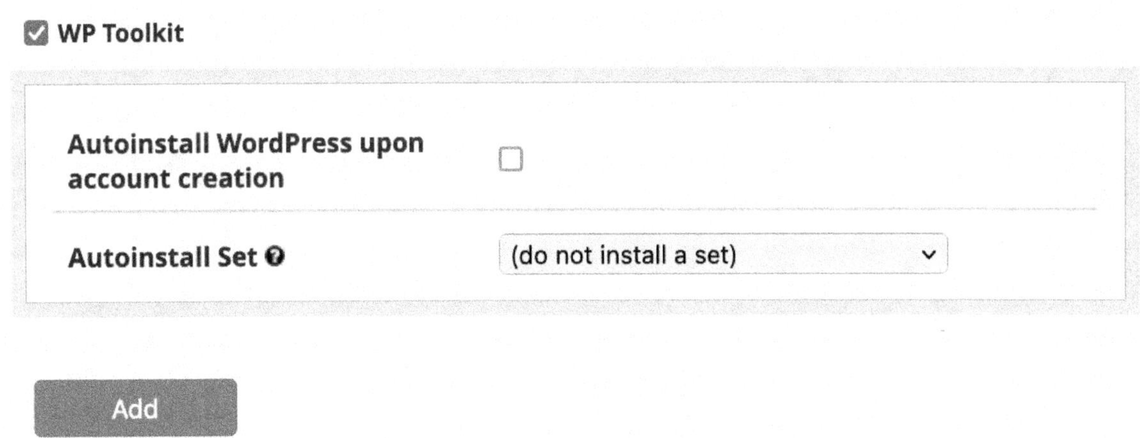

Once the plan details have been filled out, click on the **Add** button to add the plan.

20.2 Delete a Package

If there is a package that you want to delete, you can delete it from the Delete a Package interface. Select the package you want to delete from the list and click the **Delete** button.

Packages that are in use cannot be deleted. In order to delete a package that is in use, you must Upgrade/Downgrade accounts using that package to a different package first.

When a package is deleted, there is no way to recover the package. The only way to have the package as an option again is by recreating it.

Note
cPanel has a "default" plan that cannot be deleted.

20.3 Edit a Package

Packages on the system can be edited to change resources, feature lists, and so on. Package names cannot be edited once created. To rename a package, you must create a new package with the name that you would like.

To edit a package, select the package from the list and click on the **Edit** button. You can then edit values of the package and click **Save Changes**.

Accounts that are currently using the package will automatically be updated to have the changes of the plan.

20.4 Feature Manager

The feature manager allows you to create and manage feature lists you can assign to plans. For example, if you have a plan that you only want to allow mail functions, you can create a feature list that only provides access to the mail-related features.

Feature Manager

Home / Packages / Feature Manager » Feature Lists 

This interface allows you to enable and disable features and cPAddons in each user's cPanel. To assign a feature list to a package, use the Edit a Package interface. For more information, read the documentation.

- default — The system grants cPanel users access to these features by default. If you disable a feature from this list, the system will disable it in every user's cPanel that uses that list.
- disabled — cPanel users cannot access these features, and other lists cannot grant access to them.
- Mail Only — For cPanel users that can only access mail-related features, such as Email Archiving or SpamAssassin.

To create a feature list for a specific reseller account, you must prefix the list name with the reseller username and an underscore.

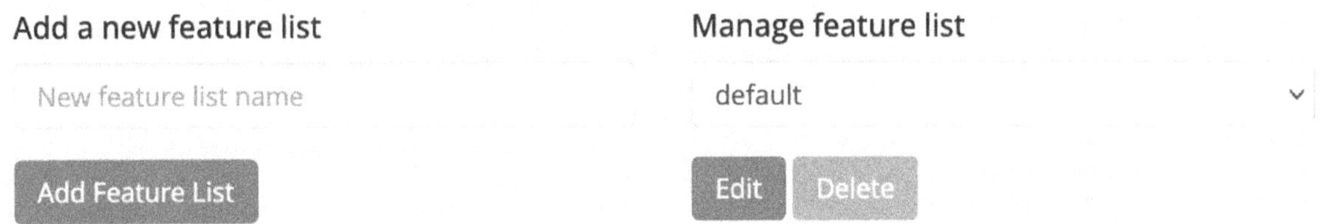

By default, cPanel includes a default feature list. While this list cannot be deleted, it can be edited. In most cases, you should use the default feature list rather than creating a separate feature list for each plan. Creating a feature list for each plan can become a hassle to manage, especially if cPanel introduces new features which must then be enabled manually in each feature list. Instead, you should create feature lists based on the types of accounts you plan to create. Like previously mentioned, a feature list for just mail-only hosting accounts or a feature list for just DNS-only hosting accounts.

20.4.1Adding a new Feature List

When you add a new feature list, start by giving it a name. Feature lists are named like packages. If a feature list is prefixed with a reseller's username, then only that reseller can use it. I suggest naming feature lists using lower case words with underscores to represent spaces (e.g. mail_only, standard_accounts, etc.).

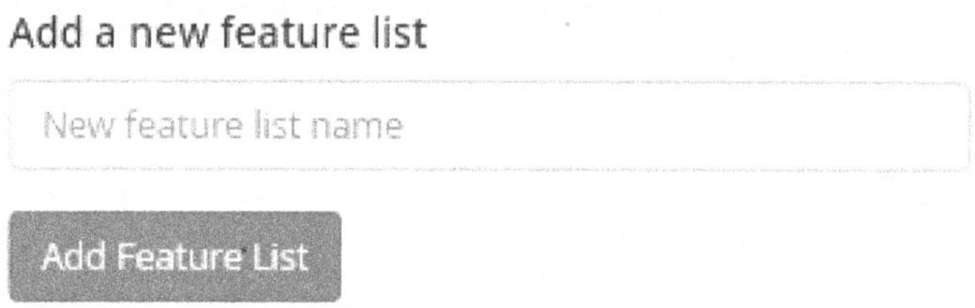

Add a new feature list

New feature list name

Add Feature List

Once you've put in a name, click on **Add Feature List.** On the next interface, you'll be presented with a list of features. By default, all features will be unchecked, so you will need to check the features you want to add to this feature list.

Feature Manager

Home / Packages / Feature Manager » Edit Feature List

This interface allows you to enable and disable features and cPAddons in each user's cPanel. For more information, read the documentation.

- [ ] Select all features for: mail_only

Search

- [ ] Addon Domains
- [ ] Address Importer
- [ ] Agora Shopping Cart
- [ ] Alias Domains
- [ ] Analog Stats
- [ ] Apache Handlers
- [ ] Apache SpamAssassin™
- [ ] Apache SpamAssassin™ Spam Box
- [ ] API Shell (for developers)
- [ ] API Tokens
- [ ] Application Manager
- [ ] Autoresponders
- [ ] AutoSSL
- [ ] Awstats
- [ ] Backup Manager
- [ ] Bandwidth Stats
- [ ] BoxTrapper
- [ ] Calendars and Contacts
- [ ] Change Language
- [ ] Change Style
- [ ] Configure Greylisting
- [ ] Contact Information
- [ ] cPanel Market
- [ ] CPU and Concurrent Connection Usage
- [ ] Cron Jobs
- [ ] Default Address
- [ ] Directory Privacy
- [ ] Directory Selection Popup
- [ ] Disk Usage Viewer
- [ ] Dynamic DNS
- [ ] EA4 - Allow PHP 8.1
- [ ] EA4 - Allow PHP 8.2
- [ ] EA4 - Allow PHP 8.3
- [ ] Email Accounts
- [ ] Email Archiving
- [ ] Email Deliverability (Authentication)
- [ ] Email Delivery Route (deprecated)
- [ ] Email Disk Usage
- [ ] Email Domain Forwarding
- [ ] Email Filtering Manager
- [ ] Email Routing (MX Entry)
- [ ] Email Trace
- [ ] Encryption (PGP/GPG)
- [ ] Error Log
- [ ] Error Pages
- [ ] File and Directory Restoration
- [ ] File Manager
- [ ] Forwarder Manager
- [ ] FTP Account Manager
- [ ] FTP Settings
- [ ] Git™ Version Control
- [ ] Hotlink Protection
- [ ] Images
- [ ] Index Manager
- [ ] IP Blocker
- [ ] Latest Visitors

Username	Hostname	OS	cPanel Version
root	alexander.nodespace.dev	AlmaLinux v8.9.0 STANDARD kvm	120.0.8

Search Tools and Accounts (/)

- [ ] ModSecurity™ Domain Manager
- [ ] MultiPHP INI Editor
- [ ] MultiPHP Manager
- [ ] MySQL
- [ ] Optimize Website
- [ ] Password & Security
- [ ] Perl Modules
- [ ] PHP Pear Packages
- [ ] PhpMyAdmin
- [ ] PhpPgAdmin
- [ ] PostgreSQL
- [ ] Raw Access Logs
- [ ] Redirects
- [ ] Ruby on Rails
- [ ] RubyGems
- [ ] See PHP Configuration
- [ ] Server Status Viewer
- [ ] Site Publisher
- [ ] Site Quality Monitoring
- [ ] Site Software
- [ ] Sitejet Builder
- [ ] SSH Access & Terminal
- [ ] SSL Host Installer
- [ ] SSL/TLS
- [ ] SSL/TLS Wizard
- [ ] Subdomain Stats
- [ ] Subdomains
- [ ] Theme Switching
- [ ] Track DNS
- [ ] Two-Factor Authentication (Google Authenticator)
- [ ] Update Notification Preferences
- [ ] User Manager
- [ ] Virus Scanner
- [ ] Web Disk
- [ ] Webalizer
- [ ] Webmail
- [ ] WP Toolkit
- [ ] WP Toolkit Deluxe
- [ ] Zone Editor (A, CNAME, MX)
- [ ] Zone Editor (AAAA, CAA, DMARC, SRV, TXT)

Save Cancel

When you are happy with your selections, you can click on **Save** and then edit a hosting plan and apply the feature list to that plan. Make sure you test changes because you may find out that you forgot a feature in the sea of checkboxes.

The features are organized alphabetically. There are also some features that are split between multiple checkboxes. One example is the Zone Editor. You will find that there are two zone editor options – one that will allow users to edit "basic" DNS record types A, CNAME, and MX and a second one which will allow more "advanced" DNS record types AAAA, CAA, DMARC, SRV, and TXT.

While, personally, I have always allowed all my customers full access to cPanel, you might decide that you want to have some "basic" accounts that limits the number of features available and more advanced packages that open things up.

20.4.2 Delete a Feature List

To delete a feature list, on the main feature manager page, select the feature list under the "Manage Feature List" dropdown menu and find the list that you created. Click on the **Delete** button.

Manage feature list

mail_only

Edit Delete

Keep in mind you can only delete a feature list if it's not in use. Switch any packages and users that are assigned a feature list to the default feature list before deleting.

Note
While you can edit the default feature list, it cannot be deleted.

20.4.3 Edit a Feature List

You can edit a feature list by going to the Feature Manager main screen and then selecting the list you want to edit from the Manage Feature List dropdown menu and then selecting the **Edit** button. This will take you to the page with all the features. You can then make any adjustments as needed. When you click the **Save** button, the feature updates will immediately be applied to all users and packages assigned with that feature list.

Keep in mind too that you may need to occasionally edit a feature list whenever cPanel introduces a new feature and your users don't immediately see it. You will probably find the feature is on the feature list unchecked.

21 DNS Functions

This chapter will investigate the DNS functions made available to you either as a server administrator or as a reseller user. WHM gives you some extra flexibility when it comes to managing DNS by removing some of the safeguards that are normally applied to standard users. Keep that in mind when you use the tools in this section. DNS has become critical for the modern internet. If you accidentally make a change that you didn't mean to change, you can cause temporary downtime for one or more users.

Understand DNS is much more complicated under the hood. In this chapter, I will go into a bit of depth about DNS, but at the same time I am still intentionally keeping it simple. But the fact of the matter is, if you're hosting websites, you're going to need to know more about DNS beyond A, AAAA, TXT, CAA, CNAME, SRV, and MX records.

21.1 Add a DNS Zone

First, we need to define what a DNS Zone is. In system administrator talk, a DNS zone is simply a collection of DNS records for a domain name. For example, "nodespace.com" can be a DNS zone on a server. Inside this zone, there can be other DNS records for "nodespace.com."

In WHM, adding a DNS zone to an account allows the account to manage the DNS for that domain name.

When you go to Add a DNS Zone, you will see several fields. You will need to put in an **IP Address** that will be assigned to the root domain name. Next, type in the **Domain Name** and then finally, assign it to an account by selecting the account. Keep in mind you don't have to assign it to an account. If you don't assign the zone, then the account owner will not be able to manage it, just the root user.

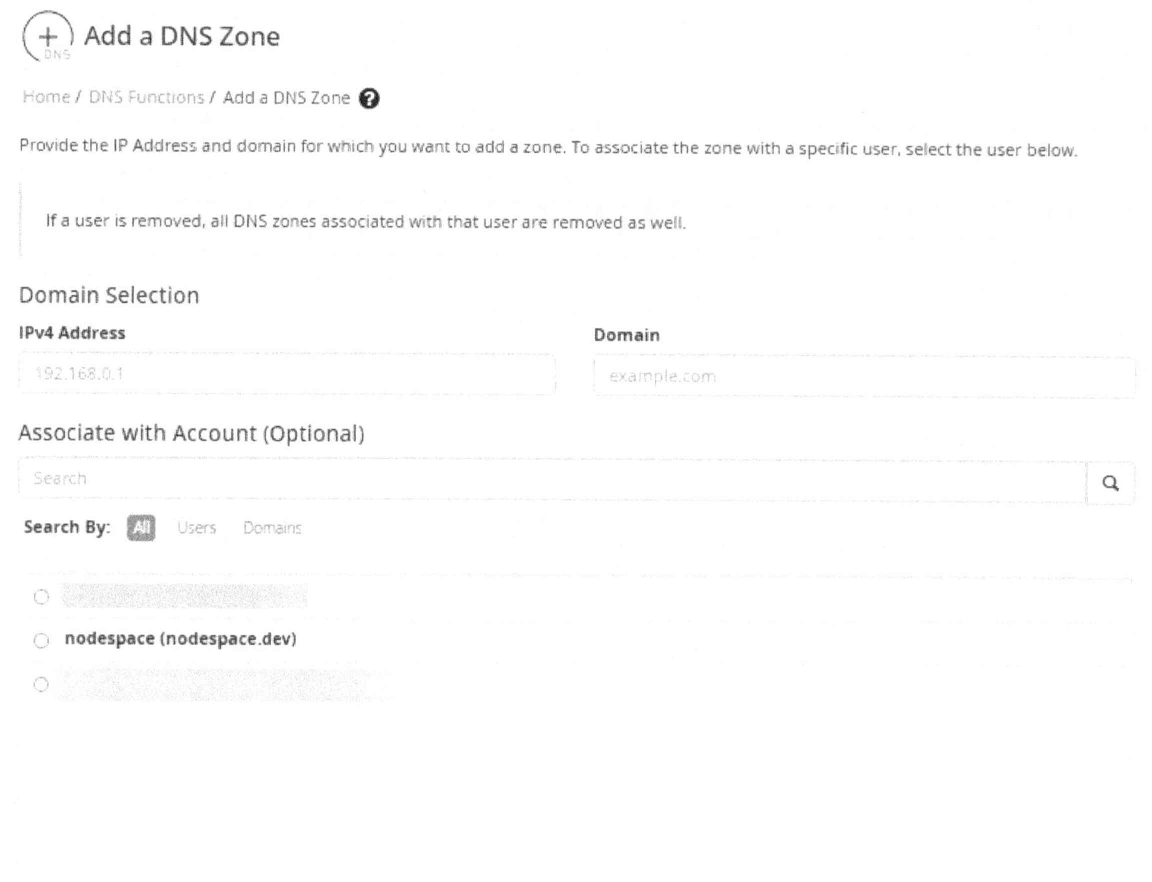

Once a Zone is added, it can be managed by the user in their Zone Manager. When a zone is added, it is neither a parked domain nor an addon domain. It is in essence, just DNS hosting.

21.2 Add an A Entry for your Hostname

When you update the hostname for your server, this tool will allow you to either create or update a DNS entry on your server for the hostname with the main IP address of the server. This makes sure that the server knows how to reach itself and the server will act as the authoritative source for the server's hostname.

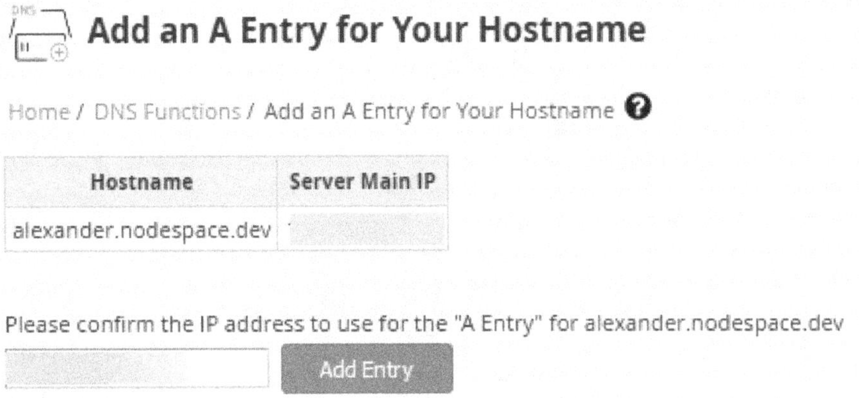

Add an A Entry for Your Hostname

Home / DNS Functions / Add an A Entry for Your Hostname

Hostname	Server Main IP
alexander.nodespace.dev	

Please confirm the IP address to use for the "A Entry" for alexander.nodespace.dev

Add Entry

21.3 Delete a DNS Zone

Caution!

Before you delete a DNS zone, make sure you know if it is still in use or not. In most cases, you will not need to delete a DNS zone manually as the system will delete it automatically. For example, if you're deleting a parked or addon domain from a cPanel account, the DNS zone will automatically be deleted unless the system was instructed to keep the DNS zone. Deleting a DNS zone manually can cause unintended consequences. Proceed with caution.

When you go to the Delete a DNS Zone interface, you'll be presented with a list of DNS zones on your server. If you setup your server using the cprapid.com domain, you will see your server's IP address in a subdomain format along with any other domains on your server.

Generally, the cprapid.com subdomain can be deleted if you have switched everything over to a hostname and domain name that you control.

You can delete this DNS zone by checking it in the Choose Zones To Delete box. Then click on delete.

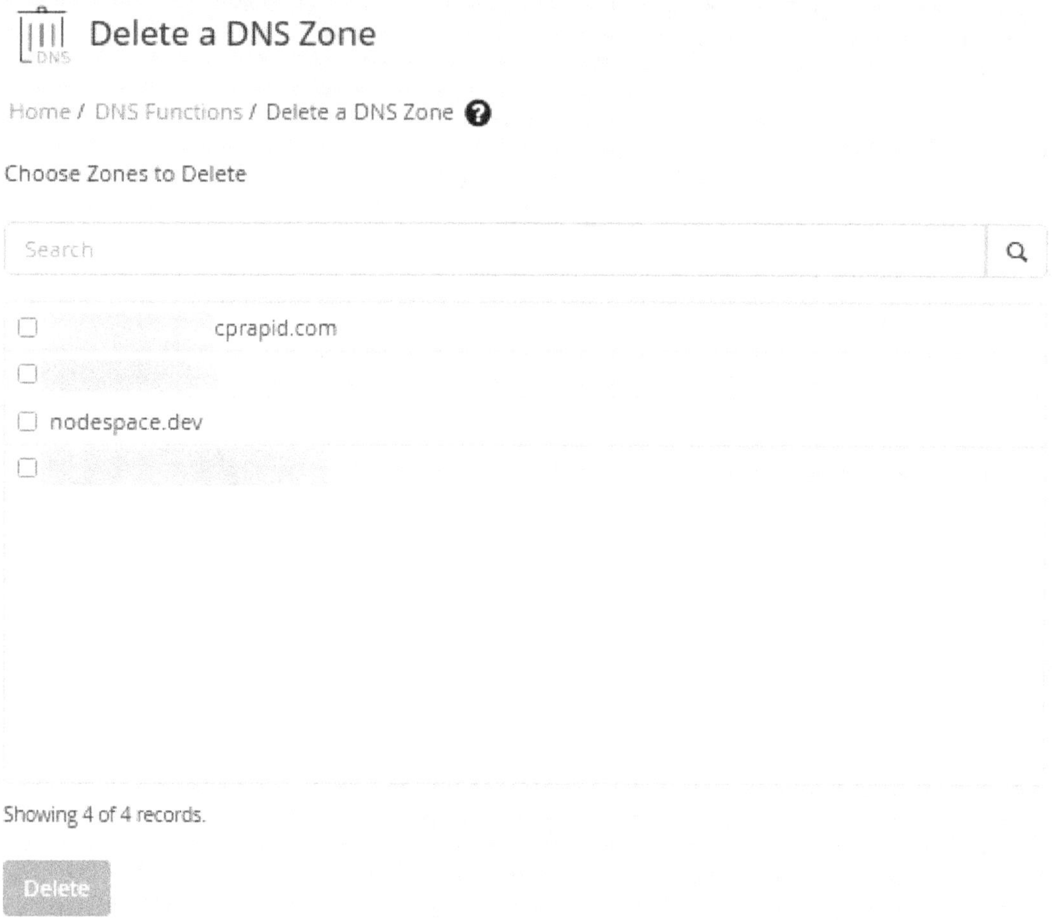

Delete a DNS Zone

Home / DNS Functions / Delete a DNS Zone

Choose Zones to Delete

Search

cprapid.com

nodespace.dev

Showing 4 of 4 records.

Delete

Keep in mind that once a DNS zone is deleted, it cannot be restored except if you're backing up DNS zones.

21.4 DNS Zone Manager

The DNS Zone Manager interface should look very familiar if you're used to working with it in cPanel. In fact, it basically is the exact same interface that your clients and customers use for managing their domains. The only exception is that you will have access to all features, including the advanced features, that your clients and customers may not have full access to (see Feature Lists in Chapter 20). You will also see every DNS zone on the system. The exception being if you are a reseller, you will only see the DNS zones for the accounts that you own.

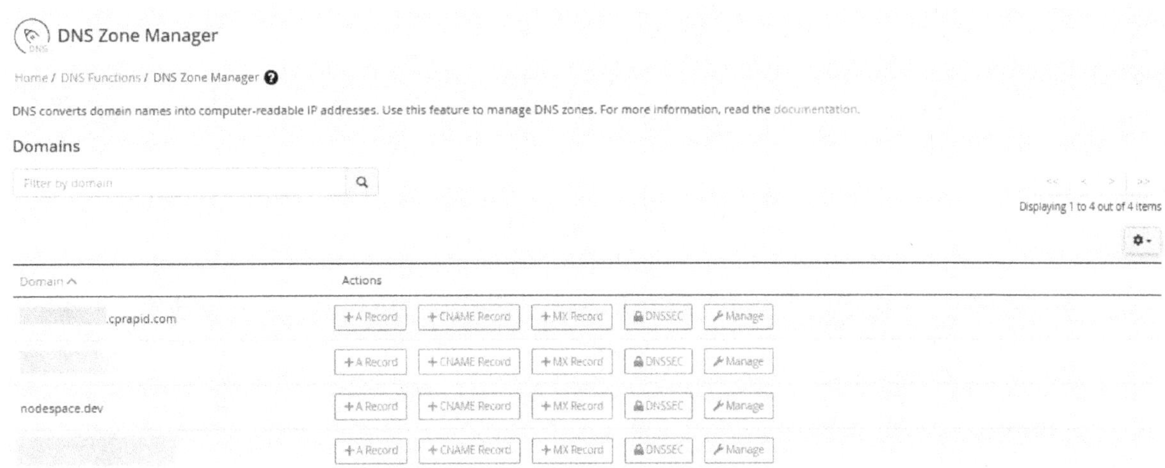

Under the **Actions**, you will have the same quick actions for managing a domain – Add an A record, CNAME record, MX record, DNSSEC, and then finally a button to manage the entire zone. If you click on **Manage**, you will be able to manage the entire DNS zone. You will see all the DNS records in the zone.

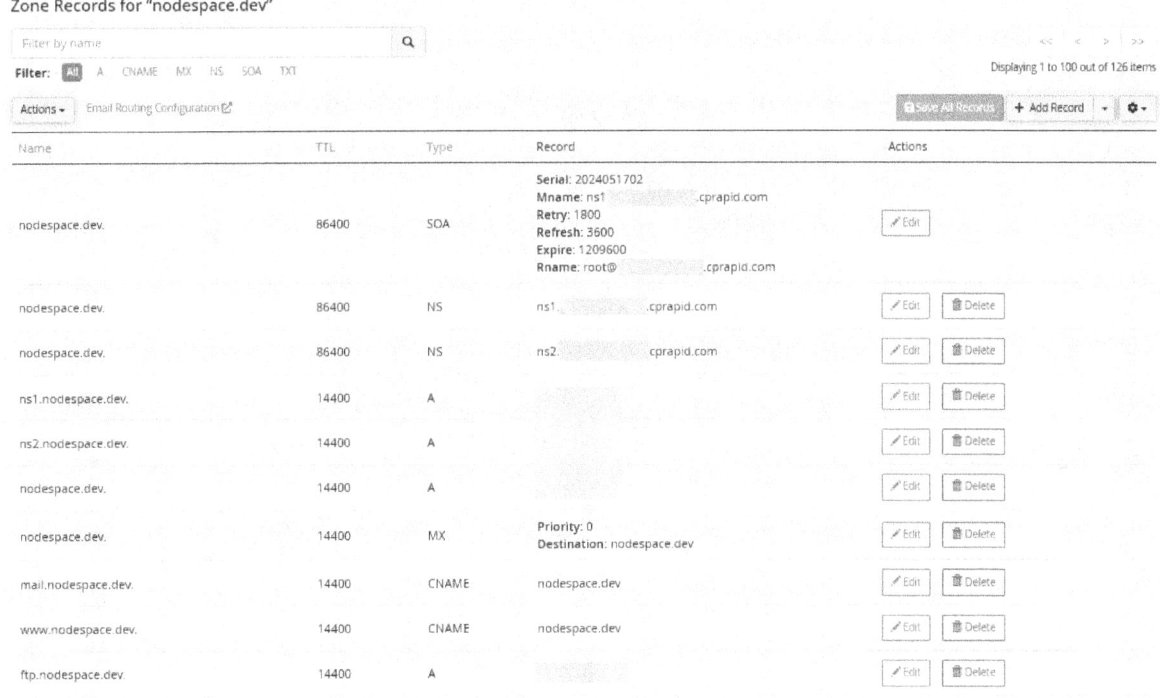

When you view a DNS zone from within WHM, you are going to see some additional records that make DNS function that you won't see from the front end. The most important record that you need to be careful when editing and cannot be removed is the **SOA** record. This is a special record. It stands for Start of Authority, and it tells DNS who is responsible for the DNS zone. There are several fields in this that are important and can help you resolve DNS issues. Two fields you may edit are:

- **Mname**: This is the primary authoritative nameserver for the domain. If you added a domain while using the cprapid.com domain, you'll find an invalid nameserver entry.
- **Rname**: This is the email address of the person responsible for the DNS zone. Typically, this will be `root@<serverhostname>`.

You are advised to leave all other entries as is and do not edit these fields. You will notice that the serial number cannot be edited. This is because the serial must be unique per zone update (e.g. adding or changing the zone requires the serial to be updated) so the system handles this for you.

21.4.1Adding a DNS Record

You can add DNS records of all kinds for your clients if they do not have the ability to do it themselves. If you click the down arrow next to the **New Record** button, you'll get a list of all the records you can add.

Add "A" Record
Add "AAAA" Record
Add "AFSDB" Record
Add "CAA" Record
Add "CNAME" Record
Add "DMARC" Record
Add "DNAME" Record
Add "DS" Record
Add "HINFO" Record
Add "LOC" Record
Add "MX" Record
Add "NS" Record
Add "NAPTR" Record
Add "PTR" Record
Add "RP" Record
Add "SRV" Record
Add "TXT" Record

When you click the appropriate record type, DNS Manager will insert a new line and allow you to enter the required information for the DNS record type.

There are some things you need to know about cPanel's DNS records that may be different from other DNS software and platforms that you have used in the past.

- If you are instructed to add an "@" record, this means "root" and would be the name of the zone that you are modifying. For example, if you are instructed to add a TXT record for @ with the value "VERIFY-12345", you will add a TXT record with the name "example.com." (switch example.com with your domain) and don't forget about the dot at the end of the domain. cPanel will add this dot for you, but it's a good habit to get into.
- cPanel requires all records to be the same TTL. This means that you cannot have one TXT record be 5 while another TXT record has a TTL of 14400.
- Remember if you edit the MX record to a remote system, update the domain's email routing configuration.

21.4.2 Deleting a DNS Record

If you need to delete a DNS record, you can remove it by clicking on the **Delete** button in the row that contains the record.

Remember that once a DNS record is deleted, there is no way to restore the record except for recreating the record manually.

Deleting a record that is still in use may cause unintended downtime for any service that uses that record.

21.4.3 Editing a DNS Record

You can edit a DNS record after it has been created. Click on the **Edit** button next to the record you want to edit. You can edit all parts of the record, including the name, TTL, Type, and the record value. Be sure that you do not cause a conflict by adding multiple records that should not exist. You may inadvertently cause service issues. For example, if you change the root domain's A record to a CNAME, you may break services that rely on this record.

21.5 Edit Zone Template

For VPS/Dedicated Servers
The information in this section applies to VPS and dedicated servers.

cPanel gives you the ability to edit zone template files for simple zones, standard zones, and standard zones that use a shared IP address.

Note
In the normal course of business, you will not need to change these zone templates. These should only be modified if you use custom DNS configurations.

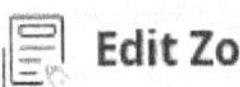

Edit Zone Templates

Home / DNS Functions / Edit Zone Templates

The Zone Template Editor will allow you to edit the default zones that are used when creating DNS entries. (Unless you have a custom setup, you do not need to edit these.)

simple - Domains with an A entry only
standard - Domains on a dedicated IP address, parked domains, and addon domains
standardvirtualftp - Domains on a shared IP address

Custom DNS zone templates will **not** affect subdomains you add to a cPanel account and DNS zone templates will **only** apply when you create new zone files. Any existing zones will not have any changes made to them if you modify the template.

The following variables are available in template files:

Variable	Description
`%cpversion%`	The version of cPanel & WHM.
`%domain%`	The domain name.
`%ftpip%`	The domain's FTP server's IP address.
`%ip%`	The domain's IPv4 address.
`%ipv6%`	The domain's IPv6 address.
`%maildomain%`	The hostname of the server that handles the domain's mail.
`%nameserver%`	The primary nameserver's hostname for the primary NS record.
`%nameserver2%`	The secondary nameserver's hostname for the secondary NS record.
`%nameserver3%`	The tertiary nameserver's hostname for the tertiary NS record.
`%nameserver4%`	The quaternary nameserver's hostname for the quaternary NS record.
`%nameservera%`	The primary nameserver's IP address.
`%nameservera2%`	The secondary nameserver's IP address.
`%nameservera3%`	The tertiary nameserver's IP address.
`%nameservera4%`	The quaternary nameserver's IP address.

Variable	Description
`%nameserverentry%`	The primary nameserver's hostname for the glue record. Your system will use this hostname as a registered nameserver for the autocreateaentries setting.
`%nameserverentry2%`	The secondary nameserver's hostname for the glue record. Your system will use this hostname as a registered nameserver for the autocreateaentries setting.
`%nameserverentry3%`	The tertiary nameserver's hostname for the glue record. Your system will use this hostname as a registered nameserver for the autocreateaentries setting.
`%nameserverentry4%`	The quaternary nameserver's hostname for the glue record. Your system will use this hostname as a registered nameserver for the autocreateaentries setting.
`%nsttl%`	The nameserver's Time to Live (TTL).
`%reseller%`	The reseller who owns the domain. Important: If a reseller owns the domain and has created their own DNS zone template files, your domain will apply these templates when you create it.
`%rpemail%`	The contact email address.
`%serial%`	The zone record's serial number.
`%ttl%`	The domain's TTL.

21.6 Email Routing Configuration

Every domain and subdomain on a cPanel system can send and receive email by default. To properly route email in various use cases, the Email Routing Configuration tool allows you to change the email configuration for a domain.

This tool will also allow you to modify the MX record for a domain or subdomain.

To use this tool, first select the domain or subdomain from the list. Click on **Edit.** When you are in the edit mode, you will have a screen that will let you change the email routing and the MX entries.

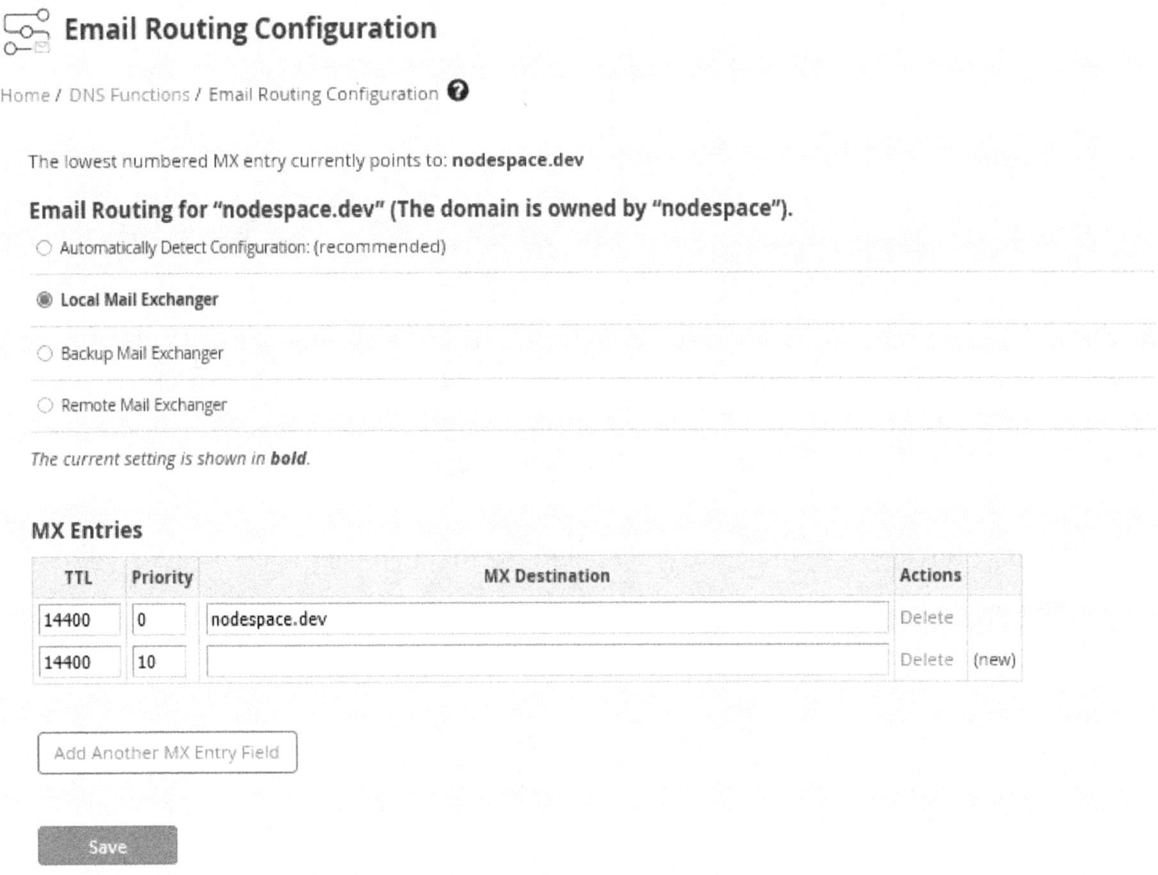

Email routing is made up of the following options:

- **Automatically Detect Configuration** – This is recommended, and it will allow cPanel to determine the best method to use automatically.
- **Local Mail Exchanger** – This cPanel server handles the email for this domain/subdomain. The system will always use itself.
- **Backup Mail Exchanger** – This system is a backup email system. The system will use a lower priority MX destination before using itself.
- **Remote Mail Exchanger** – This system does **not** handle email for the domain/subdomain. It will use the MX record(s) provided for all email. You

would use this option if you're using an external email provider such as Office 365, Google Workspaces, or Zoho Mail.

This tool will allow you to manage the MX records for the selected domain or subdomain as well. You can adjust the existing entries, or you can add more if required. Once you are done, click on **Save** and allow DNS changes to propagate.

21.7 Enable DKIM/SPF Globally

For VPS/Dedicated Servers

The information in this section applies to VPS and dedicated servers.

Back in cPanel version 62 (released in January 2017), the system started provisioning SPF and DKIM on new accounts by default. But accounts that were setup before this feature was added will not have SPF and DKIM enabled by default. You can use this tool to enable DKIM and SPF on these older accounts.

DKIM SPF **Enable DKIM/SPF Globally**

Home / DNS Functions / Enable DKIM/SPF Globally 

As of cPanel & WHM version 62, the system provisions SPF and DKIM for new accounts by default. However, the system does not automatically provision these DNS records for existing accounts. When you enable this feature, the system will create SPF and DKIM DNS records for all accounts and domains. If a domain currently possesses an SPF record, the system will append the appropriate IP address from the /var/cpanel/mainip file to the existing record. However, the system will not modify existing DKIM records.

Do not edit any nameserver configuration files during this process.

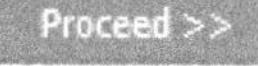

The system will not modify any existing DKIM records if it detects them. For SPF records, it will append the account's IP address (whether it is shared or dedicated) to the existing SPF record, if one is detected.

21.8 Nameserver Record Report

For VPS/Dedicated Servers

The information in this section applies to VPS and dedicated servers.

This is a report that cPanel will generate nightly or when you transfer in an account from another server. This information does **not** always reflect the status of your server's functional and in-use nameservers or domains. This report returns information based on the server's local DNS zones, as well as localhost lookups of those records.

This report will help you fix domains that might potentially be having any DNS issues as well as making sure they point to the proper nameservers. For example, if a domain is using external DNS, you will see the nameserver listed here. If you click on **Edit Zones**, you will be taken to the DNS Zone Manager where you can then update the domain's record to point to the proper nameservers.

21.9 Park a Domain

The Park a Domain interface will allow you to park a domain on top of an existing domain for an account (i.e. create an alias domain). From the first column, you will select the domain where you want to have the new domain parked.

In the second column, type in the domain name you want to park on top of the selected domain. Click on **Submit** to park the domain.

 **Park a Domain**

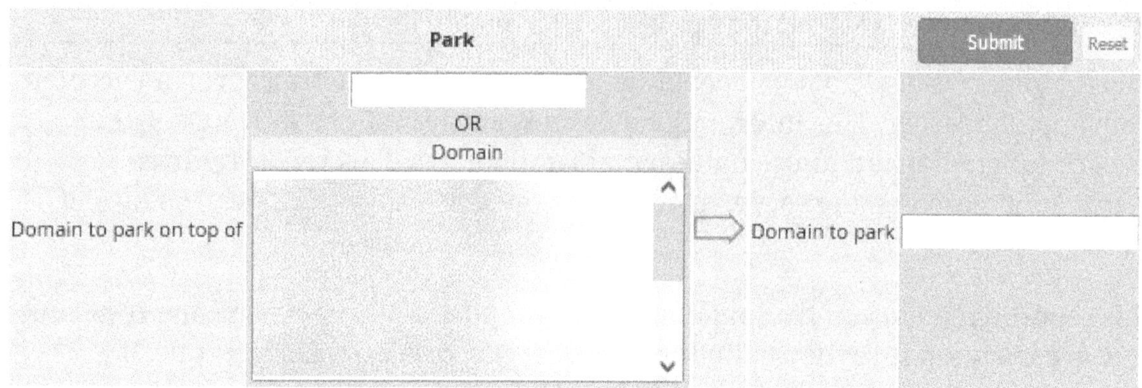

This interface will bypass some restrictions that are typically in place on the frontend cPanel interface for users. These bypassed restrictions are:

- WHM will **not** enforce that the domain name being parked is actually registered.
- WHM will **not** enforce that the domain name have its nameservers updated to point to the cPanel server.

Keep these restrictions in mind to make sure users aren't asking you to park domains they have no right to use.

21.10 Perform a DNS Cleanup

For VPS/Dedicated Servers
The information in this section applies to VPS and dedicated servers.

This feature will allow you to clean up duplicated DNS records on your system.

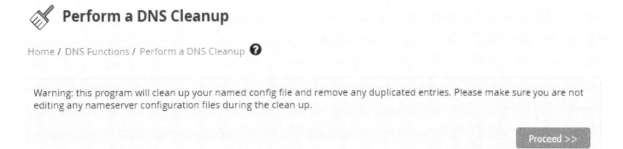

 **Perform a DNS Cleanup**

Home / DNS Functions / Perform a DNS Cleanup 

Warning: this program will clean up your named config file and remove any duplicated entries. Please make sure you are not editing any nameserver configuration files during the clean up.

Proceed >>

Before you click on **Proceed**, you need to keep the following in mind:

- Do **not** modify nameserver configuration files while this process runs.
- **Only** run this process (or the `/usr/local/cpanel/scripts/cleandns` script) on servers that use BIND or PowerDNS nameservers. Do not run this process on servers that use any other nameserver.

When the cleanup is done running, you will see a summary of the number of cleaned zones.

21.11 Set Zone Time to Live (TTL)

This interface will allow you to set the value for TTL in one or more selected DNS Zones. The TTL specifies how long a DNS server caches a record before it requests an update from the authoritative nameserver, measured in seconds.

The value that you enter must be a positive integer. Negative numbers are not permitted. The default TTL is 14,400 seconds.

If you have a DNS cluster setup and you do not want to synchronize the TTL across the DNS cluster, check the **Do Not Sync Changes...** box. Finally, click **Set TTLs** to update all records to the specified TTL.

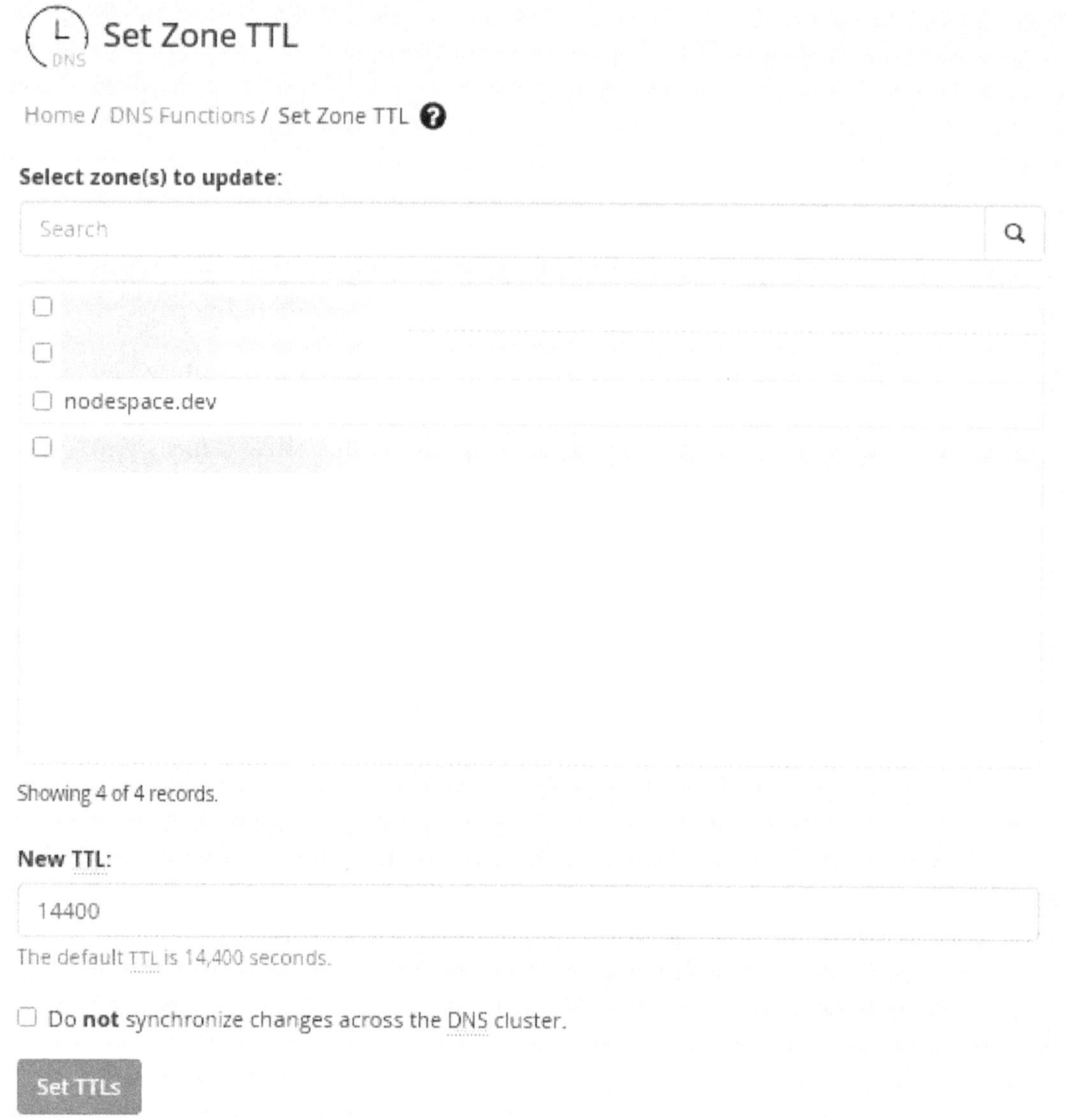

21.12 Setup/Edit Domain Forwarding

For VPS/Dedicated Servers

The information in this section applies to VPS and dedicated servers.

This is meant to be a temporary measure, for example redirecting a domain during website maintenance.

This feature also requires that you have multiple IP addresses on your system. **Due to IP address shortages, in most cases you will not be able to use this feature as most server providers are only offering a single IPv4 address with servers now.**

For permanent domain forwarding, please reference Park a Domain.

To set up a domain forwarder, start by clicking "**Click to Create**." Next, click "**Setup Forwards**." In the Domain column, enter the domain whose visitors you want to redirect. Then, in the Redirection URL column, enter the domain or subdomain to which you wish to redirect these visitors. Finally, click "**Save Map**." A confirmation message will appear, indicating that the setup is complete.

To disable domain forwarding, click on **Click to remove domain forwarder**.

21.13 Synchronize DNS Records

For VPS/Dedicated Servers
The information in this section applies to VPS and dedicated servers.

This interface will allow you to synchronize DNS Zones across servers in your DNS cluster. This helps prevent invalid or old data from being sent. There are several synchronization methods available to you.

- **Synchronize one zone to this server.** When this is selected, only one zone will be compared with the same zone on all servers. The newest one will be copied to this server.
- **Synchronize all zones to this server only (optional: Synchronize zones that are not configured on this server).** All zones will be compared with the same zones on all servers in the cluster and the newest ones will be copied to this server.
- **Synchronize one zone to all servers.** When this is selected, only one zone will be compared with the same zone on all servers. The newest one will be copied to all servers in the cluster.
- **Synchronize all zones to all servers (optional: Synchronize zones that are not configured on this server).** All zones will be compared with the same zones on all servers in the cluster and the newest ones will be copied to all servers in the cluster.

Click on **Synchronize** to start the task.

Synchronize DNS Records

Home / DNS Functions / Synchronize DNS Records

Synchronizing DNS Zones ensures all servers in the cluster use the latest version of each DNS Zone. This prevents invalid or old data being sent in response to DNS queries.

Choose synchronization method

○ **Synchronize one zone to this server only**

(e.g. example.com)

One zone will be compared with the same zone on all servers in the cluster and the newest one will be copied to this server only.

○ **Synchronize all zones to this server only**

☐ **Synchronize zones that are not configured on this server**

All zones will be compared with the same zones on all servers in the cluster and the newest ones will be copied to this server only.

○ **Synchronize one zone to all servers**

(e.g. example.com)

One zone will be compared with the same zone on all servers in the cluster and the newest one will be copied to all servers in the cluster.

◉ **Synchronize all zones to all servers**

☐ **Synchronize zones that are not configured on this server**

All zones will be compared with the same zones on all servers in the cluster and the newest ones will be copied to all servers in the cluster.

Synchronize

22 Database Services

Since cPanel installs a LAMP stack, the Database Services tools will allow you to interact with the installed database server. By default, this has been MySQL but cPanel is starting to support MariaDB as an option. As MySQL and MariaDB are compatible with each other, the tools in this section will work with both MySQL and MariaDB, depending on which one is installed on your server.

22.1 Change Database root Password

For VPS/Dedicated Servers
The information in this section applies to VPS and dedicated servers.

This interface will allow you to change the database root user password. By default, when the database was installed, cPanel automatically chose a very secure password. This root password is different from your server's root password and generally doesn't need to be changed. However, if you do find that you need to change it, you need to update it from this interface as cPanel needs to know about the root password to perform maintenance.

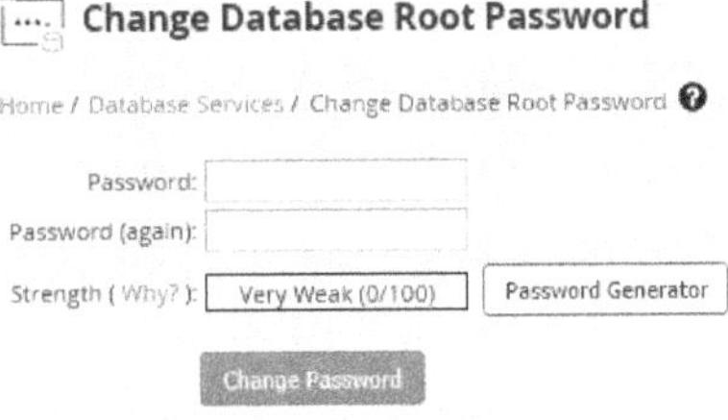

Note: By default, the database root password is set to a random string. You should set this to something that is very hard to guess. You do not need to remember this password unless you plan to connect manually to the database server as the root user.

If you do change this password, make sure you set it to something *very* secure that is difficult to guess. You do not need to save this password unless you plan to manually connect to the database server as the root user.

22.2 Change Database User Password

This tool will allow you to select a database user on the system and then change its password.

Change Database User Password

Home / Database Services / Change Database User Password

Database User: nodespace_ce
Password:
Password (again):
Strength (Why?): Very Weak (0/100) Password Generator

Change Password

Use caution when changing a database user's password. By doing so, you may break a client or customer's application or website.

22.3 Database Map Tool

For VPS/Dedicated Servers

The information in this section applies to VPS and dedicated servers.

This feature allows server administrators to grant ownership of database objects (databases and database users) to a cPanel user. The cPanel user who owns a database can access and manage it through the cPanel interface. You can only use this feature to grant ownership of databases that no cPanel account currently owns. You cannot use it to transfer ownership of a database between two cPanel accounts.

From the Account Selection menus, select either the domain or username of the cPanel user who will own the database objects that you specify. You can also use the Account Search By text boxes to search the list by domain or username. Click **Select**. The Update Database Map interface will appear.

In the **Database users** text box, enter a comma-separated list of database users that you wish for the cPanel user to own. In the **Database names** text box, enter a comma-separated list of databases that you wish for the cPanel user to own. Click **Submit**.

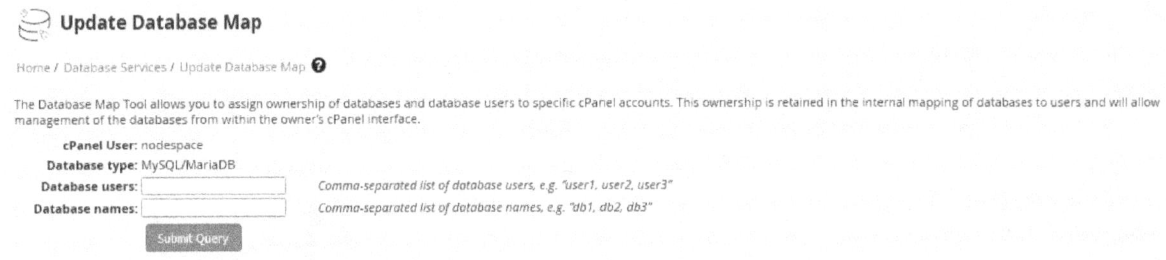

Update Database Map
Home / Database Services / Update Database Map
The Database Map Tool allows you to assign ownership of databases and database users to specific cPanel accounts. This ownership is retained in the internal mapping of databases to users and will allow management of the databases from within the owner's cPanel interface.
cPanel User: nodespace
Database type: MySQL/MariaDB
Database users:
Comma-separated list of database users, e.g. "user1, user2, user3"
Database names:
Comma-separated list of database names, e.g. "db1, db2, db3"
Submit Query

22.4 Edit Database Configuration

For VPS/Dedicated Servers

The information in this section applies to VPS and dedicated servers.

This is a user-friendly interface that allows you to make changes to MySQL or MariaDB configuration.

When you specify sizes in this interface, you can use the following units:

- K – Kilobytes
- M – Megabytes
- G – Gigabytes
- P – Petabytes
- E -Exabytes

If no file size unit is provided, the system will default to bytes.

When you make changes to the configuration using this interface, the database server will restart automatically.

22.4.1Database Optimization

This interface suggests optimized database values for you based on your MySQL or MariaDB usage. You can also manually apply the suggested optimizations to individual settings. These optimizations are general suggestions and may not result in increased database performance for all use cases.

OPTIMIZE DATABASE

Want to improve your database's performance? Click the optimize icon next to a setting to see a custom recommendation.

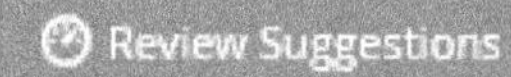

Click on **Review Suggestions** to see what WHM suggests.

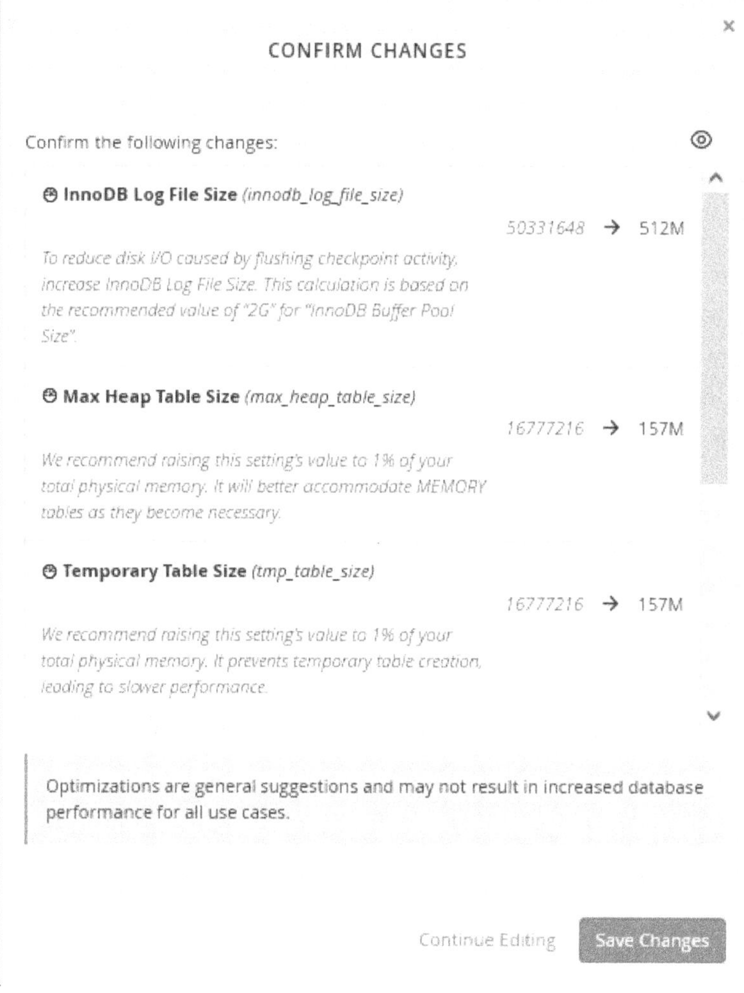

If you want to use the suggestions, click on **Save Changes**.

22.4.2 Configuration Settings

Setting	Description
General Logging	This setting enables or disables the general query log. The query log contains information for data processed by the MySQL server. This setting is available in MySQL and MariaDB.
General Log File	This setting allows you to specify a custom name for the general log file. This setting is available in MySQL and MariaDB.
InnoDB Buffer Pool Chunk Size	This setting defines the size of the buffer that InnoDB uses to write to the log files on disk. This setting is available in MySQL and MariaDB. Note: MariaDB **only** supports this setting on versions 10.2 and later.
InnoDB Buffer Pool Instances	This setting specifies the number of InnoDB buffer pool instances. InnoDB Buffer Pool Instances help reduce contention and improve concurrency. This setting is available in MySQL and MariaDB. Note: • This setting **only** takes effect when setting the InnoDB buffer pool size to 1GB or more. • MariaDB deprecated this setting in version 10.5. • MariaDB removed this setting in version 10.6.
InnoDB Buffer Pool Size	This setting defines the InnoDB buffer pool size. The InnoDB buffer pool is the memory area where InnoDB caches table and index data. This setting is available in MySQL and MariaDB.
InnoDB Log Buffer Size	This setting allows you to specify the InnoDB log buffer size. The InnoDB log buffer holds data in memory before

Setting	Description
	the system writes it to the log files. This setting is available in MySQL and MariaDB.
InnoDB Log File Size	The InnoDB log file defines the size of each log file. This setting is available in MySQL and MariaDB.
InnoDB Sort Buffer Size	This setting defines the size of the InnoDB sort buffer. The InnoDB sort buffer sets the following values: • The sort buffer size for online DDL operations that create or rebuild secondary indexes. • The length of the temporary log file when recording concurrent DML. • The size of the temporary log file read buffer and write buffer. This setting is available in MySQL and MariaDB.
Interactive Timeout	This setting allows you to specify the number of seconds the server waits for an idle connection before closing it. This setting is available in MySQL and MariaDB.
Join Buffer Size	This setting defines the minimum size of the buffer for plain index scans, range index scans, and joins that perform full table scans. This setting is available in MySQL and MariaDB.
Key Buffer Size	The key buffer size is the size of the buffer used for index blocks. The key buffer is also known as the key cache. The key buffer holds the index blocks used by MyISAM tables. This setting is available in MySQL and MariaDB.
Error Log File Name	This setting allows you to specify the name of the Error Log. This setting is available in MySQL and MariaDB.
Error Log Verbosity	This setting allows you to specify the level of verbosity in the error log. Note:

Setting	Description
	This setting is **only** available on MySQL version 5.7 or later. This setting is not available on MariaDB.
Log Warnings	This setting allows you to specify which additional warnings are logged. Larger numbers increase verbosity. This setting is available in MySQL and MariaDB.
Log Output	This setting allows you to specify the format of the general log and slow query log output. More than one setting can be active. This setting is available in MySQL and MariaDB.
Long Query Time	This setting specifies the maximum number of seconds a query can run before it is logged to the slow query log file. This setting is available in MySQL and MariaDB. Note: This setting accepts decimal values and has microsecond precision.
Max Allowed Packet	This setting allows you to specify the maximum size of one packet or any generated/intermediate string. This setting is available in MySQL and MariaDB.
Max Connect Errors	This setting allows you to specify the number of failed connection attempts before the server blocks the connection. This setting is available in MySQL and MariaDB. Note: This setting does not protect against brute force attempts.
Max Connections	This setting allows you to specify the maximum number of concurrent `client` connections. This setting is available in MySQL and MariaDB.
Max Heap Table Size	This setting allows you to specify the maximum size to which user-created `MEMORY` tables are permitted to grow. This setting is available in MySQL and MariaDB.
Open Files Limit	This setting allows you to specify the maximum number of `file descriptors` available for use. This setting is available in MySQL and MariaDB.

Setting	Description
Performance Schema	The Performance Schema is a tool to help a database administrator do performance tuning. This setting is available in MySQL and MariaDB. Note: All MySQL Performance Schema settings also work in MariaDB.
Query Cache Size	This setting allows you to specify the amount of memory reserved for caching query results. This setting is available in MySQL and MariaDB. Note: MySQL deprecated this setting in version 5.7.
Query Cache Type	This setting determines query cache behavior for all clients that connect to the server. This setting is available in MySQL and MariaDB.
Read Buffer Size	This setting does the following: • Each `thread` that does a sequential scan for a `MyISAM` table allocates a buffer of this size for each table it scans. • Determines the memory block size for `MEMORY` tables. This setting is available in MySQL and MariaDB.
Read Random Buffer Size	This setting allows you to specify the size of the read random buffer. The read random buffer reads rows from the `MyISAM` table in sorted order after a key sort. This setting is available in MySQL and MariaDB.
Slow Query Log **Note:** **In MariaDB version 10.11 and later, this**	This setting allows you to enable or disable the slow query log. Enable the slow query log to find queries that take a long time to execute. The slow query log consists of the following:

Setting	Description
setting is ***Log Slow Queries.***	• SQL statements that take more than the specified `long query time` seconds to execute. • Queries that examine fewer than the `min_examined_row_limit` value. This setting is available in MySQL and MariaDB.
Slow Query Log File Name	This setting allows you to specify the name or full path of the slow query log file.
Sort Buffer Size	This setting defines the following: • The sort buffer size for `online DDL` operations that create or rebuild secondary indexes. • The amount by which the temporary log file is extended when recording concurrent DML during an online DDL operation, and the size of the temporary log file read buffer and write buffer. For more information about sort buffer size, read the MySQL or MariaDB documentation.
SQL Mode	MySQL and MariaDB can apply different SQL Modes depending on the value of this setting.
Thread Cache Size	This setting allows you to specify the number of `threads` the server stores in a `cache` to use. This setting is available in MySQL and MariaDB
Temporary Table Size	This setting allows you to specify the size of internal, in-memory, temporary tables. The temporary table size does not apply to user-created `MEMORY` tables. This setting is available in MySQL and MariaDB. Note:The value of `Max Heap Table Size` will override this setting if it is a smaller value.

Setting	Description
Wait Timeout	This setting allows you to specify the maximum number of seconds the server waits on an idle connection before closing it. This setting is available in MySQL and MariaDB

Table Source: https://docs.cpanel.net/whm/database-services/edit-database-configuration/#configuration-settings-for-mysql-and-mariadb

22.5 Manage Database Access Hosts

For VPS/Dedicated Servers
The information in this section applies to VPS and dedicated servers.

This interface allows you to permit remote hosts (or servers) to access databases on your server or to access are mote database server that you configured via the Manage Database Profiles interface.

In the text box, enter the hostnames of remote hosts that you want to allow access to your server's databases. You can specify these hostnames as fully qualified domain names (FQDN) or as IP addresses. When using FQDNs, ensure they are in all lowercase letters. To add these hostnames to each user's access list, you have two options: either click the link to automatically add the hostnames to each cPanel user's access list or ask your cPanel users to go to cPanel's Remote Database Access interface to add the hosts themselves.

22.6 Manage Database Profiles

For VPS/Dedicated Servers

The information in this section applies to VPS and dedicated servers.

This interface enables you to manage multiple MySQL or MariaDB profiles, each defining the connection information for either a local or remote database server. You can also designate which profile is active, determining how the root database user connects to databases and where new users and databases are created. Using a remote server can be beneficial for managing busy servers or servers with large databases, as it allows you to offload database-related tasks to a remote server.

Remote servers can include other cPanel & WHM servers running MariaDB or MySQL, dedicated MariaDB or MySQL servers, and Amazon Relational Database Service (RDS). This feature supports active connections only to servers running MySQL versions 5.6, 5.7, and 8.0, as well as MariaDB versions 10.1, 10.2, 10.3, 10.5, and 10.6. Additionally, any remote MySQL or MariaDB servers must have a `/root/.my.cnf` file containing the MySQL or MariaDB root user and password.

When you create a new MySQL database in cPanel & WHM, the server uses the active MySQL profile to determine its connection information. For example, if the active profile named user connects to host example.com, new MySQL databases will be created on the example.com server. However, this feature does not automatically transfer MySQL databases or data when you change remote servers. For instance, if you have a database named example created under the active user profile connected to example.com, this database will not automatically transfer to a new server if you switch the active profile to user2 connected to not.example.com.

To connect an existing database to new servers, you must manually copy it and update the configuration files on the target server. For example, if you move an existing WordPress database to a remote server, you need to manually copy the database to the remote server and then update the WordPress configuration files to use the new remote server.

22.7 Manage Database Users

This interface allows server administrators to retrieve a list of database users, each user's database, and which account owns each database user. The server administrator can use this interface to rename database users.

Use caution when changing a database user's username. You may break a client or customer's application or website by doing so.

22.8 Manage Databases

This interface allows you to view the cPanel-managed databases on your server, including each database's engine and the user who owns each database. Additionally, you can use this interface to rename databases. The maximum length for a database name is 64 characters. However, because of the way cPanel & WHM stores MySQL database names, each underscore character counts as two characters toward this limit. If you enable database prefixing, the maximum length for the database name is 63 characters, including the database prefix and the underscore character, with each additional underscore requiring another two characters.

Renaming a MySQL database can be risky, so it is strongly recommended to create a backup of any MySQL database you intend to rename. The renaming process will terminate all active connections to the database, and you will need to manually update configuration files and applications to use the new database name. Larger and more complex databases will require additional time to rename.

MySQL does not allow direct renaming of a database. Instead, when cPanel & WHM "renames" a database, the system performs the following steps: first, it creates a new database; then, it moves data from the old database to the new one; next, it recreates grants and stored code in the new database; and finally, it deletes the old database and its grants.

There are warnings to consider:

- If any of the first three steps fail, the system will return an error and attempt to restore the database's original state. If the restoration process fails, the API function's error response will describe these additional failures.

- In rare cases, the system may successfully create the new database but fail to delete the old database or grants. In such cases, the rename action is treated as a success, but the API function will return warnings about the failure to delete the old database or grants.

22.9 phpMyAdmin

phpMyAdmin is a tool that allows you to manage databases through a web interface. When you click on **phpMyAdmin**, WHM will launch a new tab that will load phpMyAdmin. Please see https://www.phpmyadmin.org for more information on how to use it.

22.10 Repair Databases

This interface allows you to attempt to repair database tables that may have become corrupt. To repair a database, select the desired database from the Users list and click "**Repair Database**."

22.11 Show Database Processes

For VPS/Dedicated Servers
The information in this section applies to VPS and dedicated servers.

This interface lists all of the processes that currently run on any database on your server.

22.12 Upgrade Database Version

For VPS/Dedicated Servers
The information in this section applies to VPS and dedicated servers.

Upgrade Database Version (Step 1 of 5)

Home / Database Services / Upgrade Database Version

This interface allows you to upgrade your database server to a newer version. This interface will automatically upgrade your database installation to newer point releases (the third number in the version string) because these upgrades involve little risk to your users' data. Upgrades to new major releases (the first two numbers in the version string) are more involved because there is a substantial risk of data loss. This interface attempts to walk you through the major release upgrade process.

Information

Although in-place upgrades are generally safe, you should always perform a full database backup before you begin the upgrade process.

Please note that downgrades to previous versions are unsupported. After you upgrade your system to a newer version, it may be impossible to switch back.

Current Version

MySQL 8.0.37

Select a Version

	Version	Release Date	End of Life Date
◉	**MySQL 8.0** Recommended Installed Features: • Roles exist now for easier user management. • Support for MySQL Server Components. • Spatial Data support. • Release Notes	April 19, 2018	April 1, 2026

Continue

This interface allows root users or resellers with root-level privileges to manage MySQL or MariaDB version upgrades, such as upgrading from MySQL 5.7 to 8.0. After selecting your server's MySQL or MariaDB version, WHM will automatically keep your database engine up-to-date by applying vendor-released patches to your installation.

Before upgrading your database, version or switching from MySQL to MariaDB, it is crucial to back up your server's databases.

There are several limitations to consider when upgrading or installing MySQL or MariaDB:

- MariaDB is considered an upgrade from MySQL. Once you switch to MariaDB, reverting to MySQL is not possible.
- The MySQL sha256_password plugin is not supported for MySQL 5.7, MySQL 8, MariaDB 10.2, or MariaDB 10.3.

- This feature does not support downgrading database engine versions. It is strongly advised against attempting to downgrade MySQL or MariaDB.

If CloudLinux's MySQL Governor is installed on your server, MySQL upgrades will not work through this interface. Refer to CloudLinux's MySQL Governor documentation to understand the implications of removing MySQL Governor.

Important warnings include:

- Upgrading from MySQL 8 to MariaDB 10.x is not possible due to incompatibilities between these versions. Consult MariaDB's documentation for more information.
- During the cPanel & WHM installation process, system administrators can choose either MySQL or MariaDB. For more details, refer to the Installation Guide.

To upgrade or reinstall your server's version of MySQL or MariaDB, follow these steps:

1. Select the version of MySQL or MariaDB you wish to upgrade or reinstall.
2. Click **Continue**. The interface will present warning messages and validate the `/etc/my.cnf` file.
3. Check each warning box to acknowledge your awareness of the potential upgrade consequences.
4. Click **Continue**.
5. Choose the type of upgrade you want to perform:
    - Unattended Upgrade: Automatically upgrades MySQL or MariaDB.

- Interactive Upgrade: Guides you through the upgrade process step-by-step.

6. Click **Continue** to proceed to the upgrade process interface. You can toggle the Autoscroll output checkbox to change whether the output display scrolls as the upgrade runs. If you chose the Interactive Upgrade type, the interface will prompt you through each step and may provide additional instructions to complete before continuing.

7. After the upgrade completes, the interface will display a message indicating whether the upgrade succeeded or if there are errors that need to be addressed.

23 IP Functions

For VPS/Dedicated Servers

The information in this section applies to VPS and dedicated servers.

The IP functions tools will allow you to manage some of the networking on your server. Such tools will allow you to manage IPv6 and IPv4.

Note

IPv6 support on cPanel is still new and is being developed as IPv4 is deemed "legacy" and is slowly deprecated.

Warning!

Due to networking requirements, you **cannot** run an IPv6-only cPanel & WHM server. You **must** have at least one IPv4 address.

23.1 IPv6 Ranges

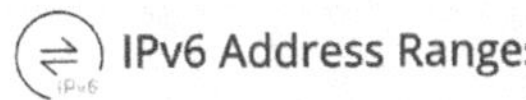

Home / IP Functions / IPv6 Ranges

This feature allows you to add, edit, and delete an IPv6 address range. An IPv6 address range is a group of several IPv6 addresses and uses the following format:

- The range should be a shortened IPv6 address that ends with a slash (/), followed by a number which indicates the network portion of the IPv6 address range.
- The most common network portion will be /64. The network portion might be as low as /48, or as high as /128, which would be a single IPv6 address.
- For example: 2001:db8:1a34:56cf::/64

When you assign an IPv6 address to a user, you will choose a range that you added here.

Add Range Cancel

IP Range Details	Actions
There are currently no ranges.	

This interface allows you to add or remove an IPv6 address range from the server. You must add at least one IPv6 address range before assigning dedicated IPv6 addresses to a user in WHM's Assign IPv6 Address interface. An IPv6 address range cannot include the server's shared IP address, and the system will not allow a shared IP address to be set within any configured IPv6 address range.

Before using this interface, ensure that IPv6 is functioning properly on your server.

The `cpsrvd` daemon must listen on IPv6 addresses for IPv6 to work on a cPanel & WHM server. To enable this, set the "**Listen on IPv6 Addresses**" option to "On" in the System section of WHM's Tweak Settings interface.

23.1.1 Add an IPv6 Range

To add a range of IPv6 addresses, follow these steps:

1. Click "**Add Range**."
2. Enter a name for the IPv6 address range in the "Range Name" text box. The name must be 64 characters or fewer.
3. Enter the IPv6 address range in the "Range" text box. An IPv6 address range consists of a shortened IPv6 address, followed by a slash (/) and a number indicating the network portion of the IPv6 address range. For example: **`2001:0db8:1a34:56cf::/64`**.

Important

Do not add an IPv6 address range that includes the main IPv6 address set in WHM's Basic WebHost Manager Setup interface.

You must add your gateway individually before adding the full gateway range and set the gateway to RESERVED so that the system does not assign this IP address to an account. For example:

`2001:0db8:1a34:56cf::/128 RESERVED`

`2001:0db8:1a34:56cf::1/128 RESERVED`

4. Select one of the following range types from the "Range Type" menu:
   Available: You can distribute the addresses in this range to users on your server.
   Reserved: You cannot distribute the addresses in this range to users on your server. If you select Reserved, WHM's Assign IPv6 Address interface will not list the range.
5. Enter a description of the IPv6 address range in the "Range Notes" text box, which must be 256 characters or fewer. Click "**Add Range**" to add the IPv6 address range or click "**Cancel**" to close the form.

23.2 Add a New IP Address

Add a New IP Address

Home / IP Functions / Add a New IP Address

Please contact your hosting or network provider for an IP address or range of IP addresses. They can also provide you with a subnet mask for the address or addresses.

You may add one or more new IP addresses to the system below. To add multiple IP addresses, use one of the following IP range formats:

- Class C CIDR (e.g. 192.168.4.0/25).
- IP Address Range (e.g. 192.168.4.128-255)

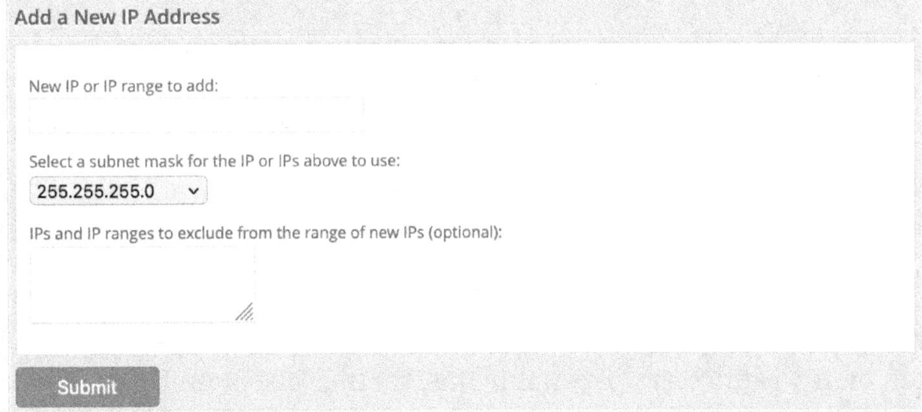

This interface allows you to add IP addresses to your IP address pool, which can be used when assigning a static IP address to a new account.

To add one or more IP addresses in the "Add a New IP Address" table, follow these steps:

1. Enter the IP address or addresses in the "New IP or IP range to add" text box. If you are in 1:1 NAT Mode, enter the local IP address, not the public IP address. If the "New IP and IP range to add" value uses Class C CIDR format, you must use a mask range between 24 and 30.
2. Enter the subnet mask in the "Select a subnet mask for the IP or IPs above to use" text box. Note that an incorrect subnet mask may cause networking issues for your server or other servers on your network. If you do not know the

correct subnet mask for this IP address or IP address range, consult your hosting or networking provider.
3. Enter any IP addresses to exclude in the "IPs and IP ranges to exclude from the range of new IPs" text box.
4. Click "**Submit**" to add the IP address or addresses.

When you add an IP address, the system attempts to add an alias of that IP address to the main network interface. This process rebuilds the IP address pool, which resides in the `/etc/ipaddrpool` file. The system stores IP addresses in the `/etc/ips` file, and the `ipaliases` service activates these IP addresses when the server starts.

23.3 Assign IPv6 Address

Before using this interface to assign dedicated IPv6 addresses, you need to ensure the following:

- Enable IPv6 on the server and use WHM's IPv6 Ranges interface to add IPv6 ranges. If no IPv6 ranges have been added to the server, a message indicating "No IPv6 ranges have been added" will be displayed.
- For IPv6 to function properly on a cPanel & WHM server, the cpsrvd daemon must listen on IPv6 addresses. To enable this, set the "Listen on IPv6 Addresses" option to "On" in the System section of WHM's Tweak Settings interface.

To assign a shared IPv6 address to one or more users, configure a shared IPv6 address in WHM's Basic WebHost Manager Setup interface. Do not assign a shared IPv6 address within an IPv6 range, as the system will block any such addresses.

Using this interface to assign IPv6 ranges will erase any IPv6 addresses previously assigned to the selected users via other methods.

If a warning appears indicating that "Apache must be recompiled" or "Apache should be recompiled" at the top of this interface, recompile using EasyApache 4.

To assign an IPv6 address to the selected account, follow these steps:

1. Select the desired IPv6 address range from the "Enable this account with an IPv6 address from the selected range" menu. Ensure the selected range includes available addresses. To assign the server's shared IPv6 address to an account, select "The server's shared IPv6 address." This address will function as a shared, rather than dedicated, address. Note that your server may use a Stateless Autoconfigured Address (SLAAC) determined by your MAC address, which changes if your hardware changes. For instance, replacing your ethernet card will result in a new IPv6 address, causing the old address's VirtualHosts to use the incorrect IPv6 address.

2. Click "**Enable Account**." When you enable IPv6 on an account, the system binds that IPv6 address to your server and adds a AAAA record for the DNS zone on the domains owned by the account. An enabled account retains its IPv6 address information even if you enable it again with a different IPv6 address range.

23.4 Configure Remote Service IPs

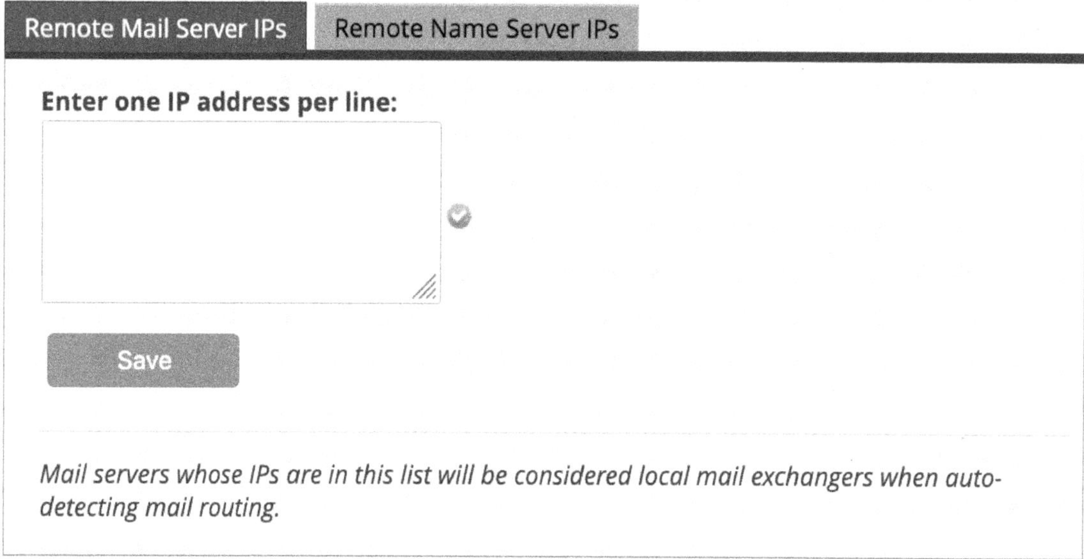

This interface allows you to specify remote mail server and nameserver IP addresses that the system will then consider as local addresses.

23.5 Remote mail server IP addresses

This feature allows you to specify the IP addresses of remote services that handle mail for one or more domains. For example, you can use this feature to specify the address of a third-party spam filter service.

The system stores these entries in the `/etc/ips.remotemail` file as a line-separated list.

23.5.1 Add mail server IP addresses

To add remote mail server IP addresses, follow these steps:

1. Click the "**Remote Mail Server IPs**" tab.
2. Enter the IP addresses you want to add in the provided text box, with one address per line.
3. Click "**Save**."

To remove remote mail server IP addresses, delete the entries you no longer want to use from the text box.

23.5.2 Remote nameserver IP addresses

This feature allows you to specify the IP addresses of remote nameservers used by your system. For example, you can use this feature to enable users to create remote parked or addon domains by specifying the nameservers' IP addresses. It is only necessary to add one of the nameservers for the domain, not all of them. Note that if you add the IP address of the domain itself (different from the nameserver's IP address), the system will not authorize that domain.

The system stores these entries in the `/etc/ips.remotedns` file as a line-separated list. If you use remotely clustered DNS nameservers, you must manually add the IP addresses.

23.5.3 Add remote nameserver IP addresses

To add remote nameserver IP addresses, follow these steps:

1. Click the "**Remote Name Server IPs**" tab.
2. Enter the IP addresses you want to add in the provided text box, with one address per line.
3. Click "**Save**."

To remove remote nameserver IP addresses, delete the entries you no longer want to use from the text box.

23.5.4The Allow Remote Domains option

To allow users to create remote parked or addon domains while overriding the nameservers listed in the Configure Remote Service IPs interface, enable the "Allow Remote Domains" option in WHM's Tweak Settings interface.

Warning: For security reasons, it is strongly recommended not to enable this option. If you do enable it, you must also enable the "Prevent cPanel users from creating specific domains" option in WHM's Tweak Settings interface.

23.6 IP Migration Wizard

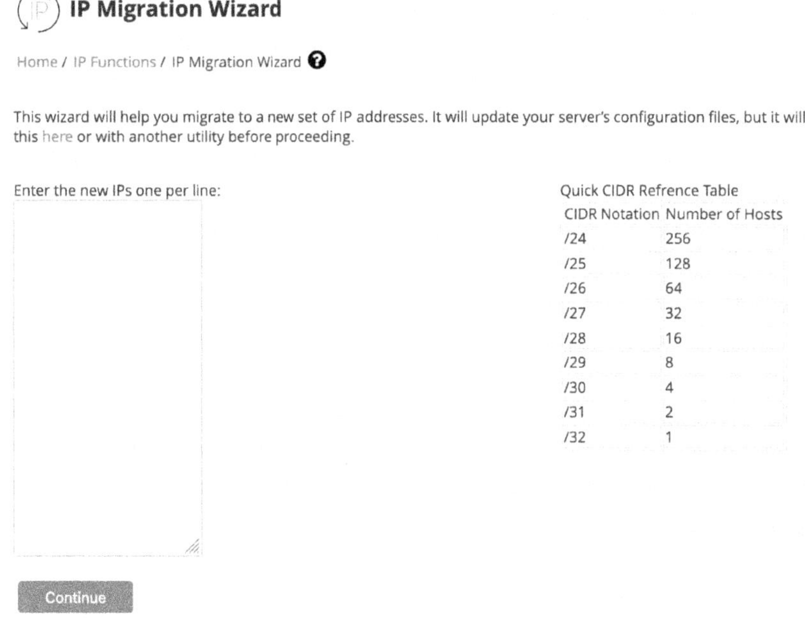

IP Migration Wizard
Home / IP Functions / IP Migration Wizard
This wizard will help you migrate to a new set of IP addresses. It will update your server's configuration files, but it will not bind the new IP addresses. You will need to do this here or with another utility before proceeding.
Enter the new IPs one per line:
Quick CIDR Refrence Table
CIDR Notation Number of Hosts
/24 256
/25 128
/26 64
/27 32
/28 16
/29 8
/30 4
/31 2
/32 1
Continue
Notes: When adding multiple IP addresses, you must use Class C CIDR format or 192.168.0.1-254 format.
Valid examples: 192.168.4.128/25, 192.168.3.5-10, 192.168.99.55-230

The IP Migration Wizard helps you change the IP addresses of the cPanel accounts hosted on your server. It can also be used to change your server's primary IP address, which is particularly useful if you move your server to a different subnet or datacenter.

To change the IP addresses of multiple accounts, follow these steps:

23.6.1 Step 1: Enter the new IP addresses

1. Enter new IP addresses in the text box, with each address on a separate line. You can use CIDR notation to enter multiple IP addresses, such as `192.168.0.20/25`.
2. Click **Continue** to proceed to Step 2.

23.6.2 Step 2: Confirm the translation

1. Review all information in the interface to ensure its accuracy.
   - The wizard assigns a new IP address for each current IP address on the server.
   - If you enter more new IP addresses than currently exist, the system discards the extra addresses.
   - If you enter fewer new IP addresses, the system assigns all available new IP addresses and displays an editable text box for accounts needing a new IP address. If left blank, those accounts retain their old IP addresses.
2. Click **Continue** to proceed to Step 3.

23.6.3 Step 3: Download the translation matrix

1. To view a list of each domain's administrator username, old IP address, and new IP address, right-click **Click Here to Download an IP Translation Matrix** and select **Save Link As**.
2. Click **Continue** to proceed to Step 4.

23.6.4 Step 4: Convert the configuration files

In this step, the system updates the Apache configuration file, the FTP server configuration file, and cPanel internal data files. The Apache configuration file will include both old and new IP addresses for each virtual host, allowing visitors to access the website through both updated DNS records and the old, cached IP address.

Click **Continue** to proceed to Step 5.

23.6.5 Step 5: DNS Migration

This step updates the DNS zone files and automatically takes you to the next interface. Watch for any error messages during this step.

23.6.6 Step 6: Wait 48 hours

Log out of WHM and wait 48 hours for DNS records to propagate. After 48 hours, navigate to WHM's IP Migration Wizard interface (Home » IP Functions » IP Migration Wizard) and click **Click Here to proceed to Step 7**.

23.6.7 Step 7: Additional steps to clear the old IP addresses

In this step, the wizard removes the old IP addresses from the Apache configuration file. When the process finishes, click **Click Here**. A new interface will announce that the IP address migration process is complete. To completely remove the old IP addresses, follow these steps:

23.6.7.1 Step 7a: Remove the old IP addresses from this system

Click the **Show or Delete Current IP Addresses** link to open the interface in a new window and remove the old IP addresses. Note that you can only delete IP addresses created with WHM's **Add a New IP Address** interface. IP addresses controlled by the operating system cannot be removed.

23.6.7.2 Step 7b: Update your system's startup scripts to reflect the new main IP address

Your system's startup scripts assign the IP address used as the primary network interface. The operating system determines how these scripts are configured. Run the **`ifconfig -a`** command at the command line to see your current IP address and the assigned interface.

To assign your new IP address to the primary network interface on a dedicated server, follow these steps:

1. Edit the appropriate file in the /etc/sysconfig/network-scripts/ directory to remove the old IP address and add the new one. For a dedicated server, eth0 is the most common primary network interface.
2. Restart the network with the **`/etc/init.d/network restart`** command. It is recommended to have a technician available at the server console to address any issues during the restart.
3. After restarting the network service, run the **`ifconfig`** and **`ping`** commands to verify that all IP addresses are available.

23.6.7.3 Step 7c: Change your licensed IP address

This step must be performed immediately after completing the previous step. Until this step is done, the cPanel, WHM, WebDAV, and Webmail interfaces will not be available. Websites, FTP, and email services through desktop mail clients will not be affected.

For WebPros International, LLC direct customers:

1. Log in to your cPanel Store account.
2. Under **Orders**, click **View My Licenses**. The Manage Licenses interface will appear.
3. Under **Actions**, click the pencil icon. A new interface will appear.
4. Click **Edit IP**.
5. Enter the new IP address.
6. Click **Save Changes**.

If you obtained your license elsewhere (e.g. from your hosting provider or a third-party license reseller), contact them to update your server's licensed IP address.

23.6.7.4 Step 7d: Configure WHM to use the new IP address for new accounts

After clicking **Server Setup**, WHM's Basic WebHost Manager Setup interface will open in a new window. To configure the shared IP address, follow these steps:

1. Click the **Basic Config** tab.

2. Enter the new IP address in the **The IP address (only one address) that will be used for setting up shared IP virtual hosts** text box.
3. Click **Save Changes**.

If resellers have a different main IP address, update the IP address in WHM's Reseller Center interface. To update the main IP address for a reseller, follow these steps:

1. Click **Manage Main Shared/IP-less IP**.
2. Select the reseller to modify from the menu.
3. Click **Submit**.
4. Select the desired IP address from the menu.
5. Click **Save**.

23.6.7.5 Step 7e: Ensure DNS and reverse DNS are configured properly

Your hosting provider must set the reverse DNS entries for your server. However, your new main IP address should already point back to the server's hostname. To ensure the hostname points to the new main IP address, navigate to WHM's DNS Zone Manager interface.

23.6.7.6 Step 7f: Revise custom configurations

Ensure that custom configurations in WHM do not use the old main IP address. For example, update the following customizations:

- Custom sender IP addresses for Exim in the `/etc/mailips` file.
- Custom DNS templates in WHM's Edit Zone Templates interface.

23.7 Rebuild the IP Address Pool

This feature scans the server's bound IP addresses to find any that are not linked to a domain. If the system identifies any available, unused IP addresses, it returns those addresses to the IP address pool. When new accounts are created, cPanel & WHM uses addresses from this pool.

To rebuild the IP address pool, click **Proceed**. After the scan is complete, the interface displays the number of free IP addresses in your IP address pool.

23.8 Show IP Address Usage

This feature lists how your system uses IP addresses.

23.9 Show or Delete Current IP Addresses

This feature displays the IP addresses that are bound to your server. It also allows you to delete these IP addresses from the server.

23.10 Show/Edit Reserved IPs

This feature allows you to reserve an IP address that is in your address pool. When you reserve an IP address, you cannot assign it to newly created accounts. This is useful if, for example, you do not want the system to automatically assign a specific IP address to a new account as a dedicated IP address.

24 Software

This chapter goes into details about managing the software on your server. This includes both cPanel/WHM and the Linux operating system.

24.1 Install a Perl Module

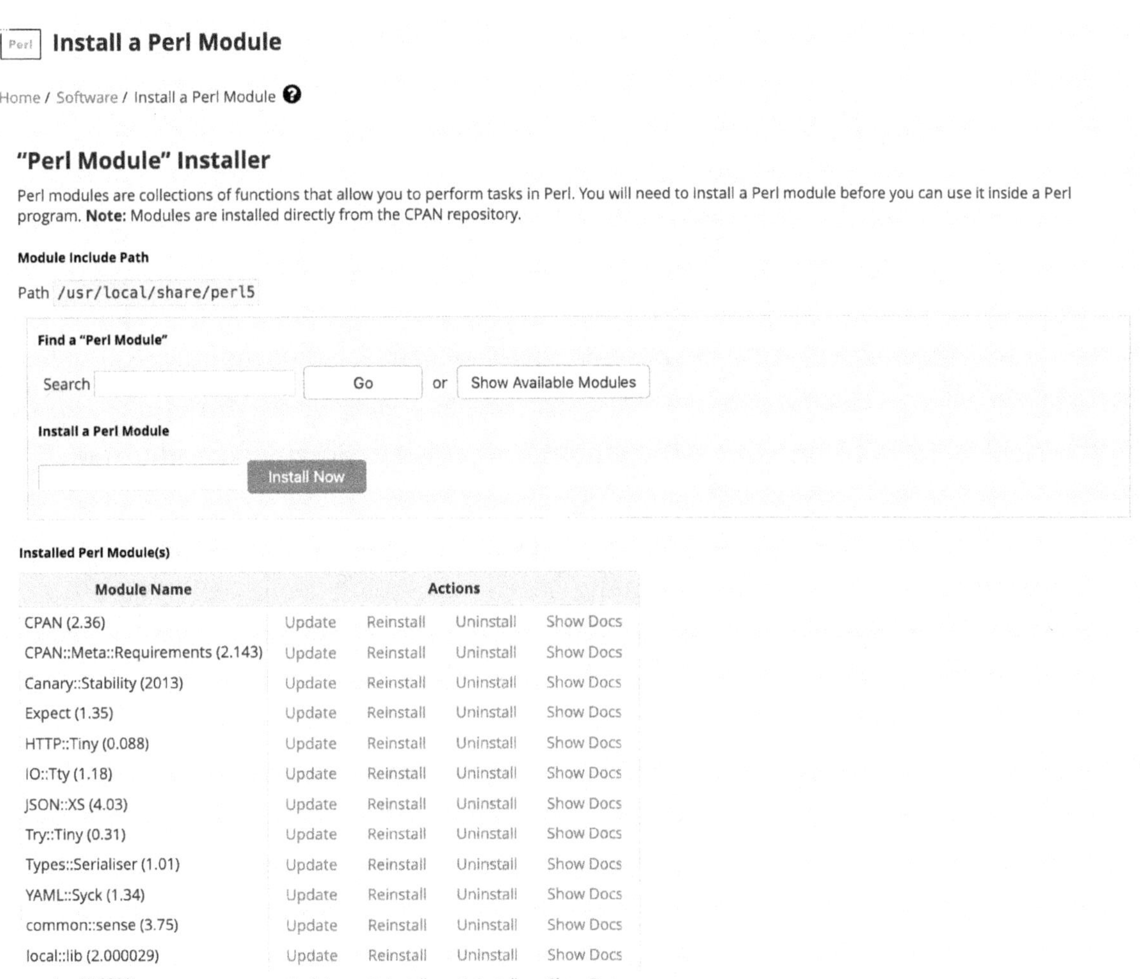

Perl **Install a Perl Module**

Home / Software / Install a Perl Module

"Perl Module" Installer

Perl modules are collections of functions that allow you to perform tasks in Perl. You will need to install a Perl module before you can use it inside a Perl program. **Note:** Modules are installed directly from the CPAN repository.

Module Include Path

Path /usr/local/share/perl5

Find a "Perl Module"

Search Go or Show Available Modules

Install a Perl Module

Install Now

Installed Perl Module(s)

Module Name	Actions			
CPAN (2.36)	Update	Reinstall	Uninstall	Show Docs
CPAN::Meta::Requirements (2.143)	Update	Reinstall	Uninstall	Show Docs
Canary::Stability (2013)	Update	Reinstall	Uninstall	Show Docs
Expect (1.35)	Update	Reinstall	Uninstall	Show Docs
HTTP::Tiny (0.088)	Update	Reinstall	Uninstall	Show Docs
IO::Tty (1.18)	Update	Reinstall	Uninstall	Show Docs
JSON::XS (4.03)	Update	Reinstall	Uninstall	Show Docs
Try::Tiny (0.31)	Update	Reinstall	Uninstall	Show Docs
Types::Serialiser (1.01)	Update	Reinstall	Uninstall	Show Docs
YAML::Syck (1.34)	Update	Reinstall	Uninstall	Show Docs
common::sense (3.75)	Update	Reinstall	Uninstall	Show Docs
local::lib (2.000029)	Update	Reinstall	Uninstall	Show Docs
version (0.9930)	Update	Reinstall	Uninstall	Show Docs

A Perl module is software written in the Perl programming language, often used in scripts. To properly integrate a Perl module into a script, you need to retrieve the module from a central repository and install it on your server.

To search for and install a Perl module, follow these steps:

1. Use one of the following methods to find the desired module:
    - Enter a search term in the available text box and click **Go**.
    - Click **Show Available Modules** to list CPAN-provided Perl modules.
2. The interface displays the following information for all displayed modules:
    - **Module Name**: The module's name and version number.
    - **Description**: A description of the module.
    - **Actions**: The actions that you may perform for that module.
3. Click the install icon next to the module you wish to download and install.
    - To view a module's documentation, click **Show Docs** for that module.
    - If you did not find the desired module, enter a new keyword in the Search text box and click **Go**.

24.2 Install Distro Packages

For VPS/Dedicated Servers
The information in this section applies to VPS and dedicated servers.

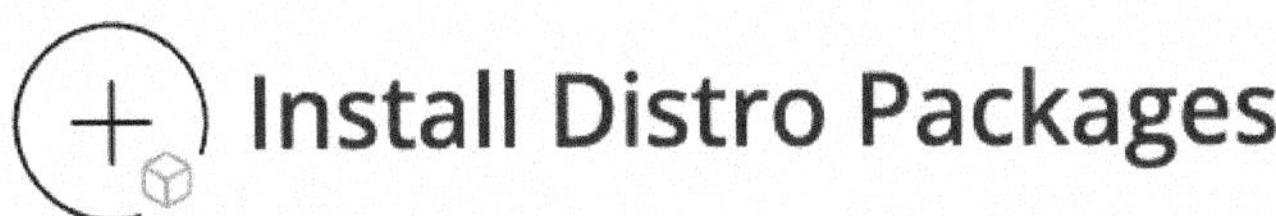

Home / Software / Install Distro Packages 

Provide a partial package name:

Search pattern | Search

Enter a search pattern for the package name you would like to install.

To install a package, follow these steps:

In the **Provide a partial package name** text box, enter the name of the package you wish to install. Click **Search**. In the search results table, click **Install** for the package you wish to install. The interface will display the installation process.

24.3 Module Installers

For VPS/Dedicated Servers

The information in this section applies to VPS and dedicated servers.

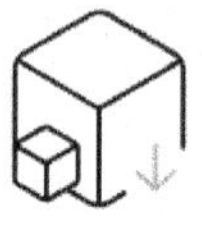

Module Installers

Home / Software / Module Installers 

The Following Language Module Installs are installed:

	Language	Actions
php	PHP Extensions and Applications Package	Manage
php	PHP PECL	Manage
	Perl Module	Manage
	Ruby Gem	Manage

This WHM feature provides access to four interfaces that you can use to find and install modules for PHP, Ruby, and Perl. You can use the modules that you install, for example, in custom scripts.

24.4 MultiPHP INI Editor

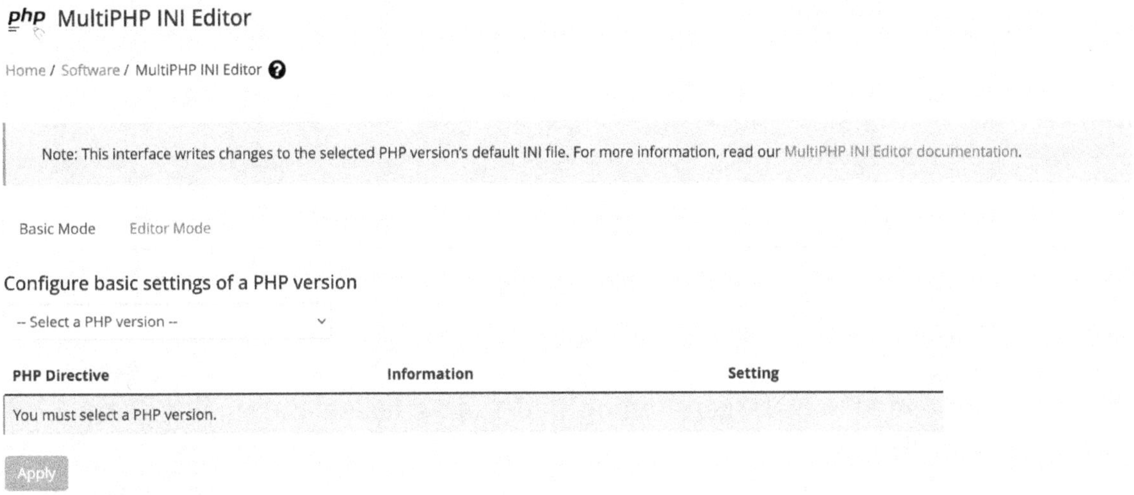

php MultiPHP INI Editor

Home / Software / MultiPHP INI Editor

Note: This interface writes changes to the selected PHP version's default INI file. For more information, read our MultiPHP INI Editor documentation.

Basic Mode Editor Mode

Configure basic settings of a PHP version

-- Select a PHP version --

PHP Directive	Information	Setting
You must select a PHP version.		

Apply

To configure your PHP settings, select the desired PHP version from the menu. This loads the directive values from the **php.ini** file for that PHP version. Adjust the settings as needed and click **Save**. The system saves these settings in the **/opt/cpanel/<your_php_package>/root/etc/php.ini** file, where **<your_php_package>** is the name of your PHP package.

Key directives include:

- **allow_url_fopen**: Enable URL-aware fopen wrappers. Default: Enabled.
- **allow_url_include**: Enable URL-aware fopen wrappers for include(), include_once(), require(), require_once(). Default: Disabled.
- **asp_tags**: Use ASP-like tags. Default: Disabled.
- **display_errors**: Display errors. Default: Disabled.
- **enable_dl**: Allow dynamic loading of PHP extensions at runtime. Default: Disabled (recommended to leave disabled due to security risks).
- **file_uploads**: Enable HTTP file uploads. Default: Disabled.
- **magic_quotes_gpc**: Automatically escape certain characters with a backslash. Default: Disabled.
- **max_execution_time**: Maximum time (in seconds) a script can run. Default: 30 seconds.

- **max_input_time**: Maximum time (in seconds) to parse input data. Default: -1.
- **max_input_vars**: Maximum number of input variables per request to prevent DoS attacks. Default: 1000.
- **memory_limit**: Maximum memory a script can allocate. Defaults based on system memory:
    - 1 GB: 32M
    - 2-4 GB: 64M
    - Over 4 GB: 128M
- **post_max_size**: Maximum size of post data, affecting file uploads. Default: 8M. Recommended to be larger than **upload_max_filesize** and smaller than **memory_limit**.
- **register_globals**: Convert GET or POST input into variables. Default: Disabled.
- **safe_mode**: Enable safe mode for security. Default: Disabled.
- **session.save_path**: Directory for storing PHP session files. Default: `/var/cpanel/php/sessions` with subdirectories for each PHP version.
- **session.gc_maxlifetime**: Maximum lifetime (in seconds) of a session file. Default: 1440 seconds (24 minutes).
- **session.gc_probability**: Not required as a cron job cleans session files. Default: 0.
- **session.gc_divisor**: Not required as a cron job cleans session files. Default: 0.
- **upload_max_filesize**: Maximum file upload size. Default: 2M.
- **zlib.output_compression**: Enable compression of pages when the browser supports gzip or deflate. Default: Disabled.

For more detailed information on each directive and additional settings, refer to the PHP-FPM documentation and other relevant resources.

24.5 MultiPHP Manager

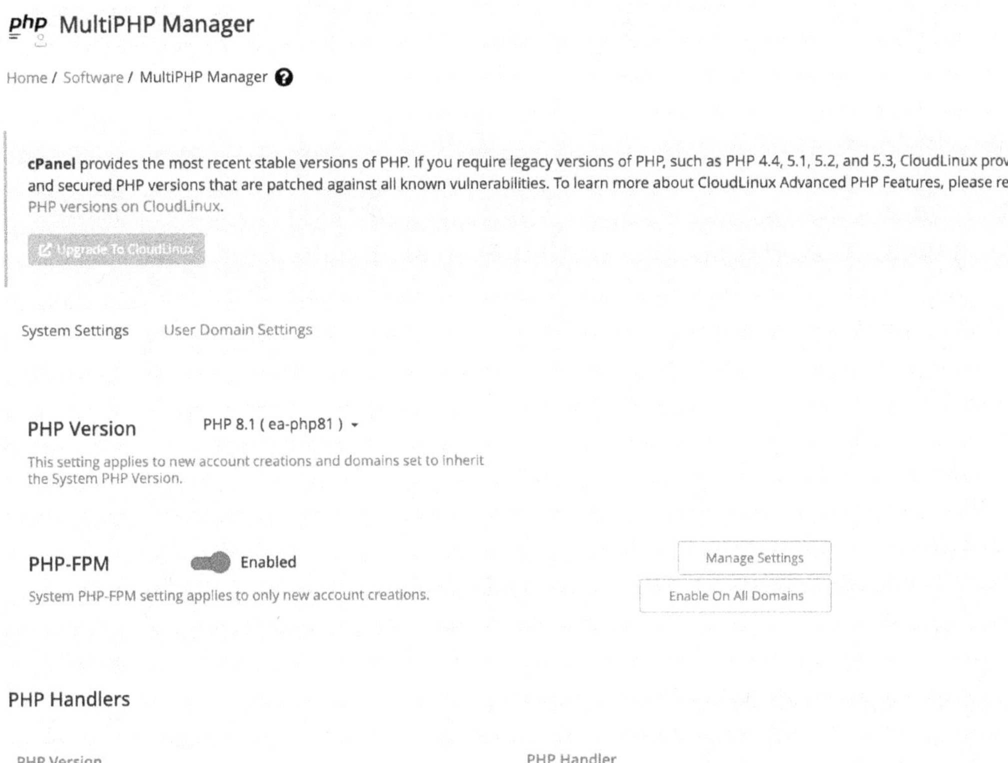

This interface allows you to easily manage the PHP and PHP FastCGI Process Manager (PHP-FPM) configurations of your system and your cPanel accounts.

24.6 System Settings tab

In this tab, you can configure your system-level default PHP settings.

24.6.1.1 PHP Version

To set the system's default version of PHP, select your desired PHP version in the menu.

If you select a deprecated version of PHP, the system will display a warning message. Click *Apply Deprecated Version* to continue.

This setting determines the version of PHP assigned to any new account that you create. Changing this setting does **not** alter any account's PHP version, unless it is set to inherit its PHP version from the system.

24.6.1.2 PHP-FPM

To set whether the system uses PHP-FPM by default, set the toggle to either **Enabled** or **Disabled**. Changing this setting does not alter any existing account's PHP-FPM settings. To configure your system's PHP-FPM settings, click **Manage Settings**. The System PHP-FPM Settings interface will appear.

24.6.1.2.1 Enable PHP-FPM for all domains

To enable PHP-FPM on your system, set the toggle to "Enabled." If your system has enough memory, you'll be prompted to enable PHP-FPM for all domains. Click "Enable" to proceed, and the system will activate PHP-FPM on all domains. You can view the conversion process by clicking "conversion log." If PHP-FPM is already enabled, click "Enable On All Domains" to activate it on all domains, or you'll see a warning if there is insufficient memory. For detailed information, refer to the PHP FastCGI Process Manager - PHP-FPM documentation.

24.6.1.2.2 System PHP-FPM Settings

In this interface, you can adjust the system's PHP-FPM settings, which include two sections: PHP-FPM Pool options and PHP-FPM INI Settings. For domain-specific pool options and PHP INI directives, click the PHP-FPM Settings button next to the domain in the User Domain Settings tab. You can click "Show Help Text" for more details on each setting.

After configuring your PHP-FPM settings, you have the options to:

- Update: Save your settings.
- Validate Settings: Check if your settings are valid.
- Reset Settings: Revert changes to their saved values.

To exit, click "Go Back to System Settings." For further information, refer to the PHP-FPM documentation.

24.6.1.2.3 PHP-FPM Pool options

The PHP-FPM Pool options section lets you configure automated worker pools for your system. You can adjust several settings, including:

- Max Requests: The maximum number of requests a process can handle before spawning a new one, with a range from 1 to 10,000,000, and a default of 20.
- Max Children: The maximum number of PHP-FPM processes the server can create, ranging from 1 to 10,000, with a default of 5.
- Process Idle Timeout: The duration, in seconds, a process can remain idle before being terminated, ranging from 1 to 10,000,000, with a default of 10.

24.6.1.2.4 PHP-FPM INI Settings

The PHP-FPM INI Settings section allows you to configure php.ini directives for your server and control whether users can override these settings. The settings you can manage include treating URLs as files (`allow_url_fopen`), logging errors (`log_errors`), recognizing PHP code within short tags (`short_open_tag`), disabling specific PHP functions, and setting the error reporting level. To prevent users from changing these settings, select the "Block domain from changing the setting" checkbox, which applies the `php_admin_value` directive. Without this selection, the system uses `php_value`. For more information, refer to the PHP-FPM documentation[6].

24.6.1.3 PHP Handlers

The PHP Handlers section allows you to choose the PHP handler for each PHP version installed on your server. To change a handler, simply select the desired handler from the menu next to the corresponding PHP version.

24.7 User Domain Settings tab

In this tab, you can customize PHP settings for individual users. The table provides details about each domain, including the domain name, account name, PHP version

[6] https://docs.cpanel.net/knowledge-base/php-fpm/configuration-values-of-php-fpm/

(and whether it inherits this version), and PHP-FPM status. To see more information about a domain, click the arrow next to its name. You can update the PHP version, enable or disable PHP-FPM, or set the domain to inherit its PHP version. To change settings for multiple domains simultaneously, select the checkboxes next to the domains and choose to set the PHP version, inherit, or disable PHP-FPM.

24.7.1.1 Set a domain's PHP version

To set a domain's PHP version, select the desired PHP version from the menu next to the domain. Changing a domain's PHP version also changes the PHP version for any domains inheriting from it. For more on PHP inheritance, see the PHP Inheritance documentation.

To set a domain to inherit its PHP version, check the "Inherit" box in the PHP Version column, then click "Apply." The system will show "Inherit" and the inherited PHP version, with PHP-FPM marked as unavailable.

To assign a specific PHP version, uncheck "Inherit," choose the PHP version from the menu, and click "Apply." The system will display the selected PHP version and allow you to set the domain's PHP-FPM status.

24.7.1.2 Set a domain's PHP-FPM status

To enable or disable PHP-FPM for a domain, toggle the setting to "Enabled" or "Disabled." For multiple domains, select the desired domains and click "Disable PHP-FPM." Note that you cannot change PHP-FPM settings for a domain if its PHP version is set to "Inherit" or if PHP-FPM is not supported for that PHP version.

24.7.1.3 PHP-FPM Settings

To configure a domain's PHP-FPM settings, click "PHP-FPM Settings," which opens a new interface. Note that this option is only available if PHP-FPM is enabled for the domain. For more details on each setting, click "Show Help Text." After configuring, you can choose to:

- Update: Save your settings.
- Validate Settings: Ensure your PHP-FPM settings are valid.
- Reset Settings: Revert changes to their saved values.

To exit, click "Go Back to User Domain Settings." For more information, refer to the PHP-FPM documentation.

24.7.1.3.1 PHP-FPM Pool options

The PHP-FPM Pool options section lets you configure automated worker pools for your domain. You can adjust the following settings:

- Max Requests: The maximum number of requests a process can handle before spawning a new one, ranging from 1 to 10,000,000, with a default of 20.
- Max Children: The maximum number of PHP-FPM processes the server can spawn, between 1 and 10,000, with a default of 5.
- Process Idle Timeout: The time, in seconds, a process can remain idle before being terminated, from 1 to 10,000,000, with a default of 10.

24.7.1.3.2 PHP-FPM INI Settings

The PHP-FPM INI Settings section allows you to configure php.ini directives for a domain and control whether users can override these settings. You can configure options such as treating URLs as files (`allow_url_fopen`), logging errors (`log_errors`), recognizing short PHP tags (`short_open_tag`), specifying the error log location, disabling specific PHP functions, and setting the error reporting level. To prevent users from changing these settings, select the "Block domain from changing the setting" checkbox, which sets the directive with `` `php_admin_value` ``; otherwise, it uses `` `php_value` ``. For more details, refer to the PHP-FPM documentation on managing php.ini directives and user pool configurations.

24.8 NGINX Manager

For VPS/Dedicated Servers

The information in this section applies to VPS and dedicated servers.

Home / Software / NGINX® Manager

NGINX®

Reverse proxy with caching

Installing NGINX will enable NGINX caching on all user accounts by default. When the installation is complete, you can change this setting in the NGINX Manager interface. For more information, read our documentation NGINX reverse proxy with caching.

Install

WHM's NGINX Manager lets you install, uninstall, and manage your NGINX server with reverse proxy and caching capabilities. You can also manage server caching from this interface. To install NGINX, click "**Install**" to open a new interface. If the `ea-nginx-standalone` package is on your server, you'll be prompted to install NGINX with reverse proxy caching. Click "**Switch to NGINX Reverse Proxy Mode**" to proceed. The system will install NGINX, configure all accounts to use it, and enable caching by default. Once installation is complete, click "**Go to NGINX Manager**" to access the System Settings tab.

24.9 System Settings

This section of the interface is used to manage your NGINX server with various actions. You can enable caching by default for new accounts and those without explicit settings by toggling "Use Caching by Default." Note that changing a user's caching status overrides the system default. You can also clear the cache for all users, restart the NGINX server, rebuild the NGINX configuration, reset users to the system default configuration, and uninstall the NGINX Reverse Proxy from your server.

24.10 User Settings

This interface section allows you to manage NGINX settings for your users, displaying a table with usernames and their NGINX caching status. To find a specific user, use the search box. To adjust a user's caching status, toggle the switch next to their username. For multiple users, select the checkboxes next to their usernames or the top checkbox to select all visible users, then click "**Enable NGINX Cache**" or "**Disable NGINX Cache**." To clear a user's cache, click "**Clear Cache**" next to their username. For multiple users, select the checkboxes and click "Clear NGINX Cache."

If you want users to manage their own NGINX caching status, enable the "EA4 - Allow enabling/disabling NGINX caching" option in WHM's Feature Manager interface, which activates the NGINX Caching toggle in cPanel.

24.11 Rebuild RPM Database

RPM **Rebuild RPM Database**

Home / Software / Rebuild RPM Database 

This will attempt to rebuild your rpm database if it has become corrupt. This procedure can take 1-30 minutes depending on the speed of this machine.

Proceed >>

If you are experiencing issues with updating your system and are noticing errors about a RPM database corruption, rebuilding the RPM database might resolve those issues. This tool performs an automated way to rebuild the RPM database.

24.12 System Update

For VPS/Dedicated Servers

The information in this section applies to VPS and dedicated servers.

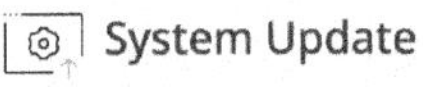

Home / Software / System Update

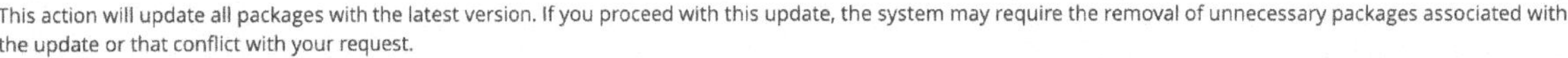

Include kernel packages

Update

This feature will run the `dnf update` command on Enterprise Linux servers. By selecting the "Include Kernel Packages" box, the server may require a reboot to complete the update. Click on **Proceed** to start the update process.

24.13 Update Server Software

For VPS/Dedicated Servers

The information in this section applies to VPS and dedicated servers.

Update Server Software

Home / Software / Update Server Software

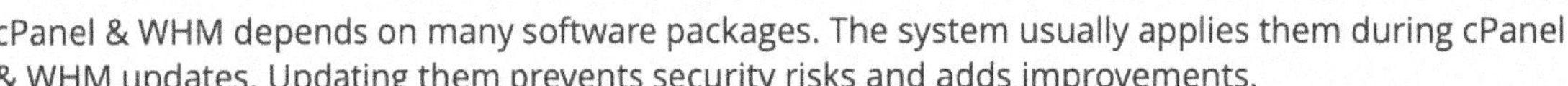

cPanel & WHM depends on many software packages. The system usually applies them during cPanel & WHM updates. Updating them prevents security risks and adds improvements.

To run a manual update, perform the following step:

Proceed >>

This interface allows you to manually update software dependencies that your operating system installed and which cPanel & WHM requires in order to run.

24.14 EasyApache 4

For VPS/Dedicated Servers

The information in this section applies to VPS and dedicated servers.

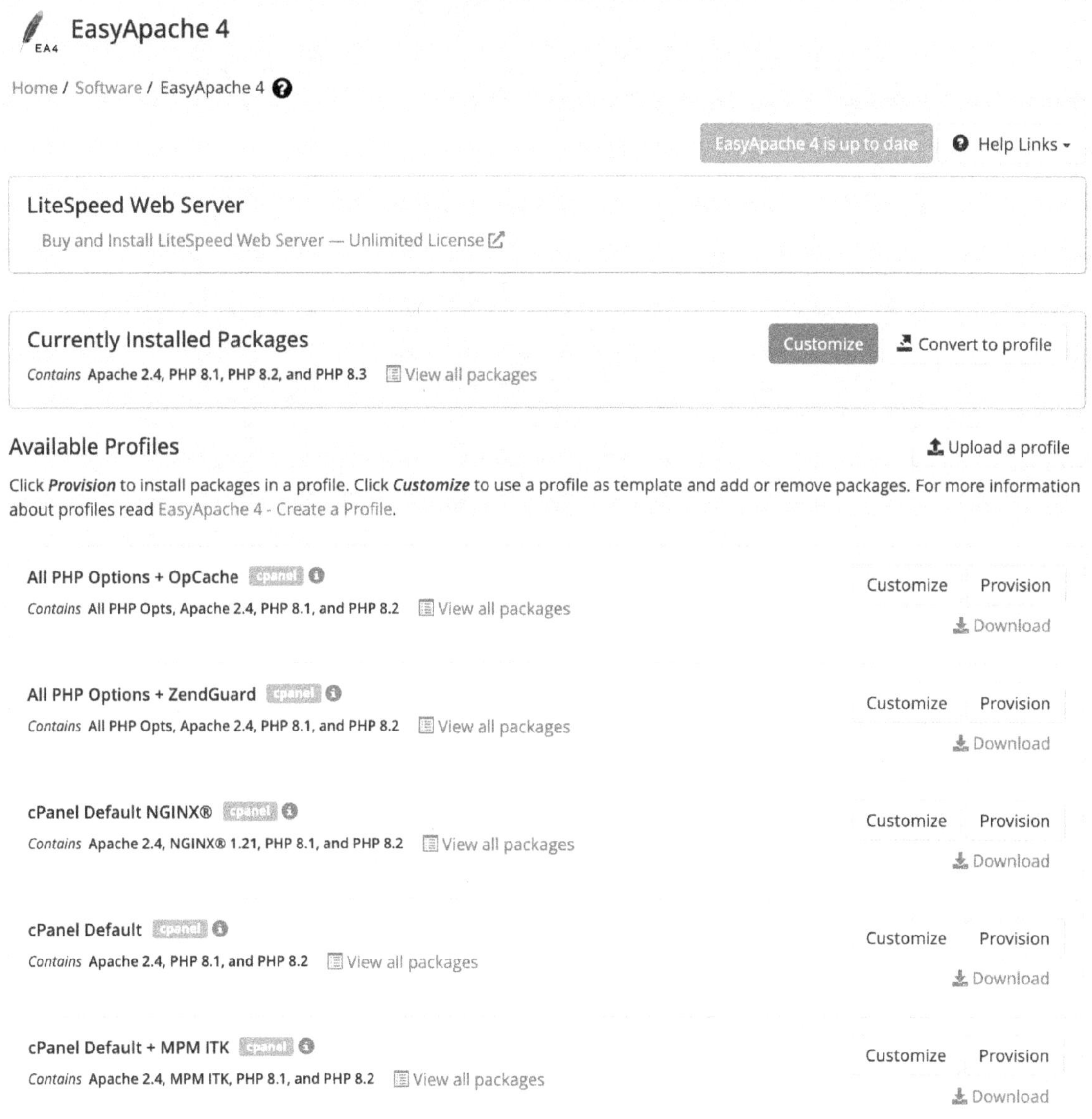

EA4 EasyApache 4

Home / Software / EasyApache 4

EasyApache 4 is up to date   Help Links

LiteSpeed Web Server

Buy and Install LiteSpeed Web Server — Unlimited License

Currently Installed Packages   Customize   Convert to profile

Contains Apache 2.4, PHP 8.1, PHP 8.2, and PHP 8.3   View all packages

Available Profiles   Upload a profile

Click ***Provision*** to install packages in a profile. Click ***Customize*** to use a profile as template and add or remove packages. For more information about profiles read EasyApache 4 - Create a Profile.

All PHP Options + OpCache   cpanel   Customize   Provision

Contains All PHP Opts, Apache 2.4, PHP 8.1, and PHP 8.2   View all packages   Download

All PHP Options + ZendGuard   cpanel   Customize   Provision

Contains All PHP Opts, Apache 2.4, PHP 8.1, and PHP 8.2   View all packages   Download

cPanel Default NGINX®   cpanel   Customize   Provision

Contains Apache 2.4, NGINX® 1.21, PHP 8.1, and PHP 8.2   View all packages   Download

cPanel Default   cpanel   Customize   Provision

Contains Apache 2.4, PHP 8.1, and PHP 8.2   View all packages   Download

cPanel Default + MPM ITK   cpanel   Customize   Provision

Contains Apache 2.4, MPM ITK, PHP 8.1, and PHP 8.2   View all packages   Download

This interface allows you to update and install Apache, PHP, and other components of your web server.

24.14.1 Customizing Existing Profile

If you need to add additional PHP modules, Apache modules, or other additional packages, click on **Customize** to begin customizing the existing profile.

24.14.1.1 Apache Multi Processing Modules

Apache Multi-Processing Modules (MPMs) control how Apache handles HTTP requests and manages processes, influencing the web server's performance, scalability, and resource management.

By default, cPanel will install Apache with the Prefork MPM. You can switch between each MPM by switching the toggle switch. Only one MPM can be active at a time.

24.14.1.1.1 Prefork MPM

The Prefork MPM creates a separate process for each incoming request, with each process handling one connection at a time. This MPM ensures stability and compatibility with non-thread-safe libraries, as each child process operates independently. The isolation provided by separate processes means that if one process crashes, it does not affect the others. However, this comes at the cost of higher memory usage because each process requires its own memory space. Prefork is less efficient in handling high traffic compared to threaded MPMs, making it suitable for low to moderate traffic sites or those requiring non-thread-safe applications.

24.14.1.1.2 Worker MPM

The Worker MPM uses multiple child processes, each with multiple threads. Each thread can handle an individual request, allowing for better resource utilization and scalability. This MPM is more efficient in memory usage than Prefork because threads within the same process share memory space. Worker MPM is well-suited for high-traffic environments where efficient handling of numerous requests is essential. However, it requires that all modules and libraries be thread-safe. The primary drawback is that if a thread crashes, it can potentially impact other threads within the same process, though overall it provides a good balance of performance and stability.

24.14.1.1.3 Event MPM

The Event MPM builds upon the Worker MPM by optimizing the handling of keep-alive connections. In this setup, dedicated threads manage connections that are kept open but are idle, freeing up other threads to handle new requests. This improves performance and reduces memory usage for sites with a high number of long-lived connections. Event MPM is ideal for high-traffic sites where many clients maintain open connections, such as those using WebSockets or serving long-polling HTTP requests. Like Worker, it requires thread-safe modules, and while it offers enhanced performance for certain workloads, it shares similar risks regarding thread crashes affecting others in the same process.

24.14.1.2 Apache Modules

EasyApache 4 will let you install Apache modules easily. Apache Modules let you add additional features and functionality to the Apache web server.

There are over 100 Apache Modules, so it's impossible to list all of them here, but I will touch on some good modules to add:

- mod_remoteip[7] – This module will restore visitor IP addresses if websites are using Cloudflare or another reverse proxy.
- mod_pagespeed[8] – This is a module that will help make websites faster. Review the documentation as it may not always be necessary to add this.
- mod_brotili[9] – This module will enable Brotili compression.

---

[7] mod_remoteip Documentation: https://httpd.apache.org/docs/2.4/mod/mod_remoteip.html

[8] mod_pagespeed Documentation: https://www.modpagespeed.com/

[9] mod_brotili Documentation: https://httpd.apache.org/docs/2.4/mod/mod_brotli.html

24.14.1.3 PHP Versions

EasyApache 4 will allow you to install (or remove) the latest stable versions of PHP. These versions are shipped from cPanel so you are limited to the versions that cPanel provides. To install a PHP version, enable the toggle switch next to that version.

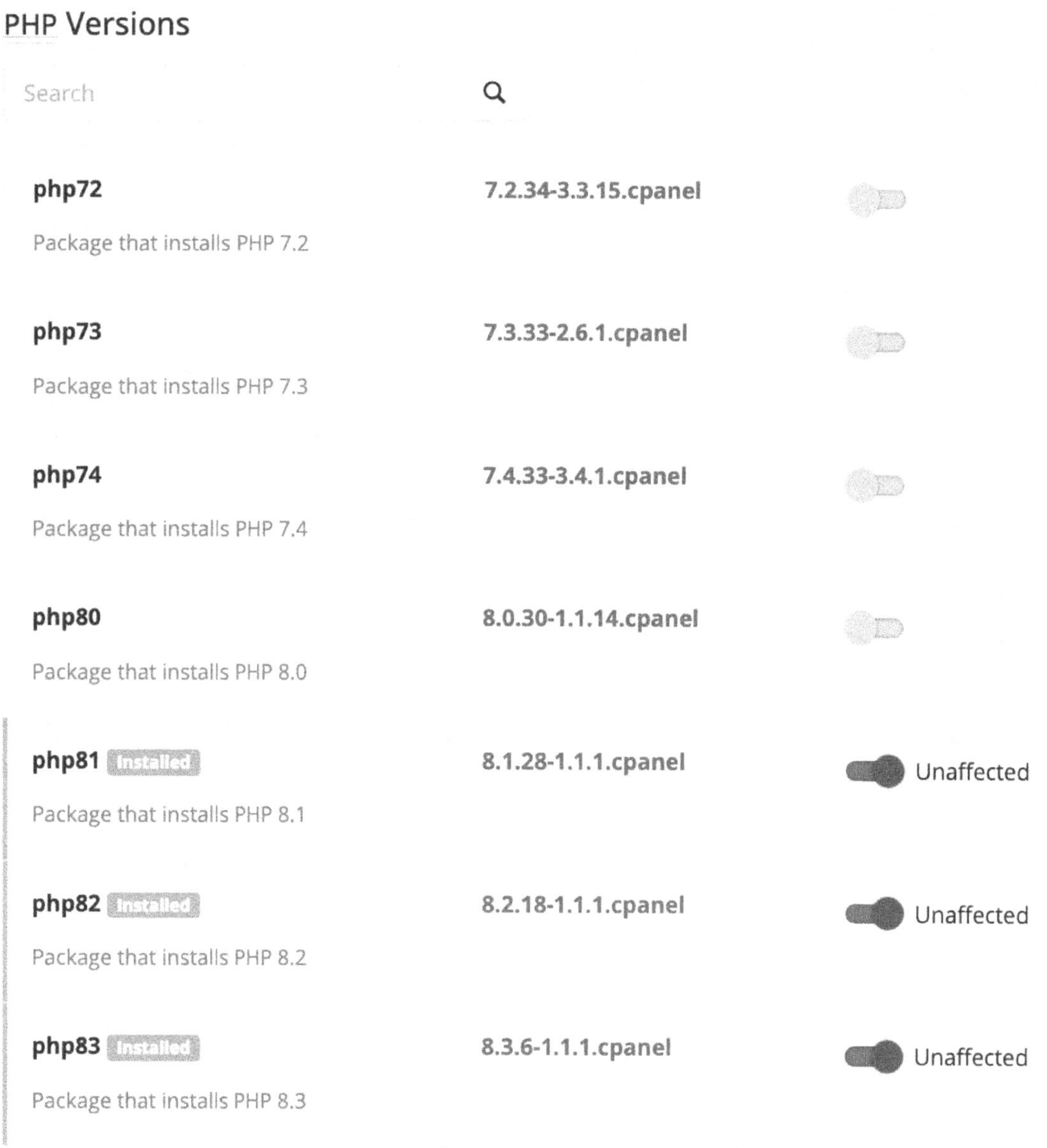

PHP Versions

Search

php72 7.2.34-3.3.15.cpanel
Package that installs PHP 7.2

php73 7.3.33-2.6.1.cpanel
Package that installs PHP 7.3

php74 7.4.33-3.4.1.cpanel
Package that installs PHP 7.4

php80 8.0.30-1.1.14.cpanel
Package that installs PHP 8.0

php81 Installed 8.1.28-1.1.1.cpanel Unaffected
Package that installs PHP 8.1

php82 Installed 8.2.18-1.1.1.cpanel Unaffected
Package that installs PHP 8.2

php83 Installed 8.3.6-1.1.1.cpanel Unaffected
Package that installs PHP 8.3

As of this writing, cPanel supports PHP 7.2, 7.3, 7.4, 8.0, 8.1, 8.2, and 8.3. Versions prior to 8.1 are not actively being supported by The PHP Group and cPanel does not provide any additional security updates. If you require security updates or older versions of PHP, you will need to install CloudLinux, which does provide older versions of PHP as well as security updates.

When you install another PHP version, you will have the option to select the PHP version and extensions or just the PHP version. It is recommended to select the PHP version and extensions. This will enable all extensions that are enable for other PHP versions (assuming that all the extensions exist for that version).

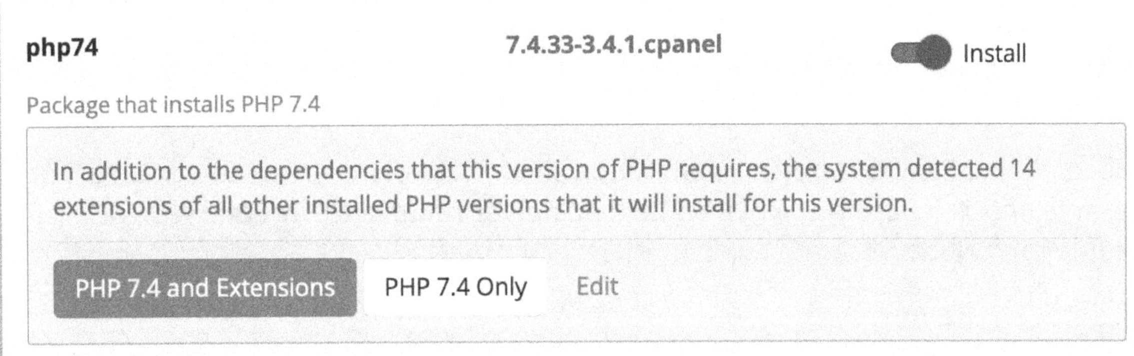
php74
7.4.33-3.4.1.cpanel
Install
Package that installs PHP 7.4
In addition to the dependencies that this version of PHP requires, the system detected 14 extensions of all other installed PHP versions that it will install for this version.
PHP 7.4 and Extensions
PHP 7.4 Only
Edit

Older PHP Versions

PHP 7.x has been **End of Life** for a while now, but a lot of popular web software may not have been updated to support PHP 8.x yet. If you find that you need an older PHP version, you should aim to use PHP 7.4.

24.14.1.4 PHP Extensions

Adding PHP extensions will vary based on the applications that you or your clients are installing. To install an extension, you toggle it on and to remove an extension, toggle it off. Each version of PHP contains its own extensions.

cPanel will install most used extensions by default with the default PHP versions. If you install another PHP version, you will need to install the PHP extensions for that version (see 24.14.1.3).

IonCube Loaders

If you need IonCube loaders for running encrypted PHP code, PHP 8.x only has loaders available as of the time of this writing:

- PHP 8.1 (IonCube 12)
- PHP 8.1 (IonCube 13)
- PHP 8.2 (IonCube 13)

PHP 7.4 has IonCube 10, 11, and 12.

24.14.1.5 Phusion Passenger

In this section, you can add any Ruby packages to enable Ruby applications.

24.14.1.6 Additional Packages

This section of EasyApache 4 contains additional packages that can be installed. For example, this is where you will be able to install or remove NGINX and NGINX modules and Node.js.

24.14.1.7 Review

Once you have made selections, the review section will allow you to view what packages will be added or removed. Click on the **Build** button to make the changes and rebuild the Apache configuration.

25 Email

I call email a necessary evil. Just like printers and fax machines, I don't think email will ever truly go away. We rely on it for everything, and this chapter will dive into the email management and troubleshooting tools that will help you make managing email on cPanel a little easier.

An Important Note About Email:
As you are probably aware, spammers love email. Web hosting providers and data centers do not love spammers. Some data centers have completely restricted email from their networks. If you're running an email server, you will find out that these services will no longer work. If you are unfortunate enough to be in one of these data centers, here are some things you can do:

- Ask that you have SMTP (port 25) access enabled for your server. However, get ready for this to be an uphill battle and you may have to accept "no" as an answer.
- Use a third-party SMTP relay service such as MailChannels but understand that you will have to configure your server and pay for this service. The good news is, MailChannels provides instructions on how to do this for cPanel servers.
- Move to a data center that does not block SMTP access[10].

25.1 Email Deliverability

Nothing is worse than finding out that your email has gone into the spam folder of the intended recipient. The Email Deliverability tool will help you find these issues before they become problems.

This section will walk you through several checks.

[10] A lot of providers are planning on removing or restricting SMTP access so check with a potential data center or hosting provider's sales team. Public cloud providers such as Azure, AWS, Digital Ocean, and others, block SMTP access and you must either use a third-party service or use their own SMTP service (usually for an additional fee).

25.1.1 Mail HELO

The first check that this tool will do is make sure your mail HELO is set properly. This should resolve to your server's hostname. If it does not, you will need to update your **Reverse DNS record** (commonly called **rDNS**) or ask your hosting provider to update it for you.

25.1.2 DKIM

The system will automatically setup and configure DKIM which stands for **DomainKeys Identified Mail**. It is a cryptographic email authentication method that helps prevent spammers and other malicious users from impersonating a domain.

DKIM works by having a private key on the server that the email is "signed" with and then your DNS has a DKIM record with a public key that is validated against the signed message. If it passes, then the server is authorized to send that message and the chances of it going into spam are low.

Google and Yahoo require email sent to them uses DKIM as of February 2024.

25.1.3 SPF

SPF stands for **Sender Policy Framework,** and it is another way to validate that a particular server is allowed to send email on behalf of a domain. This is a text record that is added to your domain, and it tells mail servers if the message they received came from a server authorized to send on behalf of your domain. While wildly simplified, the exchange looks like this:

Mail Server: "I just received a message from example.com from the server 100.65.72.24. Are they authorized?"

Example.com SPF: "Yes, I have 100.65.72.24 as an authorized sender."

Mail Server: "Sounds good, this message is legitimate then!"

And the mail server will deliver it as normal. However, if the server does not pass the check, SPF will suggest that the mail server either hard fail it or soft fail it. It depends on the server whether it will send it to spam or reject the message outright.

Google and Yahoo require email sent to them uses SPF as of February 2024.

25.1.4Reverse DNS (PTR)

This section allows you to view and verify a domain's current pointer (PTR) record. A PTR record is a DNS record that resolves an IP address to a domain or hostname. The server uses this record to perform a reverse DNS (rDNS) lookup to retrieve the associated domain or hostname. A PTR record requires an associated A record. If your rDNS is not set or is incorrectly set, contact your hosting provider for assistance.

25.2 Filter Incoming Emails by Country

For VPS/Dedicated Servers
The information in this section applies to VPS and dedicated servers.

This is a security and anti-spam prevention measure on cPanel. You can select if a certain country should be allowed to send email to your server. For example, if the server is for your business and you are not doing business with anyone outside of the United States, Canada, and/or Mexico, you may want to block all other countries.

Use this feature sparingly as it can sometimes cause false positives if an IP address was reallocated from another region. IP geographic information can take a few months to properly update in all databases.

25.3 Filter Incoming Emails by Domain

For VPS/Dedicated Servers
The information in this section applies to VPS and dedicated servers.

This is a global blocklist filter. Any domain name entered, this list will have their messages rejected by the server and they will not reach any recipients on the server. This list also supports wildcards. When entering wildcards, you must enter asterisk (*) then the domain. For example, if you wanted to block every ".shop" domain from sending email to your server, you can enter "`*.shop`" on the list.

25.4 Greylisting

For VPS/Dedicated Servers

The information in this section applies to VPS and dedicated servers.

Greylisting is another anti-spam protection device that is common amongst mail servers. When a mail server that is not trusted attempts to send an email to the server, the server will temporarily reject the message. If the email is legitimate, the sending server should try to send the message again. After enough time has passed, your server will accept the message for delivery. Spammers typically don't wait to resend mail, so if the server rejects the message, it will move on. However, a legitimate email server will generally attempt to resend the message.

Enabling greylisting is recommended, however users should be made aware that it will cause slight delays in receiving emails if the server hasn't received email from the sending server in a while. These delays can be anywhere from 5-10 minutes. You can always "trust" a server and bypass it from greylisting.

25.5 Mail Delivery Reports

This feature is incredibly useful when trying to troubleshoot why an email didn't make it to the intended recipient. You can search based on several options and then drill down into the messages. There are several icons that will show you the event at a glance.

Success – The email was delivered successfully.

Filtered – The system filtered the email.

Unknown – The email's status is unknown, or delivery is in progress.

Deferred – The system deferred the email.

Error – The system encountered a delivery error.

Rejected – The system rejected the email at SMTP time. This can be because an RBL includes the sender's server, or the server contains an insecure configuration.

25.6 Mail Queue Manager

For VPS/Dedicated Servers

The information in this section applies to VPS and dedicated servers.

This tool will let you view and manage the outbound mail queue on the server. The mail queue is where messages are stored if they have not yet been delivered to their destination. Generally, messages should only spend a limited amount of time in the mail queue. Many messages in the mail queue can indicate a mail sending problem. Some common issues are:

- The receiving server will not accept mail from your server and isn't allowing it to connect (either through a network issue or a firewall issue)
- Your data center or network operator is not allowing SMTP traffic outbound
- Any other configuration issue.

It is a recommended that you make a habit of checking that you check the mail queue for issues daily. When you encounter an issue, it's also generally a good idea to clear the mail queue otherwise your server will flood receiving servers with messages. Some data centers will see the flood of email messages coming from your server as a potential issue and may further restrict SMTP traffic or suspend your network all together.

25.7 Mail Troubleshooter

This is a built-in troubleshooting tool that will allow you to enter an email address and then trace it. You can see if your server is able to make the required connections to send email. This tool will not guarantee or check that your email will make it to the inbox of your recipient. Rather it will show you the server can at least send to the recipient.

For example, I put in our test Gmail address:

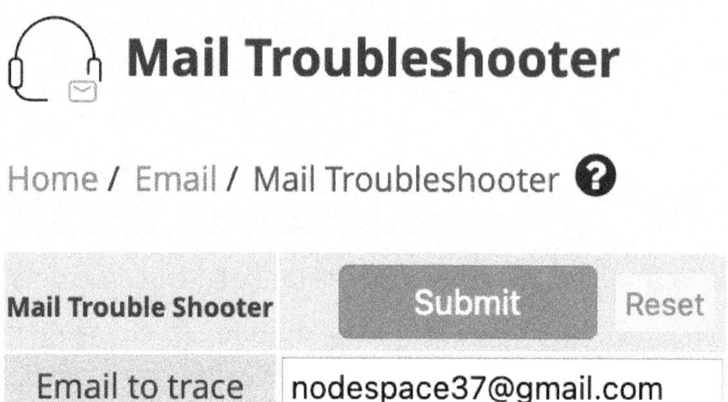

After submitting the email, the response from the troubleshooter shows us that everything looks good for all the MX records, and we should have no problem sending email from this server to the recipient.

Mail Troubleshooter

Home / Email / Mail Troubleshooter 

nodespace37@gmail.com
dkim_lookuphost via gmail-smtp-in.l.google.com [142.250.105.27] MX=5 dnssec=no

nodespace37@gmail.com
dkim_lookuphost via alt1.gmail-smtp-in.l.google.com [172.217.197.27] MX=10 dnssec=no

nodespace37@gmail.com
dkim_lookuphost via alt2.gmail-smtp-in.l.google.com [108.177.12.26] MX=20 dnssec=no

nodespace37@gmail.com
dkim_lookuphost via alt3.gmail-smtp-in.l.google.com [172.253.62.26] MX=30 dnssec=no

nodespace37@gmail.com
dkim_lookuphost via alt4.gmail-smtp-in.l.google.com [64.233.186.27] MX=40 dnssec=no

Map Legend

Icon	Meaning
	Mail Routing Error
	Filter/Alias File
	SMTP Destination

25.8 Mailbox Conversion

For VPS/Dedicated Servers

The information in this section applies to VPS and dedicated servers.

This tool will allow you to convert an account's mailbox format. cPanel defaults to using the maildir format, but if you have accounts that need to use the mdbox format, you can use this tool to convert them.

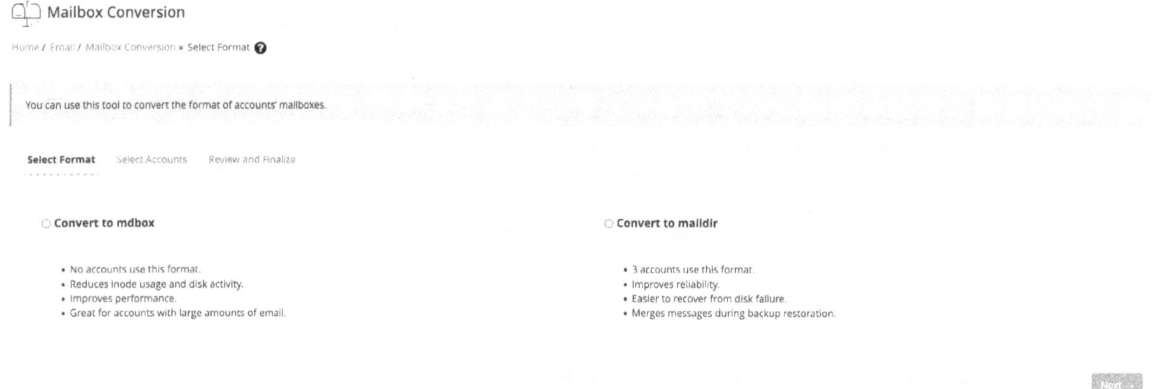

Keep the following in mind:

Maildir format uses flat files, which will cause systems with large mail archives to exhaust their inode resources quickly. Mdbox format will store multiple messages in a file and uses a simpler indexing scheme. Since it requires fewer files, it reduces inode usage significantly.

If you do convert an account from maildir to mdbox, do **not** delete the `/storage` directory or the `/mailboxes` directory. The system **requires** these directories.

25.9 Repair Mailbox Permissions

Occasionally, users will muck about with the permissions of files and directories in their accounts even though they should be warned not to. If you do have a user that is receiving permission issues in regard to their email, the Repair Mailbox Permissions tool will attempt to inspect mailbox ownership and attempt to repair any permission issues that might exist.

 **Repair Mailbox Permissions**

Home / Email / Repair Mailbox Permissions 

This function will inspect mailbox ownership and permissions and attempt to fix any issues that may exist.

Proceed >>

When you click on **Proceed**, the system will check every mailbox on the system.

25.10 Spamd Startup Configuration

For VPS/Dedicated Servers

The information in this section applies to VPS and dedicated servers.

This screen will allow you to change the startup options for the Apache SpamAssassin daemon.

The following table describes the available options:

Option	Description	Default value
Allowed IPs	To only allow connections from specific IP addresses to access the spamd daemon, enter a comma-separated list of IP addresses in the *Allowed IPs* text box. If you do not enter a value, the spamd daemon allows connections from any IP address. Warning: If you restrict access to the spamd daemon, you **must** include the local IPv4 address (`127.0.0.1`) to ensure that the `chkservd` daemon can access the spamd daemon. Also, if you use IPv6 on your server, you **must** also include the local IPv6 address (`::1`). If you do not include these IP addresses in the Allowed IPs list, the `spamd` daemon will fail.	`127.0.0.1,::1`
Maximum Connections per Child	Defines the maximum number of connections that a `spamd` child process may have. After a `spamd` child process reaches the maximum number of connections, the `spamd` daemon will abandon the child process.	`200`
Maximum Children	Defines the maximum number of child processes that a `spamd` process can spawn at startup.	`5` Note:

Option	Description	Default value
	Note: The `/usr/local/cpanel/scripts/vps_optimizer` script optimizes this value for the amount of memory on your server.	On Virtual Private Server (VPS) systems, this option defaults to `3`.
TCP Timeout	Defines the amount of time, in seconds, that the `spamd` daemon waits before it abandons a TCP connection. If you set the value to `0`, the `spamd` daemon will not abandon TCP connections.	`30`
TCP Child Timeout	Defines the amount of time, in seconds that a child process waits before it abandons a TCP connection. If you set the value to `0`, the `spamd` daemon child processes will not abandon TCP connections.	`300`

25.11 View Mail Statistics Summary

This is a reporting tool that will allow you to keep an eye on the email usage on your server. This report has several sections to give you an overview of what is happening on your server.

25.11.1 Grand Total Summary

Grand total summary (Back To Top)

TOTAL	Volume	Messages	Addresses	Hosts	At least one addr Delayed		At least one addr Failed	
Received	87MB	6817		814	307	4.5%	1519	22.3%
Delivered	80MB	5263	5263	211				
Rejects		1411		80				
Temp Rejects		266		1				

This table will show you the volume of received, delivered, and rejected email. Volume is the amount of data, messages is the number of messages, addresses is the number of unique email addresses, and hosts is the number of unique mail-sending hosts.

25.11.2 Deliveries by Transport

Deliveries by Transport (Back To Top)

	Volume	Messages
bypassed	3017KB	181
:blackhole:	170KB	8
dkim_remote_smtp	23MB	2620
dovecot_delivery	34MB	2079
dovecot_virtual_delivery	20MB	375

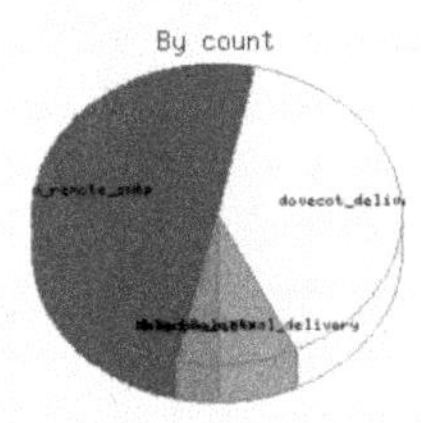

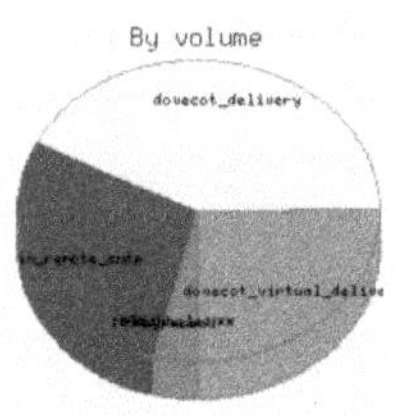

This section shows details about the mail that the Mail Transfer Agent (MTA) delivers. Local_delivery are messages delivered from one user on the server to another. Remote_stmp are messages that the system delivered from a user on the server to another user on a remote server. Virtual_userdelivery are messages the system forwarded from a virtual user (a mail forwarder) to a real user on your server. You might notice other items such as ":blackhole:" which are messages the system silently discarded.

25.12 Messages Received Per Hour

Messages received per hour (each dot is 18 messages) (Back To Top)

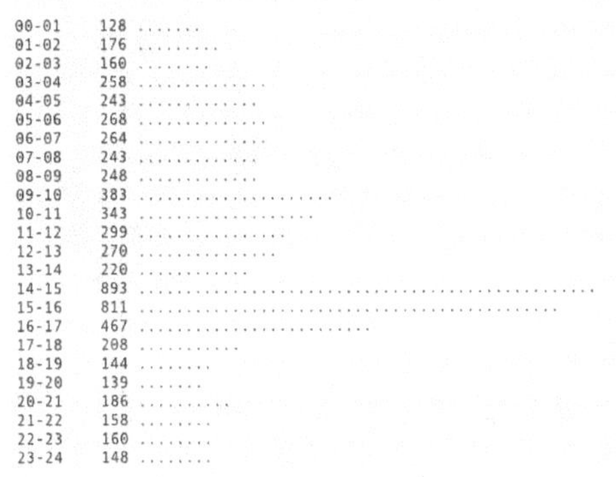

```
00-01   128 .......
01-02   176 .........
02-03   160 ........
03-04   258 ..............
04-05   243 .............
05-06   268 ..............
06-07   264 ..............
07-08   243 .............
08-09   248 .............
09-10   383 .....................
10-11   343 ...................
11-12   299 ................
12-13   270 ...............
13-14   220 ............
14-15   893 .................................................
15-16   811 .............................................
16-17   467 .........................
17-18   208 ...........
18-19   144 ........
19-20   139 .......
20-21   186 ..........
21-22   158 ........
22-23   160 ........
23-24   148 ........
```

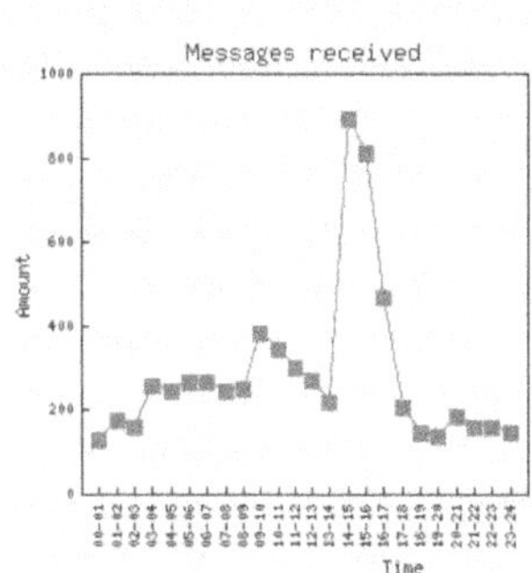

This is a chart that shows you a daily view of when your busiest email periods. For example, on this server you can see that the most email was received between 2-3PM, 3-4PM, and 4-5PM.

25.12.1 Deliveries Per Hour

Deliveries per hour (each dot is 12 deliveries) (Back To Top)

```
00-01     98 ........
01-02    143 ...........
02-03    134 ...........
03-04    214 .................
04-05    208 .................
05-06    208 .................
06-07    218 ..................
07-08    210 .................
08-09    220 ..................
09-10    306 .........................
10-11    279 .......................
11-12    266 ......................
12-13    233 ...................
13-14    184 ...............
14-15    623 ...................................................
15-16    482 ........................................
16-17    300 .........................
17-18    181 ...............
18-19    124 ..........
19-20    112 .........
20-21    156 .............
21-22    121 ..........
22-23    128 ..........
23-24    115 .........
```

This chart shows you a daily snapshot of when your server delivered email messages to users on the server. You can use this to help determine when email activity is the highest.

25.12.2 Time Spent on the Queue: All Messages

Time spent on the queue: all messages (Back To Top)

Time	Messages	Percentage	Cumulative Percentage
Under 1m	6494	95.6%	95.6%
5m	41	0.6%	96.2%
15m	14	0.2%	96.4%
30m	45	0.7%	97.0%
1h	28	0.4%	97.5%
3h	13	0.2%	97.6%
6h	3	0.0%	97.7%
12h	5	0.1%	97.8%
1d	29	0.4%	98.2%
Over 1d	123	1.8%	100.0%

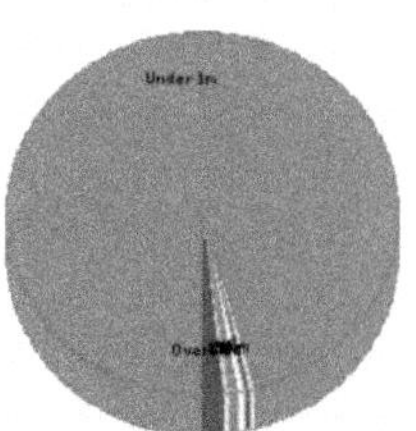

This section displays the amount of time that messages waited in your mail queues before the server delivered them. Ideally, you want most messages to be in the queue for as little time as possible.

25.12.3 Time Spent on the Queue: Messages with at Least One Remote Delivery

Time spent on the queue: messages with at least one remote delivery (Back To Top)

Time	Messages	Percentage	Cumulative Percentage
Under 1m	2529	96.8%	96.8%
5m	4	0.2%	97.0%
15m	8	0.3%	97.3%
30m	34	1.3%	98.6%
1h	16	0.6%	99.2%
3h	2	0.1%	99.3%
1d	3	0.1%	99.4%
Over 1d	16	0.6%	100.0%

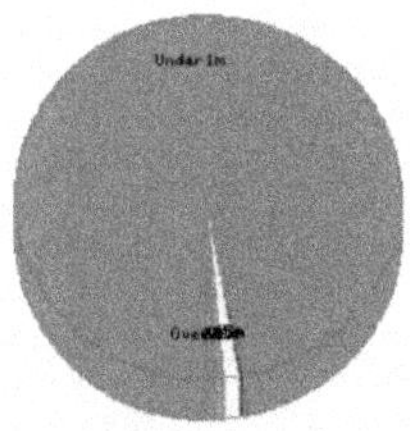

This value is like Time Spent on the Queue: All Messages except it takes into account messages that had at least one external recipient.

25.12.4 Relayed Messages

This section displays statistics about mail that the system sent from your server to remote destinations.

Warning!

Do **not** allow your server to operate as an open relay. Exim is **not** an open relay because it requires authentication for the system to send outbound messages. Messages that this section displays under *Relayed Messages* do **not** indicate that the server is an open relay.

25.12.5 Top 50 Mail Rejection Reasons by Message Count

Top 50 mail rejection reasons by message count (Back To Top)

Messages	Mail rejection reason
194	Rejected RCPT: No Such User Here"
170	Rejected RCPT: Sender verify failed
132	Rejected RCPT: root cannot accept local mail deliveries
80	Rejected MAIL: Access denied - Invalid HELO name (See RFC2821 4.1.1.1)
41	Unknown
30	Dropped: too many syntax or protocol errors
28	Rejected RCPT: "JunkMail rejected - ought.binorex.com [194.169.172.165]
21	Rejected RCPT: "JunkMail rejected - losner.clearliamendem.org [95.213.139.39]
16	Dropped: too many unrecognized commands

This table will list the reasons why a message was rejected by the error message along with the number of messages that triggered that error message.

25.12.6 Top 50 Mail Temporary Rejections by Message Count

Top 50 mail temporary rejection reasons by message count

Messages	Mail temporary rejection reason
44	Temporarily rejected connection in "connect" ACL: "Host is ratelimited (1.9/1h max:1.2)"
38	Temporarily rejected connection in "connect" ACL: "Host is ratelimited (1.8/1h max:1.2)"
36	Temporarily rejected connection in "connect" ACL: "Host is ratelimited (1.7/1h max:1.2)"
21	Temporarily rejected connection in "connect" ACL: "Host is ratelimited (1.3/1h max:1.2)"
20	Temporarily rejected connection in "connect" ACL: "Host is ratelimited (1.6/1h max:1.2)"
16	Temporarily rejected connection in "connect" ACL: "Host is ratelimited (1.5/1h max:1.2)"
16	Temporarily rejected connection in "connect" ACL: "Host is ratelimited (2.0/1h max:1.2)"
13	Temporarily rejected connection in "connect" ACL: "Host is ratelimited (1.4/1h max:1.2)"
13	Temporarily rejected connection in "connect" ACL: "Host is ratelimited (2.8/1h max:1.2)"
10	Temporarily rejected connection in "connect" ACL: "Host is ratelimited (1.2/1h max:1.2)"
10	Temporarily rejected connection in "connect" ACL: "Host is ratelimited (2.6/1h max:1.2)"
9	Temporarily rejected connection in "connect" ACL: "Host is ratelimited (2.7/1h max:1.2)"
6	Temporarily rejected RCPT: Could not complete sender verify
4	Temporarily rejected connection in "connect" ACL: "Host is ratelimited (2.1/1h max:1.2)"
4	Temporarily rejected connection in "connect" ACL: "Host is ratelimited (2.9/1h max:1.2)"
3	Temporarily rejected connection in "connect" ACL: "Host is ratelimited (2.4/1h max:1.2)"
1	Temporarily rejected connection in "connect" ACL: "Host is ratelimited (2.2/1h max:1.2)"
1	Temporarily rejected connection in "connect" ACL: "Host is ratelimited (2.3/1h max:1.2)"
1	Temporarily rejected connection in "connect" ACL: "Host is ratelimited (3.0/1h max:1.2)"

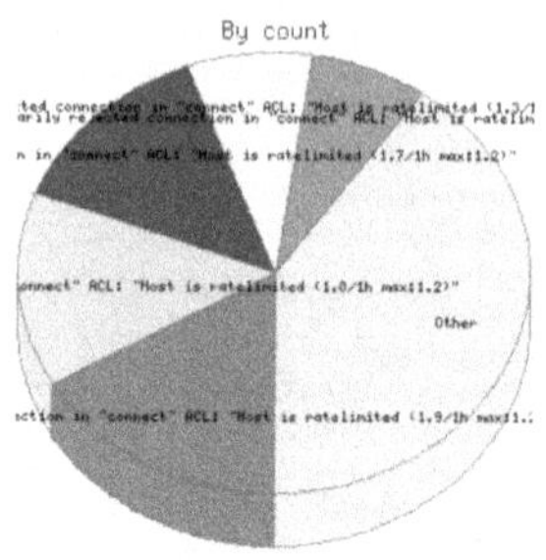

This table will list the temporary rejections by message count. The number of messages is the messages that received that error message.

25.12.7 Top 50 Sending Hosts by Message Count

This table will list the top senders to and from your server. You can use this table to help track down accounts that send a lot of email or view the servers that are sending your server a lot of email. The “local” host or domain represents all mail that your server sends.

25.12.8 Top 50 Sending Hosts by Volume

This table will display the top 50 domains that send the most data to or from your server. The “local” host or domain represents all mail that your server sends.

25.12.9 Top 50 Local Senders by Message Count

This table will list the top 50 users on this server who are sending emails, ordered by message counts.

25.12.10 Top 50 Local Senders by Volume

This table will list the top 50 users on this server who are sending email, ordered by the size of email sent.

25.12.11 Top 50 Host Destinations by Message Count

This table will list the top 50 email destinations that users on your server are sending email to, ordered by message count. The "local" host or domain are messages sent to the local server by the local server.

25.12.12 Top 50 Host Destinations by Volume

This table will list the top 50 email destinations by the amount of email that is sent to them. The "local" host or domain are messages sent to the local server by the local server.

25.12.13 Top 50 Local Destinations by Message Count

This section displays the 50 domains that receive the most messages from your server.

25.12.14 Top 50 Local Destinations by Volume

This section displays the 50 addresses on your server that receive the most data via email.

25.12.15 Top 50 Rejected IPs by Message Count

This section displays the 50 IP addresses that sent the most rejected email messages to your server.

25.12.16 List of Errors

This section lists the errors your mail server encounters, and identifies the total number of errors.

25.13 View Relayers

This interface lists users who have relayed mail. Relayed email is email a user on your server forwards to a remote account.

25.14 View Sent Summary

This feature displays the total number of message delivery attempts that each domain on your server made within a specified time and date range. You can view the number of successful attempts, failed attempts, and the total number of bytes that each domain sent.

26 System Health

For VPS/Dedicated Servers

The information in this section applies to VPS and dedicated servers.

The tools provided in the System Health section will help you keep an eye on your system to make sure it is running smoothly. It also helps secure your system from potential threats from malicious users.

26.1 Background Process Killer

Background Process Killer

Home / System Health / Background Process Killer

You can configure WHM to kill any of the following processes and send you an email when it finds one of them. Malicious users may run an IRC bouncer on their shell accounts even though this may be against your policy. WHM detects these processes correctly even if the bouncer is renamed (e.g. to something that appears non-malicious like "pine", to give the impression that the user is just reading email).

Please check the names of any programs you do not want running on your server; we recommend that you check them all since letting users run IRC bots and servers usually leads to denial-of-service attacks.

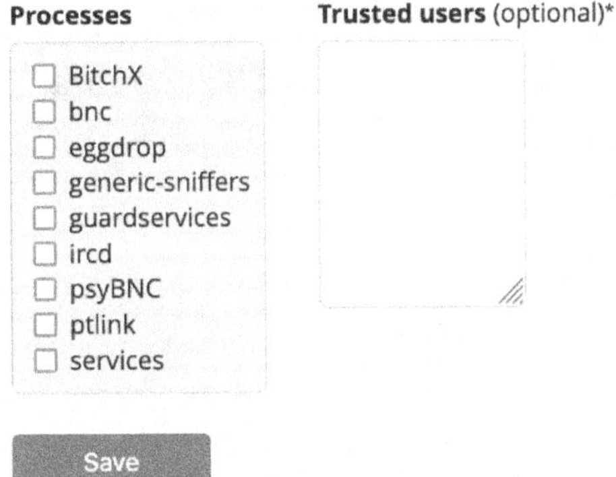

* List users that you want the process killer to ignore, one per line, in the textbox. Note that root, mysql, named, cpanel, and users with UIDs below 99 are already considered trusted and do not need to be added to this list.

This interface allows you to select processes that the system will terminate when the `upcp` script calls the system maintenance script (`/scripts/maintenance`) every night. After the system terminates a process, it will send you a notification via email.

26.2 Process Manager

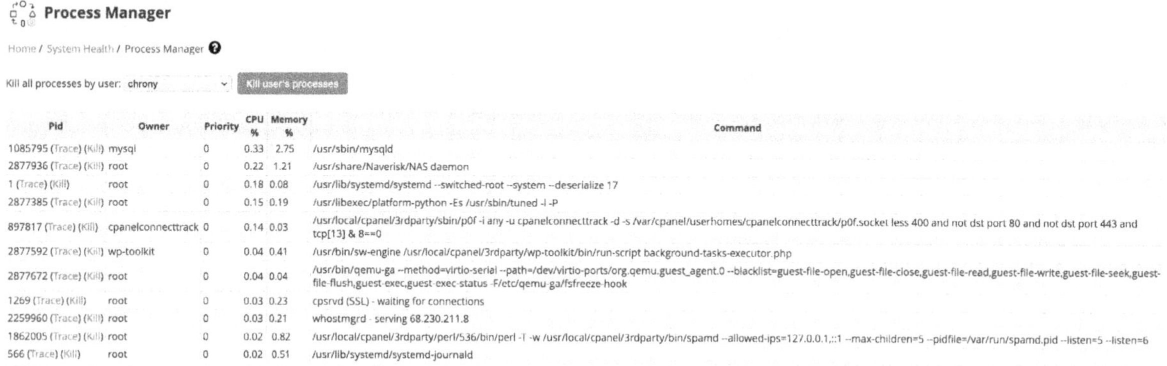

The process manager will show you what processes are running on your server and how many resources they are using. You can use this to track down runaway scripts or software that is causing your system to slow down.

This is like what you see when launching Activity Center on macOS or Task Manager on Windows. To kill a process (force quit), you can click on the **Kill** link. You can also see what a process is doing and to track it as it runs, by clicking on the **Trace** link.

26.3 Show Current Disk Usage

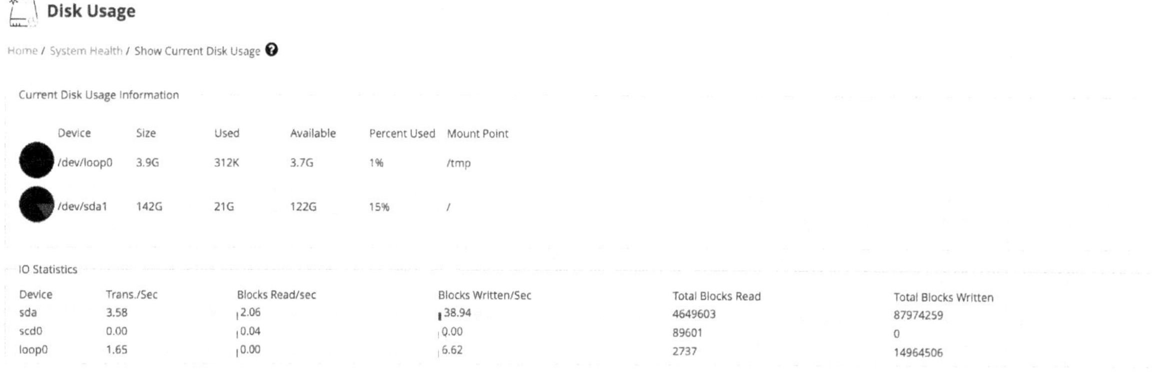

This interface will show you the current usage of your disks. You can see how much disk space is currently being used as well as the current read, write, and number of transactions per second. This can help you diagnose or troubleshoot issues related to your system disk.

26.4 Show Current Running Processes

This interface will show the processes that are currently running on your system. It is like Process Manager, except it will only show you the Process ID, name, file, current directory, and command. It will not show you usage by CPU, RAM, or allow you to manage the process.

27 cPanel

The cPanel section houses tools that will help you interact with cPanel. It contains a lot of settings for managing and working with cPanel and extending cPanel.

27.1 Change Log

This link will take you to cPanel's website and show you the change log for the current version of cPanel. You can view the version number, release date, and all the changes in this version. You can use this for tracking bug fixes or potential issues.

27.2 Customization

The customization tool will allow you to customize the main cPanel theme to fit your branding and company. This tool is also available for resellers so they can customize cPanel with their own company branding, overriding any other branding.

27.2.1 Logos

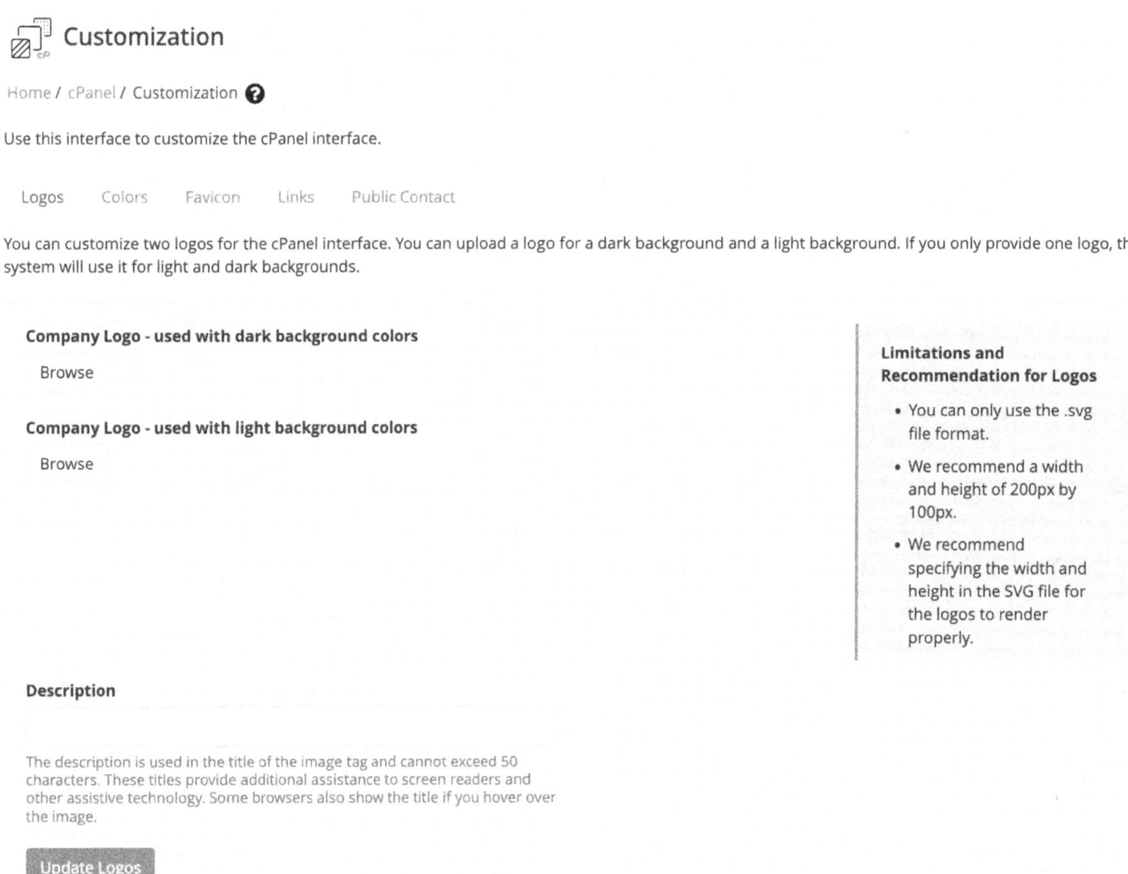

cPanel allows you to upload logos that are shown in the cPanel interface. You can provide a logo to be used with dark background colors and one to be used with light background colors. **Keep in mind that your logo must be in SVG format. PNG is not accepted.**

27.2.2 Colors

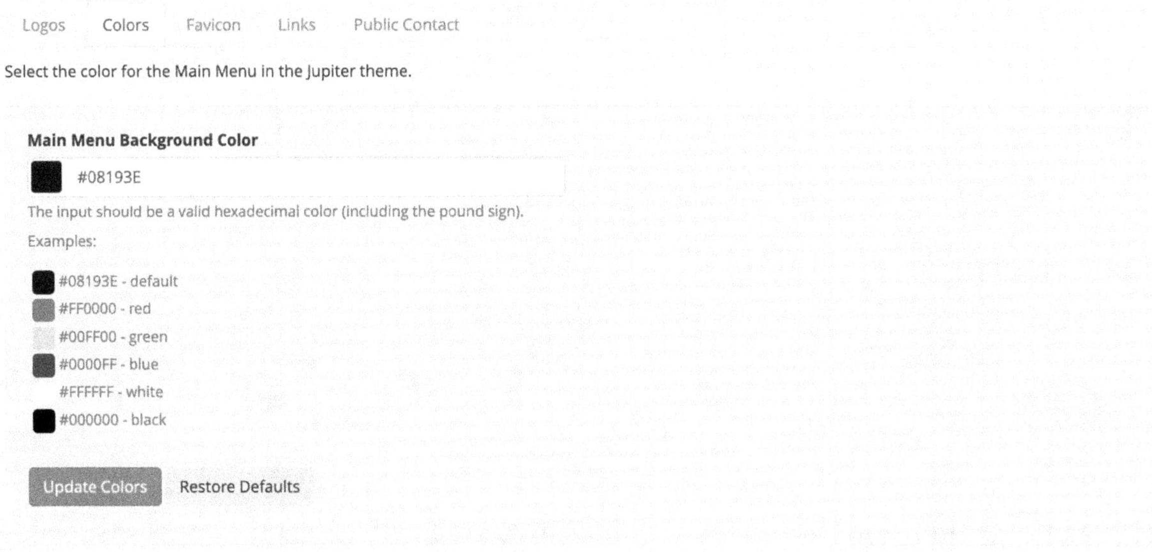

You can select the background color for the sidebar menu in the Jupiter theme.

27.2.3 Favicon

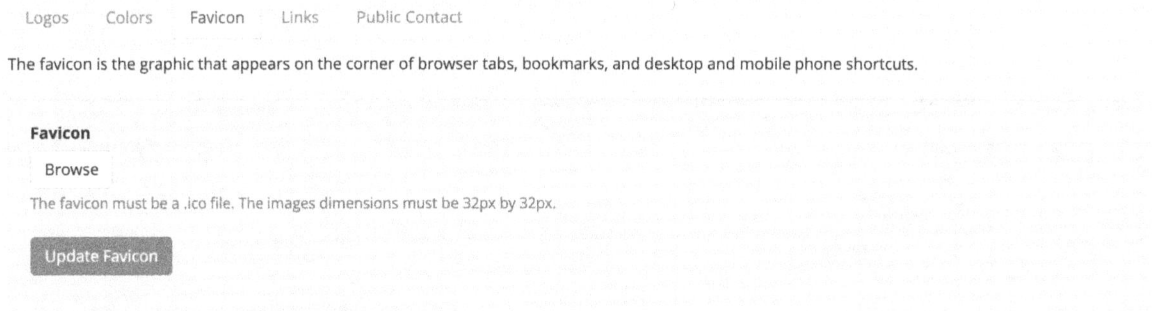

You can add a custom favicon that is shown in the user's browser. This must be a .ico file with the size 32px by 32px.

27.2.4 Links

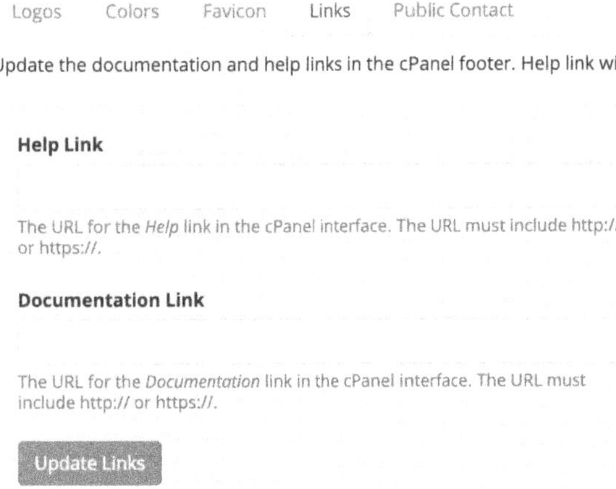

By default the Help and Documentation links in cPanel will direct to cPanel's website. By entering your own links here, you can direct users back to your own help and documentation websites. For example, you might set the help link to point to the URL of your ticketing system and the documentation link to be set to your knowledge base.

27.2.5 Public Contact

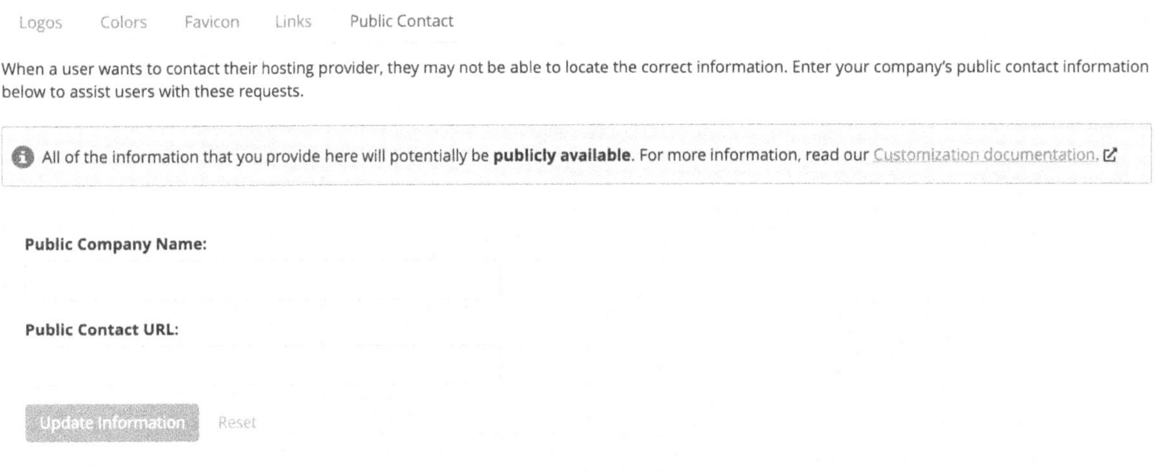

This interface will allow you to add publicly available contact information that is used on various cPanel error pages and are sometimes shown on websites (for example, account suspended page). This will direct users to your contact form. You might set this to a contact form on your website or your help desk ticketing system.

27.3 Install cPAddons Site Software

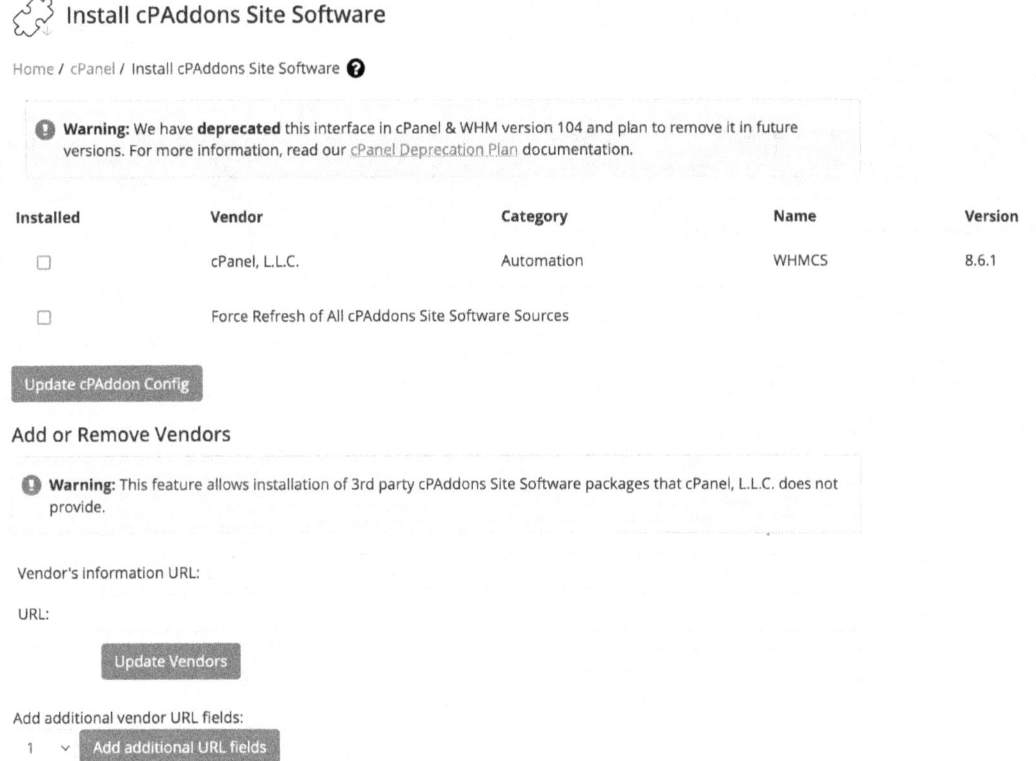

This is cPanel's homegrown "one click installer" that allows users to easily install software from third parties. 20 years ago, this section was filled with useful software. 10 years ago, it dwindled down to some popular software still used. Then over the last several years, it dropped even more, including support for WordPress as the WP Toolkit was introduced. Now, the only software natively provided by cPanel is WHMCS.

This tool is a shell of its former self and should not be used. Look into getting a license for Softaculous[11] and providing that to your users.

27.4 Manage CPAddons Site Software

This tool allows you to force updates of software that is installed with the cPAddons Site Software. This tool is a shell of its former self and should not be used. Again, look into getting a license for Softaculous and providing that to your users.

27.5 Manage Plugins

For VPS/Dedicated Servers

The information in this section applies to VPS and dedicated servers.

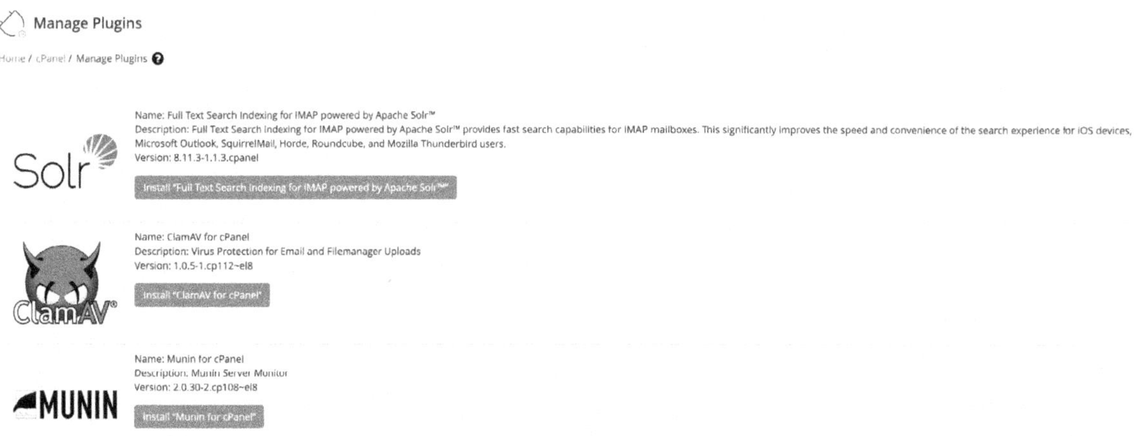

Plugins are additional features and capabilities that can be installed in cPanel to enhance its functionality. cPanel ships with some default plugins that can be installed.

- **Solr:** a full-text search indexing utility, and it will provide fast search for IMAP mailboxes. This will help users who connect to IMAP search their mailboxes

11 https://www.softaculous.com/pricing/

using iOS Mail, Microsoft Outlook, Roundcube, and Mozilla Thunderbird search their email faster.

- **ClamAV:** a free and open source virus scanner. It is needed to allow the mail server to scan email for viruses and it also allows users to scan their website files for threats.
- **Munin**: free and open source server monitoring software. If you are not using an external server monitor, Munin is a great tool to use.

27.6 Modify cPanel & WHM News

For VPS/Dedicated Servers

The information in this section applies to VPS and dedicated servers.

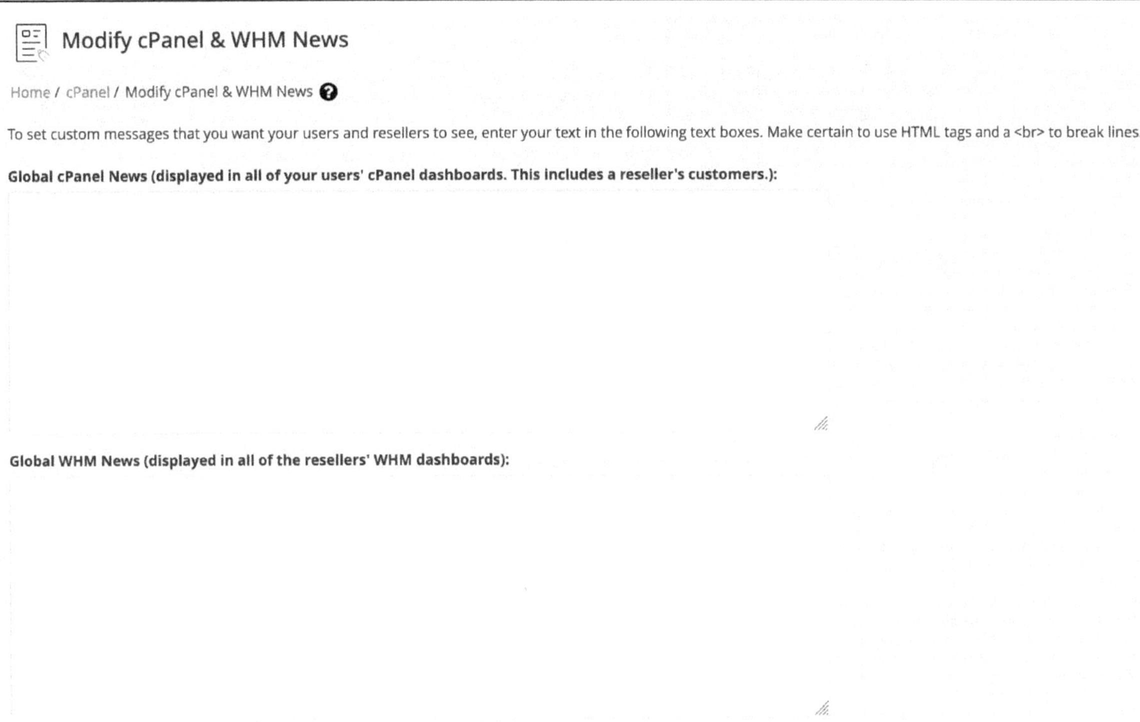

This is a system that will allow you to automatically post notifications to all your users and/or reseller users in their dashboards. You have the option to post news:

- Global cPanel – In *ALL* user's cPanel dashboards, including reseller's users

- Global WHM – In *ALL* reseller's WHM dashboards
- Reseller Customer News – In cPanel dashboards of your *reseller's users*
- cPanel News – In cPanel dashboards of your customers (reseller customers will *NOT* see this news)

These fields can accept HTML formatting. You should use this feature carefully. An email notification might be a better option.

27.7 Reset a Mailman Password

If you need to reset a mailman mailing list password, you can use this tool to select the list and then change the password.

27.8 Upgrade to Latest Version

For VPS/Dedicated Servers
The information in this section applies to VPS and dedicated servers.

Upgrade to Latest Version

Home / cPanel / Upgrade to Latest Version 

You will be upgrading to the latest **current** build.

☐ Force a reinstall even if the system is up to date.

Click to Upgrade

This tool will allow you to upgrade cPanel and WHM to the latest version without waiting for the system to automatically do it. Additionally, you can repair your installation by checking the box to force a reinstall even if the system is up to date.

28 SSL/TLS

The tools in this chapter will help you manage SSL/TLS certificates on your system.

28.1 Generate an SSL Certificate and Signing Request

This feature allows you to simultaneously generate both a self-signed SSL certificate and a certificate signing request (CSR) for a domain. You can also use this interface to generate private keys, which are essential for self-signed certificates and purchased certificates. To purchase a certificate, submit the CSR to your chosen certificate authority (CA). They will provide you with a certificate, typically in a `.zip` file via email.

28.1.1 Contact Information

To receive the SSL certificate, private key, and CSR via email, enter your email address in the Email Address text box. Then, check the box labeled "When complete, email me the certificate, key, and CSR." to receive a copy of the generated request. However, do not select this checkbox if your email service provider does not support secure mail through SSL/TLS. This is to protect your SSL/TLS certificate.

28.1.2 Private Key Options

Select the desired key from the Key Type menu. RSA, 2048-bit is default and is generally used in most applications.

28.1.3 Certificate Information

To generate an SSL certificate and CSR, follow these steps:

First, enter the domain name of the website that the certificate will secure in the Domains text box. You can use a wildcard-formatted domain name to secure multiple subdomains with the same certificate if they share an IP address. For instance, a wildcard certificate for *.example.com can secure both mail.example.com and www.example.com. You can also enter multiple domains, with each domain on a separate line. For more details on sharing SSL certificates, refer to the Manage SSL Hosts documentation.

Next, provide the full name of the city where your servers are located in the City text box. Then, enter the complete name of the state in the State text box. In the Country text box, select the country of origin for the certificate.

In the Company Name text box, enter the full name of your business. Note that some certificate authorities may not accept special characters in the Company Name and Company Division text boxes. If your company name includes symbols other than a period or comma, check with your CA to see if these characters are allowed.

Optionally, in the Company Division section, enter the name of the department or group within the company. Finally, in the Email text box, provide a secure contact email address that your CA can use to verify domain ownership.

28.1.4Shared Secret

Enter a passphrase in the box if your certificate authority requires one or if it is optional, but you want to use one.

28.1.5Create

After entering the necessary information, click "**Create**." WHM will generate and display the CSR, SSL certificate, and private key. You need to copy and paste these items into their appropriate directories. If you provided an email address, the system will also send this information to that address. Additionally, you can view the keys, certificates, and CSRs you create in WHM's SSL Storage Manager interface.

The system stores this information in specific directories on your servers: CSRs are saved in `/var/cpanel/ssl/system/csrs`, SSL certificates in `/var/cpanel/ssl/system/certs`, and private keys in `/var/cpanel/ssl/system/keys`. If you purchased an SSL certificate, be sure to provide the CSR to the issuing company.

28.2 Install an SSL Certificate on a Domain

Use this interface to install an SSL certificate on a domain, subdomain, addon domain, or the server hostname. Before you can use this feature, you **must** create or purchase a certificate, and you **must** possess the certificate's key. When you install a certificate, this interface indicates whether your certificate is self-signed. Self-signed certificates are easy targets for attackers and generate security warnings in your users' web browsers. **Only** install a self-signed certificate temporarily, until you can replace the certificate with a certificate from a valid certificate authority (CA).

28.3 Manage AutoSSL

AutoSSL is a feature that will provide free SSL certificates for your users' domains. By default, the system uses the free Let's Encrypt Certificate Authority to generate and install SSL certificates that are valid for 90 days. Let's Encrypt offers both domains per certificate and wildcard SSL certificates.

For more information about Let's Encrypt, go to https://www.letsencrypt.org.

28.3.1 Providers

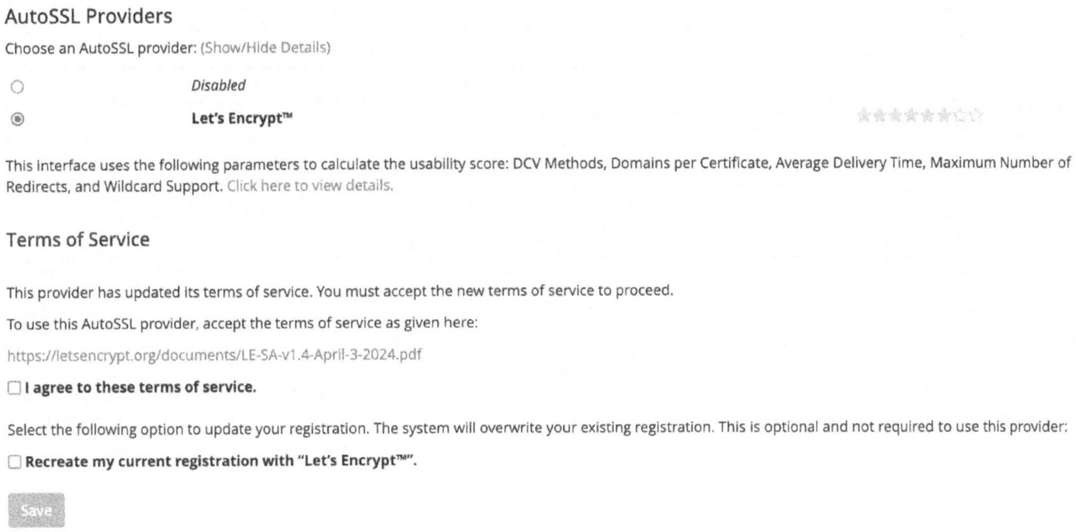

AutoSSL Providers

Choose an AutoSSL provider: (Show/Hide Details)

○ *Disabled*

◉ **Let's Encrypt™**

This interface uses the following parameters to calculate the usability score: DCV Methods, Domains per Certificate, Average Delivery Time, Maximum Number of Redirects, and Wildcard Support. Click here to view details.

Terms of Service

This provider has updated its terms of service. You must accept the new terms of service to proceed.

To use this AutoSSL provider, accept the terms of service as given here:

https://letsencrypt.org/documents/LE-SA-v1.4-April-3-2024.pdf

☐ **I agree to these terms of service.**

Select the following option to update your registration. The system will overwrite your existing registration. This is optional and not required to use this provider:

☐ **Recreate my current registration with "Let's Encrypt™".**

Save

To use Let's Encrypt, you need to register an account. This does not require creating a username and password for the service, only accepting the Terms of Service. The server will reach out and create an account for you that this server will use to order free SSL certificates.

28.3.2 Options

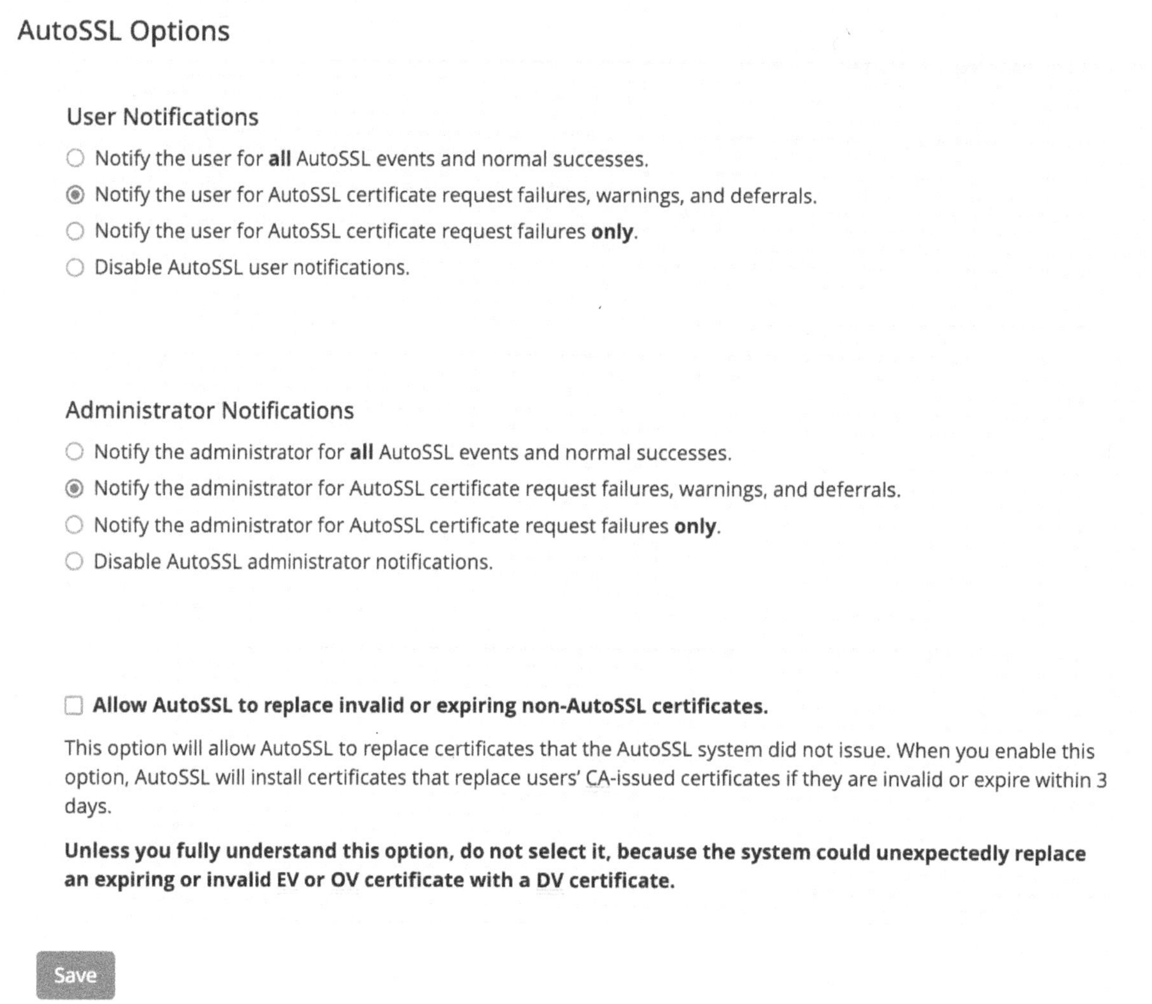

AutoSSL Options

User Notifications

- ○ Notify the user for **all** AutoSSL events and normal successes.
- ◉ Notify the user for AutoSSL certificate request failures, warnings, and deferrals.
- ○ Notify the user for AutoSSL certificate request failures **only**.
- ○ Disable AutoSSL user notifications.

Administrator Notifications

- ○ Notify the administrator for **all** AutoSSL events and normal successes.
- ◉ Notify the administrator for AutoSSL certificate request failures, warnings, and deferrals.
- ○ Notify the administrator for AutoSSL certificate request failures **only**.
- ○ Disable AutoSSL administrator notifications.

☐ **Allow AutoSSL to replace invalid or expiring non-AutoSSL certificates.**

This option will allow AutoSSL to replace certificates that the AutoSSL system did not issue. When you enable this option, AutoSSL will install certificates that replace users' CA-issued certificates if they are invalid or expire within 3 days.

Unless you fully understand this option, do not select it, because the system could unexpectedly replace an expiring or invalid EV or OV certificate with a DV certificate.

Save

AutoSSL has some useful options you may want to configure. First, you can have the server send out notifications to users regarding their certificates – whether one was installed, if there were failures or warnings, or deferrals. Sometimes these get noisy and confuse some users. You may want to consider using failures only or disabling these notifications all together.

If you do disable user notifications, it might be useful to have Administrator Notifications turned on so that you can manage any issues that arise for your customers automatically.

Another helpful feature is that you can enable AutoSSL to replace expiring certificates that were (are) non-AutoSSL provided. For example, if a user purchases an SSL certificate and in a year they forget to renew the certificate, this option will replace the invalid certificate with a free Let's Encrypt certificate until the user purchases a replacement certificate. This makes sure that their website continues to function over HTTPS without any certificate errors notifying that the SSL has expired.

28.3.3 Logs

This tab will allow you to view and inspect the AutoSSL logs. If there are any problems issuing certificates, they will be logged, and you can review this log to find out why Let's Encrypt was not able to issue the certificate.

28.3.4 Manage Users

This tab will let you configure AutoSSL for users on the server. For example, if you have a user that does not want Let's Encrypt certificates *at all*, then you can exclude them from AutoSSL.

This tool is also useful for manually forcing AutoSSL to run for a particular user, especially after any issues preventing AutoSSL from running are fixed.

28.4 Manage SSL Hosts

The Installed SSL Hosts table displays the virtual web hosts with installed SSL certificates as well as each domain's information. If the interface does not list any certificates, you **must** create and install a new SSL certificate. Expired certificates display a red circle with an exclamation mark. An icon with a red, open padlock means the indicated SSL certificate does not protect this domain while a green, closed padlock indicates the domain is protected by the SSL certificate.

28.5 Purchase and Install an SSL Certificate

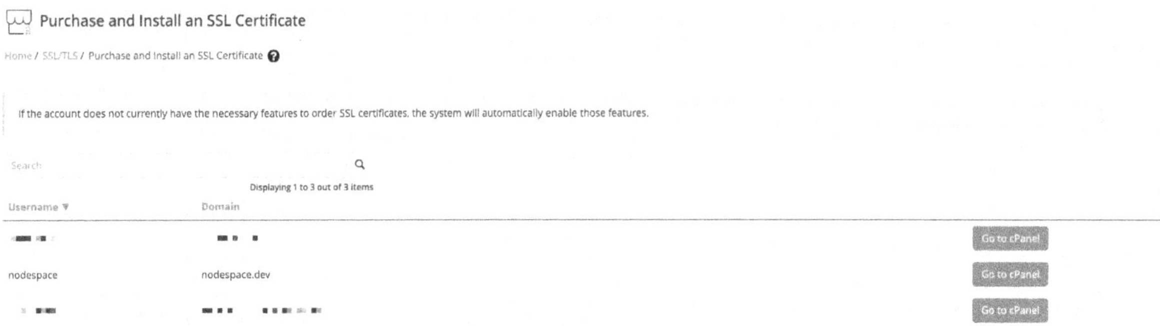

This interface allows you to log in to a user's cPanel interface to purchase an SSL certificate for them through cPanel's SSL/TLS Wizard interface.

> **Warning!**
>
> **POTENTIAL LOSS OF REVENUE!** If you are running a hosting business or sell SSL/TLS certificates to your clients, you may want to disable this feature. Since this feature takes you through cPanel, you (or your customers) will be purchasing the SSL certificate directly from cPanel. That means cPanel gets the revenue from the sale, you do not. See Chapter 29 for more details and how to ensure that you receive commission from these sales as well as the ability to adjust pricing.

When you select the **Go to cPanel** button, you will be redirected to the user's cPanel interface in the SSL/TLS Wizard. Select the domain(s) you want to secure with a SSL certificate or select the option for a wildcard certificate.

You will then be able to pick the certificate validation you want to purchase.

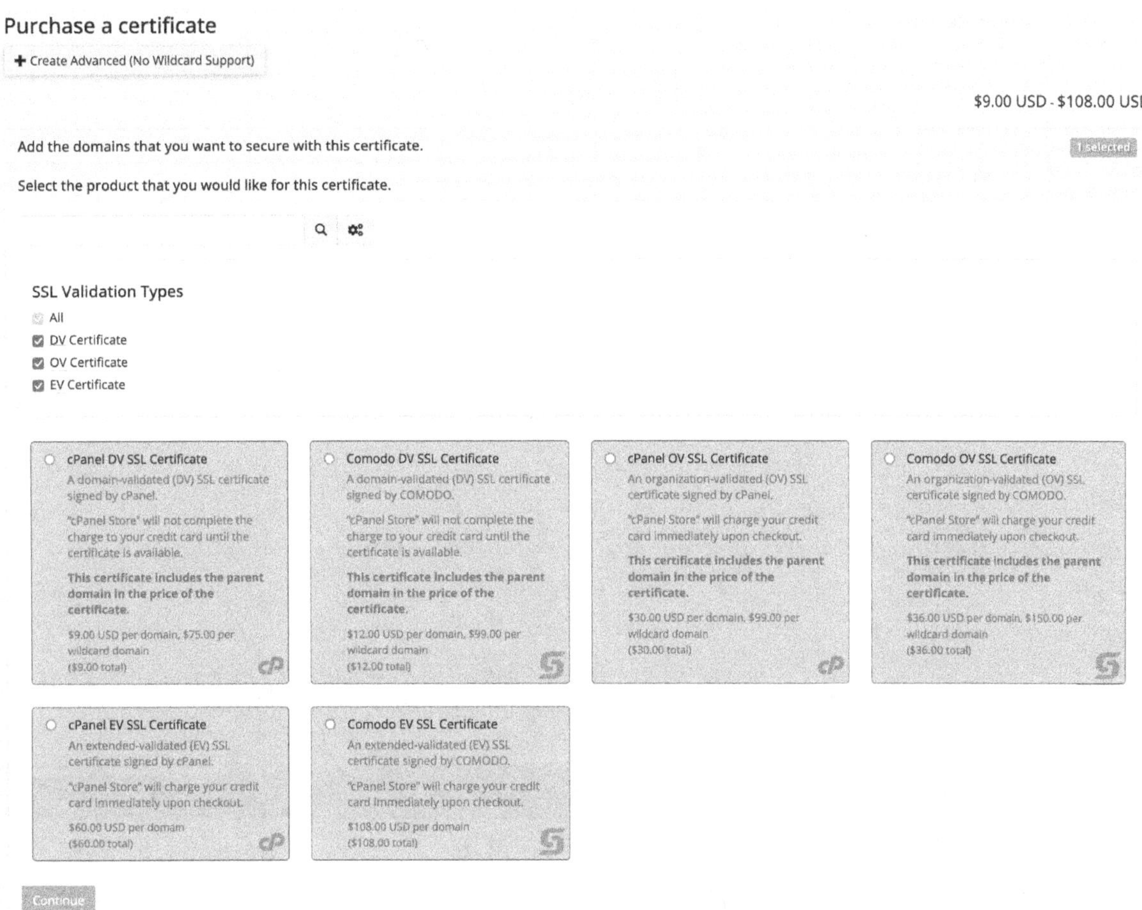

Purchase a certificate
Create Advanced (No Wildcard Support)
$9.00 USD - $108.00 USD
Add the domains that you want to secure with this certificate.
1 selected
Select the product that you would like for this certificate.
SSL Validation Types
All
DV Certificate
OV Certificate
EV Certificate
cPanel DV SSL Certificate
A domain-validated (DV) SSL certificate signed by cPanel.
"cPanel Store" will not complete the charge to your credit card until the certificate is available.
This certificate includes the parent domain in the price of the certificate.
$9.00 USD per domain, $75.00 per wildcard domain
($9.00 total)
Comodo DV SSL Certificate
A domain-validated (DV) SSL certificate signed by COMODO.
"cPanel Store" will not complete the charge to your credit card until the certificate is available.
This certificate includes the parent domain in the price of the certificate.
$12.00 USD per domain, $99.00 per wildcard domain
($12.00 total)
cPanel OV SSL Certificate
An organization-validated (OV) SSL certificate signed by cPanel.
"cPanel Store" will charge your credit card immediately upon checkout.
This certificate includes the parent domain in the price of the certificate.
$30.00 USD per domain, $99.00 per wildcard domain
($30.00 total)
Comodo OV SSL Certificate
An organization-validated (OV) SSL certificate signed by COMODO.
"cPanel Store" will charge your credit card immediately upon checkout.
This certificate includes the parent domain in the price of the certificate.
$36.00 USD per domain, $150.00 per wildcard domain
($36.00 total)
cPanel EV SSL Certificate
An extended-validated (EV) SSL certificate signed by cPanel.
"cPanel Store" will charge your credit card immediately upon checkout.
$60.00 USD per domain
($60.00 total)
Comodo EV SSL Certificate
An extended-validated (EV) SSL certificate signed by COMODO.
"cPanel Store" will charge your credit card immediately upon checkout.
$108.00 USD per domain
($108.00 total)
Continue

You will need to resolve any issues preventing the certificate from being issued. Once that is complete (or you accepted the risks of some domains not being covered), you can continue to purchase the certificate.

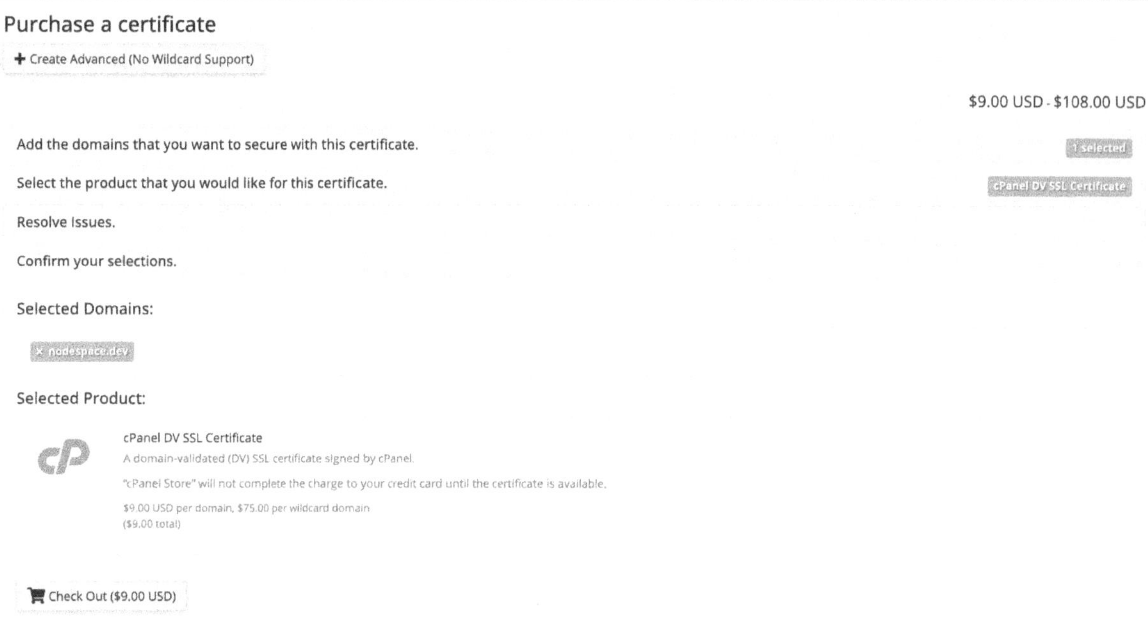
Purchase a certificate
Create Advanced (No Wildcard Support)
$9.00 USD - $108.00 USD
Add the domains that you want to secure with this certificate.
1 selected
Select the product that you would like for this certificate.
cPanel DV SSL Certificate
Resolve Issues.
Confirm your selections.
Selected Domains:
nodespace.dev
Selected Product:
cPanel DV SSL Certificate
A domain-validated (DV) SSL certificate signed by cPanel.
"cPanel Store" will not complete the charge to your credit card until the certificate is available.
$9.00 USD per domain, $75.00 per wildcard domain
($9.00 total)
Check Out ($9.00 USD)

Once purchased and validated, cPanel will automatically install the certificate on the account for you.

Reminder

The purchase of this certificate is through cPanel. While your customer will not see any cPanel branding, cPanel handles the transaction. Refer to Chapter 29.

28.6 SSL Storage Manger

The SSL Storage Manager interface provides system administrators with the ability to view detailed information about their SSL resources. In addition to viewing, administrators can also delete SSL resources listed in this interface. Caution is advised when using this feature, as it allows for the deletion of certificates and private keys. Deleting the wrong item could result in websites and services malfunctioning.

28.7 SSL/TLS Configuration

You can configure the default SSL/TLS key type for your server using this feature. The system will use the specified key type when generating SSL/TLS certificates and signing requests for all users, as well as for creating the root's SSL/TLS keys. By default, the system is set to use a 2,048-bit RSA key. If needed, you can modify this setting in the Security section of WHM's Tweak Settings interface. Additionally, cPanel users have the option to choose their own preferred SSL/TLS key type in cPanel's SSL/TLS interface, and their selection will override the system-level setting.

29 Market

The Market Provider Manager is a feature in cPanel that allows you to manage products users may purchase via the cPanel interface. By default, there is only the cPanel Store provider. You can enable or disable this option.

Under Products, you will find all the products that are offered by the enabled providers. You can decide if you want to enable or disable products as well as adjust the pricing for a product. This table will also show you your potential commission from selling products at these prices.

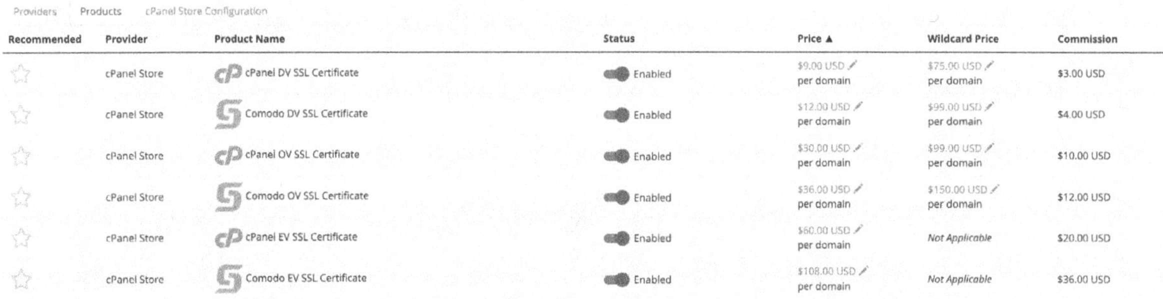
Providers Products cPanel Store Configuration

Recommended	Provider	Product Name	Status	Price ▲	Wildcard Price	Commission
	cPanel Store	cPanel DV SSL Certificate	Enabled	$9.00 USD per domain	$75.00 USD per domain	$3.00 USD
	cPanel Store	Comodo DV SSL Certificate	Enabled	$12.00 USD per domain	$99.00 USD per domain	$4.00 USD
	cPanel Store	cPanel OV SSL Certificate	Enabled	$30.00 USD per domain	$99.00 USD per domain	$10.00 USD
	cPanel Store	Comodo OV SSL Certificate	Enabled	$36.00 USD per domain	$150.00 USD per domain	$12.00 USD
	cPanel Store	cPanel EV SSL Certificate	Enabled	$60.00 USD per domain	*Not Applicable*	$20.00 USD
	cPanel Store	Comodo EV SSL Certificate	Enabled	$108.00 USD per domain	*Not Applicable*	$36.00 USD

Notice!

To make sure that you are paid for any products sold through cPanel, make sure you go to the **cPanel Store Configuration** tab and enter your cPanel Store Commission ID. For more information, go to https://go.cpanel.net/redeemcommission.

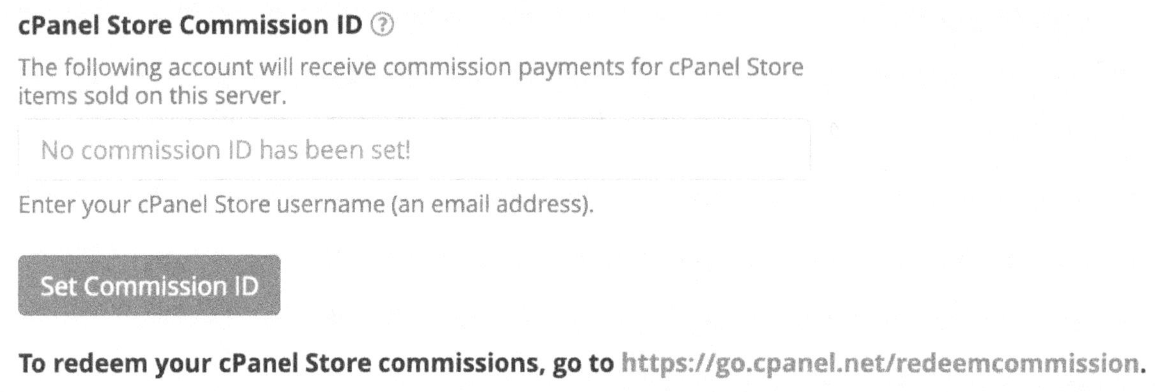

cPanel Store Commission ID

The following account will receive commission payments for cPanel Store items sold on this server.

No commission ID has been set!

Enter your cPanel Store username (an email address).

Set Commission ID

To redeem your cPanel Store commissions, go to https://go.cpanel.net/redeemcommission.

If you have another preferred way for users to order SSL certificates, you can disable this functionality by disabling the cPanel Store market provider.

30 Restart Services

For VPS/Dedicated Servers

The information in this section applies to VPS and dedicated servers.

This chapter covers the tools that will let you restart services on your server. You may need to restart a service either to apply a configuration or to resolve an error with it.

30.1 Database Server

This will gracefully restart either MySQL or MariaDB, depending on which server is installed.

30.2 DNS Server

This will gracefully restart the DNS server installed on the system (either PowerDNS or BIND).

30.3 FTP Server

This will gracefully restart the FTP server installed on the system. If an FTP server is not installed, this option will not be available.

30.4 HTTP Server (Apache)

This option will restart the Apache webserver gracefully on the system. Any existing connections will be closed out and then the server restarted.

30.5 IMAP Server

This will gracefully restart the Dovecot IMAP server.

30.6 Mail Server (Exim)

This will gracefully restart the Exim (SMTP) mail server.

30.7 Mailing List Manager (Mailman)

This will gracefully restart the mailing list (Mailman) service.

30.8 PHP-FPM Service for Apache

This will gracefully restart the PHP-FPM service.

30.9 SSH Server (OpenSSH)

This will gracefully restart the SSH service.

31 Development

The tools in the development section will help you when it comes to application development features for cPanel, whether you're developing your own applications or will provide features such as API tokens for providing developer access to cPanel and WHM.

31.1 Apps Managed by AppConfig

For VPS/Dedicated Servers
The information in this section applies to VPS and dedicated servers.

The AppConfig system configures cPanel & WHM attributes and registers WHM plugins. This book is not about developing applications for WHM, so please consult the cPanel API developer docs for assistance at https://api.docs.cpanel.net.

31.2 cPanel Development Forum

This link will take you to cPanel's Developer Forum where you can discuss cPanel development with other developers.

31.3 cPanel Plugin File Generator

For VPS/Dedicated Servers
The information in this section applies to VPS and dedicated servers.

This interface generates a plugin installation file for the cPanel interface's theme. The installation file automates the plugin installation process and stores the desired configuration for the plugin as a `.tar.gz` file in the `/var/cpanel/cpanel_plugin_generator/` directory.

Creating and developing plugins is out of scope for this book. Refer to cPanel's documentation for more information.

31.4 Developer Documentation

This is a link to https://go.cpanel.net/devdocs. Refer to this link for developer documentation.

31.5 Manage API Tokens

Whenever you need to manage software that needs to talk to and control the cPanel server, you will want to generate an API token with the appropriate level of permissions. Using an API token is more secure as it does not require you to provide a password and if you no longer use an application, the token can be revoked.

If you use business automation software such as ClientExec, WHMCS, HostBill, or similar software, then you will need an API Token to allow the billing software access to cPanel to create accounts, suspend/unsuspend accounts, terminate accounts, and collect metrics on accounts such as disk space, bandwidth, etc.

How you setup billing software or other software is not the purpose of this section, but rather the cPanel aspect.

31.5.1 Generate a Token

To provide access, you will need to generate a token. This can be done by clicking on **Generate Token.**

When you generate a token, you will need to give it a name. For example, "ClientExec" if it will be used for ClientExec.

Tip

It's a good idea to give each system its own token. That way if that token gets compromised or needs to be rotated out, it only must be done on one system.

Next, you should specify if the token should expire or not. While it is best practice to expire tokens after 12 months in case of compromise, keep in mind that once the token expires, anything using that token will need to be updated with a new token. Consider your security policy for guidance.

You can further restrict use of the token by entering whitelisted IP addresses. For example, if you enter the IP address of your billing system, then only your billing system would be able to use that token. If another system attempted to use that token, it would be denied. Remember you would need to make sure the whitelist is updated if you moved your billing system or added another system that used that specific token.

Finally, set the permissions required. Check your software documentation for guidance. If you give too few permissions, your software won't be able to get what it needs to operate. Too many, and anyone with that token can cause serious harm to the server.

For example, if you use the billing software WHMCS, you will need to give the following permissions to the token:

- Basic-whm-functions
- Basic-system-info
- Cpanel-api
- Create-acct
- Create-user-session
- Suspend-acct
- Upgrade-account
- Kill-acct
- Passwd
- Acct-summary
- List-accts
- Show-bandwidth
- Cpanel-integration
- List-pkgs
- Ns-config
- Edit-mx
- Manage-api-tokens
- Ssl-gencrt

For root users, you will need to add

- Viewglobalpackages

If you're using WHMCS' Configurable Package Addon, you will need to add

- Edit-account

And if you're offering reseller products, then you will need to add

- Everything

When you click on **Create**, you will be shown the API token. **Save the API token or add it to where it is needed because the token is only shown once! If you do not save the token, delete it and create it again.**

31.5.2 Editing an API Token

On the list of API tokens, click on **Edit** to edit the token. When editing a token, you can change:

- Token name
- Expiration date
- Whitelisted IPs
- Privileges

Click **Save** to save the changes made to the token.

31.5.3 Delete an API Token

On the list of API tokens, click on **Delete** next to the token that you want to delete. Confirm deletion of the token.

Caution!

When deleting a token, if the token is still being used by applications such as your billing software, it will not be able to manage accounts on the server anymore. Once the token is deleted, it is permanently invalidated.

31.6 Manage Hooks

For VPS/Dedicated Servers

The information in this section applies to VPS and dedicated servers.

This is a feature for cPanel developers. Please refer to the developer documentation for assistance as this is out of scope for this book.

32 Plugins

For VPS/Dedicated Servers

The information in this section applies to VPS and dedicated servers.

Plugins that are installed within cPanel can be managed from this section. This section will generally include both third-party plugins as well as plugins provided by cPanel directly.

32.1 ImunifyAV

cPanel ships with a free third-party antivirus tool called ImunifyAV. This product is quite limited, but it will scan accounts and tell you if there are any infected files. It is better than ClamAV as it is geared towards malicious PHP files, but as it is the free version, it will not do anything except notify you. You can use this interface to find infected files and attempt to manually resolve the problem. You can always upgrade ImunifyAV to Imunify360 (paid). For further information about ImunifyAV and Imuinify360, go to the product website: https://www.imunify360.com.

32.2 WP Toolkit

WP Toolkit is provided by cPanel and is installed by default. This is the backend that will allow you to manage all the WordPress installations on your server with WP Toolkit.

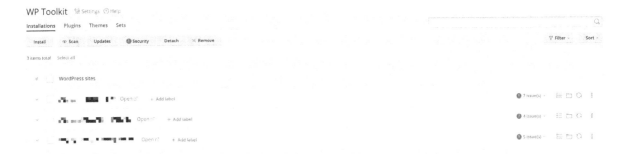

The Installations tab will allow you to view all the current installations being managed by WP Toolkit. If you want to scan the server for installations not being managed by WP Toolkit, click on the **Scan** button to add them.

The **Install** button will allow you to install WordPress on a selected domain for a user. As a root user, you will see all domains and subdomains.

The **Scan** button will allow you to scan the server for unmanaged WordPress installs and add them for management under WP Toolkit.

The **Updates** button will open a pane that will show you the sites and the updates that are currently available for those sites.

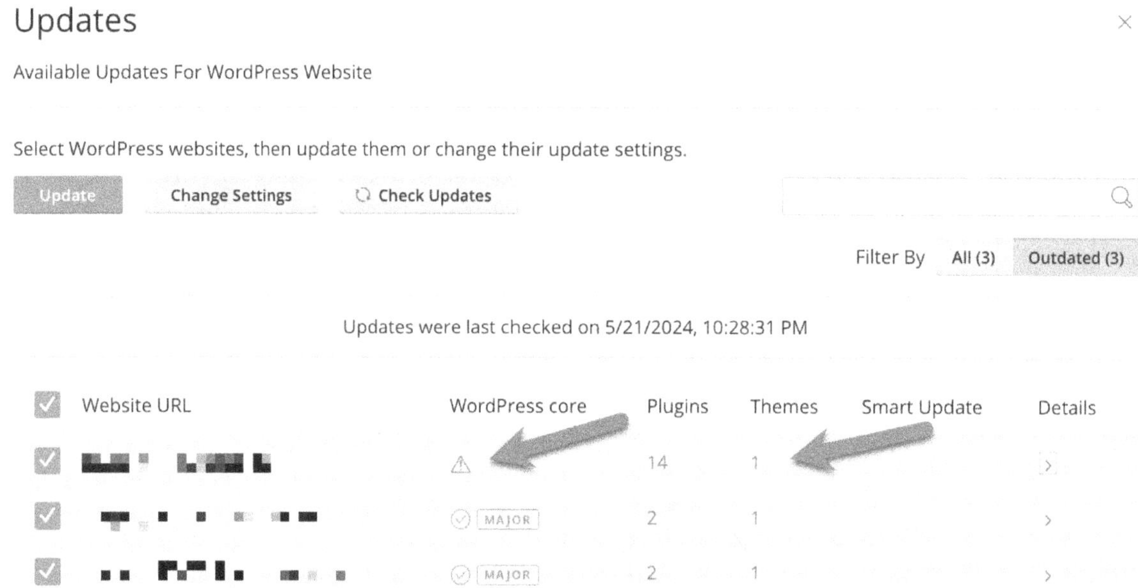

In this example, you can see one site is running an older version of WordPress and indicates that it needs an update. The sites are also missing updates for 14 plugins, 2 plugins, and 2 plugins, respectively. Each site also has a theme upgrade required. If you click on the right facing carrot under Details, you can view details about what needs to be updated on each site.

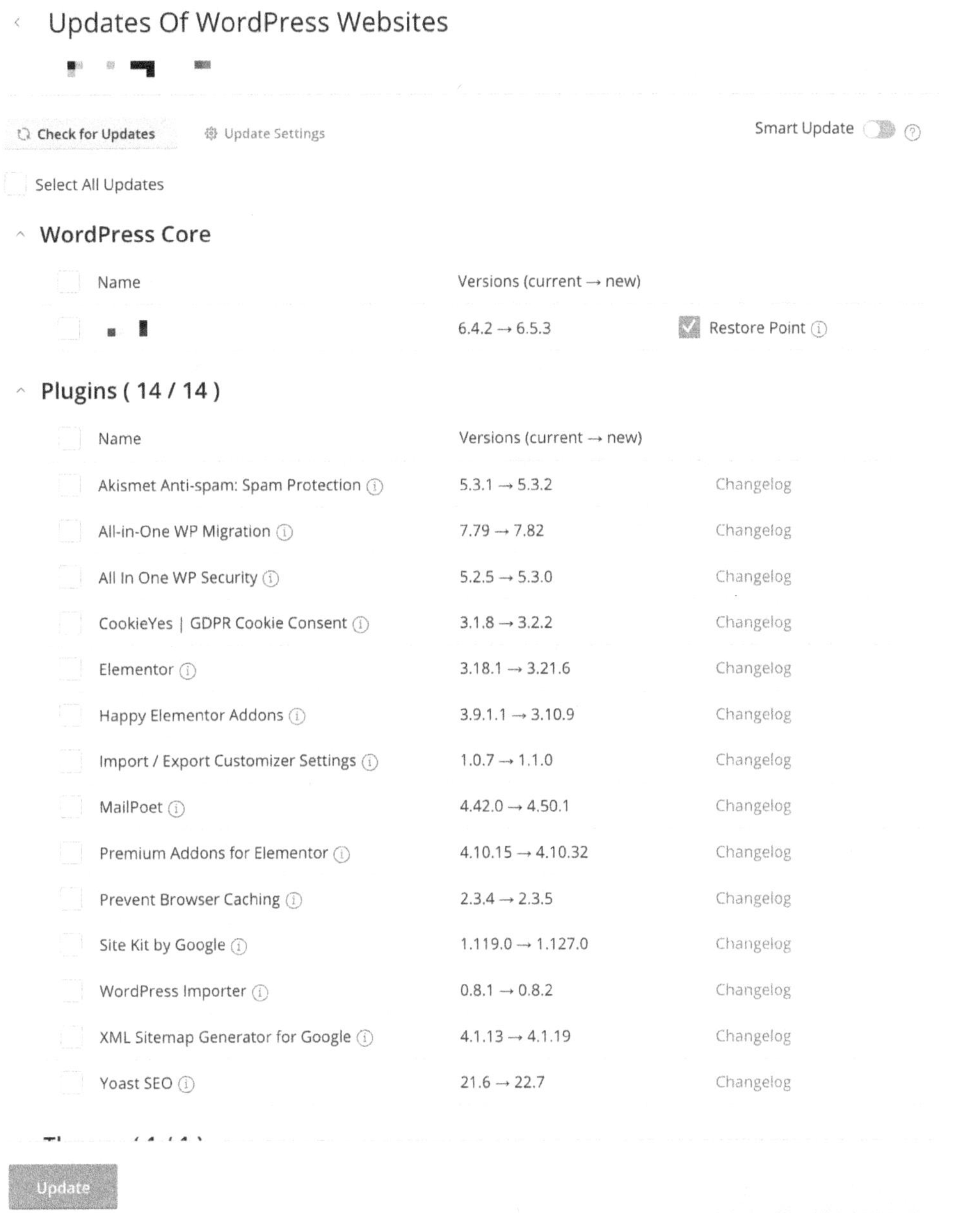

Updates Of WordPress Websites

Check for Updates   Update Settings   Smart Update

Select All Updates

WordPress Core

Name	Versions (current → new)	
	6.4.2 → 6.5.3	Restore Point

Plugins (14 / 14)

Name	Versions (current → new)	
Akismet Anti-spam: Spam Protection	5.3.1 → 5.3.2	Changelog
All-in-One WP Migration	7.79 → 7.82	Changelog
All In One WP Security	5.2.5 → 5.3.0	Changelog
CookieYes | GDPR Cookie Consent	3.1.8 → 3.2.2	Changelog
Elementor	3.18.1 → 3.21.6	Changelog
Happy Elementor Addons	3.9.1.1 → 3.10.9	Changelog
Import / Export Customizer Settings	1.0.7 → 1.1.0	Changelog
MailPoet	4.42.0 → 4.50.1	Changelog
Premium Addons for Elementor	4.10.15 → 4.10.32	Changelog
Prevent Browser Caching	2.3.4 → 2.3.5	Changelog
Site Kit by Google	1.119.0 → 1.127.0	Changelog
WordPress Importer	0.8.1 → 0.8.2	Changelog
XML Sitemap Generator for Google	4.1.13 → 4.1.19	Changelog
Yoast SEO	21.6 → 22.7	Changelog

Update

You can see which plugins and themes will be updated, the version currently installed and the current version, and the changelog. Using this interface, you can force update a site and the plugins and themes.

The **Security** button will show you a list of all the security issues within all WordPress sites on your server. You can use this interface to force an upgrade or force a deactivation of the plugin.

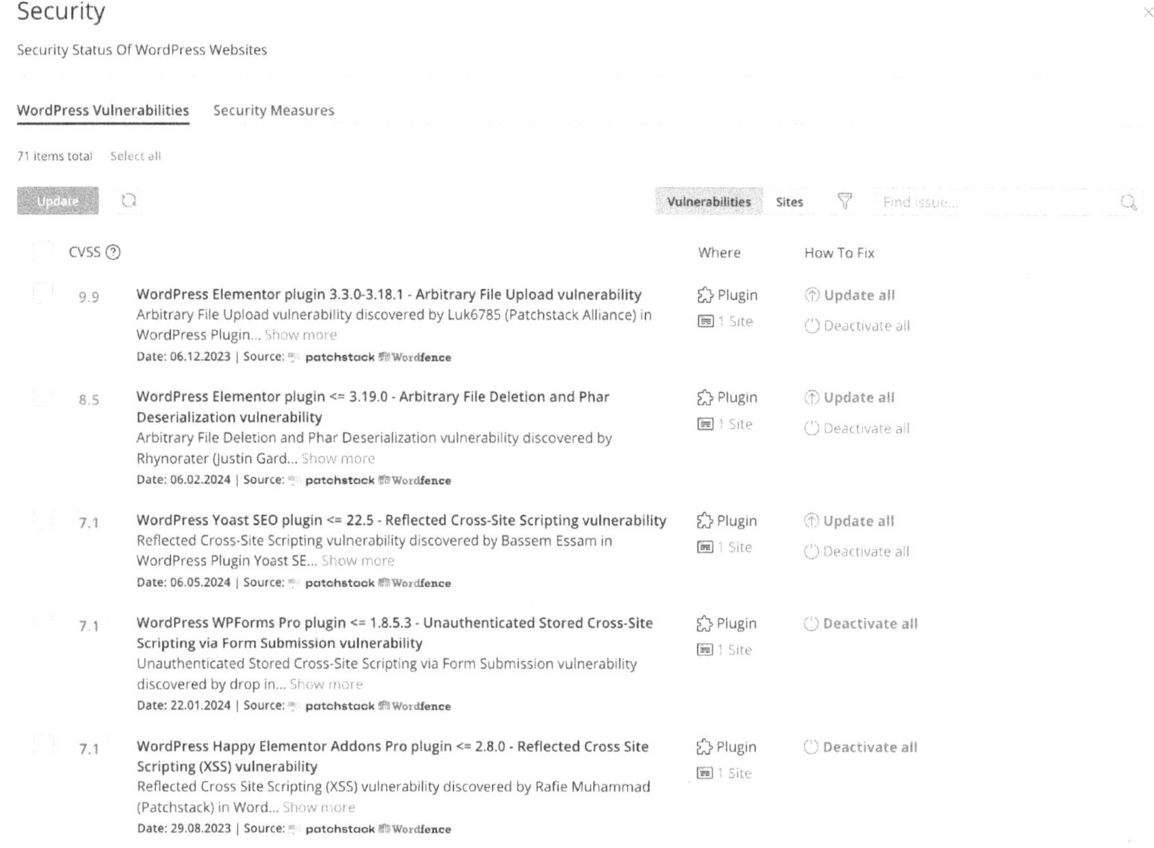

Use forced upgrades with caution. Some users may not have a current subscription to the plugin, in which case if it's commercial, the upgrade will fail. Likewise, if you deactivate a plugin, you could break a customer's website which would lead to a very upset customer. Only use these options if you are providing managed WordPress hosting or communicate with your customers in advance.

The **Detach** button will remove a selected site from management within WP Toolkit.

The **Remove** button will completely remove the WordPress installation.

The Plugins and Themes tabs will show you a list of installed plugins and themes, as well as which sites they are installed on. You will also be able to see if there is an update to a plugin or theme, if it's vulnerable, install a plugin or theme on a site, upload a plugin for installation on a site, activate/deactivate a plugin or theme, as well as uninstall a plugin or theme.

The Sets tab will let you customize the existing sets. You can add specific themes or plugins. Additionally, you can create your own custom set which will allow you to specify plugins and themes to include. When users choose your set, these items will automatically be installed on that installation of WordPress when it is installed.

Appendix – cPanel/WHM Resources

Name	URL	Notes
Softaculous	https://www.softaculous.com	One-click software installer
ClientExec	https://www.clientexec.com	Billing and hosting automation software
Blesta	https://www.blesta.com	Billing and hosting automation software
FOSSBilling	https://www.fossbilling.org	Open source billing and hosting automation software (**caution: in beta**!)
RVSkin for cPanel	https://rvglobalsoft.com/rvskin	cPanel Skin (theme)
CloudLinux	https://www.cloudlinux.com	Specialized Enterprise Linux-based operating system for web hosting
WHMCS	https://www.whmcs.com	Billing and hosting automation software

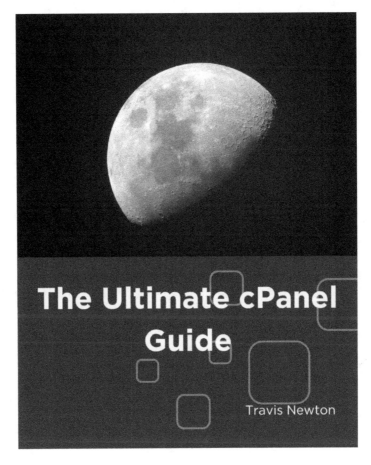

www.ingramcontent.com/pod-product-compliance
Lightning Source LLC
LaVergne TN
LVHW081328050326
832903LV00024B/1070

* 9 7 9 8 3 2 6 3 9 1 5 8 2 *